State Administration in India

Emerging Issues and Challenges

State Administration in India
Emerging Issues and Challenges

U.B. Singh

KALPAZ

First Published, 2021

Published by

Kalpaz Publications
C-30, Satyawati Nagar,
Delhi – 110052
Ph.: 011-47034999, 9811692060
www.kalpazpublications.com
E-mail: kalpaz@hotmail.com

Printed at: Gyan Press, Delhi.

Cataloging in Publication Data—DK
Courtesy: D.K. Agencies (P) Ltd. <docinfo@dkagencies.com>

State administration in India / [editor], U.B. Singh.
pages cm
Contributed articles.
ISBN 9789353243142 (HB)

1. State governments—India. 2. India—Politics and government.
I. Singh, U. B., 1953- editor.

LCC JQ298.8.S56 2021 | DDC 351.54 23

Contents

Preface

It had been my cherished desire to pay my humble honour to Professor S. K. Singh, my esteemed 'academic *Guru*'. I was pondering over the manner to fulfill this desire. One day my daughter advised me to present a book to him. I got the right clue on right time, and my quest was half completed. The subjects of Constitution of India, Indian Administration and Public Enterprises in India were his most favoured subjects at PG level teaching. These were the subjects close to his chest. After a long thought, I preferred to choose the subject of "State Administration in India"; hence, this book was conceived.

The Constitution of India in its first Article says, "India, that is 'Bharat', shall be a Union of States." The turn of events at the time of country's partition preceding the birth of free India impelled the Constituent Assembly to opt for a "Union of States" with a strong Centre, keeping away from the idea of a loose federation that had engaged the attention of the framers of the Constitution initially. The Indian Constitution is unique in its features. Among other attributes, it has several features of a 'Federation' like the dual government; distribution of powers between Union Government and State Government, supremacy of the Constitution, and final authority of courts to interpret the Constitution. On the other hand, there are several 'Unitary' features like a unified judicial system; integrated machinery for election; accounts and audit; power of superintendence of Union Government over State Government in emergencies and to some extent, even in normal times; single citizenship, etc. Thus the word 'Union of States' used in our Constitution is not a Federation of the type set up by the U.S. Constitution.

Article Two authorizes Parliament 'by law admit into the Union, or establish new State'. Article Three empowers Parliament to form a new State by separation of territory or by uniting two States or parts of States, increase and diminish the area and alter the boundaries of any State and also alter the name of any State. The Constitution defines separate legislative, financial, functional and judicial powers of the Union and States. States being responsible for running administration and execution of development programmes, the efficacy and efficiency of the administration of the entire country depends upon the vigour and competence of state administration.

State Administration

'State Administration' is defined as a system of entities created by statute and in the competence to carry out internal and external management and executive activities with responsibility assigned to state. The reference to "state" here denotes country sub-divisions which are officially known as "states", and should not be confused with a "sovereign state".

Part-VI of the Constitution deals with the State Administration. The Fifth Schedule contains the provisions regarding the administration and control of scheduled areas and scheduled tribes in a state, while the Sixth Schedule consists of provisions connected with the administration of tribal areas in the states of Assam, Meghalaya, Tripura and Mizoram.

The executive powers of the state vest in the Governor who is appointed by the President for a term of five years. He holds office during the pleasure of the President. These powers are exercised by him either directly or through the officers subordinates to him. However, many a times the decisions of the Governor become a centre of controversy. The contentious issue of the role of Governor had been discussed at length by the Commissions on Centre-State Relations and very important recommendations were made; but their implementation remained prerogative of the Central Government.

In the state administration there is a 'Council of Ministers' whose main function is to aid and advise the Governor in the exercise of his functions. At the head of the council of ministers there is the Chief Minister. The state government enjoys authority to make laws on List- II— State List (Seventh Schedule), and to run the administration accordingly. The power of the state government on the List-III—- Concurrent List is limited or qualified. The decisions of council of ministers headed by the chief minister are generally intended for attaining the political goals of the party in power. Sometimes, political interest overshadows overall development.

A 'Secretariat' is the nerve-centre of the state administration. It consists of career bureaucrats. Experienced and efficient bureaucrats (Secretary / Principal Secretary) sit at the top of every department. The most important function of the secretary/principal secretary is to advise the minister in policy-making affairs. These public servants generally remain neutral, but their advice helps in achieving the ambition of the political masters. All the government departments combined form the secretariat (each House of the State Legislature has a separate secretariat of its own).

There are several ministers in a state government and each minister is the head of a department, sometimes even many more. The minister is the political executive of a department and plays the important role in policy-making affairs. In discharging this function he is assisted by an experienced bureaucrat (secretary). There is a fixed limit about the number of ministers but no rule exists about the number of departments that will constitute a secretariat. The number of departments varies from state to state. Normally there are more than fifty-sixty (even more) departments in a state secretariat. There is thus found overlapping in their functional jurisdiction and hence many a times exists lack of clarity in their roles and responsibilities. ***This needs a rethinking on departmentalising and amalgamating several departments entrusted with similar nature of functions in one. The restructuring may be a way to achieve 'minimum government, maximum governance'.***

In state administration the Chief Secretary is the most important person. He is called the "king of the secretariat". The main task of the chief secretary is to aid and advise the Chief Minister in the discharge of his/her administrative functions. He acts as the main link between the Chief Minister and all the departments. If in the judgment of the Chief Minister a person happens to be efficient and able, that person is selected for this most crucial post. In many cases senior bureaucrats are found lobbying and seek favour from influential ministers for his selection to this coveted post. ***Sometimes selection of a chief secretary remains in cloud. The appointment of junior officer in the guise of merit or on other considerations demoralises senior bureaucrats. The matter of appointment of the chief secretary needs a churning and constituting a high level selection committee under the chairmanship of the Chief Minister of the state, Chief Justice of the High Court and the Secretary to Government of India in the Ministry of Personnel as members may be thought of.***

'Directorates' are the executive arm of the state government. They translate into action the policies that are framed through the State Secretariat. It acts as an executive agency of the department. The funds allotted for the departments are spent through the directorate on implementation of policies and programmes determined by the government. ***The experiences show in many cases directorates are not effective at all. They are not suitably manned. Many directorates are often headed by a junior officer. Thus there is a dire need to strengthen them as they are the main link between the department and the field units.***

The 'state civil service' personnel are recruited through the state public service commission. These services are primarily meant for the state. Every state has well-organized services to cater to the needs of dissimilar sectors of governmental activity in non-technical and technical spheres. The personnel of the state services operate in subordination to the members of the All India Services. They constitute the middle stage of the state administrative system. ***Some heart burning however between both the services, sometimes, hammers the smoothness in state administration. An attempt has been made to evolve a common stream. This has been achieved***

through inducting a sure percentage of the State Services personnel into the All India Services.

Centre-State Cooperation

Part-XI of the Constitution distinctly makes the provisions regarding relation between the Union and the States. This framework of relationship between Centre and States had worked fairly smoothly till mid-sixties and the institutions created under or inspired by the Constitution for this purpose enjoyed complete trust and respect of all concerned. This harmonious functioning was, perhaps, possible because this period was characterized by, by and large, a single party (Congress Party) domination of the Governments both at the Centre and in most of the states. The General Elections in 1967 were followed by the formation of non-Congress Government in a number of states. Simultaneously, it was also the beginning of a period when coalition politics started at state level and the coalition governments were formed in many states. This was the time when the regional political parties wanted to create their own niche in their respective regions. There were wide spread demands particularly from non-Congress and other regional parties led governments for providing greater autonomy for the states in their functioning.

Politically, however, with the rise of regional parties and coalitions, states seemed to gain the upper hand in many matters. Centre's powers of intervention also came to be circumscribed by several judicial pronouncements. The *Janata* Party that came into power at the Centre in the post-emergency period in 1977 was a coalition essentially of the parties that were opposed to the Congress Party, though not carrying the same, and in many cases, totally different political ideologies. At the same time with a host of non-Congress governments in the states, there was obvious clamour and demand for greater autonomy for the states. With a weak coalition at the Centre and with its constituents coming from totally different political backgrounds, the *Janata* Party regime proved a short lived one and the people once again voted the Congress Party to power in 1980 at the Centre with a very large majority. However, non-Congress Government in the states at the time also started putting up a united front, demanding more administrative and fiscal autonomy. This led to, on many occasions, disharmonious relationship between the Union and the State governments.

Due to its unique features, our Constitution lays down a quasi-federal polity. Granville Austin has called our 'Federation' a 'Cooperative Federalism' due to the need for close cooperation between the Union Government and the State Governments. In a system of multi-level governance, as of ours, operating essentially in a federal framework harmonious relations between the Centre and the States (and States and the

Local Governments) are critical for the stability, security and economic development of the country. Harmonious relationship between the Centre and the States will always be a key to the unity and integrity of this great country; particularly at time when with multi-party governments are found operating both at the Union and State levels. The emergence of one party (BJP) led (NDA) governments since 2014 at the Centre, and domination of strong regional parties in many states inspired the Central Government to initiate advocating of 'Cooperative and Competitive Federalism'. Unexpectedly, the National Democratic Alliance (NDA) led by the *Bhartiya Janta* Party (BJP) returning to power in 2019 led 'Cooperative Federalism' to be perverted to 'Non-Cooperating Federalism' or sometimes to 'Conflicting Federalism'; creating administrative complexities in the country. Both the groups (ruling NDA and Congress led UPA along with other opposition parties) have reasons in one another's support. This situation is a blow to the harmonious relations between the Union and opposition parties led state governments. Maintaining a harmonious relationship between these two Constitutional Units is a major concern of the day.

Commission on Centre-State Relationship

In the last seven decades since the Constitution has come into force one hundred and four amendments (as of January 2020) have taken place, with several of these having direct bearing on Centre-State relations. So far, two Commissions for studying Centre-State Relations have been constituted. The first Commission was constituted by Parliament on March 24, 1983, headed by Justice R.S. Sarkaria, a retired Judge of the Supreme Court of India. The Sarkaria Commission submitted its two volume reports in 1988.

In pursuance to the commitment made in the National Common Minimum Programme of the UPA government, the Government of India decided to set up another Commission on Centre-State Relations in September 2005.The Commission consisted of a full-time Chairperson and four fulltime members. The Commission, however, actually got constituted in April 2007 under the chairmanship of Justice Madan Mohan Punchhi (Retd.) former Chief Justice of India. The Commission submitted its multi-volume reports on March 31, 2010.

These commissions have thoroughly studied almost all aspects of creating and maintaining harmonious relationship between the Union and States.

Administrative Reforms Commissions

The Government of India has appointed two Administrative Reforms Commissions for reviewing the public administrative system of India so far. The first such Commission was established on 5 January 1966 under the chairmanship of Morarji Desai. Later on K. Hanumanthaiah became its chairman when Desai became Deputy Prime Minister of India. It prepared and submitted its reports on 20 subjects in mid-1970s.

The Second Administrative Reforms Commission was constituted on 31 August 2005 under the chairmanship of Veerappa Moily for revamping the public administrative system in the country. The Commission submitted 15 reports on different subjects between 2006 and 2009.

Both the Commissions reviewed State Administration thoroughly in their exclusive reports.

Review the Working of the Constitution

A National Commission to Review the Working of the Constitution, popularly known as Justice Venkatachaliah Commission was set up by the Government of India (Vajpayee Government) on 22 February 2000 for suggesting possible amendments to the Constitution. It submitted its report in two volumes on 31 March 2002.

Emerging Issues

First time, in 2014, BJP led National Democratic Alliance (NDA) formed the government at its own (the Vapayee Government was a coalition) at the Centre. In those elections opposition parties shrank in numbers. The subsequent 2019 General Elections brought surprises and NDA succeeded to return to powers with a thumping majority to BJP. Opposition parties further reduced in numbers. This led to political scenario witnessing an upheaval after 2014 and 2019 General Elections in the country. The large majority to NDA partners, especially BJP, against the imagination of opposition parties, led to unfold old, contentious and communally and politically sensitive grave issues which have presumably resulted into multifold attack on federal fabric and harmonious relationship between the opposition-led governments in the States and the NDA led government at the Centre. Many state governments have passed resolutions opposing non-implementation of a law passed by Indian Parliament. Many state governments and organizations have approached to the Supreme Court of India seeking its intervention. Besides, a few selective civil society organizations in many states have been aided and abetted to hold gatherings and embrace anti-Central government sloganeering.

In the backdrop of these political developments in the country, there is an opportune time especially for academics to dissect and diagnose the issues emerged since 2019. On scanning, it is found that a lot of literature has been produced on subjects like, Centre-State (fiscal, political) Relations, Role of Governor, use of Article 356, etc. Hence, some latest emerging issues and challenges thereof, which are leading a path for rethinking role of states in our federal structure, have been chosen for deep discussion. Such of these focussed issues are explained hereunder.

Citizenship Amendment Act (CAA), 2019

The Indian Citizenship Act, 1955 was enacted to provide for the acquisition and determination of Indian citizenship. There have been several amendments to this Act in past, but the protests against the current Citizenship (Amendment) Act, 2019 have been going on for quite some time, with most protesters (allegedly especially from vested interests in civil society) having little idea of what they are protesting about.

The Government Notification mentions that 'trans-border migration of population has been happening continuously between the territories of India and the areas presently comprised in Pakistan, Afghanistan and Bangladesh since partition of India in 1947. The constitutions of these countries provide for a specific state religion. As a result, many persons belonging to Hindu, Sikh, Buddhist, Jain, Parsi and Christian communities have faced persecution on grounds of religion in those countries. Many such persons (in *lakhs*) have fled to India to seek shelter and continued to stay in India even if their travel documents have expired or they have incomplete or no documents. Such migrants are regarded as illegal migrants and ineligible to apply for Indian citizenship. Under the current Amendment (CAA 2019) the illegal migrants who have entered into India up to the cut of date of 31.12.2014, the Government shall grant the certificate of registration or certificate of naturalisation subject to such conditions, restrictions and manner as may be prescribed.

'The amendment further seeks to protect the constitutional guarantee given to indigenous populations of North Eastern States covered under the Sixth Schedule to the Constitution and the statutory protection given to areas covered under the Inner Line Permit System'.

The passage of the Citizenship (Amendment) Act (CAA), 2019 has galvanised more concerted regional opposition. Their apprehension, though not unfounded, is that it may open the door for preparation of National Population Register (NPR) and then ultimately National Register of Citizens (NRC). Many state governments and opposition parties have opposed the move and approached to Supreme Court of India for cancellation of the CAA, 2019. Opposition parties-led state assemblies (West Bengal, Kerala, M.P.(erstwhile Congress led government), Rajasthan, Punjab, and Chhattisgarh) have resolved their refusal to implement this law passed by the Parliament. This unprecedented move by many state governments has led to a conflicting situation and a constitutional crisis, apart from vitiating the harmonious and cooperative relationship between the Union and opposition-led State governments.

National Population Register (NPR)

The National Population Register (NPR) is a list of all the people residing in India. It is prepared as per the provisions of the Indian Citizenship Act, 1955, and the Citizenship (Registration of Citizens and Issue of National Identity Cards) Rules, 2003. The listing is done at the local, sub-district, district, state and national level. Every "usual resident of India" is required to register in the NPR.

In 2010, the NPR was created for the first time with the names of 119 *crore* residents of India. This data was further updated in 2015 by linking with biometric information from *Aadhaar* database. ***It is proposed to also include more details such as the place of birth of the parents, last place of residence and the serial number for official documents in the NPR planned for 2020. The non-cohesive and sometimes contrasting statements by BJP leaders and even by some junior (Union) ministers have added fuel to the fire. In spite of repeated explanations from the top most authorities in the Union Government about rationale of including additional details in the forthcoming NPR exercise, the opposition remains apprehensive.***

National Register of Citizens (NCR)

The National Register of Citizens (NCR) is a register of all Indian citizens whose creation is mandated by the 2003 Amendment of the Citizenship Act, 1955. Its purpose is to document all the legal citizens of India so that the illegal migrants can be identified and deported.

Assam, being a border state with unique problems of illegal immigration, had a Register of Citizens created for it in 1951 based on the 1951 census data. However, it was not maintained afterwards. The Illegal Migrants (Determination by Tribunal) Act, 1983 was then passed by the Parliament, creating a separate tribunal process for identifying illegal migrants in Assam. However, the Supreme Court struck it down as unconstitutional in 2005, after which the Government of India agreed to update the Assam Register of Citizens (RC). Following unsatisfactory progress on the process of updating the Assam RC for over a decade, the Supreme Court started directing and monitoring the process since 2013-2014. The final updated RC for Assam was published on 31 August 2019 rendering millions potentially stateless.

It is in the air that the Government of India may plan to implement it(NRC) for the rest of the country in 2020. The Government has denied any such move in near future, but opposition parties have been creating a hue and cry, and try to establish a link between ensuing NCR(for the whole country) with seeking additional details of citizens in NPR, 2020.

Article 370 of the Indian Constitution

Article 370 (Temporary provisions with respect to the State of Jammu and Kashmir) of the Indian Constitution gave special status to Jammu and Kashmir. The Article was drafted in Part-XXI of the Constitution: Temporary, Transitional and Special Provisions. The Constituent Assembly of Jammu and Kashmir, after its establishment, was empowered to recommend the Articles of the Indian Constitution that should be applied to the state or to abrogate the Article 370 altogether. In exercise of the powers, as conferred by clause (3) of Article 370 of the Constitution, the President, from time to time, has made a series of Orders with the concurrence of the Government of the State of Jammu and Kashmir. The Constitution Presidential Order of 1950, officially The Constitution (Application to Jammu and Kashmir) Order, 1950, which came into force on 26 January 1950 contemporaneously with the Constitution of India, was superseded by the Presidential Order of 1952. The Presidential Order of 1952 was published on 15 November 1952. After discussions, the 1952 Delhi Agreement was reached. After consultation with the state's Constituent Assembly, the 1954 Presidential Order was issued, specifying the Articles of the Constitution that applied to the state. The Presidential Order of 1954, officially The Constitution (Application to Jammu and Kashmir) Order, 1954 came into force on 14 May 1954 was a comprehensive order seeking to implement the 1952 Delhi Agreement. The Order of 1954 added to the Constitution a new Article 35A which empowered the state's legislature to define 'permanent residents' of the state and provide special rights and privileges to those permanent residents. These privileges included ability to purchase land and property, ability to vote and contest elections, seeking government employment, among others. Thus Article 370 along with Article 35A defined that the Jammu and Kashmir state's 'residents live under a separate set of laws, including those related to citizenship, ownership of property, and fundamental rights'. As a result of this provision, citizens from other states (non-permanent residents) could not purchase land or property, enroll for higher education and get benefits of heath care in Jammu & Kashmir.

In addition to these original Orders, forty-seven other Presidential Orders were issued between 11 February 1956 and 19 February 1994, making various other provisions of the Constitution of India applicable to the state of Jammu and Kashmir. All these Orders were issued with the 'concurrence of the Government of the State' without any Constituent Assembly.

The effects of the Presidential Orders issued since 1954 had been to extend 94 of the 97 subjects in the Union List to the state of Jammu and Kashmir, and 260 of the 395 Articles of the Constitution of India. Of the 'Concurrent List', twenty-six of the forty-seven items applied to Jammu and Kashmir, the state had exclusive right to legislate on those matters. The right to legislate on elections to state bodies also rested with the state.

Preamble and Article 3 of the erstwhile Constitution of Jammu and Kashmir stated that 'the State of Jammu and Kashmir is and shall be an integral part of the Union of India.' Article 5 stated that 'the executive and legislative powers of the state extend to all matters except those with respect to which Parliament has power to make laws for the state under the provisions of the Constitution of India.' The constitution of Jammu and Kashmir was adopted on 17 November 1956 and came into force on 26 January 1957.

On 5 August 2019, the Government of India issued a Presidential Order superseding the 1954 Order, and making all the provisions of the Constitution applicable to Jammu and Kashmir based on the resolution passed in both Houses of Parliament. Following the resolutions, a further Order was issued on 6 August 2019 declaring all the clauses of Article 370 except clause (1) to be inoperative.

In addition, the Jammu and Kashmir Reorganisation Act, 2019 was passed by the Parliament, enacting the division the State of Jammu and Kashmir into two Union Territories to be called Union Territory of Jammu and Kashmir (with an assembly) and Union Territory of Ladakh (without an assembly). The reorganisation took place on 31 October 2019. The constitution of Jammu and Kashmir was rendered infructuous by The Constitution (Application to Jammu and Kashmir) Order, 2019 issued by the President on 5 August 2019.

Many opposition parties have been opposing the abrogation of Article 370 and bifurcation of Jammu and Kashmir into two Union Territories in August 2019. Some opposition parties and a few individuals have approached to the Supreme Court of India and challenged the move (abrogation and bifurcation) of the Union Government.

State Finances

The Constitution envisages clear fiscal relationship between Union and States. States are assuming greater responsibility in governmental spending in the country. States primarily rely on three sources for financing their expenditure: (i) own resources, (ii) transfers from the Central Government (through Finance Commission), and (iii) borrowings. Own resources of states have undergone a major shift since 2017 with the implementation of Goods and Services Tax (GST), under which states transferred a major part of their taxation powers to the GST Council. Many s***tates (opposition ruled) often express their resentments over devolution criteria, conditionalities, financing of programmes and rates of GST. In this context, we look at***

recent developments that affect state finances and the trends in various components of state finances.

Local Governments

The powers and functions of the Union and the State Governments are specified in the Constitution. They function independently in their own spheres. Of course, there is an area of overlapping responsibility and there are certain powers of superintendence. The subject of Local Government falls in the State List (Entry 5). Local Governments (urban and rural) enjoy limited autonomy—fiscal, functional, and administrative as defined by the state government. It differs from state to state. As a result of 73rd and 74th Amendments to the Constitution (1992), a third type of government—Local Government (*Panchayats* and Municipalities) has been constituted; and thus another 'Federation (State and Local Governments) within the Federation (Union and State Governments)' has been created. Consequently, Part-IX (The *Panchayats*) has been inserted by repealing Part-IX dealing with territories in Part D of the First Schedule; and a new Part-IXA (The Municipalities) has also been inserted.

These Amendments provided Local Government Institutions constitutional status, with the hope that they would function as a third type of governments, but they remained in the State List. Although the local governments were expected to perform functions on a scale (functions codified in Eleventh Schedule (*Panchayats*) and Twelfth Schedule (Municipalities) larger than before, their access to tax powers and borrowing remained limited. The transfer system (through State Finance Commissions and Central Finance Commissions) did help to alleviate the regional disparities in the levels of living and in public services to some extent, but sharp imbalances still remained. ***In an attempt to counter the possible ill-effects on fiscal discipline, conditionalities came to be used increasingly with transfers by Central Finance Commissions. The Democratic Decentralisation ensuring presence of deliberative (elected) wing has occurred, but commensurate measures in connection with Administrative Decentralisation are missing. Besides, co-relationship between functions, finances and functionaries is totally non- existent. These institutions suffer from inadequate, unsuitable and inefficient human resources with no clarity in their roles and functional responsibilities. The recommendations of Second Administrative Reforms Commission were a welcome move but the then (UPA) Union Government rejected out rightly. It is high time that those recommendations should be reconsidered afresh and implemented and the Constitution be amended further and a new 'Local Government List' (in addition to Union, State and Concurrent Lists) should be inserted in it. This step can only ensure real autonomy to the Local Governments as envisaged by the 73rd and 74th CAA.***

Crisis Management

State administration plays a crucial role in mitigating and preventing disaster—natural or man-made; epidemic or endemic or pandemic. Relief management is the primary responsibility of state administration with the help of district administration and local government institutions. During the current global pandemic (COVID-19) the efficacy and efficiency of state administration have been on great stake. The Corona virus has ruined many economies in the world including ours. Luckily, in our country states have been able to tame the deadly effects of this pandemic to a great extent, while many other countries are struggling hard. This pandemic, by and large, added strength to our federal polity. The states have generally followed the Central guidelines of long lockdowns for curbing the spread of virus. Though some hiccups do exist. Many opposition-led state governments, especially West Bengal, Kerala, Maharashtra and Punjab have not moved along accusing Centre for its partisan behaviour. The concern of opposition-led state governments is mainly related to non-release of sufficient funds to meet this pandemic, besides GST compensation from the Centre.

The state government, district administration and local government units should be empowered trained and adequately equipped with modern latest techniques and technologies to fight with the current pandemic and any such disaster occurring in future. The Union Government should have more consultations with state governments (Prime Minister do make regular consultations with the Chief Ministers). Their funds related issues should be considered and sorted out amicably. However, political gains should not overshadow such a fatal pandemic situation.

E-Governance

E-governance is the application of information and communication technology (ICT) for delivering government services, exchange of information and communication transactions. It is a two-way protocol. Through e-governance, government services are made available to citizens in a convenient, efficient and transparent manner. The launch of Digital India initiative by the Union Government has a vision to transform the country into a digitally empowered society. Our concern is to study the extent of transparency and efficiency occurred in state administration through various e-governance initiatives.

The foregone discussions to tracing a few emerging issues create necessary opportunities for studying state administration afresh. The country is now facing demographic challenges, financial disruptions, technological developments, political disunity, restrained and disharmonious Union-States relationship, regional economic imbalances, states' disobedience on certain matters, administrative procedures and political interests sometimes overshadowing national interests. Many such issues create an environment of 'divergence, instead of convergence', and destined to dent our federal framework. Very often this situation leads to constitutional crisis. Such a mind boggling scenario in the country presents a churning opportunity by the academia. Some issues pertaining to state administration have been well-researched thoroughly from time to time by academics, commissions and committees, and a lot of literature is available on these subjects. In this backdrop, I thought proper not to touch those issues, though still important and relevant. I took the recent emerging issues and requested my fellow academics to throw light on the state of state administration in context of these new emerging issues. The current pandemic (COVID-19) has drawn attention of many scholars. A good number of scholars preferred the allied subjects like gender mainstreaming, tourism administration, skill development, smart city, social security, administrative challenges, etc—subjects compatible to their interest and specialization; but also important functional aspect.

I got enormous and enthusiastic response to my request from fellow academicians of repute from across the country. They made it convenient to favour me with their scholarly papers despite all the odds—academic and social (health, education) during the long lockdown and thereafter due to fatal pandemic. I express my sincere gratitude to them all. With all the humility, I express my deep sense of gratitude especially to senior academicians (Professor P.N. Gautam (Shimla) and Professor S.N. Singh (Lucknow), contemporary to Professor Singh, and are in quest of joining the octogenarian club, for their invaluable contribution. This is a token reflection of their sheer love and affection towards me. I humbly accept their blessings. My special thanks to those learned fellows also who unwillingly could not accede to my request for certain reasons. I gracefully accept their good wishes. I am also thankful to my friend Dr. R. K. Trivedi for helping in selection of *shlokas*. I am indebted to all the books, journals, wikipedia, websites, reports of government commissions and committees, government notifications, etc. and their authors to whom I have consulted and quoted extensively.

Last but not the least, I am thankful to M/s Gyan Publishing House, New Delhi for bringing out the volume in a record time.

U.B. Singh

Shikshak Diwas, 2020 Lucknow

The Honour

PROFESSOR S.K. SINGH

Professor of Public Administration

Lucknow University, Lucknow

Professor S.K. Singh, my esteemed 'academic *'Guru',* initiated me to the teaching career, and guided me in doctoral and post-doctoral research works. I was his first proud scholar of Ph.D. and second of D.Litt. I am obliged to him for compassionately helping and guiding me even in framing sub- themes and identifying potential contributors without any query. This befits a True *'Guru'*. He is always proficiently available to guide their disciples. His blessings have been guiding and inspiring me and shaping my personality. Esteemed Professor Singh, a man of impeccable personality is not known only for his resolute principles, self-contained nature and strict discipline, but for his generosity, self-effacing and humane behaviour. **My *'shat shat Pranam'* to him.**

अखण्डमण्डलाकारं व्याप्तं येन चराऽचरम्।
तत्पदं दर्शितं येन तस्मै श्री गुरवे नमः।।

अज्ञानतिमिरान्धस्य ज्ञानाञजनशलाकया।
चक्षुरुन्मीलितं येन तस्मै श्रीगुरवे नमः।।

अखण्डानन्दबोधाय शि यसन्तापहारिणे।
सच्चिदानन्दरूपाय तस्मै श्रीगुरवे नमः।।

शि याणां मोक्षदानाय लीलया देहधारिणे।
सदेहेऽपि विदेहाय तस्मै श्रीगुरवे नमः।।

स्थावरजङ्गमंव्याप्तं येन कृत्स्नंचराऽचरम्।
तत्पदं दर्शितं येन तस्मै श्री गुरवे नमः।।

Controbutors

Professor P.N. Gautam, Retd. Professor of Public Administration, Himachal Pradesh University, Summer Hill, Shimla.

Professor S.N. Singh, Emeritus Professor, Department of Public Administration, Lucknow University, Lucknow.

Professor R. K. Mishra, Director, Institute of Public Enterprise, Hyderabad.

Professor S.K. Jaiswal, Head of the Department of Ancient Indian History & Archaeology, University of Lucknow, Lucknow.

Professor V. Gnaneshwar, Former Professor, Regional Centre for Urban and Environmental Studies, Osmania University, Hyderabad.

Professor Lalrintluanga, Dean, School of Social Sciences, Mizoram University, Aizawl, Mizoram.

Professor S. Chandran, Former Professor of Political Science, Vinayaka Missions University, Salem (Tamil Nadu)

Professor Neelima Deshmukh, Senior Fellow ICSSR, Dr.Babsaheb Ambedkar College of Law and Retd. Prof. of Public Administration & Local Govt., RTM Nagpur University, Nagpur.

Dr. V. Bijukumar, Associate Professor, Centre for Political Studies, Jawaharlal Nehru University, New Delhi.

Professor M.A. Hussein, former Professor of Political Science, Sri Venkateswar University, Tirupati, Andhra Pradesh.

Professor N.V.R. Jyoti Kumar, Head of the Department of Commerce, Mizoram University, Aizawl, Mizoram.

Professor Rajbir Singh Dalal, Chairperson, Department of Public Administration, Chaudhary Devi Lal University, Sirsa, Haryana.

Dr. A. Sridhar Raj, Associate Professor, Institute of Public Enterprise, Hyderabad.

Dr. Abhinav Sharma, Associate Professor, Department of Political Science, Banaras Hindu University, Varanasi

Professor C. Devendiran, Department of Social Work, Mizoram University, Aizawl , Mizoram.

Dr. Chaganti Nagaraja Rao, Senior Faculty, Centre for Urban Development Studies, Dr. M.C.R. Human Resource Development Institute, Jubilee Hills, Hyderabad, Telengana.

Dr. S. Vijay Kumar, Head & Associate Professor (Retd.), Department of Economics, Kakatiya Govt. College, Hanamkonda, Kakatiya University, Warangal (Telangana).

Dr. A. K. Singh, Assistant Director, Regional Centre for Urban & Environmental Studies, Lucknow University, Lucknow.

Dr. Pawan Kumar Banta, Consultant at N G Os, New Shimla.

Krishna Pratap Singh, Research Scholar, Department of Political Science, Banaras Hindu University, Varanasi.

Jyoti Bikash Chakma, Research Scholar, Department of Commerce, Mizoram University, Aizawl, Mizoram.

Dr. Ravindra Singh, Assistant Professor, Department of Social Work, Dr Bhimrao Ambedkar College, University of Delhi, Delhi.

Ms. V. Anupama NRI, Habsiguda, Hyderabad

1

Covid-19 and Polemics of Indian Federal Polity

— *P.N. Gautam*

Introduction

The corona virus disease called as Covid-19, a worldwide pandemic had its origin in China. This virus first appeared in November 2019 in Wuhan city of China. The first case of Covid-19 in India was reported on January 30, 2020. India currently has the largest number of confirmed cases in Asia, and has the third highest number of confirmed cases in the world after the United States and Brazil with the number of total confirmed cases. Central and state governments of India took many preventive, informative, curative and financial steps to fight the pandemic. Country has passed through three lockdown and three unlock phases from 24th March, 2020 to the end of August, 2020.

The United Nations (UN) and the World Health Organization (WHO) have praised India's response to the pandemic as 'Comprehensive and robust,' terming the Lockdown restrictions as aggressive but vital for containing the spread and building necessary healthcare infrastructure. The Oxford COVID-19 Government Response Tracker (OxCGRT) noted the government's swift and stringent actions, emergency policy making, emergency investment in healthcare, fiscal stimulus, investment in vaccine and drug R&D. It gave India a score of 100 for its strict response. Michael Ryan, chief executive director of the WHO's health emergencies programme noted that India had tremendous capacity to deal with the outbreak owing to its vast experience in eradicating smallpox and polio. In June, India was ranked 56th of 200 countries in COVID-19 safety assessment report by Deep Knowledge Group. Though, other commentators have also raised concerns about the economic fallout arising as a result of the pandemic and preventive restrictions.

Present paper discusses how the central and state governments of India fight the pandemic of Covid-19 which exhibits the real polemics of Indian federal polity. It discusses nature of Indian federalism, efforts made and problems faced by the central and state governments. It also makes suggestions for effective fight against the Covid-19 and for developing healthy cooperative federalism.

Nature of Indian Federalism

India is a federal democratic republic with a strong centre designed purposely by the founding father of the Constitution in view of the historical background. Division of powers between the Centre and the states has been meticulously mentioned in the Seventh Schedule of the Constitution (Article 246). Division has been done according to three lists. List-I is Union List, containing 97 items, on which the Central government makes laws. List-II is State List, containing 66 items on which the state governments make laws. List-III is Concurrent List having 47 items on which both the central as well as state governments can make laws[1]

However, in case a law made by a state is contrary to a law made by the Centre, the law made by the state shall be repugnant to that extent. Then there are also provisions which allow a state government to request the Parliament to make a law with respect to that state even on the subjects which fall in the State List. According to the Article 356 of the Constitution the central government has the power to declare emergency. If the President, on receipt of report from the Governor of a State or otherwise, is satisfied that a situation has arisen in which the government of the State cannot be carried on in accordance with the provision of the Constitution, he may assume the functions of the government of the State and declare that the powers of the legislature of the State be exercised by or under the authority of Parliament. All this make the Central government very strong in India.

Central Government Fights Covid-19

Continuing our discussion on the Covid-19, we may say that according to the entry number 6 of the State List of the Seventh Schedule of the Indian Constitution, 'public health' is a state subject. At the same time "Prevention of the extension from one State to another of infectious or contagious diseases or pests affecting men, animals or plants" is in the 29th item of the Concurrent List of the Schedule on which both the state and central governments have the jurisdiction. The Centre also used the provisions of the Disaster Management Act, 2005 and the Epidemic Diseases Act, 1897 to fight against the virus.

The Epidemic Diseases Act 1897, is a 125 year old British colonial era law, is the main legislative framework at the Union level for the prevention and spread of dangerous epidemic diseases. It was enacted to "tackle the epidemic of bubonic plague that broke out in the then Bombay state at the time." It has been "historically used to contain the spread of various diseases — swine flu, cholera, malaria and dengue." Section 2A of the Act empowers the union government to take necessary measures and prescribe regulations to deal with dangerous epidemic disease at ports of entry and exit. Under section 2, states are empowered to take special measures or promulgate regulations to deal with epidemics within their jurisdictions. Thus, any state government, when satisfied that any part of its territory is threatened with an outbreak of a dangerous disease, and upon determination that the ordinary provisions of the law are insufficient for the purpose, may adopt or authorize all measures, including inspection of travelling persons and quarantine, to prevent the outbreak of the disease.

The Central government ordered first 21-day lock down on March 25th to contain the spread of the virus in the country. The government took proactive measures to control its spread in India. Movements of the people from their houses were restricted. All the intra and inter-state transport services, railways services and air services were suspended. All cross-national borders were sealed. All the educational institutions like schools, colleges, universities, etc. were closed. Gyms, malls, clubs, hotels, community halls, religious places, etc. were shut. Only essential services like supply of food items, provision of water, electricity, hospital facilities, etc. were allowed. It suspended all visas except for diplomats and employment. It conducted heavy screenings and mandatorily quarantined incoming International travellers. All this was done to save the country from the community spread of the virus.

To curb the growing panic and to safeguard the people from rumors, the government provided authentic information on the virus, its spread, preventions, guidelines, helpline numbers, registered cases, death tool, etc. on the Ministry of Health's official website. The government introduced the *Arogya Setu* mobile application to educate the people about the virus and help them make informed decisions amid the crisis. The government designated 72 centres across the country for the diagnosis and treatment of the virus. To provide for more isolation wards, the government converted 20,000+ railway coaches into isolation stations. Meanwhile, the Centre has also ramped up steps to develop a vaccine for the pandemic.

Some of the efforts made by the Central government, as pointed out by Jayant Sinha in his article "Moving resolutely towards post-pandemic future published in The Hindu may be mentioned here: "Soon after the lockdown was announced, the Prime Minister announced the *Pradhan Mantri Garib Kalyan Yojana* — a massive relief package for the needy. Through this programme, around 80 crore fellow citizens are being provided rations through the Public Distribution System. This has saved them money and put cash in their pockets. Over 20 crore *Jan Dhan* women account holders have received INR 30,654 crore directly into their bank accounts. Around 2.3 crore construction workers have got INR 4,313 crore, while 2.8 crore beneficiaries in the National Social Assistance Programme have received INR 2,815 crore. Almost 10 crore farmers have received INR 40,000 crore as income support through the PM *Kisan Samman Nidhi*. Over 4 crore households are benefiting from the expanded Mahatma Gandhi Employment Guarantee Act scheme. Thus the rural economy has received over INR 2 lakh crore of cash directly into beneficiary accounts just from the Central government. Micro, Small and Medium Enterprises (MSMEs) and large corporates have also been provided substantial relief through coordinated action between the Reserve Bank of India (RBI) and the government. Compliance filings and tax payments were extended by several months. Borrowers received a loan moratorium of six months. Moreover, the RBI has cut rates by 115bps and pumped in more than INR 9 lakh crore in liquidity into the financial system; INR 3 lakh crore have been made available as guaranteed collateral-free loans for MSME borrowers. The National Bank for Agriculture and Rural Development (NABARD), Small Industries Development Bank of India (SIDBI), National Housing Bank, and Non-banking financial companies have all been provided refinancing facilities. The RBI has undertaken vast long-term repo operations to bring down the yield curve. As a result of all these policy actions, credit markets have stabilised, credit is available, and spreads have come down to normal levels. After these relief measures were rolled out, the government introduced the *Atmanirbhar Bharat* revival package. Following the adage that a crisis is a terrible thing to waste, the Prime Minister has launched bold policy reforms in agriculture, defence production, electronics manufacturing, coal mining, and the public sector. These reforms position India for the future and generate confidence among business people and investors."[2]

State Governments Fight Covid-19

All the state governments, including the non-BJP governments, and Union Territories followed the lock-down instructions. Some of the non-BJP state governments, like Punjab, Kerala and Telangana, ordered lockdown even before the Central government asked for the lockdown. Section 2A of the Epidemic Diseases Act 1897 empowers the Union government to take necessary measures and prescribe regulations to deal with dangerous epidemic disease at ports of entry and exit. Under section 2, states are empowered to take special measures or promulgate regulations to deal with epidemics within their jurisdictions. Some states and Union Territories, thus, issued emergency measures and regulations (Karnataka being the first State to issue regulations) for their own jurisdictions in pursuant to the Epidemic

Disease Act to deal with COVID-19: The Delhi Epidemic Diseases, COVID-19 Regulations, 2020, The Maharashtra Epidemic Diseases COVID-19 Regulations, 2020, Punjab Epidemic Diseases, COVID-19 Regulations, 2020, The Himachal Pradesh Epidemic Disease (COVID-19) Regulations, 2020 are some of the such regulations issued by the states.

These regulations and measures varied but included provisions on duties and obligations of hospitals and laboratories, powers of district administrations to implement containment measures (sealing off geographical areas, barring entry or exit of containment area, designating quarantine facilities, and closure of schools, offices, etc. and banning mass gatherings), and combating COVID-19 related misinformation. State/Union Territory governments, thus, took many actions to strengthen community surveillance, quarantine facilities, isolation wards, adequate PPEs, trained manpower, rapid response teams for management of COVID-19.

Migrant Labour Crisis and Covid-19

Lockdowns imposed by the Central and state governments led to the migrant labour crisis. With factories and workplaces shut down due to the lockdown, millions of migrant workers hailing from the states of Uttar Pradesh, Bihar, West Bengal, Jharkhand and Chhattisgarh had to suffer with the loss of income, food shortages and uncertainty about their future. There were no trains, buses or other vehicles to go back to their home states. Thousands of them then began walking back home, with no means of transport due to the lockdown. In response, the Central and State Governments took various measures to help them, and later arranged transport for them. More than 300 migrant workers died due to the lockdown, with reasons ranging from starvation, suicides, exhaustion, road and rail accidents, police brutality and denial of timely medical care.

The Supreme Court of India, recognising the problems faced by migrants stranded in different parts of the country, reviewed transportation and relief arrangements made by the governments. On June 9, the Court directed Central and state governments to complete transportation of remaining stranded migrants and expand focus of relief measures to facilitate employment for returning migrants. The Central and state governments did take several steps to provide transportation, free food, some work through MNREGA, etc. But this was not sufficient. Then there some conflicts between the Centre and state governments, especially were with the non-BJP ruled states like West Bengal and Maharashtra, in providing relief to the migrant labour. So much so, that on 26 May, the Supreme Court admitted that the problems of the migrants had still not been solved and that there had been "inadequacies and certain lapses" on the part of the governments. It thus ordered the Centre and states to provide free food, shelter and transport to stranded migrant workers. It can, thus, easily be concluded that both Centre and states failed to devise a coherent and holistic plan of action to avert the migrant crisis.

Critique

Fight against Covid-19 has thrown a lot of light on the working of federalism in India. An article entitled as "Reaffirm cooperative federalism" published in The Hindu on 13th May, 2020 talks about the nature of Indian federalism and federal issues accentuated during the Covid-19 pandemic. The writers are of the view that "India's success in defeating **Covid-19** actively rests upon Centre-State collaboration. However, some recent developments have revealed fissures in Centre-State cooperation. As it is the States which act as first responders to the pandemic, supplying them with adequate funds and autonomy becomes a pre-requisite in effectively tackling the crisis. This requires the Centre to view the States as equals, and strengthen their capabilities, instead of increasing their dependence upon itself. In this context, Covid-19 poses a litmus test for the federal structure of India, whose nature is already a matter of debate amongst constitution experts."[3]

Let us discuss some financial issues accentuated during the Covid-19 pandemic. During various lockdown phases and even unlock phases the sources of states' revenue have dried up. Position of following sources of revenue is worth mentioning in this connection:-

- Majority of states' revenue comes from liquor sales, stamp duty from property transactions and the sales tax on petroleum products.
- However, their expenditure such as on interest payments, social sector schemes and staff salaries remain unchanged.
- Moreover, states are now called upon to spend more on beefing up their health infrastructure and on Covid-19 measures, including testing, treatment and quarantining.
- States' GST collections have also been severely affected with their dues still not disbursed by the Centre.

Some of the following other institutional financial handicaps which the states face in the present federal system also came to light during this pandemic:-

- According to the FRBM Act, states cannot borrow from the market over a certain limit.
- The PM-CARES relief fund has been put under the ambit of Corporate Social Responsibility (CSR) contributions. However, contributions to the 'Chief Minister's Relief Fund' or 'State Relief Fund for Covid-19' do not qualify as admissible CSR expenditure. This directly disincentivises donations to any Chief Minister's

Relief Fund; diverts crores in potential State revenues to PM-CARES; and makes the States largely dependent upon the Centre.

- The suspension of MPLADS and diversion of the funds to the Consolidated Fund of India may not be in concurrence of cooperative federalism, as it discourages locally tailored solutions by the MPs.
- The Disaster Management Act, 2005 envisages the creation of a 'National Plan' under Section 11, as well as the issuance of binding guidelines by the Centre to States under Section 6(2), in furtherance of the 'National Plan'. However, section 11(2) of the Act mandates State consultations before formulating a 'National Plan'.

The above scenario has made the states in India fully dependent on the Union government for finances.

Views of Kabir S. Ghosh in his article, Erosion of fiscal federalism in times of Covid-19, published in The Hindu Business Line deserve to be quoted here: "As India's battle against Covid-19 completes two months, worrisome trends in Centre-State relations have come to the fore. With Prime Minister Narender Modi steamrolling policies on cash-strapped States, the fiscal demands of fighting the current pandemic have put extraordinary pressures on State finances. From imposing pan-India policies on subjects strictly within the States' domain, prohibiting sale of alcohol, withholding of GST compensation, denial of State disaster funds from the benefit of CSR contributions to the suspension of MPLADS, the Modi government has ensured a consolidation of fiscal powers not only threatening fiscal federalism, but the very foundations of the federal structure evolved over the past decades."[4]

Some light on the political dimension of Indian federalism in the context of fight against Covid-19 also need to be discussed here to have the clear picture of its polemics.

On the outbreak of Covid-19, in the beginning, when Prime Minister Narendra Modi gave a call for a people's curfew and then a three-week national lockdown, all state governments even those run by opposition parties backed the move and enforced the lockdown — some, in fact, even encouraged the PM to take such a step. States also backed the second phase of the lockdown — from April 15 till May 3. All the states willingly followed the Centre's lead in view of the severity of the pandemic. The fact that the PM himself had a series of interactions with the chief ministers prior to lockdowns helped in giving a sense of a more consultative and consensual approach. There were differences of course (the most obvious being the one between the Centre and West Bengal), but the big picture was one of a degree of coordination.

But this period of harmony was over by the third phase of lockdown and slowly politics returned to its normal dimension by both the Centre and Opposition-ruled states openly articulating their differences. The West Bengal government led by Mamata Banerjee and Maharashtra government led by Uddhav Thackeray, were the first to point out their differences with the Centre especially on the issue of migrant labour and arranging for their journey back to their home states. The states also began feeling that extended lockdown has lost much of its utility and caused heavy economic strain. On fighting Covid-19, the Centre pulled up some of the more severely affected states for inadequate testing, gaps in the contact tracing process, and not having prepared the health infrastructure enough. States, especially those governed by non-BJP parties, in turn; saw this as the Centre deflecting blame for its own shortcomings. On finances, states felt aggrieved at the delay in the payment of compensation due to them under the Goods and Services Tax regime; they also expected the Centre to provide a greater financial cushion in these times. The Centre felt that by relaxing borrowing limits for states and making it conditional on a set of reforms has helped the states.

The game of political credit and blame has now come to its full play. Now from the Prime Minister (PM) down to each Chief Minister (CM), all political leaders in the country are trying their best to be seen well in dealing with the pandemic. Views of Mani Raj in his blog in The Times of India deserve to be quoted in the present context: "The return to political competitiveness is not necessarily negative. It is through contestation that democracy evolves and decisions get better. But partisan politics has adverse effects too, particularly when the nation needs to battle the crisis as one. What is, however, clear is that this competition, in the wake of the pandemic, will inaugurate a new phase of Indian federalism. The new balance of power between the Centre and states is not yet clear, but can be the most important political fallout of the crisis."[5]

On the bright side of the Indian federalism, it may be mentioned that the PM began holding consultations with the chief ministers of various states, before issuing orders for extension of lockdown. In fact by the third phase of lockdown and now, with Unlock 1, 2 and 3 in process, states got more and more say in decision making. It is now up to the state governments to decide which area would be declared a containment zone and which would not be. This cooperation went a step further, with the public seeing considerable interactions between home minister Amit Shah and Delhi chief minister, Arvind Kejriwal. These arch-rivals on the political field have held meetings more than once to discuss and check the spread of Covid-19 and make available beds in Delhi hospitals for Corona patients.

Suggestions

The constituent assembly in India studied various democratic federal models in the world and formulated a system suited uniquely to India's needs. Further, it is argued that a "strong centre" does not necessarily presuppose weak states. As a result, India adopted 'cooperative federalism' — essentially defined by administrative cooperation between the Centre and states and among states. Therefore, both Union and states should work together to tackle the Covid-19 pandemic and strengthen the spirit of cooperative federalism. According to K.R. Vignesh Karthik, "A desire to go for a command-and-control approach led from the Centre will lead to a square peg in a round hole situation that would aggravate miseries on ground. In fine, the pandemic has come to serve as a perfect case study to revisit the idea of federalism in India and start action towards undoing the prevalent centralising tendencies in the Indian polity and governance."[6]

Some of the following suggestions deserve to be noted for developing a healthy cooperative federalism model in India:-

- The Covid-19 pandemic can be handled better if the Centre follows a bottom up approach and allows states to make decisions about lockdown and all health related issues. This will bring about a sense of empowerment among state governments. Both the Centre and the states should try to rise above party politics and take the pandemic head on. Mud-slinging and blaming one another should be sincerely avoided. Hopefully, the Corona virus will teach a lesson to the political class to rise above their narrow party interests to fight effectively against the virus.
- As PM-CARES relief fund is an avenue of expenditure under the ambit of Corporate Social Responsibility (CSR) contributions, similarly, contributions to the 'Chief Minister's Relief Fund' or 'State Relief Fund for COVID-19' should also qualify for CSR expenditure. This will give fine tuning to the spirit of cooperative federalism and at the same time enhance the financial capability of the states to fight the pandemic.
- The limit imposed by the FRBM Act must be relaxed so that states who are falling short of funds can borrow money to combat the pandemic and revive the economy. These borrowings can be backed by sovereign guarantee by the Union Government.
- As per the need of hour, the Centre should provide money to states so that they can take necessary action to deal with the crisis at state level.
- As a matter of generous gesture, the Centre should direct FCI to move the grains from the go downs to states.
- A successful approach to tackle the crisis would still need centre's intervention and guidance in a facilitative manner, where the Centre would communicate extensively the best practices across states,

address the financial needs effectively, and leverage national expertise for scalable solutions.

- Nobel laureate Abhijit Banerjee recently in an interview discussed the federal relations between the Centre and state and has advised the Central government to not plan the lockdown activities and expenditure management for the states, and instead the primary lookout for the Centre should be to transfer money to the states to make them capable to revive their economy according their state-specific requirements. It should be noted that the constitutional body of Finance Commission also recommended fiscal transfer keeping the state priorities as one of the factors for consideration and hence the Centre should not arbitrarily legislate, execute or transfer money to the states according to its own views and opinions about the states. The demands for relaxation of the mandated three percent fiscal deficit under Fiscal Responsibility Management Act, 2003 should be considered by the centre in this- exceptional situation.

Summing Up

The fight against Covid-19 by the Central government and state governments has brought many aspects of the polemics of Indian federalism. It has clearly shown us the elements of cooperation, competition and conflict in the working of our polity. Strong Centre has taken bold steps by providing informative and curative help and guidance to the states. The states, on their part, have followed various calls given by the Centre for lockdowns and un-lockdowns. They have also taken various measures suggested by the Centre to fight the pandemic. States have also learnt the ways of fighting the pandemic from the successful methods adopted by other states. The Centre has given some financial packages to enable the states to fight the pandemic. The states ruled by the non-BJP governments have clearly shown their resentment against the Centre for not providing them the necessary facilities in coping with the migrant labour crisis and also not providing them with the equipment to fight the Covid-19. They have also criticised the centre for not providing them their Goods & Services Tax (GST) dues, withdrawal of MPLADS funds and not extending them the benefits of Corporate Social Responsibility (CSS) to the Chief Ministers' Relief Funds. States are also demanding special financial packages to fight the Covid-19. The Centre needs to consider the genuine demands of the states. Suggestions given as above need to be implemented sincerely. More open dialogue between the Centre and states is the need of hour. It will help India not only develop a true cooperative federal state and mature democratic polity, but also enable India to the pandemic effectively and expeditiously.

To conclude, the views of Prof. Balramulu deserve to be quoted to address the problem of Covid-19: "Presently both the Central and state governments are not seriously addressing the health concerns of the people and leaving it to the individuals and private sector, persistence of corona viruses across the country. Private hospital managements are charging exorbitantly, and thus many people are deprived of health services." He further suggested, "Both the governments should allot more budgets to the health sector. State governments need to strengthen the primary health care system and make that accessible to the poor. Governments should monitor and control private hospitals."[7]

Notes

1. The Constitution on India, Seventh Schedule.
2. Jayant Sinha, The Hindu, Moving resolutely toward post-pandemic future, p. 6.
3. Pranav Verma and Sughsh Joshi, The Hindu, Reaffirm cooperative federalism, May 13, 2020, p. 6.
4. Thehindubusinessline.com/opinion/erosion-of-fiscal-federalism-in-the-times-of-covid19/ article. 21670568.ece. May 25, 2020.
5. Mulak Raj, Timesofindia.indiatimes,com>Blogs>India Blogs Covid Times: Federalism in a new form.
6. K.R. Vigneh Karthik, a doctoral researcher at King's College London has tweeted through his tweet @krvtweets.
7. prof.balarumulu@gmail.com; 25 Aug, 2020.

2

STATE ADMINISTRATION IN INDIA
Role in Development Administration and Pandemic Management

— A. Sridhar Raj & R K Mishra

Introduction

From Government to Governance, is the fundamental shift that has been happening in Indian political structure in the recent years. The state governments have been emerging as an important tool for the central government to carry out their constitutional mandate. The concept of *power sharing* gave way to *responsibility sharing* in the Indian context. Kuldeep Mathur has expanded the ambit of governance who stated that, "Governance is concerned with the changes taking place in the organization of the state and its relationships with private sector and civil society."(Mathur: 2016)

The Constitution of India has given due importance to the state governments in India by calling Indian polity as a "Union of States" which means that the states are an integral part of the federal structure. The state governments act as limbs of the central government extending well into the hinterland of the country. The makers of the Indian Constitution were aware of the fact that India was highly pluralistic, multi-lingual and multi-racial. Given such diversity of the states, the Constitution provided enough autonomy and flexibility for the state governments to address specific needs of each state.

Subhash Kashyap opined that "A citizen is more intimately concerned with the state administration and the powers available for the state to look after his interests."(Kashyap: 1997) The state governments are pivotally placed in the Indian federal structure to act as a link between the citizens and the central government. Although, the Constitution of India has provided for a strong central government, the state governments are positioned to serve the citizens from a holistic perspective.

State Administration: The Execution Arm for Development

The state administration is responsible for ameliorating the living conditions of the poor and downtrodden sections of the society. Towards such objective, the state administration shoulders responsibilities which enhance the overall living standards of the citizens. In fact, the developmental plans of the Government of India are dependent upon the state administration for their successful execution. According to Krishna Tummala, "all developmental programmes of the Center since independence are entirely dependent upon the sub-national governments for their execution."(Tummala: 1994)

A similar sentiment was echoed by Maheshwari with regard to the role and importance of the state governments. He opined that, "The state governments have been entrusted with a large number of functions which extend to both regulatory and development administration. Internal security is the state government's direct responsibility which covers, in addition, to nation building activities like agriculture, animal husbandry, public health, cooperatives, education, minor irrigation, etc. Indeed, most line functions, which are of direct concern to the citizens are with the state government, which make them a very powerful level of the federal system."(Maheshwari: 1991)

It is but natural that the state administration is laden with all those responsibilities where the citizens *find and feel* the government every day and everywhere and in the words of Nicholas Henry, it is *Big Democracy and Big Bureaucracy*.(Henry: 2003)

Although, the central government is the overall guardian of the country, the Constitution and the citizens, the state governments carryout the development mandate for the citizens. The institution of public administration is more visible for the citizens at the state level than at the central level. Hence, the development orientation of the state is felt at the state level, as the central government's role is restricted to that of an advisor and guide. The following statistics provide a glimpse as how the state governments address the myriad needs of the citizens:

- 28.7 percent of households in India have at least one member covered under a health insurance or health scheme
- 84.75 percent of people who demanded employment under MGNREGA were provided the employment in rural India
- One rural household is covered under PDS for every low income rural household where monthly income of highest income earning member is less than Rs. 5000
- 221 governmental health workers per 1,00,000 persons with Kerala having highest rate of 762

- Highest immunization coverage is found in Punjab with 89 percent for the children in the age group of 12-23 months
- 81.15 percent of school teachers in India are professionally qualified
- 75.83 percent of eligible children are enrolled into school at elementary and secondary level
- 82.72 percent rural households have Individual Household Toilets
- 71.8 percent of rural population in India has access to safe and adequate drinking water

  (*Source:* SDG India Index, Baseline Report, 2018, Niti Aayog, Government of India)

The above data provides a glimpse of the state of development in the country and the credit for this accomplishment of the goals goes to the state governments. One of the stellar success stories of state administration successfully providing piped drinking water facility to all the villages and municipal areas in the state is Mission *Bhagiratha* in the state of Telangana.

Mission *Bhagiratha*: A Case Study of Drinking Water Supply in Rural Areas

The Government of Telangana launched the Mission *Bhagiratha* project with the objective of providing each house a tap connection which can mitigate the problems of accessing drinking water for the people. The Mission *Bhagiratha* was conceived by the Government of Telangana with an outlay of Rs. Rs 45,028 crores covering a geographical of 1.11 lakh sq.km. benefitting a population 2.72 crores in the state. The government has decided to lay pipeline network of 1,460 lakh kms. which is equal to three times the circumference of the earth. The major objectives of the Mission are given below:

- Sourcing water from major rivers or reservoirs fed by these rivers
- Purify the raw water in nearby Water Treatment Plant
- Pump treated water to the sumps at the highest points
- Transmit from the highest point through secondary pipeline network to all the habitations by gravity (98 percent)
- Distribute to each house hold through a modern, rationalized intra village network by providing tap connections to each household

The Mission was so successful that the Prime Minister appreciated the state administration for taking up a humungous project to provide drinking water to the people of Telangana.

Centre and State Relationship

The Drafting Committee of the Indian Constitution described the Indian polity as federal in structure but preferred to call it 'Union of States'. However, there are many unitary features. There are many unitary trends which were deliberately inserted in the Constitution of India to curb regional and linguistic challenges. The Constitution of India is popularly described as 'Quasi-Federal', 'unitary state with subsidiary federal features', 'a federation with a strong centralizing tendency'. Many scholars firmly believe that to a large extent that the Union is strong *vis-à-vis* the state governments.

When the state of Telangana was formed with Hyderabad as its capital city, the state of Andhra Pradesh formed a new capital city and named it Amaravati. The Ministry of Home Affairs has the final approval say in approving the name of the capital city and the same thing happened in the case of Amaravati.

This implies that the Union Government has riding powers over the state governments in many cases. In the distribution of revenue resources, the Union's tax resources are greater than those of the States. Revenues collected by the Union are allocated to the States, on the basis of recommendations by the Finance Commission. The States are dependent on the Center for grants in-aid.

The legislative powers between the Union and the States are enumerated into three lists namely the Union List, the State List, and the Concurrent List. The Seventh Schedule of the Constitution specifies the exclusive powers of the Center in the Union list, exclusive powers of the States in the State List and those falling under the joint jurisdiction of both the Union and the State are placed in the Concurrent List. Residuary powers are vested in the Union.

Union List: This List includes subjects which have national importance and the laws enacted in these subjects are the exclusive domain of the central government like external affairs, armed forces, railways, national highways, etc.

State List: The List includes all those activities which can be conveniently handled by the state government and this is the level at which the citizens come into contact with governance. Some of the items include law and order, agriculture, prisons, public health and sanitation, education, etc.

Concurrent List: This is the List where the subjects are covered both by the central and the state governments. However, the final say rests with the central government.

Centre and State Coordination: Inter-State Council

The framers of the Constitution were wise enough to provide all the mechanisms for better coordination between the central and the state governments. A provision to set up an Inter State Council for harmonizing the relationship between the national and the sub-national governments exists. The Inter State Council established is a forum for effective coordination and cooperation between the units in the federal system. It was established to provide a platform for both the Union and the States to discuss and deliberate on matters of common interest.

The Council is comprised of the Prime Minister, all the Chief Ministers, the Administrators of Union territories, Governors of States under President's Rule, six Union Ministers of Cabinet rank in the Union Council of Ministers, nominated by the Prime Minister and two Ministers of Cabinet rank in the Union Council of Ministers to be nominated by the Prime Minister as permanent invitees. The Council addresses various issues like advising upon disputes which arising between the state governments, discussing the subjects in which some or all of the states have a common interest and recommend for better coordination between the central and the state governments.

However, despite all the good intentions of the founders of the Constitution, things did not go well with the central government often interfering the functioning of the state administration. In fact, many states were annoyed with the central government's directives from time to time which were not liked by the state governments. To enhance better coordination between the central and the state governments, there were a few attempts in the form of Committees and Commissions, with the mandate of surveying the landscape of Union and State Relationship.

In the year 1969, a Committee headed by P.V. Rajamannar was appointed by the Tamil Nadu government to examine the working of the Center-State relations. The Committee observed that "there are unitary trends and in the allocation of powers there is a strong bias and tilting of the scales in favour of the Center." The Committee recommended for the abolition of the Planning Commission. The Government of India took almost 50 long years to abolish the Planning Commission and replace the same with NITI *Ayog*.

In the year 1983, another Commission was set up under the chairmanship R.S. Sarkaria, to study the Center-State relations. The Commission advocated 'cooperative federalism' and greater financial autonomy for the states. The Commission also suggested that the Article 356 should be used sparingly and the Governors of the states appointed be non-political.

The second Commission on Centre-State relations was constituted in 2006 under the chairmanship of Justice (Retd.) Punchhi which submitted its report in 2010.

The Federal Structure during Pandemic Times

Great Britain is a unitary state with Parliament as the highest legislative body. The ministries are the basic administrative units which are under the control of the minister. The minister is a member of the Parliament and is handpicked by the Prime Minister for heading the ministry. The minister is responsible for taking decisions pertaining to the ministry concerned with the help of the Secretary. Secretary is the administrative head of the ministry and assists the minister in policy decisions and also monitors the execution of the decisions. "The standard arrangement is for each ministry is to be headed by a minister responsible before Parliament for all ministry affairs."(Heady: 1996) Since, Britain is a unitary state, the power is held in the Centre; however, some powers are devolved to Scotland, Wales and Northern Ireland.

The United States is a federal state with Presidential form of government with the states forming strong sub-national governments at the state level. The balance of power between the Federal Government and the State Governments has been undergoing shifts from time to time depending upon various factors like the President, economic conditions, wars, etc. The COVID- 19 has brought out various legal and political dimensions about the federal structure and the overriding power of the Federal Government over the State Governments.

In fact, during such critical health emergency situations, the acrimony between the President and various Governors of the states particularly the Governor of New York has opened up the debates about the powers of the Federal Government. The New York Governor in a scathing criticism about the President said, "If he's sitting home watching TV, may be he should get up and go to work". On the other hand, the President rebuked the New York Governor, "Governor Cuomo should spend more time "doing "and less time "complaining". Get out there and get the job done. Stop talking."

The acrimony between the President and the Governor is pointer to the lack of coordination between two institutional heads during the health emergency. The acrimony is a pointer to the fact that the federal structure in the United States has failed to function in unison. The Federal Government and State Governments are at logger heads about the responsibility of containing the Corona virus.

In India, with a billion plus population, the Central and the State Governments have acted in unison to tackle the Corona Virus through a nation-wide lockdown. The state governments have been heeding the advice of the central government and have been carrying out the advisories from central government from time to time. In fact, the simple act of lighting lamps, a call given by the Prime Minister was actively supported by the

Chief Ministers of many states, with many Chief Ministers lighting the lamps in support of the clarion call given by the Prime Minister.

During the Pandemic times, the state governments are in the forefront and the support is extended by the central government. In India, the state governments have acted in coordination with the central government. A number of online conferences between the central government and the state governments point to the fact that India could address the Corona Pandemic in a better way than the United States.

State Administration: Pandemic Times

The COVID- 19 video conference between the Prime Minister and the Chief Ministers of different states was eagerly awaited by the people. The Chief Ministers provided valuable inputs and insights to the central government about the Ground Zero situation. The Chief Ministers gave valuable suggestions to the Prime Minister as what could be the next steps in overcoming the challenges faced by the COVID- 19 in different parts of the country. In fact, the role of the central government during the pandemic has been that of an *'advisor'* and the state government played the role of the *'executioner'*. The Prime Minister lauded the stupendous endeavors of the state governments in mitigating the challenge of the Corona Virus spread in the country. The responsibility of slowing the spread of the virus rested on the shoulders of the state administration in a country with a population of more than 1.35 billion people.

Of course, the state administration, all over the country, had been busy supplying the *essential goods and services* to the people so that they do not run out of stocks of food grains and essential items. The state administration, in some states, supplied free ration, free food, free medical supplies apart from handling the Corona Virus by testing, quarantining, diagnosing and treating the virus suspects and actual patients. The state administration right from the Chief Minister to the lowest level employee has shouldered the responsibility of saving people on one hand and providing the necessary supplies on the other hand. In fact, many Chief Ministers had gone overboard by assuring, a number of times, and the people in their states as not to worry about the pandemic.

The Government of Telangana had charted new path in rural areas for mitigating the problems of the farmers in the rural areas. The Government had decided to buy all the produce in the rural areas from the *Rabi* Crops in the village itself through Primary Agricultural Credit Societies (PACS). In fact, the farmers were assured that the Government would buy every grain from the field which has really gone well for the rural farmers in the state of Telangana.

The Punjab Government too provided free hand to the farmers for farmers by catering to their agricultural needs. The Uttar Pradesh Government deployed more than one thousand buses for transporting the migrant workers from the NCR to different parts of Uttar Pradesh. These humungous efforts of the state administration in different parts of the country during the cataclysmic Corona Virus pandemic speaks volumes about the efforts of the state administration in mitigating the impact of the virus. These illustrations are mere symptomatic about the role of the state administration in the governance structure of the country with a billion plus population to be *fed, clothed and housed.*

Governance is viewed as the exercise of political, economic and administrative to manage the affairs of the country for the pursuance of the social and economic wellbeing of the citizens. According to the United Nations, governance embraces all methods used to distribute power and manage public resources and the organizations that shape government and execution of policy. It encompasses the mechanism, the processes and the institutions through which the citizens and groups articulate their interests exercise their legal rights meet their obligations and resolve their differences. And in a country like India governance happens at the state level and state administration plays a critical role towards governance and good governance.

State Administration: Polity and Structure

The Constitution of India provides for a two-tier Government, one at the Union-level and the other at the State-level. The system of government in states is organized on the similar pattern to that of the Central government. The Constitution of India lays down a uniform structure for the State government and stipulates a parliamentary form of government similar to that of the Center. In accordance with the parliamentary framework of the Union government, the state governments also have two forms of Executive–the Constitutional head and the real executive.

The State executive consists of Governor and Council of Ministers with Chief Minister as its head. The Governor, known as State Executive is appointed by the President of India. Though the nominal executive authority is vested in the Governor, the Chief Minister and the Council of Ministers exercise the real executive authority. They are collectively responsible to the State Legislature. The States Legislature consists of Legislative Assembly and Legislative Council. Most states have only one House (unicameral legislature). The State Legislatures make laws for the concerned states on the subjects mentioned in the State List.

The Role and Functions of Governor

Governor is the executive head of the State and all the executive action of the State are taken in his name. The Governor holds a Constitutional position much like that of the President of India. Under Article 153 of the Indian Constitution, each state has a Governor. According to the Constitution the same individual can be appointed as the Governor of two or more States.

The Governor, unlike the President, is not elected but is appointed by the President. According to Article 155 of the Constitution, the President of India appoints the Governor for a term of five years. He may be appointed as the Governor for one or more States. Though the tenure of the Governor is five years, according to Article 156(1) of the Constitution, the Governor holds office during the pleasure of the President i.e., he can be recalled or dismissed or transferred to another state before the expiry of the term.

According to Article 361 of the Constitution, the Governor enjoys the following immunities and privileges: (a) "The Governor shall not be answerable to any court for the exercise and performance of the powers and duties of his office or any act done or purporting to be done by him in the exercise and performance of powers and duties; (b) No criminal proceedings whatsoever shall be instituted or continued against the Governor of State, in any court during his term of office; (c) No process for the arrest or imprisonment of the Governor of State shall be issued from any court during his term of office; and (d) No civil proceedings in which relief is claimed against the Governor of a State, shall be instituted during his term of office in any court in respect of any act done or purporting to be done by him in his personal capacity, whether before or after he entered upon his office as Governor of such State, until the expiration of two months after notice in writing has been delivered to the Governor".

The Constitution vests all the executive powers in the Governor. According to Article 163 of the Constitution, the Governor while discharging his duties is to be guided by the aid and advice of the Council of Ministers. The Governor has executive, legislative, financial and judicial powers.

Executive Powers: The Executive power of the State is vested in Governor. The administration of the state is carried in the name of the Governor by the Council of Ministers. Under Article 164, the Governor appoints the leader of the majority party in the Legislative Assembly as the Chief Minister. The Governor on the advice of the Chief Minister appoints other ministers. He can remove any minister on the Chief Minister's advice. It becomes the duty of the Chief Minister of the State to inform the Governor all the Government decisions pertaining to the administration of the affairs of the State and proposals of legislation.

Further, the Chief Minister must furnish the information relating to administration or proposals for legislation, if the Governor demands. The Governor has the power to appoint the Advocate General of the State, the

Chairman and members of the State Public Service Commission. The Governor is consulted by the President with regard to the appointment of the Judges for the High Court of the State. He nominates one-sixth of the members to the Legislative Council in the State (if such a council exists in that particular State). He can also nominate a representative of the Anglo-Indian community to the Legislative Assembly, if he is thinks that this community is not sufficiently represented in the House.

The Governor exercises his discretionary powers 'if any bill passed by the State Legislature is in question with effect of the powers of the union or contravene with the provisions of the Constitution or may not be in the national interest'. In such case, the Governor may differ with the Ministry and reserve that particular bill for the consideration of the President. For instance, the then Governor of Kerala differed with the Communist Government led by E.M.S. Namboodiripad and withheld the bill for the consideration of the President, as he felt that it affected the rights of the minorities protected by the Constitution.

In the dismissal of the Ministry also the Governor can exercise his discretionary powers, if he is convinced that the Ministry is engaged in activities, which may jeopardize national security or solidarity. Apart from the above mentioned discretionary powers, the Governor while discharging Constitutional functions such as: Decision on a question of disqualification of a legislator (Article 192 (1); Discharge of his statutory non-governmental functions, for example, functions entrusted to him as Chancellor of Universities. He can exercise his own judgment. Moreover, the Governor also has the right to be kept informed of all Cabinet decisions and the State administration. He may also call for any information from the Chief Ministers.

Legislative Powers: Apart from the executive powers, the Governor also exercises the following legislative powers. According to Article 168 of the Constitution, the Governor is part of the State legislature. As the administrative head of the State, the Governor has power to summon, prorogue, and dissolve the Legislative Assembly of the State (Article 174). He has to summon sessions of the legislature so that a gap of six months does not intervene between its last sitting in one session and the date appointed for its first sitting in the next session.

He addresses the Legislature at the beginning of its first session every year. The Governor promulgates/issues ordinances, when the Legislature is not in session (Article 213). The ordinance issued by the Governor has the same force and effect as an act of the State Legislature. But all such ordinances cease to operate after the expiration of six months. The Governor can also withdraw the ordinance at any time.

Every bill passed by the State Legislative Assembly cannot become a law until and unless the Governor gives his consent. When the Governor receives a bill passed by the State Legislature, they are four options before the Governor: (a) He can send bills for the consideration of the President; (b) Withhold his assent; (c) Give his assent to the Bill; and (d) Except in case of the Money bill, the Governor can return any bill to the Assembly for its reconsideration. The Governor of a state may reserve any Bill for the consideration of the President. However, when a bill is returned by him to the Legislature for reconsideration, if it is again passed by the Legislature in its original or amended form, the Governor is bound to give his assent to it.

Governor also has the power to nominate members of the Anglo-Indian community to the Legislative Assembly. The Governor can also nominate 1/6th part of the total members of the Legislative Council from among persons having specialized knowledge or practical experience in respect of literature, science, art, and social service (if there is a *Vidhan Parishad* / Legislative Council in a state). One should note that in the recent past, the Government of Andhra Pradesh has abolished the Council of States, albeit the opposition parties have termed the act as anti-democratic.

Some of the other legislative powers of the Governor are: he can decide matters relating to the disqualification of a member of the legislature if a voter challenges the member's election. Similarly, the annual reports submitted by the State Public Service Commission and Auditor-General to him are placed before the legislature for its consideration.

Financial Powers: All demands for grants are placed before the Assembly on the recommendations of the Governor. The state Finance Minister presents the annual Budget showing the estimated receipts and expenditure for the next financial year in the name of the Governor. All bills that the state legislature passes must receive the assent of the Governor. The Governor can reserve a non-money bill for consideration to the President and has the power to promulgate ordinances. The Governor is not authorized to refuse his assent in case of money and finance bills. The Governor can also make advances from the Contingency Fund of the State, to meet the unforeseen expenditure with the approval of the legislature.

Judicial Powers: According to Article 161 of the Constitution, "the Governor of a State can grant pardon and reprieve, and to suspend, remit or commute the sentence of any person convicted of any offence against any law relating to a matter to which the executive power of the State extends". But this power has to be exercised by the Governor on the advice of the Council of Ministers. Governor is consulted by the President in the appointment of the judges of the State High Court (Article 217). He appoints and transfers judges of the subordinate courts. He also inspects the working of the courts in the state. He has the power to carry out the administration of Scheduled Areas with Scheduled Tribes therein.

The Changing Role of Governor

The role and importance of Governor of the state had changed in the recent past for multiple reasons – political, demographic and technological. Politically, the governments at the central and state levels have witnessed political stability. Unlike the yesteryears, where the Office of Governor was highly misused by the party at the Center, for making and unmaking of the state governments, it has been observed that the Governor has stopped playing the role of arbiter of making and unmaking of state governments.

There have been many instances in the past where the Governors who owed their allegiance to the Center were hand in glove with the central government. The Governor involved in political parleys and often provoked the Chief Ministers deliberately which led to bad relationship between the Chief Ministers and Governors on many occasions. In the state of united Andhra Pradesh, the role of Ram Lal, the then Governor was instrumental in the removal of the Chief Minister N. T. Rama Rao. He installed a puppet Chief Minister which led to hue and cry against the Office of Governor.

However, the judgment of the Supreme Court in the S.R. Bommai *versus* Union of India made it clear that the Office of Governor can be subjected to judicial review. The Court laid down a number of guidelines to curb the Centre's capacity to dismiss a state government, and upheld the federal structure enshrined in the Constitution. The ruling laid down the law that the only way to determine support enjoyed by a particular state government would be by means of a floor test. Also, the court ruled that the validity of a proclamation of President's Rule is subject to judicial review. Given the stable political conditions at the central and state level due to clear cut mandate for the governments, there is no much room for the Governors to play political gambles.

The voter demographic too has changed with the increasing number of young and vigilant voters who are very shrewd to give right mandate for the political parties. There is no much indecisiveness and wavering among the voters who evaluate the performance of the state government and then vote. Coupled with such change, the technological changes – social media, has become a new tool for the citizens in expressing their views. The actions of the government are critically evaluated by the netizens on the social media which has become a dampener on the Governors to violate the constitutional and legal provisions.

The Council of Ministers and the Chief Minister

Every state has a Council of Ministers, with the Chief Minister as its head, which aids and advises the Governor in the conduct of the affairs of the State (Article 163). The Chief Minister of a State occupies a position to that of the Prime Minister at the Center. The Council of Ministers is headed by the Chief Minister. The Governor appoints the leader of the majority party in the state Legislative Assembly as the Chief Minister. On the advice of the Chief Minister the Governor appoints ministers and allocates the portfolios. The Council of Ministers is collectively responsible to Legislative Assembly (Article 164).

Even though the Governor is considered as chief executive of the State, in practice Council of Ministers of the state exercises the real executive power. The Council of Ministers formulates various polices, initiates legislation and coordinates the work of the different agencies of the Government. They implement policies of the Government with the assistance of the bureaucracy. A minister has to be a member of any of the Houses of State Legislature within six months from the date of his appointment otherwise he ceases to be a minister. The salaries and allowances of ministers are such as the State Legislature from time to time prescribed by the law. There are three different categories of ministers in the state: Cabinet Ministers, Ministers of State, and Deputy Ministers.

Collective Responsibility: The Council of Ministers are collectively and individually responsible to Legislative Assembly of the State, i.e., the ministry comes into office, and relinquishes it collectively as a team. They are collectively responsible to the assembly for various acts of omission and commission. They remain in office as long as it enjoys the confidence of the House. It can be removed by a vote of no-confidence. All the ministers must abide by the cabinet decision and support them in the Legislature as well as outside. In simple terms, the ministry sails or sinks together. Even if a Cabinet Minister might oppose any particular decision, he must go by the decision of the Cabinet and support the decision, otherwise he must quit the ministry.

The position of the Chief Minister in the Council of Ministers as the real executive is equivalent to that of the Prime Minister, in the State. The Chief Minister is the leader of the majority party in the Legislative Assembly and is the head of the state Council of Ministers. He is the real administrator of the state. He is the chief spokesperson of the Government. The Chief Minister remains in office as long as he enjoys the support of the majority members in the Legislative Assembly.

The Chief Minister is the real head of the State government. Based on the advice of the Chief Minister the Governor appoints – Cabinet Ministers, Ministers of State, Deputy Ministers. The Chief Minister selects the Ministers, and he also allocates the portfolios to the Ministers. He can reorganize or reshuffle his ministry as and when he deems it necessary. He presides over the Cabinet meetings and coordinates the activities of different departments. He can seek the resignation of any or all the ministers; and in case of defiance by any minister, he can advise the Governor to dismiss a minister.

The Chief Minister can recommend the dissolution of the Legislative Assembly even before the expiry of its term. The Governor can dissolve the *Vidhan Sabha* on the advice of the Chief Minister. The sessions of the Legislative Assembly are summoned and prorogued by the Governor on the advice of the Chief Minister. Appointments of high officials are made on his recommendation by the Governor. He communicates to the Governor all decisions of the Council of Ministers relating to the administration of the affairs of the state and proposals for legislation (Article 167).

He also furnishes to the Governor such information relating to the administration of the affairs of the State and proposals for legislation as the Governor may call for (Article 167).He acts as a link between the Council of Ministers and the Governor. Similarly he also acts as a link between the Legislature and his ministers. Being leader of the majority party, the Chief Minister ensures that Legislature passes all the bills moved by the government. All the bills, resolutions etc. must have his prior approval before being placed in the Legislature. He appoints the whips and sees that the orders are carried out.

The Changing Role of Chief Minister

The Chief Minister has donned the role of the Chief Executive Officer of the state administration and every Chief Minister is acting upon the opportunities for economic development and growth of the state. In fact, the Chief Ministers are addressing the industry captains from time to time highlighting the facilities offered by the state administration along with tax incentives and subsidies in different forms.

The Government of Telangana, which is in the forefront of integrating Information and Communication Techologies (ICTs) with state administration has come out with TS-iPASS. The "Telangana State Industrial Project Approval and Self-Certification System (TS-iPASS) Act, 2014" (Act No.3 of 2014) provides for speedy processing of applications for issue of various clearances required for setting up of industries at a single point based on the self-certificate provided by the entrepreneur and also to create investor friendly environment in the State of Telangana. The TS-iPASS provides hassle free services to the industries for the approval of the new projects.

Attracting capital and industries has become the new mantra for the Chief Ministers. The Uttar Pradesh Government has come out with industry-friendly state through its media advertisements to attract capital for the industrial development of the state. The Chief Minister of Andhra Pradesh was instrumental in KIA Motors of South Korea to start its automotive plant in the state of Andhra Pradesh. Therefore, the role of the Chief Ministers is not just doling out goodies for the citizens but act as a galvanizer for resources for the development of the state for better opportunities for the people.

Concluding Observations

The state administration has come to play an important role in the 21st century as they no longer are a part of the a strong central government command with one party ruling all over the country. The state administration in all the states has emerged as a strong bureaucratic bloc imbibed with individuals with professional approach and technological awareness. The state administration has gradually evolved aftermath the internet revolution and most of the state governments are conducting their official activities through web based platforms.

Many state administration departments have developed their own web based applications which in turn have altered the way the state is administered. For that matter, the Chief Ministers and the Governors of the State have their own twitter accounts which are an indication of how the state administration has gobbled up the opportunities provided by the emerging technologies.

The Chief Ministers are not just political professionals but have donned the role of CEOs for their states and always responsive to the needs of the citizens. With the ever vigilant media hovering 24x7 modes, the Chief Ministers have become alert in conducing the governmental affairs more seriously. Even the Governors have started behaving with dignity and decorum unlike the Governors of the yesteryears who were mere stooges in the hands of the ruling party at the Center. The COVID- 19 is a classic example of how the state administration has undergone a metamorphosis with the Chief Ministers focusing on catering to the needs of the people on one hand and mitigating the COVID-19 pandemic; all of which point towards a vibrant state administration.

References

- Heady, Ferrel (1996): Public Administration: A Comparative Perspective, Marcel Dekker Inc, New York, p. 240.
- Henry, Nicholas (2003): Public Administration and Public Affairs, Prentice Hall, New Delhi, p. 2.
- Kashyap, C. Subhash (1997): Citizens and the Constitution, Publications Division, Government of India, New Delhi, p. 240.
- Maheshwari, S.R. (1991): Theories and Concepts in Public Administration, Allied Publishers, New Delhi, pp. 210-211.
- Mathur, Kuldeep (2016): From Government to Governance, A Brief Survey of the Indian Experience, National Book Trust, New Delhi, p. 6.
- Tummala, K. Krishna (1994): Public Administration in India, Allied Publishers, Mumbai, p. 240.

3

Techniques of Statecraft in Ancient India as Depicted in the Manusmriti

— *S.K. Jaiswal*

Introduction

The techniques of statecraft in ancient India (when concept of modern nation and states was not in existence, kingdom was treated as nation state), Manu offers in his *Manusmriti* are the guidelines to a king for the administration of internal and external affairs. The book closely examines the problems of administration, state, finance, economic planning, justice and foreign relations including diplomacy, espionage and warfare. Manu seems to be fully aware of the practical problems of public administration and his book discusses almost every aspect of polity and administration and claims relevance to the modern world.

The book comprises twelve *Adhayayas* (chapters) consisting of 2694 *Slokas* (couplets). The first, second, seventh, eighth and ninth are useful for the topics of techniques of statecraft. The texts followed by *Medhatithi* and *Kulluka* are used in this work. The eminent scholars have placed this work between first century BC to third century A.D.

Like *Arthasastra*, Manu has mentioned seven constituents of state in his *Manusmriti*. They are the king, the ministers, the capital, the realm, the treasury, the army and the ally-

स्वाभ्यमाव्यौ पुरं राष्ट्रं कोशदण्डौ सुहन्तथा।
सप्त प्रकृत्यो ह्येता सप्तांडग राज्यमुत्यते।[1]

The King

These constituents constituted the wealth of the state[2] and this *saptanga* theory of state bears some resemblance to the modern definition of state. The king and his kingdom were the primary elements of the state. Manu considers the *swami* or the sovereign power the most important of the seven components of state. He has accepted the divine origin of kingship. It is said that the God created the king of kingship. It is said that the God created the king protect the whole world from anarchy.

अराजके हि लोकेऽस्मिन्सर्वतो विद्रते भयात्।
रक्षार्थमस्य सर्वस्य राजानम सृजतप्रभुः।।[3]

At another place Manu further states that the King was created by *Prajapati*, taking all elements from *Indra (the king of gods), Anila (the Air), Yama (the god of Death), Arka (the Sun), Agni (the Fire), Varuna (the god of Dains), Chandra(the Moon)* and *Vittesa* (*Kuber, the treasurer of gods*). King was thus full of divine powers.

इन्द्रानिल यमर्काणमगनेश्च वरूणस्य च्।
चन्द्रवित्तेशयोश्चैव मात्रा निर्हव्य शाश्वती।।[4]

It is to be noted that only good and noble kings were regarded as divine and bad impious ones were considered as demonic. If king did not act up to the rules of *dharma* i.e. duty he could be deposed, disobeyed or killed. A.S. Altekar has rightly observed: "It was felt that the king's status would become higher and tendency to obey the states orders strangers, if the head of the state was represented as divine; but when the question of duties and responsibilities of the king at issue, his divinity did not afford him any immunity or privilege. If he was bad in character and remiss in performing his duties, he became demoniac and not divine."[5] The origin of kingship, as a matter of fact, lay in search for a smooth life in the society devoid of troubles and turmoil.

Council of Ministers

The king is advised to keep a council of ministers for smooth functioning of the state. The Hindu law provides that the king cannot act without the cooperation of ministers. Manu calls a king foolish who would attempt to carry on the administration by himself.[6] He further says that the king must have ministers and that in their midst and along with them he has to consider ordinary and extraordinary matters of state.[7] Further, he remarks that even the smallest task cannot be accomplished by a single person. How then, he questions, can the great works of the king which involve great issues he accomplished without the assistance of ministers.

अपि यत्सुकरं कर्म तदप्येकेन दुष्करम्।
विशेशतो सहाचेनं किंतु राज्ये महोदयम्।।[8]

Ministers undoubtedly played a significant part in the proper functioning of the government and Manu like the other political thinkers[9] has regarded the council of advisors as the most important apparatus of administrative machinery. He has also stated that the king used to hold secret consultation with his ministers in the assembly hall or *Sabha* after the dispersion of the common people there from.[10] He further holds the council of ministers should consist of seven or eight ministers.

Internal Administration

The ancient political thinkers are of the opinion that without the *Janapada (districts)* the state cannot exist. Kautilya has opined in this connection that in the settlement of new territories the village should comprise 100 to 500 families and that the *Sthaniya* (neighbourhood) which is largest unit in the *Janapada* should consist of 800 villages.[12] Manu states that a *Gulma* (police station) to be established in the centre place of two or three or five villages, and a *Samgrahan* in the centre of villages-

द्वयोस्त्रपाणां पंचानाम मध्ये गुल्मधिष्ठितम् ।
तथा ग्रामशनानां च कुर्यद्राष्टस्य संग्रहम ।।[13]

It is to be noted that Manu has explained very clearly that the state should be established in such a place where the land is not marshy, delightful yielding the grains etc. for livelihood where the *Aryans* are settled and where the neighbouring kings are subdued.[14] The idea is the land should be fertile, so the people can earn their livelihood by agriculture, as it was the main occupation in India. Subduing the neighbouring is, bringing the neighbouring under the king's control.[15] It is generally required by ancient texts that mainly the producing class should inhabit the state.[16] The progress of the state undoubtedly depended on the extension of its territory and the setting up of different administrative units.

The importance of forts has also been discussed by ancient political thinkers. It is in the fort *(Durga)* where the treasury and army were kept. Functions like secret war, the upkeep of the army, the reception of allies and driving out of enemies were carried out from here. Like the *Mahabharata*[17] and *Puranas*[18] Manu[19] has described six types of forts-

(i) *Dhanva durga-* a fort surrounded by desert

(ii) *Mahi durga-* a fort make of stones or bricks

(iii) *Jala durga-* a fort surrounded by some rivers or lake used for different purpose

(iv) *Vriksha durga-* a fort which was built in the midst of a forest surrounded by trees

(v) *Sena durga-* a place of safety formed by placing the army in particular position

(vi) *Giri durga-* a fort on the mountain or surrounded by mountains on all sides

Manu is also of the opinion that the king should make his residence in any one of six *durgas* mentioned above.

धन्तदुर्ग महीदुर्ग भस्दुर्ग वाहीमेव वा।
नरदुर्ग गिरिदुर्ग वा समाद्धीतय वसंत्पुरम।।[20]

Durga or fort played a role of key significance in defense and warfare in ancient times, serving as refuge against pressure of raiders and invaders. The king might withstand a siege for long by entrenching himself in the fort. The present set up law and order has undergone radical changes but the importance of forts exists even to this day.

Tax Administration

All the activities of the state and the army were totally dependent on the *kosa (treasury)*. There were possibilities of many troubles without the *kosa* (treasury) and it was the chief source that makes the performance of virtuous acts possible. The king was always expert to pay the first attention to *kosa* (treasury). A.S. Altekar is of opinion that sound finances are absolutely necessary for the stable and prosperous state.[21] B.A. Saletore is of the view that for the protection of the state sound finance is essential. He says that the theory of public finance in ancient India was intimately linked with the theory of protection.[22] Manu states that *kosa* (treasury) and the government of the realm depend on the king.[23] The treasury was regarded as the barometer of sound administration. The political thinkers of ancient India have laid down some important principles of taxation. It is worthwhile to mention that revenue was received both in cash and in kind. The thinkers have observed that taxes should be reasonable and equitable, neither too excessive to be felt as an oppressive burden by the people nor too little to affect the stability the state itself. Manu has stated that the king should not squeeze his subjects by collecting excess taxes-

यथा फलेन युज्येत राजा कर्ता च कर्मणाम्।
तथावेक्ष्य न पो राष्ट्रे कल्पयेत्सततं करान्।।[24]

At one place he has advised the king to take to right direction – neither to cut off his own roots by not realizing taxes and duties, nor to cut off the roots of people through excessive greed.[25] He has mentioned several types of taxes like *bali* (offering), *Sulka (fee)*, *dand*a (penalty), *bhaga(share)* etc. The king is advised to receive taxes from the traders and merchants. He had to get one-sixth of honey, ghee, medical herbs, salt, fruits, vegetables etc. in the form of tax.[26] But Manu does not mention the name of officers who had responsibility to collect the taxes.

Defence

Defence against external aggression has been considered one of the most vital functions of the state. The army and fort always played an important role in resisting aggression. The four fold troops of army are called '*Chaturangabla*'(having four divisions of army) – (i) *Padatibala*- the infantry, (ii) *Gajabala* – the Elephants (iii) *Asvabala*- the cavalry and (iv) *Rathabala*– the chariots. *Senapati,* the commander of the army was the incharge (commanding) officer of the four-fold -troops. Manu has discussed two chief officers of the army – *Senapati* (captain) and *Baladhyaksha* (commander). *Senapati* (captain) seems to be the chief of all the troops and the *Baladhayksha* (commander) was a general, the leader of single troop –

सेनापति बलाक्ष्यक्षौ सर्वादिक्षु निवेशयेन् ।
यतश्च भमाशडेकत्प्राची तां काल्प येद्दिराम् । ।[27]

The military department, according to Manu, was under the supervision of one *amatya* or minister and ambassador of king was responsible for peace and war.[28] Thus the army was required to be maintained by ancient kings and it was most important component that provided stability to everything in the state.

Foreign Relationship

Diplomacy also occupied a place of vital importance in international affair like in modern time. The importance of *mitra* (friend) has been discussed on one of the seven organs of a state. Manu has pointed out that the king with land and gold cannot make as much progress as he can with the help of dependable friends.[29] The land, gold and friendship are considered to be the products of war and diplomacy respectively.[30] Before employing the '*denda*' i.e., declaring the war six measures are said to be taken for the well being of the country. These measures are – *Sandhi* (peace), *Vigraha* (enmity), *Asana* (staying quiet), *Yana* (expedition), *Samsraya* (submission) and *Dvaidhibhave* (dual policy)-

संधि च विग्रहं चैव यानमासनमेव च ।
द्वैद्यीभावं संश्रयं च सडगुणांष्चिन्तयेत्सदा । ।[31]

Inter-State relation in ancient India was broadly based on three traditional principles: the *mandala* (a group of kingdoms) theory,[32] the *Shadgunya* or six fold policy[33] or seven *upayas* or expedients.[34]

Administration of Justice

The administration of justice was regarded as a sacred duty of the king. He was expected to honour the dignity of law and establish the reign of Justice. Manu states that if a king punishes the criminal and he is sentenced to each he will go to *svarga* (heaven) on suffering the punishment.[35] Manu has referred to several officers in his ninth *adhyaya* (chapter) of the *Smriti*. He advocates that it is not possible except through *danda* (corporal punishment) to check and control sinners because thieves and other are sinners by nature and they move secretly an earth-

न हि दण्डासे भौक्यः कर्तु पापविनिगुहः।
स्तेनानां पापबुद्वीनां निमृतं चरतां क्षितौ।[36]

Manu has referred to several types of thieves such as conspires, bribers and selfish wrong doers.[37] He wants that the king shall scrupulously protect the seven constituents of the state and he has therefore to suppress ruthlessly all those who act against it.[38] He seems to very much ruthless on those who destroy public property such as tanks, temples, store of weapons and so on.[39] At one place Manu states that the king shall proclaim his own rules after carefully examining the rules of country, *Jatis* (caste) and the eternal rules of *Kulas* (race, tribe)-

जाति जानपदान्धर्मान श्रेणीन्धर्माक्ष धर्मवित्।
समीक्ष्य कुलधर्माक्षे स्वधर्म प्रतिपादयेन्।[40]

It is to be noted that Manu has specifically referred to the kingly law, and has also suggested its great importance and superiority over the other rules of *Jati* (caste), *Kula* (race) etc. Kingly law, even in the days of Manu did not depend upon the sweet will of the man in power.[41] The king in ancient India was not free to administer justice according to his own will but was to follow the rules of *Dharmasastra* (holy writ, jurisprudence) that is the path of impartiality.

Conclusion

Thus, Manu has discussed each and every aspect of polity and administration in ancient India. He not only gives a systematic exposition of the main principles of administration but also makes an attempt at giving principles of better political life. Like Kautilya he accepts the importance of king and his sovereignty, He is undoubtedly more practical and progressive in the field of administration. His principles related to administration are also useful in modern times and applicable for efficient administrators.

References & Footnotes

1. Manusmriti 9.294, (Here after Manu)
2. We notice some inconsistency with regards to the number of these Angas of the state. The Santiparve of the Mahabharata, at one place, mentions Ashtanga Rajya but it has not specified the eight constituents. (Mahabharata, Santiparva 122.8) The Vishnudharmottara Purana mentions only seven constituents of the state but at one place (Vishnudharmottara Purana II 145.3) it substitutes Sama and

Dana for Svami and Amatya. The order in which Kautilya enumerator them is as follws – Swami, Amatya Janapada, Durga, Kosa, Danda and Mitra. (Asthasastra, 6.1) The Matsya Purana, too, accepts these constituents of the state and discussed them in the same order. (Matsya, Purana, 220.19)

3. Manu VII 3, 42.
4. *Ibid.,* VII 5.
5. A.S. Altekar, State and Government in Ancient india, Delhi 1958, p. 92.
6. Manu VII 30-31.
7. *Ibid.,* VII 54-57.
8. *Ibid.,* VII 55.
9. Mahabharata, 12.106.II, Matsya Purana, 215.3, Kamandaka 13.25 Nitivakyamrita of Somadeva Suri, 18.1, 4.
10. Manu VII 146.
11. *Ibid.,* 54. 7.
12. Arthasaṣtra, II. 1.
13. Manu. 7.114.
14. *Ibid.,* 7.69.
15. See P. Shashi Rekha, Ancient Indian Administration, Cosmo publications, 1996, p. 93.
16. Matsya Purana, 217.1.2, Vishnudharmottara Purana II, 226.2. It is also suggested that those who create trouble among the components of the state should be several punished with either death or annihilation. Agni Purana, 225.12 and 223.13.
17. Mahabharata, Santi Parva, 87.1.5.
18. Matsya Purana, 217.6-7, Agni Purana 222.4-6., Vishnudharmottara Purana, 2.26, 6-9,3.232, 16-21.
19. Manu – 7.70.
20. *Ibid.*
21. A.S. Altekar, op.cit. p. 262.
22. B.A. Saletore, Ancient Indian Political Thought and Institutions, Asia Publishing House, 1963, p. 441.
23. Manu. 7-65.
24. *Ibid.* 7-128.
25. *Ibid.* 7-139.
26. *Ibid.* 7. 127-28, 130-32.
27. *Ibid.* 7-189.
28. *Ibid.* 7-65.
29. *Ibid.* 7-208.
30. Kulluka, Manu, 7 206-207.
31. Manu. 7. 160.
32. The Mandala theory set forth the rules and principles which guided the conduct of ancient Indian rules in regard to inter-state relations, see Usha Mehta, Usha Thakkar, Kautilya and his Arthasastra, New Delhi, 1980, p. 58. This theory is

said to be "the most notable contributions of the ancient Indian to the development of the world political thought." U.N. Ghoshal, "The system of inter-state relations and of foreign policy in the early Arthasastra state, Ancient India, pp. 137.138. In Mandala there are twelve primary kings. Five kings in front, four in the rear one madhyam and udasin and one conqueror. See Aradhna Parmar, Techniques of State Craft A Study of kautilya Arthasastra, New Delhi 1987, p. 203. The whole structure of modern international diplomacy seems to be based on this ancient theory. See G.P. Singh, Political Thought in Ancient India, New Delhi 2005, p. 127.

33. Six – fold policy or six- fold methods of diplomacy have been defined in the Arthasastra, Manusmriti, Karnandakanitisar, Vishnudharmottara and Agni Puranas. Also see S.K. Jaiswal, Polity and Administration in the Matsya Purana, Jaipur, 1996, p. 173.
34. The Ancient Literature has stated that the king should resort his policies through seven means namely Sama, Bheda, Dana, Danda, Upeksha, Maya and Indrajala. See Ghandiji Roy, Diplomacy in Ancient Indian, New Delhi, 1981, pp. 157-178. Also see S.K. Jaiswal, Hindu Rajasastra (Hindi), Delhi, 1994, pp. 237-242.
35. Manu., 8-318.
36. *Ibid.* 9. 263
37. *Ibid.* 9.259-60
38. *Ibid.* 9. 278-279
39. *Ibid.* 9. 278-280
40. *Ibid.* 8. 4
41. See R.S. Betai, Evolution of Law of Crimes in Ancient India, Delhi, 2003, p. 124.

4

The Role of Governors in State Polity with special reference to Uttar Pradesh

— S.N. Singh

Introduction

The political institutions of modern India have their roots in the British *Raj* and the office of the Governor too has its historical roots in that period. After independence, India opted for a parliamentary democratic polity that too was, in a sense, a continuation of the British legacy. The Constitution of India, the fundamental law of the land, formally provided for institutions, their power and position, which were to govern the future India. In this context, it may be noted that the Constitution created a "Union of States", a political framework that was federal in nature. The federal system thus, opted initially consisted of two tier structure the Union and the constituent states with defined power and status. At the Union level, the Constitution provided that there shall be a President with all the executive powers, though these powers are ceremonial in nature as the real executive authority rested in the Prime Minister and the logical expectation being that he represents the will of people. There are thus, two types of executives, viz., the nominal and the real, one represented by the President and the other by the Prime Minister.

Almost similar constitutional provisions can be seen at the state level too, though there may be certain departure so far as the power and position of State Governors are concerned. Similar in the sense that he heads the state executive with powers vested in him. At the same time there are certain powers which seem to be exclusive to the Governor. But, by and large, the Constitutional position is that the Governors are nominal executive for all practical purposes whereas as the Chief Minister of the State is the real executive as he enjoys the powers under the Constitution. In spite of such constitutional power and position, the governors have played significant role in the body politic of the states. It is pertinent to note that the role of Governor has been changing over the years. Many a times we have observed that governors have tried to influences the politics and administration of the state which created a sort of problem between the relationship of the Governor and the Chief Minister. After Independence particularly we notice a drastic change in their roles. The performance of the Governors over the past seven decades shows that some governors went by the rule book while others have been proactive. The reign of some of them has been non-controversial while that of some others raised eye brows in different quarters. In view of such different and varied opinion about the role of the governors, we thought to rationally assess the role of the governor vis-à-vis state politics and administration. We propose to confine the scope of the paper to *Uttar Pradesh* as it is not only India's largest State but a politically important as well. Also we leave the reference of earlier period between 1937 to 1947 and 1947 to 1950 from the present discussion. As a matter of fact the State of Uttar Pradesh formally came into being when the Constitution of India became operative from 26th of January, 1950. In view of this we propose to cover the subject of the role of the Governors during post-1950 period and confine our observations to this period only.

Term of Governors in *Uttar Pradesh*

During the last seventy years of its existence, the State of *Uttar Pradesh* has witnessed twenty five Governors who headed the State. The first incumbent of the *Raj Bhawan* (office of the governor) of *Uttar Pradesh* was H.P. Modi who took oath of office of the Governor on 28th of January 1950 and remained in office till June 11, 1952. Thus, the first Governor of the State could serve the State only for about one and half years after which we had K.M Munshi who took the oath of office on June 2, 1952. Though he was only the second head of the State, he completed the full term in office. This is how we find the tenure of the Governors of the State wherein out of the twenty five only eight could complete their full term in office whereas the rest could not complete their tenure and had to leave beforehand. The list of the Governors with their term of office is annexed at the end of the paper for ready reference. Most of the Governors of the State could not complete their full term in office for reasons more than one and we shall briefly to look into those factors which have generally affected not only the tenure of the governor in U.P but their position and the role vis-à-vis the politics and governance in the state.

Looking at the position of Governor, it can be argued that he occupies a constitutional position and we can also see him as a representative of the central government in the states. This keeps influencing and affecting his position as well as powers. Though the Constitution provides for a five year term, at the same time it also provides that he shall hold office during the pleasure of the President whom he represents in the State and who is also his appointing authority. Ever since India began its political journey with a parliamentary democracy and the federal polity, the relationships between the Centre and the States have continuously been a subject of debate for various reasons. We can observe that initially for a couple of decades of our governance were dominated by one party system with Congress party that remained at the helm of affairs and there was not much of controversy as it had its Government at the Centre as well as in most of the States. This provided the Congress party to set the rules of the game as it felt politically convenient wherein the Governors had their own share of responsibility in holding the forte with the Centre. However, subsequent decades of political development in India provided a different environment particularly after Lal Bahadur Shastri's death. India could see some kind of political instability when Congress party was split and one faction was headed by Indira Gandhi and the other was headed by Morarjee Desai. The scenario settled after Indira Gandhi appeared on the political scene as a leader with the support of the majority. But in the States, the problem of political stability persisted which provided scope for the Centre to enforce and manage affairs of the State through the Governors. It was often alleged that the Congress government at the Centre is trying to intervene in the internal affairs of the States and the Governors are helping such moves.

In *Uttar Pradesh* too on several occasions such situations have occurred in the past wherein the *Raj Bhawan* was trying to impose the Centre's agenda on the States generally against the wishes of the Chief Ministers. Since *Uttar Pradesh* has been at the centre of the government and politics in the country, most political parties had their agenda set on the State to serve their own political interest. We shall, however, not be going into each and every such political development wherein the Governors in Uttar Pradesh exceeded their brief in order to serve the political ends of the government at the Centre, but would only mention a few instances wherein such complaints had come in public view.

Some Important Critical Instances

One would like to mention here the case when the State into President's Rule for the first time since a democratic government came into existence. It was a question of proving majority by the State government headed by Charan Singh in the year 1968. It was alleged that Charan Singh Government has lost majority and therefore President's Rule was imposed on 17th Feb, 1968 which continued till 26 Feb, 1969. It was a period when B. Gopala Reddy was heading the State. It was subsequently alleged that the Governor had certainly traded on the domain of the legislative in coming to this subjective conclusion that the Charan Singh's ministry had lost the confidence of the majority without its strength being actually tested on the floor of the House which had been convened to meet within the next four days. This was not justified[1]. After the constitutional crisis in *Uttar Pradesh*, the President appointed a Committee of Governors to study and formulate norms on the rule of the Governor under the Constitution. It may be pertinent to briefly mention some of the major recommendations of the Committee to make our discussion relevant. The recommendations thus, were[2]:

(i) A Governor has the right to dismiss a ministry if the Chief Minister shirks his primary responsibility of facing the Assembly within the shortest time to test the confidence of the legislature in him.

(ii) The test of confidence should normally be left to a vote in the Assembly.

(iii) If an alternative ministry can be formed which in the Governor's view can command a majority in the Assembly, he must dismiss the ministry in power and install an alternative ministry in office.

(iv) If formation of such a ministry is not possible, the Governor will be left with an alternative but to make a report to the President under Article 356 and to recommend at the same time the dissolution of the Assembly.

(v) On the Governor's discretion, the Committee observed that right from the commencement of the Constitution, it has been recognized that in the choice of the Chief Minister the Governor's decision under Article 164(1) is final and based entirely on his unfettered judgment.

There were couple of more recommendations, but we leave them as they may not be relevant in our present discussion. The above recommendations of the Committee of the Governors seem to have faith in the Governor's wisdom and his judgment on the matters political. In view of the above the decision of the Governor to dismiss the Assembly and to recommend for the President's Rule in the State can still be debated. We leave this incident here and move to other instances to enrich the discussion. Before moving further, one would like to make a mention of large scale defections that were taking place in the country including *Uttar Pradesh* which affected the culture as well as the dynamics of the politics. It eroded the democratic values and affected the politics and governance both. It was a period of political uncertainty that encouraged such kind of *Aaya Ram - Gaya Ram* politics prevailing in the late sixties and seventies affecting several states in the country. One would not like to expand this as this any farther as this was only to suggest the kind of politics we were in during those decades.

So far we have been through two decades of our parliamentary democracy and federal polity wherein some trends are already visible. The decades of seventies is marked with such trends. It was a period where

Dr. Chenna Reddy, himself an active politician from *Andhra Pradesh* took over as the Governor of the *Uttar Pradesh* on October 25, 1974 and continues till October 1, 1977. It was a period when for some time Hemwati Nandan Bahuguna was the Chief Minister and later the State was under the President's Rule from 30 November, 1975 to 21 January, 1976 after which Narayan Dutt Tiwari had become the Chief Minister of the State. Again we find the Tiwari Government being dislodged on 30th april, 1977 and President's Rule imposed in the State which continued till 23 June 1977. The President's Rule ended when Ram Naresh Yadav of *Janata* Party took oath of office of the Chief Minister on 23rd June 1977. His government continued till 27 Feb, 1979. We will not go further on this state of political journey of the State, will take up again when need be. It is suffice to observe here that this was period of high political drama and a sort of political uncertainty in the State. It may be noted here that this was also a period when Mrs. India Gandhi was the Prime Minister of the country and she was facing tremendous pressure from the opposition parties which were continuously challenging her authority. This was also a period when Jai Prakash Narain was leading the movement called 'Total Revolution' against political corruption in the country. This was also a period when Mrs. Gandhi imposed Emergency in the country, consequently all the political activities ceased and large number of leaders were arrested and put behind bar. Its impact was far reaching and *Uttar Pradesh* too had its own share of pain and sufferings. During this period Dr. Chenna Reddy was Governor of the State and was allegedly proactive and that may have suited to his style of politics as it was a period of national Emergency too. We shall not expand on this further and would like to move ahead.

It is not that only during Congress party Government at the Centre or in the States such a scenario prevailed. Even the *Janata* Party when came into power after 1977 general elections people voted in their favour after the Emergency, rejecting Mrs. Gandhi and Congress. We could witness similar situation prevailing. Moreover, these were also not the early lessons of our parliamentary democracy as they could be seen further as we go ahead in our political journey. We can note couple of instances during the nineties and later to support this argument. Before we look into these instances we may mention here the report of the Sarkaria Commission which examined in detail the question of relationship and balance of power between state and Central governments and suggest changes within the framework of the Constitution. However, the discretionary powers of the Governor offer him or her vast liberty of actions. The Commission was appointed in June 1983 and submitted its report in 1988. The Commission recommended, by and large, status quo in the present scenario[3]. Some years in between passed by.

We now take up issue developing after 1997 general election in *Uttar Pradesh*. In the state after the Assembly elections held in October 1997, no political party got majority. In a 425 member House, the BJP emerged as the single largest party and had strength of 176, *Samajwadi Party* 134, and BSP and its combine 100. The State was still under the President's Rule. The Governor did not invite the single largest party, the BJP to form the Government. Instead, he recommended to the Centre for imposing the President's Rule, as according to him, no party was able to form a stable government. The Governor with the convenience of the Centre ignored the electoral mandate and recommended for the imposition of President's Rule. The Centre acted on his report and imposed President's Rule in the State. The reliability of Presidential Proclamation was challenged in the Allahabad High Court. A Division Bench of three judges of the High Court held that the Presidential proclamation imposing President's Rule under Article 356 was unconstitutional "based on irrelevant and extraneous ground" and hence liable to be quashed. The matter went to the Supreme Court, instead of hearing the appeal on merit, the highest court directed that if an attempt is to form a ministry in the State, it would have no objection. After this a BJP and BSP coalition ministry was installed in the State. But on October 20, 1997, the BSP withdrew its support from the BJP Government[4]. Even later, we observe such kind of political development in *Uttar Pradesh* wherein the Governor and the Chief Minister have been engaging themselves, may be owing to pressure from the Centre. The political overtones were witnessed when Romesh Bhandari was the Governor and later he submitted his resignation.

Gradually we see India entering into the twenty first century with its parliamentary democratic governance model which also marks an occasion for celebrating the golden jubilee of successful governance. With this the State of *Uttar Pradesh* too entered into similar mode of governance. It did pass through certain phases of political uncertainty wherein the role of Governors came into focus. There were instances during these fifty years of democratic governance in *Uttar Pradesh* wherein Governors seem to have been proactive and seem to have acted on the behest of the Central Government. Many a times it could have been in the Congress regime, but instances are also there during the non-Congress regime as well. We would now prefer to sum up the discussion of the role of the Governor, but before that one would like to mention as how the non-Congress government and so also the Governor functioned during the last two decades or so in managing the affairs of the State.

Looking at the political scenario in *Uttar Pradesh* we notice that there was no Congress government for the last more than two decades. The State was governed by non-Congress political outfits. As a matter of fact the political power rotated between *Samajwadi* Party and the *Bahujan Samaj Party* (BSP). But we find little change so far as the role of *Raj Bhawan* is concerned. It has remained active and proactive depending upon the Central government's, intention. Without going into the details of the various regimes, one is reminded of period when Akhilesh Yadav was the Chief Minister and Ram Naik was the Governor of State. During this period *Raj Bhawan* appeared to be quite concerned over the law and order situation in the State and the Governor kept a close eye on the situation often reminding the Chief Minister about the same. But the situation changed when BJP came to power and Yogi Aditya Nath became the Chief Minister. Though the question of law and order persisted but the *Raj Bhawan* was active but not proactive. Such political developments and actions do come under public domain. It is not that any one political party used the office of the Governor to their political convenience; we have instances where the Congress, the BJP and NDF have been playing the same game when in power and criticizing when in opposition.

Summing Up

With above brief explanation and observation, we would sum up the discussion about the role of Governors with special reference to *Uttar Pradesh* by saying that since *Uttar Pradesh* has been the most important State for various reasons, most of the political parties wanted to have a control in the politics and government in order to control the same at the Centre. During the last seventy years or so we are witness to situations wherein Governors preferred to act on the behest of the Centre rather than Constitutional propriety. There is hardly any change as even today we have Governors who are continuously looking towards the Centre rather than the political morality and ethical governance. It is easier to blame when in opposition but be in the same boat when in power. This is duality of political parties and there seems to be little hope for any correction in near future. Let us see.

References

1. Pandey, Dr. J.N. (2015): Constitutional Law of India, Central Law Agency, Allahabad, p. 596.
2. *Ibid.*
3. *Ibid,* p. 599
4. *Ibid.*

Annexure
List of Governors in Uttar Pradesh

	Name		*Tenure*
1.	Sri H.P. Modi	-	January 28, 1950 to January 1, 1952
2.	Sri K.M. Munshi	-	January 2, 1952 to January 9, 1957
3.	Sri V.V. Giri	-	January 10, 1957 to June 30, 1960
4.	Dr. B.R. Rao	-	July 1, 1960 to April 15, 1962
5.	Sri Bishwanath Das	-	April 16, 1962 to April 30, 1967
6.	Sri Gopala Reddy	-	May 1, 1967 to June 30, 1972
7.	Sri S.K. Verma (Acting)	-	July 1, 1972 to November 13, 1972
8.	Sri Akbar Ali Khan	-	November 14, 1972 to October 24, 1974
9.	Dr. Chenna Reddy	-	October 25, 1974 to October 1, 1977
10.	Sri G.D. Tapase	-	October 2, 1977 to February 27, 1980
11.	Sri C.P.N. Singh	-	February 28, 1980 to March 31, 1985
12.	Mohd. Usman Arif	-	March 31, 1985 to February 11, 1990
13.	Dr. Satyanarain Reddy	-	February 12, 1990 to March 26, 1993
14.	Sri Moti Lal Vora	-	March 27, 1993 to May 2, 1995
15.	Mohd. Safi Quarishi	-	May 3, 1995 to September 18, 1996
16.	Sri Romesh Bhandari	-	September 19, 1996 to March 16, 1998
17.	Mohd. Safi Quraishi	-	March 17, 1998 to April 19, 1998
18.	Sri Suraj Bhan	-	April 20, 1998 to November 23, 2000
19.	Sri Vishnu Kant Shastri	-	November 24, 2000 to July 2, 2004
20.	Sri Sudarshan Agrawal	-	July 3, 2004 to July 7, 2004
21.	Sri T.V. Rajeshwar	-	July 8, 2004 to July 27, 2009
22.	Sri B.L. Joshi	-	July 28, 2009 to July 17, 2014
23.	Sri Aziz Quaraishi(Acting)	-	July 17, 2014 to July 21, 2014
24.	Ram Naik	-	July 22, 2014 to July 19, 2019
25.	Anandiben Mafatba Patel	-	July 20, 2019 – Continued till date

5

The Citizenship Amendment Act and Refugee Question in India

— V. Bijukumar

Introduction

The passing of the Citizenship Amendment Bill (CAB), 2019 evoked mixed response not only in Northeast region, but also in other parts of India as a whole. While it generated great ethnic anxieties among the people of the region, the protagonists of the Bill justified it as a legal protection for the persecuted non-Muslim minority communities in the country. The *Bharatiya Janta Party* (BJP)-led National Democratic Alliance (NDA) government, with its brute majority in the *Lok Sabha* and politically managed strategy in *Rajya Sabha*, could pass the Bill citing it as its electoral promise in the manifesto of 2019. However, the opposition against the Bill was strong and louder from the opposition parties and the people opposing the Bill. The CAB amended the Citizenship Act, 1955, conferring citizenship to persons belonging to minority communities, namely, Hindus, Sikhs, Buddhists, Jains, Parsis and Christians from Afghanistan, Bangladesh and Pakistan. The Act was enacted to provide for the acquisition and determination of Indian citizenship. Under the existing provisions of the Act, persons belonging to the minority communities, such as Hindus, Sikhs, Buddhists, Jains, Parsis and Christians from Afghanistan, Bangladesh and Pakistan, who have either entered into India without valid travel documents or the validity of their documents have expired, are regarded as illegal migrants and hence ineligible to apply for Indian citizenship.

Who is a Refugee?

The issue of granting citizenship to religious minorities coming as refugees to India often warrants understanding the category called 'refugee'. Refugees are dispossessed people and the most vulnerable group anywhere in the world. They are forced to leave their state of nationality and seek asylum in another for security and better life conditions. They are not only deprived of nationality, but also denied human dignity and basic entitlements. Dispossessed of the right to membership in a political community, refugees seek to enter into the space of other political community by re-establishing a new political obligation. Citizenship rights are accessible to nationals only within the territory. The entitlement to rights of citizens is related to the national boundaries and once the individual is outside, she/he may lose rights. In most countries, refugees are not considered as citizens, forcing them to live as suspicious human beings in the eyes of the native communities and the state. A refugee faces stigma and humiliation and lacks resources and influence in the power structure. Hannah Arendt described refugees as "the most symptomatic group in contemporary politics" (Arendt, 1986: 277). According to her, "a refugee used to be a person driven to seek refugee because of some act committed or some political opinion held" (Arendt, 1994:264). She further argues that the suffering of refugees is the result of the adaptation of the national model by the heterogeneous state, which has generated enormous tensions. In her essay, We Refugees, Arendt gives a personal account of the condition of German Jews fleeing the Third Reich (Arendt, 1994: 110—119). Refugees are not often considered as full citizens as they are deprived of civil, political and social rights by the host country. Marshall defined citizenship in terms of civil, political and social rights. The civil aspect of citizenship "is composed of the rights necessary for individual freedom – liberty of the person, freedom of speech, thought and faith, the right to own property and to conclude valid contracts, and the right of justice" (Marshall, 1950: 11).

Addressing the Refugee Question

The passage of CAB rekindled an academic interest on India's longstanding approach of extending asylum to refugees. While the supporters of the Bill argue for granting citizenship rights to the persecuted minorities except Muslims from the neighbouring countries of India, the opponents view that it reverses India's longstanding position of giving asylum to the refugees without considering their religious background. Although India was not a signatory to the 1951 UN Convention Relating to the Status of Refugees (and extended in the 1967 protocol), which has 144 signatories, it always took a more humanitarian and moral approach to the refugee question. According to the 1951 UN Convention, refugees are individuals, who owing to a "well-founded fear of persecution" for reasons of political opinion, race, religion, nationality or membership in a particular social group are outside their country of nationality and are unable or, as a result of such fear, unwilling to return to it". While considering refugee protection is largely related to human security, the Convention contains numerous provisions like the right to protection from refoulement, or forced return, the right to protection against unlawful expulsion or detention, the right to employment and education, access to the courts and freedom of movement. The Universal Declaration of Human Rights (UDHR) recognises the right to freedom of movement across boundaries: a right to emigrate (Article 13). While Article 14 of UDHR emphasises the right to enjoy asylum under certain circumstances, Article 14 (1) reiterates that "everyone has the right to seek and to enjoy in other countries asylum from persecution". Article 34 emphasises restoring refugees to dignity and ensuring the provision of human rights includes an approach that would lead to their integration in the host country. Although all liberal democratic countries are signatories to the 1951 UN Convention of Refugees (1967 Protocol), India, the second-largest liberal democracy, moved to morality than legality in its approach to refugee question. Article 15 of UDHR states that "no one shall be arbitrarily deprived of his nationality nor denied the right to change his nationality".

There is no legal compulsion for the host country to protect refugees, unless it ratifies the 1951 UN Convention and 1967 Protocol. Sometimes, the moral or humanitarian obligation forces state (like India) to give asylum to the refugees, even though it has not ratified the UN Convention. India has one of the largest refugee populations in South Asia. The Registration of Foreigners Act, 1939, The Foreigners Act 1946 and The Foreigners Order 1948 deal with the treatment of foreigners in India. Article 2 of the Registration of Foreigners Act, 1939 defines a foreigner as "a person who is not a citizen of India". Even though, refugees are not granted citizenship rights separately, the Constitution guarantees certain fundamental freedoms to all persons including refugees as citizens. The State guarantees judicial protection and institutional redressal of their grievances. On many occasions, the Supreme Court of India observed the plight of certain refugees and directed the State to improve their material well-being. Even the institutions like the National Human Rights Commission (NHRC) intervened in the humanitarian issues related to refugees.

India followed a uniform treatment of refugees without any distinction made on the basis of religion, ethnicity and regional considerations. All asylum seekers were given equal opportunity. Since its independence, India showed its generosity to refugees across its borders, like the Tibetans, Afghans, Myanmarese, Tamils in Sri Lanka, Buddhist Chakmas from the Chittagong Hill Tracts of Bangladesh. In the wake of political trouble in neighbouring Burma, nearly 75,000 ethnic Chin Refugees came to India and mostly settled in Mizoram. Post-independence, India witnessed migration of refugees to the country due to partition. The occupation of Tibet by China in the late 1940s witnessed mass exodus of Tibetans to India. The Citizenship Amendment Act 1951 raised the issue of India's position on refugees. In 1959 India witnessed influx of refugees from Tibet, including their spiritual leader Dalai Lama. Although India had to confront

China in many occasions on this issue, it provided land settlements, social services and educational opportunities for Tibetan refugees. More than one lakh Tibetan refugees fled to India and resettled in India, especially in Karnataka, Himachal Pradesh, Arunachal Pradesh, Uttarakhand, West Bengal and Jammu and Kashmir. The Report of the Ministry of Home Affairs claimed that it has spent an amount of Rs. 26.81 crore upto 31st December 2015 on resettlement of Tibetan refugees (Government of India, 2016: 271). In 1971 India witnessed massive influx of refugees from East Pakistan. In the 1970s, there was a massive exodus of refugees from East Pakistan, which concentrated in Tripura, Assam, and West Bengal. Although India faced demographic imbalances and ethnic conflict in the border states of West Bengal, Tripura, Assam and Meghalaya, it took a more humanitarian approach irrespective of the religious character of the refugees. In the 1980s, ethnic cleansing of Rohingyas in Myanmar led to their massive influx to India. The Ministry of Home Affairs claimed that "due to ethnic violence and disturbed conditions in Sri Lanka 304,269 SriLankan refugees have entered India in various phases between July 1983 and August 2012 and mostly settled in Tamil Nadu (Government of India, 2016: 269).

Although India took a humanitarian approach to refugee asylum, it always desisted from ratifying the 1951 UN Convention Relating to the Status of Refugees (and extended in the 1967 protocol), stating that it has reservations about the sovereignty of India. Besides citing national security concerns for not signing the Convention, India always hinged on morality over legality on refugee issue, justifying its stand that not signing the Refugee Convention means that it believed humanity cannot be legalised. As a result, India does not have a national law on refugees.

Framing a National Refugee Policy

In the post-partition situation in the country, nationalist leaders such as Mahatma Gandhi, Sardar Patel and Jawaharlal Nehru reiterated India's commitment to asylum to refugees across the border. In 1959, Nehru, with reference to the Tibetan refugees, spelt in Parliament three principles: (i) refugees will be accorded a humane welcome; (ii) the refugee issue is a bilateral issue; and (iii) the refugees should return to their homeland once normalcy returns there. In 1999, speaking in a symposium, Justice K. T. Thomas of the Supreme Court said that "a comprehensive legislation for refugee protection is a legal necessity, as it is a problem which every civilized country should deal in a humane manner".[5]

In December 2015, Shashi Tharoor, Member of Parliament, introduced a Private Member's Bill called the Asylum Bill, 2015 to provide for the establishment of a legal framework to consolidate and harmonise India's refugee policies. However, the Bill could not be taken for consideration.

The intention of the Bill was to provide for the establishment of an effective system to protect refugees and asylum seekers by means of an appropriate legal framework to determine claims for asylum and to provide for the rights and obligations flowing from such status and matters connected with the Constitution. According to the Bill, a person qualifies as a refugee if he "is outside his country of origin and is unable or unwilling to return to or avail himself of the protection of that country because of a well-founded fear of persecution on account of race, religion, sex, nationality, ethnicity, membership of a particular social group or political opinion; or has left his country owing to serious and indiscriminate threats to life, physical integrity or freedom resulting from generalized violence or events seriously disturbing public order".

Politicisation and Apprehensions

The CAB's provision of granting citizenship to non-Muslim minorities from three countries involves greater political dimension than India's genuine concern for these communities. Time and again, the BJP reiterates that India is the "Natural home of persecuted Hindus". In fact, prior to the CAB, the BJP mooted the idea of amendment to the Citizenship Act in 2003 emphasising that those Hindus who had come from Pakistan and were residing in Gujarat and Rajasthan to be given citizenship. However, the attempt was put on hold due to the intervention of the Supreme Court on certain provisions of the proposed amendment. In February 2014, when Prime Minister Narendra Modi visited Assam, he asserted that "we have a responsibility towards Hindus harassed in other countries. Where will they go? We will accommodate them here".[6] The BJP leadership, especially the party president, Amit Shah, in fact, articulated the government move as fulfilling the poll promise made during the Assam Assembly election. Shah contended that the move is in tandem with the party's election manifesto, which reaffirmed its commitment that India should be natural home for persecuted Hindus who could seek refuge here. However, invoking religious criteria for guaranteeing citizenship turned to be extending legal legitimacy for majoritarian agenda of the ruling party at the centre.

Many ethnic communities in Northeast India expressed their apprehensions on legalising the migration of refugees and extending citizenship to them. Firstly, according to them, the northeast states have scarce resources, and thereby cannot accommodate more people. Secondly, such legalised migration would endanger the cultural identity, social cohesion and feeling of belongingness. Thirdly, it may affect their political opportunities and privileges in respective states. Perhaps such apprehensions have standing on the past happenings. The tribal communities often viewed that the Northeast region had to bear the effect of the Indo—Nepal Peace and Friendship Treaty in 1950, as it contributed sizeable migration of

Nepalese in the region. The Treaty evoked ethnic anxieties of tribal communities in the region and many ethnic organisations opposed and demanded for its scrapping. Moreover, they often viewed that the migration from the East Bengal in the 1970s not only affected their economic opportunities, but also the social identities. In Tripura, for instance, the indigenous tribal community lost its numerical strength, resources, political representation and employment opportunities due to the migration of Hindu Bengalis from Eastern Pakistan to the state. Although states like Mizoram, Nagaland and Arunachal Pradesh come under the purview of the Sixth Schedule of the Constitution and protected by the Inner Line Permit (ILP), illegal migration continued unabated. It often leads to low-intensity conflicts in certain localities between the indigenous tribal communities and the migrant population. In fact, such ethnic apprehensions forced many northeastern states to demand ILP protection for the state, so that they would be protected from citizens of other countries. For instance, the CAB rekindled the longstanding demand for ILP protection for the hilly states largely inhabited by the Khasis, Garos and Jaintia tribal communities.

Problem of Local Integration

Although the Citizenship Amendment Act (CAA) now legally facilitates the granting of citizenship and accommodation of persecuted non-Muslim religious minorities in India, it has raised the problem of local integration, as they have to be settled in certain localities along with the existing communities. In fact, modern nation-states are facing a problem of integration of refugees and native citizens in the same footing. The idea of multicultural citizenship often faces the problem of bringing a balance between the rights of the indigenous and refugees. The integration of migrants and ethnic minorities faces problems. The host communities often block other communities, as the resources and positions would be taken by the refugees from other countries. The native population continues to suffer from widespread poverty and discrimination. The resistance to local integration is not only the threat of losing the identity of the host community, but also has material aspects too. Perhaps the task before the nation-state is bridging the gap between the citizens and refugees. The main hurdles of local integration include: resistance to settlement from the host community, resource allocation to settlers, allocation of land and lack of political will. Refugees are often considered as internal enemies, and hence the host country often faces the problems of their integration. Refugees and natives are often in conflict over survival. The host countries also face the problems of the repatriation of refugees to homes of their origin. In many cases, most of the refugees do not want to return. The growing apprehension is that the refugees would, in course of time, outnumber the indigenous people and take away their resources and positions and impoverish the cultural fabric and heritage of the local communities. Benhabib argues "the crises of the nation-state, along with globalization and the rise of multicultural movements, have shifted the lines between citizens and residents, nationals and foreigners" (Benhabib, 2005: 674). According to her, "socio-economic equality is itself a precondition for the effective exercise of democratic citizenship rights. The equal value of liberty for citizens can be realized only if they also have access to and enjoy a bundle of rights and entitlements which are necessary for them to lead lives of human dignity and autonomy" (Benhabib, 2004: 111).

The UN Convention on Refugee in 1951 focuses on the importance of citizenship in achieving local integration. Local integration is a process whereby refugees become full members of their host community and it is often promoted as a decent solution to the problem. Lucy Hovil talks about two levels of local integration—de facto and de jure. According to her, "De facto integration is an informal process that takes place primarily at a local level whereby refugee individuals or groups negotiate belonging in the locality in which they are living. Integration takes place on a spectrum and can function on multiple levels—whether economic, social, cultural, and, at times, political—and is strongly context specific" (Hovil, 2014: 489). Hovil says that "the relationship between refugees and the host population (often including local government officials) is key to their ability to integrate locally: for instance, their legitimacy to live in the area might be built on localized understandings of belonging that transcend national identities, or through recognition of refugees as a potential asset" (Hovil, 2014: 489). According to her, "de jure local integration, on the other hand, is primarily about national belonging (despite the misleading notion of 'local'). It is represented by the formal process of obtaining a new citizenship and is an overtly political process. This acquisition of a new national identity represents, at least in theory, the gateway to rights as citizens of that state" (Hovil, 2014: 489). In her opinion, government often evades this approach. As Hovil states that "…formal citizenship does not necessarily translate into inclusion for former refugees: the legitimacy to belong is a far more complex process. On the one hand, local belonging is unstable without national recognition; localized forms of integration have the potential to be undermined should external circumstances change. On the other, national citizenship holds little promise if individuals and groups fail to be accepted within a particular locality" (Hovil, 2014: 489).

Ranabir Samaddar talks about the policy on refugee protection based on care. According to him, "in terms of a policy on refugee protection by the state and a study of such policy, these three questions would mean to: (a) definition of the term 'refugee' and its scope; (b) the concept of 'non-refoulement' and its scope; and (c) the administrative-judicial machinery to determine the status of a shelter-seeker as a refugee and once determined, the question of assistance the shelter-seeker needs" (Samaddar, 2003: 23). The success of resettlement depends very much on the integration of those refugees who are resettled with their host community. However, often the native people feel that the outsiders coming into a political community would deprive them of the privileges of a citizen. Such apprehensions have wider repercussion when it is perceived that members of the political communities are members of a cultural community as it affects the cultural fabric of the country. Often the stereotyping of the refuges as strangers poses a threat to the national security and peace and order of the host country.

The non-Muslim minority communities from neighbouring countries, who are acquiring citizenship, would face the problem of local integration, and it is more acute in the northeastern states of India. When India witnessed the mass migration of Bengalis including Hindus from Eastern Pakistan in the 1970s, these Hindu Bengalis often face social rejection by the Hindu Bengalis who earlier settled in India. For instance, there are often the problems of integrating Hindu Bengalis who came from East Pakistan and Hindu Bengalis who originally settled in India in West Bengal and Northeastern states like Tripura, Assam and Meghalaya. In many occasions, their social identity and material existence is questioned by the so-called original Hindu Bengalis. In majority of the northeastern states, except Tripura, the Hindu Nepalese are pushed back to certain village enclaves and are thereby preventing their integration with the local tribal communities.

Conclusion

Refugee asylum often turns out to be a contentious political issue not only in India, but also across the world. Since lakhs of people seek asylum in many countries every year, there is a need for ethical scrutiny of the issue. There is considerable currency for the demands for protecting the rights of the asylum seekers. Refugee asylum sometimes raises moral questions, when the host country is a liberal democratic one. It is often seen as the liberal democracy's moral response to the question of asylum.

Despite being a liberal democratic country, India has not enacted a national refugee law. However, it gives asylum to refugees as a humanitarian gesture. In the absence of a specified refugee policy, it is the discretion of the state, often the government of the day, to recognise some people coming from other countries as refugees and to give citizenship to them. This ambiguity leads to partiality on the part of the state in granting citizenship, as often the ruling dispensation acts in accordance with its political agenda. An editorial in a national daily suggests that "Rather than make these calculations it would have been infinitely better if India had a national policy on refugees or was a signatory to the 1951 refugee convention under which signatories are obliged not to send refugees back to where they have a well-founded fear of persecution. It is often viewed that absence of a clear-cut refugee policy leads to different approaches to different communities in India and often politically used for political advantage. In the absence of a coherent policy such issues will continue to be derailed in *ad hoc* manner, driven by ideological-political considerations".[7]It is argued that "along with the tentative and imperfect judicial response, the other major cause for this distressing repudiation of judicial and constitutional mandate is the conspicuous absence of any defined statutory framework or even a policy on refugees" (Bhattacharjee, 2008: 73). In the light of the lack of a compressive refugee policy, India has to do two things—-passing of a National Refugee Policy and signing 1951 UN Refugee Convention, which probably prevents the ruling dispensation's attempt to legalise its toxic politics of majoritarianism.

Notes

1. The Pioneer, 14 November 1999.
2. "Exclusionary Intent", The Hindu, 13May 2015.
3. *Ibid.*

References

- Arendt, Hannah (1986), The Origin of Totalitarianism, London: Andre Deutsch.
- Arendt, Hannah (1994),The Jewish Writings, New York: Schoken Books.
- Benhabib, Seyla (2004), The Rights of Others: Aliens, Residents, and Citizens, Cambridge: Cambridge University Press.
- Benhabib, Seyla (2005), "Borders, Boundaries, and Citizenship", PS: Political Science and Politics, Vol. 38, No.4, pp. 673—677.
- Bhattacharjee, Saurabh (2008), "India Needs a Refugee Law", Economic and Political Weekly, Vol. 43, No. 9, March 1—7, pp. 71—75.
- Government of India (2016), Annual Report 2015—16, New Delhi: Ministry of Home Affairs.
- Hovil, Lucy (2014), "Local Integration" in Elena Fiddian-Qasmiyeh, Gil Loescher, Katy Long, and Nando Sigona (eds.), The Oxford Handbook of Refugee and Forced Migration Studies, Oxford: Oxford University Press, pp. 488—498.
- Marshall, T. H. (1950), Citizenship and Social Class and Other Essays, Cambridge: Cambridge University Press.
- Samaddar, Ranabir (2003), "Introduction; Power and Care: Building the New Indian State", in Ranabir Samaddar (ed.), Refugees and the State: Practices of Asylum and Care in India, 1947—2000, New Delhi: Sage Publications, pp. 21—68.

6

Culture and Governance: Recent Trends in Tamil Nadu

— *Subramaniam Chandran*

Introduction

In modern democracies, governance is largely based on the constitutional law and specific set of rules. The executive part of government sometimes faces resistance of society on cultural grounds. The role of opposition consolidated in a systematic way to escalate the resistance reflecting the interests of the people. There is also cooperation from the people when the interests are recognized by the government. However, the multicultural social structure is a challenging endeavour for bureaucracy to mediate between the power structure and the social structure. The administrative class often witnesses the governance ignores the law but goes with the cultural demands. It is believed that federalism assures comfortable power sharing between the centre and the units in the multicultural social structure. The current trends in India can be explored on three visible grounds in relation to governance: the centre enhancing and expanding its powers; the states resisting the expanding of centre's powers over the states through their cultural components; and a state of ambiguity among the permanent executives amidst these trends. The culture of governance gets enormous twist and deviation from its status quo regulation when political decisions opted for. For a multicultural society, liberalism and federalism are often considered as strength as well as comfortable. When culture is superimposed on politics and governance, many adopt the basic concepts of primordial or civil loyalties to understand the issues and of the attitudes of rulers and the ruled. When friction arises, the former is related to the rulers and the latter to the ruled. Besides, the central and the state governments witness the same sort of friction in the process of governance. In short, politics may overplay governance and vice versa. It is further complicated with the pattern of majority and minorities in protecting or upholding the interests. Tamil

Nadu remains a fertile field of study in understanding the nexus between culture and governance the position of bureaucracy to mediate the process.

Reflections on the Concept

Culture refers to a way of life. It includes the values and beliefs governing the society. It is a result of a long process of evolution reflected in its social, economic and political institutions. The administrative culture often understood in its behaviour is influenced by the values cherished by the society at large and together with the ascribed bureaucratic features. Fred Riggs initially examined the relation between society and administration through his ecological approach. He states that every culture offers both support and obstacles to change or development. There are values that support change and development. Besides, there are values, which obstruct the change and development.[1] These values are generally termed as instrumental and consummated. A society having instrumental values becomes modernized.[2] It is believed, if the civil servants have instrumental values, they will definitely work towards the development of the society. Based on these presuppositions, Indian scenario is also understood as the Hindu values influence the administrative behaviour as majority of the civil servants are Hindus.[3] It is also believed that the administrative culture reflects the distinctiveness and complexity of national and local realities. Such cultures are historical products, where past experiences, myths, and traditions have shaped psychological orientations. Any administrative culture is also conditioned by existing circumstances and challenges. Even perceptions of the past are mediated by current experience.[4]

In short, culture exists prior to governance. Liberalism and democracy accept this thesis. Authoritarian governance views culture should be defined by the rulers. Conflict can be resolved in the former belief and conflict persists in the latter. At present, no state enjoys monolithic culture but diverse or fused cultures. Conflicts come and pass away. Governance is a process and it also comes and passes away. But the culture remains. Conflicts may reappear and resolved and the cycle goes on ever. The responsibilities assumed by the administrative class remain significant and desirable as the political process implies problematic or overplays the governance with vested interests. Yet the governance is unavoidable combination of politics and administration. The concept of administrative culture is forced to take experiments in the prevailing social and political structure and behaviour.

Indian Scenario

Indian culture has strong historical roots. Surprisingly, from monarchical to colonial administration, however selective, their characteristics have their place. Moral foundation and democratic features signify in framing the

Constitution. The civil service in the post-independence era imbibed all those features of Indian culture with aristocratic tune.[5] However, the elite components have been gradually changed by opening opportunities to the backward classes and the depressed with a view to upholding social justice and empowerment to the weaker section of people at large. This has strong reflection in policy formulation. Governance moved a step forward to emphasis on citizen participation. In other words the aristocratic attitude of the administrative class began to see the dignity and the needs of the people. Governance seems to accommodate populist agenda. However, it never gave up its elitist attitude. Submissive attitude to the political executives and dominant attitude to the public is real and sometimes latent feature of Indian bureaucracy.

Political parties are used effectively to consolidate the interests of the people. Right from the formation of the Indian National Congress, demands were put forth to the colonial government. Representation in government not only in the council but also in the civil service was emphasized. The British imperialism accepted the demands and opened opportunities to Indians some extent.[6] The British legacy implies two contradictory yet conciliatory tendencies in civil service. These are: the aristocratic, elitist and subservient to the order of the Queen on the one hand; and judicious based on rule of law as directed by the government. These two tendencies remain a reality. The aristocratic-elitist attitudes of civil service comfortably continue in governance. The Indian civil service did not deviate from this situation for a long time. When politics dominates in policy formulation, the administrative class has to bear the responsibility of implementation. The real task is to understand the cultural components in governance. Ironically, the question arises whether it is the culture of the administrative class or the people in general or part. Right from the beginning of the twentieth century, during the evolution of civil service, cultural conflicts between the elite and the backward section began to spread. It reflected in political, economic and social dimensions. Equality and justice became the central concerns which attracted or warned the nationalist agenda. The British colonialism skillfully geared her civil service to play amidst the elite and the backward section of people as early when the struggle for independence began to grow.

Culture and Governance in Tamil Nadu

Two tendencies rooted in society and politics attracted the scholars in conceptualizing the government in Madras Presidency. From the beginning of the twentieth century, when the freedom movement began to intensify and the British colonialism streamlined the governance, a reaction against the elite section of the society emerged. Then the educated new elites from the backward class consolidated the support and demand their rights.

The government formed right from the first elections in 1920 raised the voice for the benefit of the backward class, then consolidated as non-Brahmins or Dravidians.[7] Three developments were visible then. The administrators were subservient to the British imperialism. The freedom fighters or the nationalist demanded more rights and freedom to the natives. The dissidents who opposed the Brahmin domination in society, in Congress and in civil service took the stand of supporting the British rule with a view to enhancing their influence. The elected political executives were only three that time. The remaining executives were appointed by the Governor. Like civil servants, the first minister, then equal to chief minister, too depended upon the mercy of the Governor. The desirable culture of them officially outlined up to show loyalty to British imperialism.

Culture embodied in social, economic and political demands gradually found more place in governance. The initial step was to empower the non-Brahmins in education and employment. As the Hindu society is strongly identified with castes, phenomenon of social status and the idea of social equality are increasingly contemplated. Though the authenticity of the idea of Aryan and Dravidian was debated at length, it became a political reality appropriated the governance significantly. The government order in 1921 popularly called as communal GO categorized the different sections of people based on castes and religions and offered reservation to fill up government jobs. It was done roughly based on the percentage of population in respective sections. From time to time the practice was restructured and widened. The concept of social justice was comfortably identified with that policy. The composition of civil service was seen as the beginning of the cultural overtones on governance. When the elite composition became gradually restructured and opened opportunities for the backward classes, the corresponding impact on policy formulation could not be ignored. The political parties dynamically supported the development. In fact the British extended its concession to the Muslim students as early in 1880s for their backwardness in education in Madras Presidency.[8] From the beginning of the twentieth century the issue of merit and social justice began to prevail in the recruitment of officials in Madras Presidency.

Historical Roots

The formation of first elected government by the Justice Party in 1920 to the recent Anna Dravida Munnetra Kazhagam (ADMK) government in 2016, Tamil Nadu contributed largely reflecting cultural aspects in policies and schemes. The bureaucracy is implementing those policies without any hesitation as if they were part of their beneficiaries. The system of reservation policy based on communal quota is the powerful policy which brought the backward and the depressed classes to the forefront of the governance. Another policy is giving prominent place to Tamil language. Glorification of the Tamil language and Tamil literature became an important practice in governance. Education to the backward and depressed classes assumed greater significance. Women empowerment also became prominent concept in social welfare policies. Except during 1937-1939 and 1952-1954 when Rajagopalachari ruled, the Congress attracted much dissatisfaction and opposition. The situation boosted the regional sentiments rooted in Tamil culture largely identified with self-respect. Termed as Dravidian ideology and criticized as separatism, culture was used to justify their demands. The governance of the Congress became unpopular when it went against the feeling of the public.[9]

The Congress then decided to rescue its power by granting authority to Kamaraj. He earned the support of E.V. Ramaswamy for his non-Brahmin identity. From 1954 to 1967, the Congress enjoyed power and survived through its constructive policies. Expanding school education to the backward and depressed classes, Tamil medium in schools and colleges, heavy industries to Tamil Nadu, agriculture and irrigation development were the major involvement of the Congress governance.[10] However, the issue of official language status to Hindi brought trouble to the Congress government under Bakthavatsalam. His moves became wrong what Rajagopalachari already failed during his tenure in 1937-1939. The prominent place given to Hindi in place of English provoked widespread agitation in Tamil Nadu. The governance was ambivalent as it should maintain law and order and at the same time it should win the trust of the people. Neither could be achieved by the Congress. It became one of the major reasons to ensure the Dravida Munnetra Kazhagam (DMK) to win in 1967. From then onwards, the DMK and the ADMK were maintained their power despite the occasional threat from the Centre. Several castes once considered as upper class now found place in backward class. The land owning and the traditional industrialist and business class are well placed in the backward class. Except the Brahmins, most of the upper class castes have no problem to support the Dravidian ideology in the label of non-Brahmin.[11]

These phenomena throw light on the links between culture and governance. Academic stand often ignores the link in real terms in order to provide sanctity and autonomy to the study of public administration. The idea of organizational culture is mostly related to the aspect of management. But the idea of administrative culture is to be understood with the political process. In real terms, administrative culture is the ways and manners of the administrative class to cope up with the ruling party and effectively manages the public and the opposition. How the administrative instruments were appropriated to weaken the opposition is another important story. The administrative class often experience frustration when conflict of interest between the centre and the state. Either the centre is not yielding or the state does not cooperate with the centre over issues or implementing policies or schemes. Both attempt to earn goodwill of the people and to enhance their power. If both reaping mutual benefits without any conflict the scenario is always welcome. The involvement of administrative class in carrying out the regulatory and developmental policies becomes smooth too. When the governor overlooks the chief minister the entire issue seems to be problematic with the administrative class as the question of loyalty in terms of de facto or de jure exists. When the state government become weak or is weakened by certain circumstances, the Centre began to play in all possible ways. In order to check those issues the DMK demanded more federal features and even state autonomy.[12] The visibility of these issues could be examined historically as well as currently.

Recent Trends in Tamil Nadu

The post-1967 era keeps opportunities for the DMK and the ADMK in maintaining their power. As the administrative class is already composed by the backward classes in large numbers, formation of any one of those parties is not viewed as problem for the administrative class. There is no cultural conflict with the political executives; however it exists in small measure. In the issues of development, regulation, corruption, misuse of powers or sycophancy, the cultural fusion between the political executives and the permanent executives obviously exist. Political appropriation of policies and schemes at the cost of public exchequer by the ruling parties is accepted by the administrative class. They know that the mercy of the political executive is needed for placement, transfer, promotion, and protect from charges and punishment. Over the period of time, the administrative class who yielded to the political executives got powerful posts and the resisters placed in routine work. Even if the former category of officials got punished, they are hopeful, as the power swings between the DMK and the ADMK. Tamil culture, Tamil language and state autonomy are prominently pronounced when the Centre extends its control and authority over the state governance. The autobiographical writings of Karunanidhi reiterated this issue strongly.[13] The Congress in the post-1967 era gradually came into terms with the DMK or the ADMK and widely accepted their cultural attitudes. The administrative class in the guise of neutrality supports their cultural overtones. Naming of the schemes, public buildings, statues of leaders, celebrations, festivals, awards and honours are marked with cultural categories of the Tamils. Any political parties going against would lose their votes in the elections. As the Congress used to have electoral alliance with either DMK or ADMK, it welcomes the aspects of Tamil culture as well.

After the formation of government by Mr Narendra Modi in 2014 at the Centre with the promising idea of Hindutva, the states which do not welcome his moves began to face troubles. What is viewed by the Centre as creative and developmental is negatively viewed by the non-BJP states. The case of Tamil Nadu is not free from such outcomes. However, the Centre could not control Tamil Nadu as long as Ms Jayalalitha headed the ADMK government. As the Bharatiya Janata Party (BJP) has weak network in Tamil Nadu, it has lot of limitations to show its power over this state. Even it could not move the administrative class with the help of the governor during her rule. The only option was to use the department of income tax and enforcement to make the state government and opposition to become subservient to the authority of the Centre. That was also absent till Jayalalitha held power. Knowing the voters, Jayalalitha did not appreciate BJP openly in electoral terms. She retained power in 2016 elections and continued to keep distance from BJP reflecting the sentiment of the larger Tamil voters. When she died on 5 December 2016, a short period of confusion persisted over the leadership of the ADMK. Two factions emerged and tried to exclude the other. The BJP found the opportunities not to mediate but to overplay the situation. The administrative class was paralyzed with confusion and fears. It is difficult to measure how much the shadow authority of Ms Sasikala played in appointments and transfers of civil servants in the name of Jayalalitha. They paid heavy price to free from the corruption case.[14] But when Sasikala played vital part after the demise of Jayalalitha, the BJP decided to stop her move. The disproportionate assets case was reappeared. The BJP facilitated to see Sasikala to be punished. Finally the case brought punishment to Sasikala and her team. The political entry of her was stopped at that time. That made the BJP easier to move the ADMK government with their own interest. Reviving the corruption cases and the income tax issues brought scare in complete terms to the political as well as permanent executives. The BJP assures corruption free governance at the Centre, it decides to unfold the corruption-ride governance at the states of non-BJP. Though the BJP has all its appreciation to the personality of Jayalalitha, it reveals the corruption of Jayalalitha. The initiation of Subramanian Swamy and the efforts of the DMK largely contributed to move the case.

The BJP and the ADMK played a sour part in affecting the sentiments of Tamils in general and the DMK in particular related to the burial site of Karunanidhi. The common sense goes that the Dravidian leaders found place in the Marina beach began with C.N. Annadurai. That was also with the effort of Karunanidhi, then chief minister of Tamil Nadu. M.G. Ramachandran and Jayalalitha were also buried in Marina. The day when Karunanidhi died, the ADMK-BJP tries to stop his burial in Marina citing the legal issue. The sentiments of the public with mourning furies resulted in the extreme hatred and anger towards the ADMK-BJP stand. M.K. Stalin was very much annoyed. The BJP supporter Gurumurthy cleverly spoke to stop burial at Marina. The BJP sympathizers themselves did not welcome his statement. The DMK went to the High Court and the court heard the case from 8 pm to late midnight. Upholding the validity of arguments put forth by the DMK counsel the court gave more consideration to the public sentiments than the fragile aspects of the legal issue. The court permitted the burial place at Marina. The last hours of public display of his body and burial activities were done overnight immediately after the verdict. For courtesy sake, the ADMK and BJP leaders visited him to pay homage. Scholars and journalists held that the ADMK-BJP partnership played unwanted and immature role in that issue which is unforgettable in the history of Dravidian movement.[15]

The influence of the Centre over the state implies to sustain the state governance till the resistance becomes wide. The BJP promoted electoral alliance with the ADMK for the 2019 Lok Sabha elections. It also facilitated the ADMK to make alliance with other parties to defeat the opposition. It was expected that the ADMK and its allies would win majority of seats. They also anticipated on the chances in the BJP cabinet. The opposition did not plunge into any nightmare but confident. The administrative class kept silent despite its knowledge of the political reality. During elections, income tax raids were going on the DMK leaders. The results of the elections shocked the BJP. Except one place the ruling ADMK lost all places to the DMK front. It is not the point to evaluate the results but the implications are important which widely covered by the media. These are: the governance of the ADMK at large is not satisfactory, the ADMK governance is directed by the BJP, uncomfortable alliance with political parties, viz, the BJP, TMC, PMK, and DMDK. On the contrary, the DMK did not experience such kind of conflict of interests with the allies. The opposition propagated that the BJP was a danger to Tamil culture and social justice. The media exposed that the leaders of the ADMK allies compromised with the BJP in making electoral alliance even if they did not have any common ground in principles. The voters belonging to their parties themselves knew the situation. The BJP took effective steps to stop distribution of money to the voters. It was largely done on the DMK allies selectively and not on the ADMK.

Tamil Nadu is witnessing enormous pressures from the Centre to subvert the Tamil culture which remains a fertile field to cherish the Dravidian parties. The state at large views that the Centre is dominant in all aspects of the governance leaving the state in weak network. In other words it gradually reduces the decision making powers of the state which have high cultural connotations. In recent times, the governor attempted to review the performance of departments and the implementation of policies. He visited places and met the beneficiaries and the implementing agencies. He spoke at length the performance of the government. Mr Banwarilal Prohit expressed his opinions on the performance of the government. He attempted to break the traditional role of the governor. The media covered his activities and views which painted his moves as politician. Usually, the governor will not act like that. It is the activity of the government specifically by the political and permanent executives. The opposition parties criticized that the governor undermined the state government and acted as the representative of the Central government or the BJP tried to subvert the role of the state administration. Ironically, the ruling ADMK welcomed such activities of the governor which clearly echoed the voice of the BJP.[16]

When the ADMK could not win seats in the Lok Sabha elections in 2019, Gurumurthy said that the political executives are incapable.[17] It aroused rage among the ADMK and countered him with words. In fact, they felt that their self-respect was hurt. The administrative class has its moral responsibility as well for whatever criticism attracted by the ministers in day to day administration. Few senior IAS officers opined that his criticism has lot of implication about the social justice cherished by Tamil Nadu.[18] The civil service during the British constituted more than eighty percent of Brahmins. Now that place is occupied by the non-Brahmins. The officer interpreted that the criticism not only leveled against the politicians but also to the bureaucrats. This view is shared by several officials who are sympathetic to the Dravidian ideology.

The introduction of NEET in the selection of students for medical education is viewed as bypassing the powers of the state. The previous evaluation based on the performance in school examination is completely ignored. The spirit of education becomes pushed away and the competitive spirit and fear comes into forefront. It created stress among the students. Suicides were attempted. Unhealthy practices happened with a view to inspect the students even to enter into the exam hall. Strict control was administered. The opposition parties as well as the ruling parties demanded exception from NEET to Tamil Nadu. Initially, the BJP leaders in Tamil Nadu also supported the demand. So far no exception was granted. Instead, the state government is persuaded to speak with the voice of the Centre time to time. Since the subject of education was brought to the concurrent list, the decision making powers of the state over the education declined.

Another move is related to the controversies in introducing Sanskrit in schools by the Central government. As far as Tamil Nadu is concerned, the compulsory introduction of Hindi and Sanskrit is viewed as the hegemony of the Centre. Sanskrit is viewed as an instrument of brining importance to the Brahmins. Tamil Nadu is historically known for its non-Brahmin empowerment in all aspects replacing the Brahmins with political power. The Congress in the past knew that and kept distance from the sensitive issues. When the draft of the New Education Policy 2019 made the Sanskrit mandatory, a widespread opposition from the Tamil Nadu was noted. The new policy undermined the importance of English. This created a spur among the non-Hindi states and scholars from different fields.[19]

With a surprise, year by year more number of students learns Hindi and takes examination conducted by Dakshina Bharat Hindi Prachar Sabha. It reported that the candidates, mostly students, who appeared for the exam, were more than 5.7 lakhs in 2019.[20] Many view that if the Centre distains from mandatory policies in cultural aspects, it can achieve what it intended for. On more sensitive issue is to damage the statue and icon of E.V. Ramaswamy, known popularly as Periyar. The persons who damaged the icon are identified as the supporters of the BJP. Gurumurthy, Subramanian Swamy, and H. Raja frequently made controversial statements arousing the sentiments of the Tamils, especially the DMK. Many learned Brahmins themselves do not entertain their remarks. Only a section of Brahmins connected with political interests welcomed them. It is believed that their unwanted behaviour reduces the level of votes originally intended for the BJP. As it is a known fact, the national wing of BJP appreciates the Tamils and their culture now and then. It also gives position to the backward and the depressed classes to stop the image that it is promoting the interests of the Brahmins. Their instrumental practice cannot be equated with actual stand. The conflict between the Brahmin and the non-Brahmin is currently become pacified, the activities of the BJP revived such sentiments. The Dravidian parties do not tolerate harsh speech against E.V. Ramaswamy in the present circumstances too.[21] Besides, a selective attack on the ideas of Tamils is envisaged now and then by the supporters of the BJP. The ruling ADMK do not usually oppose those speeches but interpret in defence of the BJP. The most recent issue is the introduction of the Citizenship Amendment Act 2019 (CAA) which is viewed danger to the Muslims. The ADMK allies speak with the voice of the BJP in support of the CAA. But the opposition grows in fast measure.[22] The BJP allies organized rallies in support of the CAA in reaction to the rallies of the opposition. Both created the problem of law and order. The emotion involvement in the rallies of opposition was obvious the police force would act with care. Any adverse move would bring problem to the ruling elites and their allies. Both action and inaction would definitely be problematic. The administrative behaviour is left with no choice in the ambivalent situation. Due to the fear of Corona virus the protest in the form of assembling and rallies are temporarily suspended.

These developments bring enormous pressures on the part of governance in maintaining law and order. The administrative class with police force has to regulate the situation without any embarrassment to the government. Moreover, they could not act on their own but with the order of the political executives. Even though they advocate so-called neutrality, their security and sentiments are at risk. They would come to conclusion that the status quo is better than the change in circumstances. Moreover, increasingly engaging in such kind of risks would slow down the regulatory administration and developmental scenario. They are easily questioned by the political executives and the public. Immediate action is largely illogical in executive and judicial spheres. But the political executives may act before thought. The administrative culture may be a safety net as well as a trap depending on the circumstances.

The BJP knows that any move to undermine the Tamil language and culture or the personalities of Dravidian movement could not be tolerated in Tamil Nadu. The Congress stopped such practice long. The BJP shows ambivalence in this case. Mr Narendra Modi appreciated the classical status of the Tamil language some times. He spoke in appreciation of Thiruvalluvar and *Thirukkural*. He called on Karunanidhi and greeted him in Tamil 'Vanakkam Sir.' He held the 93 years old veteran in his hand and invited him to his home in Delhi for taking rest.[23] Immediately a story was created that the BJP coming close to the DMK. His government made honoured and awarded celebrities from Tamil Nadu irrespective of castes, religion and gender. Then why should the DMK allies and the Muslims do not entertain the BJP in Tamil Nadu. They believed that the BJP attitude has lot of hypocrisy. Their ultimate aim is to reduce the opportunities for the non-Brahmins which would facilitate the Brahmins to enhance their power. Their show in balancing the castes has a strong motive of influencing the voters. Are the Brahmins really needed the BJP for their well-being? A careful perusal of this statement is needed to avoid any amount of illusion and to throw light on the reality. What happened to the living standards of the Brahmins in Tamil Nadu during the rule of Dravidian parties? Surprisingly both the non-Brahmins and the Brahmins enhanced their living standards. The system of communal reservation provided new opportunities to the non-Brahmins in education, jobs and even in political positions. The emergence of new capitalist class is also seen from the non-Brahmins in the past five decades. Cinema and media industry are once dominated by the Brahmins now dominated by the non-Brahmins. Ironically, several non-Tamils produce Tamil films successfully. It is a fact that due to communal quota the recruitment of Brahmins is reduced over the period of time. They could not find chances to become doctors, engineers or professors at state universities and clerks in the government service.[24]

There is other story to justify that the Brahmins in Tamil Nadu are not deprived in any way. They are one of the minority communities with high literacy rates having respectable social status historically, in spite of the sarcastic treatment of E.V. Ramaswamy and his followers on rational grounds. They keep the position of priests in temples and perform rituals in Hindu families of non-Brahmins as well. Apart from the traditional occupations, they found occupation in newspapers, magazines, Television, cinema, hotel, software, auditing, accounts, banking, and share market. The poor section of them remains confined to the temples and cooking in the nearby households. They had also opportunities in private industries of commerce and marketing and educational institutions. They comfortably found opportunities in central government sector. They found places in high qualified categories in abroad. The poverty rate is very low as several NGOs give security to their life. Hindu religious organizations of non-profit helped in great extend. Though these opportunities exist to non-Brahmins too the recognition is not as wide as the Brahmins. It is a fact that during the governance of Dravidian parties both the non-Brahmins and the Brahmins enhanced their powers, perhaps, the former with the help of government, the latter with their social push and personal effort.

The wealth distribution survey revealed that the upper castes which constitute 22.3 percent own 41 percent of total wealth in India. The backward class holds 31 percent less than their population size of 35.66 percent. The Muslims own 8 percent who constitute 12 percent of population. The SC and ST who constitute 27 percent own 11.3 percent combined. The distribution of wealth varies across the states. Of the total wealth, the highest 17.5 percent is concentrated in Maharashtra, followed by Uttar Pradesh 11.5, Kerala 7.4, Tamil Nadu7.2 and Haryana 6 percent. In Tamil Nadu more than 70 percent of the assets are owned by the top 29 percent households.[25] The Central government reservation of 10 percent to the poor upper class is criticized as it is against social justice.[26] The story of north India is completely different from Tamil Nadu. Many view that the criterion of poor is illogical. In Tamil Nadu, as among the upper class, only the Brahmins lead in the level of education, and this reservation will ultimately help the Brahmins. State sponsored concessions exist throughout the world. Nations follow the policy in one or other forms. They viewed the policy as protective discrimination in order to bring the deprived to the mainstream. The US government is known for its policy to help the black and the minorities. However, debates always to decide who is really deprived and how it should be rectified effectively. India has no exception in this case too.

Among those heavy propaganda against the BJP by the media and the opposition, and the states echoed in support of the BJP policies, the image of administrative class has its own pressures. Usually, the regulatory aspect of administration does not attract the cultural opposition in great measure. But the issues of policies affecting the status quo are viewed with alarm and generated much opposition. The media will focus the debates of policies and the public. As the actual implementation of such policies is entrusted with the administrative class it should bear the burden of resistance. It has also pressures to earn the goodwill of the government. Even if they have logical solution or alternative ideas they are easily ignored by the political executives. Alternatively they are flexible enough to appease them for their survival or reward.

It has been revealed that several IAS officers who were close to Jayalalitha and Sasikala were corrupt and misused power for mutual benefit. After the death of Jayalalitha, the income tax raid was conducted at the office of the chief secretary while the chief minister was very much in his office. Currencies and illegal documents were seized. Media exposed all those developments. The reaction of the state administration was completely absent. The opposition and the media criticized the situation as the practice itself subverted the powers of the state. It is the practice when the accused are ready to support the BJP they have the chance to drop the charges. Several raids on the pro-ADMK have no follow up actions. The DMK said that the BJP is misusing the probe agencies like the CBI, ED, and Election Commission. It further said that the ADMK government supported by the BJP is the most corruption state in India.[27] Earlier, just before the 2016 Assembly election, Amit Shah spoke that the Jayalalitha government is the most corrupt in the country and asked the people to oust in the elections.[28] The opposition revealed all those developments in recent times. In short, the administrative class is not in position to act rationally. The hierarchy is diluted with the outsiders who oversee the issues with political support. Senior IAS officers believed that parallel governance exists within their span of hierarchy and control. Sometimes, orders from hidden sources, understandably from the central authority, move the permanent executives bypassing the permanent executives. Ironically, an IAS officer informed sending of order relating to an appointment with no previous knowledge to the political executive. It is fact that the DMK allies continuously attack the ADMK-BJP led government of Tamil Nadu. Perhaps, there may be happening unexposed or the issues may be over exclaimed. A senior journalist reported that in every government two sets of bureaucrats existed. One team has the opportunities to make illegal money and the other team does not have the opportunities. Not only the administrative class but also the public at large is skeptical about the autonomy of the ADMK-led state governance. Even though a portion of loyalty goes in favour of the ruling party yet the dissatisfaction exist. The administrative class views that the game theory has its foot in cultural categories.

For some time the Tamil Nadu governor was dragged to a sensitive issue where Nirmala Devi, the college professor arrested on charges of luring four of her girl students to extend sexual favours to senior officials. The governor said that he has not even seen face of her. He continued that he has grandchildren and great grandchildren and he is already 78 years old. The efforts of the governor to protect his image are obvious. He himself ordered the case to be probed. Media persons also attracted defamation case for referring the governor.[29]

One more recent issue is the corruption in public service commission. Administrative failure is weighed more than the political involvement. It is an autonomous body in theory. However, the ruling party has the interests to appoint its chairperson and the members. It is reported that several private coaching centres have the access to the questions before the examination held. Besides, the staff in the service commission with intermediaries involved in corrupt practices. Interested candidates are selected with their systematic involvement. From selection of exam centres to the evaluation and selection, they have their cleverness and hidden role. The crime branch police revealed the facts and this practice happened for a long time. It traced the corruption right from 1996 when ADMK held power.[30] The opposition attacks that the corruption happened with the help of political executives. The ADMK said that the corruption also happened during the rule of DMK. The issue is going to be fixed with the officials rather the politicians. The accountability is largely vested with the permanent executives. Of course, share in corruption when political climate permits is not the part of administrative culture. But in reality it happened from time to time. The online exam system is another caricature. In certain centres, the supervisors themselves aided the candidates. Some used mobiles and books freely in answering the questions. Media reported these situations with authentic proofs. The commission cancelled some examinations and withheld some results. It permitted some other results even if they had the same kind of controversy. Though both the political and permanent executives are answerable to such kind of malpractice, the officials are more vulnerable. In recent years the BJP is boldly declaring that they are giving corruption free governance. It is also believed that nothing moves without the knowledge of the Central government in Tamil Nadu. Yet the recent corruption in public service commission and even in NEET examination did not support the declaration of the BJP.

There are other issues prevailed in Tamil Nadu which in which the BJP attracted severe criticism. The *Jallikattu* is a traditional sport during *Pongal* in Tamil Nadu. The sport is entertained very much as the youths showing their valour in chasing the bulls. The Central government opposed the sport as inhuman and harm to animals. But the sport is strongly connected to Tamil cultural mood. Widespread protests made the government to relax its control and permitted the sport.[31]

There are protests raised the environmental issues. These protests strongly attacked the ADMK-BJP nexus in granting permission to the environmental hazardous projects. The anti-Sterlite protest is the most horrible. The anti-Sterlite protest was led to a massacre in Thoothukudi. The protesters wanted Sterlite copper smelting unit shut down as it was causing environmental damage to the area. The demand goes since 1993 right from its establishment. When people gathered for a rally to show their opposition, 10 people were killed by police firing.[32] Protests against the exploration of hydrocarbon in Neduvasal is also the environmental issue.

Though the government stopped temporarily the BJP government at the centre is trying go with the project.[33] The Theni neutrino project is also protested by the local villagers as it is hazardous to ecosystem, though the state and central government granted permission.[34] The sentiments of the local people in particular often ignored by the ADMK-BJP government. The administrative class is pressured to go through these projects and ordered to convince the local people. The media are fast enough to dissipate these issues to the public now and then. Though there are supporting propagations, they are not as effective as the opposition. One advantage exists to the ADMK that whatever happened against the interests of the people it is the BJP- held responsibility. Thereby the ADMK retains their voters and keeps the BJP in Tamil Nadu in weak network. In other words, both the DMK and ADMK strengthen at the cost of the BJP. A question remains what extent the BJP realized this development in Tamil Nadu. These issues will be counted ultimately during elections.

The bureaucracy for the first time works under a mediocre politician who rose to the level of chief minister during the time of confusion and turmoil in the ADMK. Of course, Sasikala made him as chief minister to stop her opponent Pannerselvam who allegedly acted on the advice of the BJP at that time. Later, the two opposing factions got united and Palanisamy secured the support of the BJP too. The ADMK retained majority and the leadership of Palanisamy was not challenged within the party. The BJP continues its support politically. But the senior IAS officers reported that the Centre supervises even without the knowledge of the state. Here the administrative behaviour lapses lacking freedom and autonomy to some extent. For some times controversies revolved around the stability. Amidst these circumstances, the administrative culture of the bureaucracy also assumed mediocrity and awaits more dynamic political executives with legitimate powers. The concurrent list of the Constitution not only reduces the freedom of the political executives but also diverts the behaviour of the bureaucracy. When the Centre attempts to enhance its power over the states, the state bureaucracy has discomfort in its routine performance.

Dravidian Ideology and Hindutva

In Tamil Nadu Dravidian ideology however loosely defined or diluted is accepted politically by the DMK and the ADMK. In simple terms, it rooted in Tamil language and culture. Tamil Nadu is the place for Tamil majority and minorities speaking south Indian languages. Tamil language has its all features of classical language. It is modernized and has little influence from other languages. It still maintains its authority and sanctity when other classical languages lost their usage at large. The culture of the Tamils is civilized with moral foundations. It has due consideration for both subjectivity and rationality. It is believed that the ancient Tamil society had no caste divisions except based on geographical division of life activities. The infiltration of Aryan equated with the Brahmins was responsible for caste discrimination and social conflict. The Aryan generated religious superstitions to control the Tamils. The social and political philosophy constructed on the Tamil culture is largely known as Dravidian ideology. However, conflicting ideas always exist with appreciating tolerance. The leaders of Justice Party supported the English colonialism with the expectations that they might help to elevate the non-Brahmins. What they implied in the idea of Dravidian was also included people speaking Telugu, Kannada and Malayalam, however minority.[35] Hence the Tamil culture is synonymous with Dravidian culture with these languages without any cultural difference.

Several leaders are drawn from the South Indian origins. E.V. Ramaswamy Periyar advocated atheism and opposed the domination of Brahmins in social and educational fields. He tried to replace their domination with non-Brahmins. His ideas of social reforms, women freedom and social justice were acceptance and the government formed by the DMK and the ADMK cherished his views. However, his idea of atheism is greatly set aside and he did not face any opposition for his ideas from the non-Brahmins or the government, except a section of Brahmins openly. E.V. Ramaswamy had a strong belief that politics would do more harm than good. He kept the Dravidar Kazhagam (DK) not as political party but a social reform organization. Realizing the necessity of political authority the DMK branched from the DK. Later several offshoots appeared and the largest one is the ADMK. When the DMK and the ADMK came to power his ideas were officially put into practice. The solidarity of non-Brahmins irrespective of caste division was achieved by the Dravidian movement over the period of time. This helped the DMK and the ADMK to retain their power since 1967. There is a merit in understanding how the personalities helped in strengthening the movement and power retention. E.V. Ramaswamy, C.N. Annadurai, Karunanidhi, M.G. Ramachandran, and Jayalalitha can be lined up in this endeavour. The ADMK had no problem with the issue of Jayalalitha's Brahmin origin. She did not have any motive to deprive the non-Brahmins. There were second line, middle and bottom line leaders who developed the Dravidian parties. Their sacrifice, hard work, intelligence and relentless service paved such retention of power over the years. The administrative class is also identified with cultural categories which could not be subverted easily. Civil servants have their identity as Tamils and non-Tamils, or Brahmins, backward class and depressed class. They also have the identity based on from state service and from all-India service.[36] Several bureaucrats hailed from non-Brahmins availed the opportunities extended by the reservation policy based on the communal quota. Though most of them are sympathetic to the DMK and the ADMK, their professional neutrality cannot be questioned. Only few bureaucrats exhibit their close association with political executives. Apart from this, it helped them to consolidate their interests to pressurize the government however indirectly. Social gathering, recreation, family links and personal use of government facilities were easily done on those identities. It became a reality in all its hierarchy of personnel. The political executives have knowledge about the situation and the discretion and vested interests have their own place. This became a part of administrative culture.

The BJP rejected the construction of Dravidian and Aryan as myths. It also rejected separate and distinctive cultures within the Hindu society to weaken the Brahmins. The Dravidian ideology assures to elevate the non-Brahmins. The non-Brahmin category includes the backward, depressed and upper castes except the Brahmin minority. The Hindutva originally aims to consolidate the Hindus and to elevate them leaving the non-Hindus. Like the Dravidian ideology welcomed the Brahmins in its fold in course of time, the Hindutva begins to accept the non-Hindus of India in its fold believing their origin as Hindus. This wide coverage has lot of meaning politically though not socially. To what extent this theory can be practiced is a great question. But the BJP is confident enough to win the solidarity of the Hindu majority than the minorities of various groups. Still the Hindu majority has the promising end to give mandate to the BJP. Logically speaking, it is wasting of time to appease with the minorities for votes, as they are not consolidated. Their loyalties are fragmented and are appropriated by the regional parties at large. No doubt both the ideologies aimed to protect the majorities either the non-Brahmins or the Hindus respectively. The Dravidian ideology went a step to reduce its atheistic stand include the Brahmins in the DMK as early began by C.N. Annadurai. He tried to consolidate the support from different sections of the people. Cinema helped a lot in winning the minds of different sections of people. Like the approach of Annadurai, Vajpayee went ahead to consolidate the minorities in support of the BJP. He tried to set aside the image of Hindu majority domination. Besides, he did not question the demands of states while enhancing the communal quota. For him the survival of BJP and his government were more important than the forceful introduction of Hindutva. The opposition had free voice in the parliament and democratic norms were not affected during his tenure.

Hindutva can be traced back to the 1920s when Savarkar put forth the maxim 'Hindu, Hindi, Hindustan' remembering the European nationalism based on religious identity, common language, and racial unity.[37] Loyalty to the Hindu nation was supreme in his notion.[38] A critical milestone occurred in 1925 when Hedgewar formed the Rashtriya Swayamsevak Sangh (RSS). Hedgewar formed the RSS as a cultural organization with the purpose of strengthening Hindu society. Later, the Bharatiya Jan Sangh (BJS) was formed in 1951 as a political party. More organizations were established to foster the Hindutva, such as, the Akhil Bharatiya Vidyarthi Parishad (ABVP), the Bharatiya Mazdoor Sangh (BMS), and the Vishwa Hindu Parishad (VHP). During the coalition era the BJP oscillated between militant and moderate stances, depending on prevailing political conditions.[39] Between 2004 and 2014, the BJP occupied the opposition benches, prompting some supporters to speak openly of the party's permanent opposition status. The BJP in 2014 moved beyond the party's traditional upper caste voter base. It had made serious efforts to appeal to lower and backward castes emphasizing welfare over ideology. The campaign focused largely on issues of development, anticorruption, and good governance. However, it did not mean that Hindutva was absent from the campaign. Hindutva was applied in a targeted manner in certain times and places where it could benefit from using them.[40] The BJP knows that the bureaucracy is to be tuned to carry out its agenda not only at the Centre but also at the states. After the Mandal Commission recommendations the OBC slightly widened their place in bureaucracy. However, the composition of upper class did not give up their power. The BJP found no problem with the bureaucracy in the Central government. At the same time it maneuvers the state bureaucracy as happens in Tamil Nadu.

Hindutva lends itself to populist discourse which places a high value on the general will of the Hindus. It implies existing institutions are not the expressions of general will.[41] The challenge for the BJP government is balancing its Hindutva agenda with economic rejuvenation which increasingly seeing the failure. Many observe that Modi would aggressively move to implement pro-Hindu policies.[42] The emergence of Narendra Modi is looked with great alarm by the opposition as his government would go extreme to undermine them. It was reported by Yashwant Sinha that Vajpayee wanted to sack Modi in 2002, then the chief minister of Gujarat, on the issue of Godhra riots. But L.K. Advani opposed his decision.[43] No doubt, the BJP tries to avoid its image as serving to the interests of the upper class especially the Brahmins in Tamil Nadu. For that, it gave state leadership to woman from non-Brahmin community and to the depressed class. Despite its Hindutva policies, it tries to build an image that it is not against the interests of Tamil culture. Its image building is an instrumental exercise. The Dravidian ideology implies that Hindutva and Tamil culture are two parallel developments and the intersection may end friction rather than assimilation.

Building a temple for Rama is not viewed as anti-culture. But the introduction of Sanskrit, reservation to the upper class, the CAA, and the attack on the icon of E.V. Ramaswamy are viewed as anti-culture. Yet there is a way to build its image on the line of Dravidian ideology. If the BJP decides to follow the status quo and to keep aside those sensitive moves, it can win the trust of the people in Tamil Nadu. If it comes true, the DMK, the left and the minorities may have no conflicts in making coalition with the BJP as it happened during the time of Vajpayee. This stand will be better in view of developing the state than riding with the ADMK and its allies. Still it is believed that Narendra Modi can provide corruption free administration despite the criticism of economic failure. The bureaucrats who distain from corrupt practices largely echoed this voice. They suggest cultural solution for harmonious governance. In other words, the Hindutva should recognize the validity of diversity and tolerance. The bureaucracy in Tamil Nadu opined that the time would come to mitigate Hindutva in secular terms embedded in the social and political compulsions. The self-respect of both the Centre and the state come into terms with this move. What Dr Radhakrishnan said about Hinduism is relevant here. He said that Hinduism is a way of life. The implication is not only for the Hindus but the human in general. Hindutva may consider this implication in future as politics sometimes achieves and sometimes survives. The culture of Indian bureaucracy would inculcate the value as well.

Conclusion

The political executives come and go. Some will rule a long time. Others will have short time. The permanent executives have the span of thirty to forty years. They have the rules and laws. They have the pressures from the political executives and the opposition. They witness all the cooperation and attacks from the public. They are answerable to press and stand before the court. Ultimately they have to mediate between the Centre and the state. Amidst all those developments the governance goes with the bureaucracy even if the elected representatives absent provisionally. What sort of new meaning can be ascribed to the concept of administrative culture? It is the attitude of an official compromising with short-time political aristocrats and ultimately subservient to the interests of them with a view to protecting themselves from punishment or has a partnership with them to enhance their wealth and influence. That is the reality behind the process of governance. Their history is largely unwritten or overshadowed. But still they hold responsible for the success of governance knowing the cultural component without any politicization. They are capable of sensing the culture in pure terms as well as with politicization depending on the circumstances. They know that the BJP tries to avoid its Brahmin-oriented identity and at the same time yielding to the pressures of their interests. The administrative class knows that the Dravidian ideology, however old and diluted, it resurrects itself in circumstances promising power either to the DMK or the ADMK. May be a special definition established in academic circle but not in the real politics for the concept of administrative culture. When the BJP conceptualizes the Hindutva in one nation, one language, and one culture, the federal features are largely ignored. It also gives embarrassing situation to the regional parties nurtured in cultural aspects. The BJP is also nurtured through its greater culture called the Hindutva which is not solid in single terms. Pluralism has its place and the time is already on the way to fit to the needs of the local culture.

References

1. Riggs, Fred W. Administration in Developing Countries: The Theory of Prismatic Society, Houghton Mufflin, Boston, 1964.
2. Almond, G. A. and S. Verba. The Civic Culture Revisited, Sage, London, 1980.
3. Subramanyam A,. 'Hindu Values and Administrative Behaviour,' The Indian Journal of Public Administration, Vol. XIII, Oct-Dec. 1967, IIPA, New Delhi; also see Mathur, Kuldeep. 'Administrative Mind in a Developing Nation,' The Indian Journal of Public Administration, Vol. XXVII, No. 4, Oct-Dec, 1976, IIPA, New Delhi; Puranik. N. 'Administrative Culture: Need for Conceptual Clarity and Further Research,' The Indian Journal of Public administration, Vol. XXIV, April -June, 1978, IIPA, New Delhi.
4. Dwivedi, O. P. and J. Nef. 1998. 'Administrative Culture: A Global Perspective.' Africanus, 28(2), 1998, 5-7.
5. Maheswari, S.R. Indian Administration, Macmillan, New Delhi, 1996.
6. Misra, B.B. Administrative History of India, 1834-1947, Oxford University Press, London, 1972.
7. Chandran, S. Tamizhaga Arasiyal (Politics in Tamil Nadu), Bharathi Puthakalayam, Chennai, 2001, pp 45-46.
8. Chandran, S. 'Towards a Unified Approach of Social Justice: Merging Tradition and Modernity in Public Policy Making in India,' World Academy of Science, Engineering and Technology, 5 (5) 2011, 515-519.
9. Chandran, S. 'Traditions and Legacies at Crossroads: Rereading of Political History of Tamil Nadu,' Proceedings of the Nineteenth Annual Session of the Tamil Nadu History Congress, 2013; also see Chandran, S. Traditions Apart: Rajaji and Periyar, Sivaguru Pathippagam, Chennai, 2009.
10. Kandaswamy, P. The Political Career of K. Kamaraj, Concept, New Delhi, 2001.
11. Chandran, S. 'From Separatism to Coalition: Variants in Language Politics and Leadership Pattern in Dravidian Movement,' World Academy of Science, Engineering and Technology, 5 (3) 2011, 431-435.
12. Chandran, S. Tamizhaga Arasiyal (Politics in Tamil Nadu), Bharathi Puthakalayam, Chennai, 2001, p 174.
13. Kalaignar Mu Karunanidhi, Nenchukku Needhi, 6 vols, Thirumagal Nilayam, Chennai, 2016; also see M.R. Barnett, The Politics of Cultural Nationalism, Princeton University Press, Princeton, 1976.
14. The Hindu, 11 May, 2015.
15. The Hindu, 8 August 2018.
16. Deccan Chronicle, 17 November 2017.
17. The Hindu, 27 December 2017.
18. Based on interview from few senior IAS officers.

19. Hindustan Times, 14 August 2019.
20. Times of India, 8 June 2019.
21. The Hindu, 24 January 2020.
22. The Hindu, 19 February 2020.
23. India Today, 6 November 2017.
24. Times of India, 31 May 2019.
25. The Indian Express, 14 February 2019.
26. Economic Times, 7 January 2019.
27. Times of India, 25 June 2019.
28. The Hindu, 13 April 2016.
29. The New Indian Express, 17 April 2018.
30. The Hindu, 16 February 2020.
31. The New Indian Express, 18 January 2017.
32. The Hindu, 23 May 2018.
33. The Hindu, 8 April 2017.
34. The Hindu, 15 April, 2018.
35. Chandran, S. 'From Separatism to Coalition: Variants in Language Politics and Leadership Pattern in Dravidian Movement,' Electronic copy available at: http://ssrn.com/abstract=1859917.
36. Interview with IAS officers association in Tamil Nadu.
37. Hansen, Thomas Blom, The Saffron Wave: Democracy and Hindu Nationalism in India, Princeton University Press, Princeton, 1999, p. 78.
38. Andersen, Walter K. and Shridhar Damle, The RSS: A View to the Inside, Penguin Random House India, Gurgaon, 2018, p. 237.
39. Palshikar, Suhas, 'The BJP and Hindu Nationalism: Centralist Politics and Majoritarian Impulses,' South Asia: Journal of South Asian Studies, 38, no. 4 (2015): pp 719–735.
40. Thachil, Tariq, Elite Parties, Poor Voters: How Social Services Win Votes in India, Cambridge University Press, New York, 2014.
41. Jaffrelot, Christopher, The Hindu Nationalist Movement in India, Columbia University Press, New York, 1996, p 235.
42. Vaishnav, Milan, The BJP in Power: Indian Democracy and Religious Nationalism, Carnegie Endowment for International Peace, Washington, DC, 2019, pp 5-22.
43. Economic Times, 10 May 2019.

7

Empowering and Strengthening Rural Local Governments in Mizoram

— *Lalrintluanga*

Background

Mizoram State is situated in the extreme corner of North-East India. Until the colonisation of Mizoram by the British in March 1890 (Reid 1978:243), the ancestral land of the Mizos covered the present day's Mizoram in India and its adjacent areas in the western part of Myanmar and the eastern area of Chittagong Hill Tracts of Bangladesh.In those days, every Mizo village had a local-self-government under its own traditional hereditary Chief, called *Lal.* Absence of any central or pyramidal structure of authority to regulate relations among the different Village Chiefs enabled every Mizo village to function as a self-governing institution in which every Chief was, by custom, responsible to play an undifferentiated role as "the protector of the village life and property" (Baveja 1970:12) and "the guardian of his people, leader and defender in times of attack by the enemy and, above all, giver of food in times of scarcity" (Thanga 1978:7). Being at the pivot of a village social structure, every Mizo Chief could enjoy supreme administrative and political powers within the confine of his particular area of operation. B. Pakem who had an inside knowledge about the Mizos and their traditional self-governing system of village administration rightly said: "Each village used to be an independent unit under the concentrated power of its Chief or *Lal*" (Pakem 1981:1). Though Chieftainship was not a democratically elected rural local self-government, most of the Village Chiefs democratically exercised their authorities and decentralise some of their powers and functions to their respective hamlets called *Khawper.*[8]

The British annexation of Mizoram in 1890 had far-reaching consequences on the existing socio-economic and political life of the Mizos and the system of their grassroots' governance. Though the British rulers did not have any other concrete political or economic agenda for the Mizo tribes, they were prompted by the prevailing situation to subjugate their warlike Chiefs who intermittently carried out raids on their occupied territories in the plain areas of Assam. Initially, the British thought that one or two punitive expeditions would be able to subdue those marauding Mizo Chiefs for making the frontiers quiet. But, things proved otherwise and the British had to occupy Mizoram against their commercial interest. It was against this background that the British had set up a simple system of administration just for curtailing the mobility of the Mizo Chiefs and their subjects as far as Cachar plains of Assam. With an objective of ensuring effective administration with least expenditure in the Mizo Hills, the British authority had followed the policy of internal control of the villages by their own Chiefs and the principle was to interfere as little as possible in the day-to-day administration of the villages. Thus, under the powerful British Superintendent, the Mizo Chiefs had become mere representatives of the British Government in their own land and "the main plank of the alien rule over their own people" (Ray 1982:30).

After the British consolidation of their powers in Mizoram came the Christian Missionaries of western origin. As a part of their mission, the Christian Missionaries introduced western education. These Missionaries faced stiff opposition from the Mizo traditional Chiefs who were *ipso facto* the guardians of traditional values and cultures of the Mizo society. As a sign of their opposition to the activities of the Missionaries who always condemned drinking, some of the Mizo Chiefs "had also neglected the education of their children while the common masses were knocking at the doors of high schools and colleges" (Baveja 1970:15). The educated commoners quickly adjusted themselves to receive maximum material benefits out of the contributions made by the Missionaries and thus easily went far ahead of their traditional Chiefs in developing modern type of socio-economic and political consciousness in their society. In fact, whatsoever opportunities offered by the British administration and the Christian Missionaries in Mizoram were fully utilised by the common people. In this connection, McCall rightly said: "The main mission impact fell upon the ordinary people" (McCall 1949:14-15). Ultimately, the enlightened Mizo commoners, under the aegis of the educated elite, had daringly talked in terms of democratisation of their indigenous institution of chieftainship so that they could freely participate in the art of administration. In spite of this unprecedented political consciousness, the British administration did not allow the commoners either to express their political feelings or participate in any political activity within and outside the Mizo Hills which was declared an 'Excluded Area' by the King-in-Council in 1935. Some of the politically conscious Mizos interpreted this total exclusion from the operation of Provincial politics of Assam as a blatant denial of their democratic right by the British whereas other hill tribes in the "Partially Excluded Areas" of Assam were given democratic rights to send their common representative to the Provincial Government of Assam. In this connection, S.K.Chaube also said: "In the Mizo Hills, some 'commoners' raised a demand for representation to the Provincial Assembly of 1937. The movement was suppressed" (Chaube 1973:66-67).

In the meanwhile, the local educated group realised that there was not any "recognised system by which a commoner could raise himself to the status of chieftainship through industry" (McCall1949:98). With this understanding of their future, the educated commoners openly fought for democratisation of the polity and charged their traditional Chiefs and the British Superintendent as blocking their attainment of '*swaraj.*' In this way, the growth of political consciousness in the Mizo Hills had brought to the surface the inner contradiction between the common people and their traditional Village Chiefs, called *Lals*.

In 1940s, the British Superintendent had hinted that their rule in India was coming to an end soon. In contradiction of his earlier stand, the Superintendent had encouraged the Mizos to take greater interest in administration and politics. As the first step for educating the Mizos in this direction, the Superintendent had convened the District Chiefs' *Durbar* with the objective of involving the traditional Chiefs in the art of administration. But, the *Durbar* was structurally defective from the beginning that there was room for the common people to participate in the art of administration. Thus, the meetings and Conferences of the Chiefs under the protective authority of the Superintendent had created a feeling of unity and coordination of activities among the Chiefs. Some of the Chiefs had also become more oppressive towards their own subjects. With time slowly passed by, the traditional Mizo Chiefs had found themselves helpless to sustain their authority in the face of massive political consciousness which ultimately led to the formation of the first political party, called the Mizo Union (MU), with the permission of the Superintendent, A.R.Mac Donald, on 9 April 1946(Vanlawma 1972:86). In fact, the *ulterior* motive behind the creation of the political party by the commoners was to fight against the rights and privileges of their traditional Chiefs and their vested interests. Although the Chiefs were invited to join the new party, they had declined to join it on the ground that the emerging middle class "sought the fulfilment of its aspirations through organisation like ... the Mizo Union" (Chaube 1973:86).

When the British's transfer of powers to the Indians was about to take place, the Mizo public opinion was divided over the future status of their land. However, MU, the first local political party could come out with a concrete political demand for autonomous existence within the Assam

Province of India on the condition that "there should be liberal financial assistance from the Central Government (The Mizo Union Memorandum 1947). On the contrary, the United Mizo Freedom Organization (UMFO), which came into existence as the second oldest political party on July 5, 1947, opted to join Burma rather than India (Chaltuahkhuma 1981:42-43 & Vanlawma 1972:147-148). Meanwhile, the Constituent Assembly appointed an Advisory Committee to study the question of Fundamental Rights, Minorities and Tribal Areas in North East India which, in turn, set up an Advisory Sub-Committee on North-East Frontier (Assam) Areas and Excluded Areas, popularly known as the Bordoloi Sub-Committee, on 27th February 1947. The Advisory Sub-Committee extensively toured the Province of Assam as far as Aizawl, the Capital Headquarters of Mizoram. When the Members of Advisory Sub-Committee came to Aizawl to make an on the spot assessment of the political situation, they took evidences from different organisational representatives. In short, while giving evidence before the Sub-Committee, the representatives of MU continued to defend their stand for autonomous existence within India which irked the Superintendent, MacDonald, who also spoke before the Sub-Committee for separation of Mizoram to be the "British Protectorate or Crown Colony" outside the Indian Union.

District Council as Rural Local Government for Mizo Hills District

After hearing evidences from different representatives of the organisations in the Mizo Hills, the Bordoloi Sub-Committee had prepared and submitted its Report to President of the Constituent Assembly of India on 21st February 1948.In its Report, the Advisory Sub-Committee recommended a set-up for the administration of the Hill areas based on the concept of regional autonomy in all matters affecting their customs, forest, etc. After extensive debate in the Constituent Assembly, the recommendation of the Bordoloi Sub-Committee was adopted by the Constituent Assembly with various amendments on September 7, 1949 and was incorporated in Articles 244 and 275 of our Indian Constitution. The pattern of administration recommended by the Bordoloi Sub-Committee took shape in the outline of the Sixth Schedule to the Constitution of India. The idea behind the Sixth Schedule to the Constitution of India was "to provide the tribal people with a simple and inexpensive administrative set-up of their own which would safeguard their tribal customs and ways of life and to secure to them management of characteristically tribal affairs"(Ray 1982:93).When the Sixth Schedule to the Constitution of India was implemented by the Union Government in 1952, the erstwhile Lushai Hills District was given an autonomous district status within the Province of Assam. Thus, within five years of the day of India's Independence from the British yoke, the Mizos had begun to have a new democratic institution of decentralised governance, called the 'District Council,' in their ancestral land. In brief, the Report of the Bordoloi Sub-Committee and the subsequent deliberations in the Constituent Assembly were responsible for the materialisation of a special Schedule, known as the "Sixth Schedule" which provided for the creation of District Councils to safeguard the interests and the customary ways of life of the hill people including the Mizo tribes.

Implementation of the Sixth Schedule to the Constitution of India in Mizoram was immediately followed by the preparations for conducting democratic elections to the first District Council and April 4, 1952 was fixed as the date for the first election to the District Council (Chaltuahkhuma 1981:77). On that appointed date, democratic elections were held in which the common people and their Chiefs collectively exercised their democratic rights, for the first time, to elect people's representatives from among themselves. Thus, provision of democratic institution of decentralised governance had empowered all the *bonafide* citizens of the Mizo district to exercise their democratic rights in electing their representatives by adult franchise. In this democratic election, all the *eighteen* elected seats were contested by the MU, the first political party, and the United Mizo Freedom Organisation (UMFO). In the first democratic elections to District Council, the MU contested the election on the platform of abolition of chieftainship and integration of Mizoram with India whereas the UMFO fought the election for separation of Mizoram as proposed by the Superintendent, MacDonald.

Term of Office for the Members of District Council

The term of office for elected and nominated Members of the District Council was normally five years from the date of the first meeting of the Council after the general elections unless the District Council was sooner dissolved under paragraph 16 of the Sixth Schedule by Governor of Assam.

Formation of the Executive Committee of the District Council

In this democratic election, the MU had easily won a thumping majority by capturing seventeen seats out of the eighteen elected seats and formed the first Executive Committee (EC) of the Autonomous District Council of the Mizo Hills. Being the party in power, the EC of the District Council nominated its favourite persons to occupy all the six nominated seats who held office, like the elected Members, under the pleasure of the Governor of Assam.

Composition of the Executive Committee

According to Paragraph 6 of the Sixth Schedule to the Constitution of India, there should be an Executive Committee (EC) of the Mizo District Council to carry on the executive functions of the District Council. At the beginning, the EC consisted of the Chief Executive Member (CEM) and other two or three Executive Members (EM). The Governor of Assam should appoint any Member of the District Council elected by other newly elected Members from among themselves within forty-eight hours from the date of dissolution of the incumbent EC as the new CEM. In case of failure on the part of the elected Members of the District Council to elect their House Leader within the stipulated time frame, the Governor of Assam could appoint any one of the elected Members as the CEM. In addition, the Governor would normally appoint two or three elected Members of the District Council as Executive Members (EMs) on the recommendation of the CEM.

Allocation of Business

After completing official formality of their appointments, the CEM would allocate the aforesaid subjects to the EMs who would play their roles at the district level as if the Ministers played their roles at the State level. Accordingly, subjects such as finance, education, administration of justice, forests, agriculture, local administration, veterinary, transport, fisheries etc. would be allocated to the EMs. Thus, the CEM and his/her EMs were collectively responsible for the effective implementation of all development schemes within the jurisdiction of Mizo Autonomous District. Simultaneously, the EMs were collectively responsible for all the Executive Orders issued and policies formulated from time to time in the name of the District Council. This implies that if the CEM tendered his resignation, the EMs of the District Council stood dissolved automatically.

In short, the EC performed all the executive functions of the Council just as the Union or the State Cabinet Ministers perform their executive functions. It disposed off all matters falling within its purview and also made Rules, Regulations and Laws and all appointments with the approval of the District Council. The Executive Committee at the initiative of an EM in-charge of Finance would prepare the budget of the District Council and got it passed by the Council in its Session. Apparently, the District Council resembles a small government at the district level.

District Council's Office

Mizo District Council had its own Office which was like a mini Secretariat of the State Government today. The Administrative Headquarters of Mizo District Council was Aizawl (Previously spelled as Aijal) where its Main Office was located. The Office had Departments dealing with subjects like finance, education, administration of justice, forests, agriculture, local administration, veterinary, transport, fisheries etc. These Departments were put under the charges of the CEM and other EMs of the District Council.

There was a Secretary to the Executive Committee appointed by the CEM. He was the administrative head of the District Council's Office. The role played by the Secretary to the EC of the District Council within the district almost resembled the role played by the Chief Secretary of the State Government. There were also other subordinate officers and staff to run the civil administration of the Mizo District Council.

Mizo District Council had a District Planning Board (DPB) headed by the CEM as its Chairman. To assist the Chairman, there was a full-time Deputy Chairman who took care of the day-to-day administration of the DPB. However, the presence of this Board was not widely noticed by the people in Mizoram.

By the side of the Main Office of the District Council, there was the Office of Deputy Commissioner representing the State Government of Assam. It is, therefore, clear from the Provisions of the Sixth Schedule to the Constitution of India that the Civil Administration of the Autonomous Mizo District was placed under two authorities, namely Deputy Commissioner (DC) representing the State Government and the Executive Committee of the District Councils.

Powers and Functions

The original Sixth Schedule to the Constitution of India had provided legislative, executive, judicial and financial powers and functions to the Mizo District Council.

Legislative Functions

For the protection of customs and uplift of the Mizo tribes, the District Council had law-making powers with respect to (Aggarawala and Aiyar 1950:336-337) &Report of the Pataskar Commission 1966:146):

(a) the allotment of land for the purposes of agriculture or grazing or for residential or other non-agricultural purposes or for any other purposes likely to promote the interests of the inhabitants of any village or town;

(b) the management of any forest not being a reserved forest;

(c) the use of any canal or water-course for the purpose of agriculture;

(d) the regulation of the practice of 'jhum' or other forms of shifting cultivation;

(e) the establishment of village or town committees or Councils and their powers;

(f) any other matter relating to village or town administration, including village or town police and public health and sanitation;

(g) the appointment or succession of chiefs or headmen;

(h) the inheritance of property;
(i) marriage; and
(j) social customs.

Executive Functions

The Executive Committee (EC) was vested with the executive functions of the Mizo District Council to construct or manage primary schools, dispensaries, markets, cattle, ponds, ferries, fisheries, roads, road transports and waterways in the district (Aggarawala and Aiyar 1950:339). In addition, Sub-paragraph 1 of Paragraph 6 of the Sixth Schedule empowered the Council to prescribe the medium of instruction in primary schools and how primary schools should be run and managed within its jurisdiction.

Judicial Functions

According to the authority given by Sub-Para 4 (a) of Para 4 of the Sixth Schedule to the Constitution of India, the Mizo District Council constituted a District Council Court located at Aizawl, two Subordinate District Council Courts located at Aizawl and Lunglei (previously spelled as Lungleh) and Village Council Courts in all the Village Councils to adjudicate or try cases or customary laws in which both the parties to the dispute were tribals (Aggarawala and Aiyar 1950:338).In connection with the manpower requirement for administration of justice, the Sixth Schedule provided that the District Council Court and the Subordinate Council Courts might appoint suitable persons as the Members of Village Council Courts or Presiding Officers of such Courts and might also appoint such officers as might be necessary for administration of the laws within its jurisdiction. However, the District Council Court was not competent to hear or adjudicate cases involving offences punishable by death, transportation of life or imprisonment for not less than five years (Aggarawala and Aiyar 1950:338-339). With reference to all the suits and cases tried by the Village Council Courts and the Subordinate District Council Courts, the District Council Court acted as a Court of Appeal and no other Courts, except the High Courts and the Supreme Court of India, had jurisdiction over suits and cases decided by the Mizo District Council Court.

Financial Functions

According to Sub-paragraphs 2 and 3 of Paragraph 8 of the Sixth Schedule, the Mizo District Council had exclusive powers to assess and collect land revenues, levy and collect taxes on lands and buildings, tolls on persons, taxes on the professions, trade, callings, employments, animals, vehicles and boats, tolls on goods and passengers carried in ferries, taxes on the entry of goods into the market for sale, taxes for the maintenance of schools, dispensaries or roads (Aggarawala and Aiyar 1950:340). The District Council was also given the responsibility of framing Rules for the management of finances with the approval of the Governor of Assam.

Under Sub-paragraph 1 of Paragraph 9, the District Council was given the concurrent power to collect royalty on the licenses or leases for the extraction of minerals in the autonomous districts as granted by the Government of Assam. In case of any dispute as to the share of such royalties to be made over to the Mizo District Council, it had to be referred to the Governor of Assam who should determine the amount to be paid to the District Council. The amount so determined by the Governor in his discretion should be paid to the Mizo District Council whose decision was final. With particular reference to taxes on motor vehicles, the State Government, on behalf of the District, collected taxes from different types of motor vehicles registered within the jurisdiction of the district. Other sources of income for the Mizo District Council were: Grants-in-aid, loans and advances from the State Government.

Rural Local Governments at the Grassroots Level—Village Councils

The first Session of the District Council was held for 16 (sixteen) days commencing from 23rd June, 1952 till 10th July 1952 (Sangkima 1992:175). Elected Members of the Mizo District Council were to elect from among themselves a Chairman to conduct the business of the Council in session and also to preside over its meetings. Accordingly, the elected Members of the District Council elected one Member among themselves to be the Chairman. Mention must be made in this connection that the nominated Members of the District Council could not take part in the election of the Chairman of the District Council.

A landmark Legislation made by the first Mizo District Council was "The Lushai Hills District[9] (Village Councils) Act, 1953" which received the Assent of the Governor of Assam on 9th December 1953.[10] In sync with the MU's Election Manifesto for the establishment of democratic Local Governments at the grassroots' level in the Mizo District, the Government of Assam had enacted the Assam Lushai Hills District (Acquisition of Chiefs' Rights) Act of 1954[11] which became operative from 1st April 1954. So, in order to effectively speed up the process of implementation of democratic decentralisation at the grassroots level, "from 15th April, 1956, the rights and interests of 259 Mizo (Lusei) Chiefs and 50 Pawi-Lakher Chiefs were abolished in favour of the Government" (Poonte 1965: 4-5).

Alongside of abolition of traditional institution of chieftainship, democratic elections to Village Councils were conducted for the first time in different villages in accordance with the famous Act passed by the District

Council (The Lushai Hills District (Village Councils) Act, 1953:15). In this way, Village Councils, hitherto unknown in the Mizo society, were set up as democratic institutions to supplant the traditional system of administration at the grassroots' level in different villages. In pursuance of the Order issued by the District Authority, the first sitting of all the Village Councils in Mizoram was held on August 16, 1954 (Local Administration Department's Old Records).

Democratic institution of 'Village Council' represents Rural Local Governments at the grassroots' level in Mizoram. It can be construed that Village Council system is a democratic innovation of indigenous institution of village administration for the fulfilment of the aspirations of the politically motivated Mizo commoners who wanted to democratise their traditional power-sharing system in the Mizo society. Let us briefly examine some of the characteristic features of this democratic institution of Village Council at the grassroots' level in Mizoram.

Number of Members of a Village Council

According to the provisions of the Village Council Act of 1953 (as amended from time to time),each of the Village Councils, except those inside the three autonomous Districts in Mizoram, shall have members according to the number of houses it contains as specified below(Amended Lushai Hills Village Council Act 1953:15):

(a) For village not exceeding 100 (hundred) houses, there shall be 3 (three) members;

(b) For village with more than 100 (hundred) houses, but not exceeding 200 (two hundred) houses, there shall be 4 (four) members;

(c) For village with more than 200 (two hundred) houses, but not exceeding 400 (four hundred) houses, there shall be 5 (five) members;

(d) For village with more than 400 (four hundred) houses, but not exceeding 700 (seven hundred) houses, there shall be 6 (six) members;

(e) For village with more than 700 (seven hundred) houses, but not exceeding 1,000 (one thousand) houses, there shall be 7 (seven) members;

(f) For village with more than 1,000 (one thousand) houses, but not exceeding 1,500 (one thousand five hundred) houses, there shall be 8 (eight) members;

(g) For village with more than 1,500 (one thousand five hundred) houses, there shall be 9 (nine) members.

Term of Office

According to Rule 4(6) of the Lushai Hills Autonomous District (Administration of Justice) Rules, 1953, every Village Council would normally continue for 3 (three) years from the date of its first sitting unless dissolved under the Provision of Section 25 of the said Act (Amended Village Council Act 1953: Chap. II, 5). But, after the passing of the 73rd Constitution Amendment Act, 1992, the term of the Village Councils has been extended to 5 (five) years.

Qualifications to become a voter and contest election to the Village Council

A person is eligible for election as a member of the Village Council provided (Amended Village Council Act 1953:Chap.II, 3(2)):

(a) S/he belongs to a scheduled tribe.
(b) S/he has attained the age of 25 (twenty-five) years.
(c) S/he is a voter where he seeks elections.
(d) S/he is not a member of any other Village Council.
(e) S/he is of sound mind.
(f) a period of three years has elapsed since his conviction of an offence under the Lushai Hills Autonomous District (Administration of Justice Rules 1953), or under other laws for the time being in force in India, and if imprisoned, since his release from prison.

Unlike in the *Lok Sabha* and the State Assembly elections, the electorates for the elections of the Village Councils should include only those legitimate members of the scheduled tribes permanently staying in the State of Mizoram. In other words, only the permanent tribal residents of the State can exercise their franchise as voters in the democratic elections to those Village Councils within and outside the three Scheduled Districts of the State.

Functions of the Village Council

Every Village Council is entrusted with numerous functions and responsibilities without powers and authority. However, it is possible to conveniently divide various functions normally performed by the Village Councils into three broad groups-- administrative, executive and judicial.

(i) *Executive and administrative Functions*: In "The Lushai Hills District (Village Council) Act of 1953" (as amended from time to time), no distinction is specifically drawn between the executive and the administrative functions of the Village Council. However, the same Act paradoxically provides that the executive functions of the Village Council are vested exclusively in the office bearers, namely, the President, the Vice President and the Secretary. After analysing the powers and functions of the Village Councils as provided in the aforesaid Act, it is possible to identify the following as the executive functions of the Village Councils (Amended Lushai Hills District (Village Councils) Act of 1953,Chap.III, 23(1):

(a) Allotment of land within the boundaries of the village for *jhum* or shifting cultivation and then distribution of *jhum* plots to the villagers.
(b) Enforcement of '*Hnatlang*'[12] (Community Works) in public interest whenever the situation so demands.
(c) Clearance of inter-village roads and maintenance of internal roads of the village.
(d) Maintenance of water-tank.
(e) Clearance of *jhum*-roads and fencing of *jhum* areas.
(f) Planning of the village.
(g) Keeping record of birth and death.
(h) Fixation of rates of paddy and supply to other villages.
(i) Maintenance of graveyards.
(j) Searching out missing persons and sending out messengers.
(k) Prohibition of '*Zu*' (local drink).
(l) Construction of small minor bridges,
(m) Construction of fish dyke for community fishing,
(n) Looking after the poor and handicapped person etc.

(ii) *Legislative Functions*: Though Village Council serves as democratic machinery of governance for the people at the grassroots' level, Section 23(2) of "The Lushai Hills District (Village Council) Act of 1953" sanctions, in clear terms, certain rule-making powers to the Village Councils pertaining to the following subjects (Amended Lushai Hills (Village Councils) Act 1953: Chap.III, 23(1):

(a) Control, preservation and use of timbers and other forest products except of the reserved forests, ordinarily utilised for building purposes such as canes, sun grass, *siallu*, *thilthek*, *laisawral* etc.[13]
(b) Maintenance, preservation and improvement of good water supply.
(c) Control of stray animals within its jurisdiction and at night within the village *Ram*.[14]
(d) Prevention and control of fire within the village and the village Ram.
(e) *Ngawidawh*.[15]

(f) Sanitation and cleanliness of the village.

(g) Extraction of *Khamkhuai*.[16]

(iii) *Judicial Functions*: Section 6 of "The Lushai Hills Autonomous District (Administration of Justice) Rules, 1953"clearly gives the following judicial functions to each of the Village Councils in Mizoram. The Act provides that every Village Council should constitute within itself the 'Village Council Court' to try petty cases-both civil and criminal. The relevant paragraph of the Act states that "either the entire Village Council or at least three members of the Village Council, representing the entire Village Council, shall sit as a Village Council Court. If the entire Village Council sits as the Village Council Court, at least three of the Village Council members or more than half of its members shall be treated as forming the quorum." (Amended Village Council Act 1953, Section 6). However, it is to be noted that the Village Council Court is competent to try those 'Civil cases' arising between or among the tribals only.

In addition, the Village Council Court can try 'Criminal cases' like robbery, inflicting physical pains to other fellow human beings, broil due to intoxication, without amounting to imprisonment. In short, 'Criminal cases' that Village Council Courts can try from some Sections of Indian Penal Code (IPC) are: fighting or violence (Section160); public nuisance (Section 290); infliction of physical pains by mistakes (Section 323); restriction and confinement by force (Section 341); hurting other human beings (Section 352); robbery (Section 379); misconduct (Section 426); trespass (Section 447) and disturbance of peaceful public life due to intoxication (Section 510). In spite of the fact that the Village Council has been made competent to try minor 'Criminal cases,' it cannot give jail term to the loser of the case. The Village Council Court can only impose Rs. 500/ (Rupees Five hundred) as the maximum penalty on the loser of the case.

Scope for Empowering and Strengthening of Rural Local Governments in Mizoram-District Council and Village Councils

When democratisation of the polity took place in the wake of Indian Independence, the Mizo District Council and the Village Councils became an indispensable means of democratic decentralisation of powers and authority to the rural people in Mizoram. It is through these two democratic institutions of governance that whatever powers and functions contained in the 'The Sixth Schedule to the Constitution of India" and "The Lushai Hills District (Village Councils) Act 1953"were exercised by the people at two levels through their elected representatives. However, the relevance of these two Local Governments had been diluted almost at every stage of Constitutional development that Mizoram had ever attained which ultimately led to the extinction of District Council for the hitherto two sub-divisions namely Aizawl Sub-Division and Lunglei Sub-Division. Though these two Rural Local Governments functioning at the district and village levels had/have many strong points inasmuch as they were/are indispensable instruments for materialisation of democratic decentralised governance, each of them had/has some glaring deficiencies. In the light of the past experiences of the Mizo District Council and the Village Councils, this paper attempts to suggest measures/suggestions for empowering and strengthening the existing two Rural Local Governments in Mizoram.

(A) Rural Local Government at the District level- Mizo District Council

When the whole of Mizoram was one of the Autonomous Districts of Assam, the State Government of Assam had decentralised some of those powers and functions to the Mizo District Council provided in the Sixth Schedule to the Constitution of India.

Provision of Nomination

According to Paragraph 2(1) of the Sixth Schedule to the Constitution of India, the Mizo District Council was to nominate not more than four Members out of the total number of twenty-two seats. Sometimes, the provision of nomination was misused for reversing the majority into minority in the Council. The abuse of power of nomination for narrow party gains occasionally put the Executive Committee of Mizo District Council in a shaky position thereby leading to neglect of the real works entrusted to them.

It is, therefore, suggested that the Sixth Schedule may carefully be amended for preventing the possible abuse of provision of nominations in the existing District Councils in future.

Primary Education

Though Sub-paragraph 1 of Paragraph 6 of the Sixth Schedule empowers the Mizo District Council to establish, construct and manage primary schools and also prescribes their medium of instructions, most of the schools in the countryside of the district were run by the Council with a single teacher while few of them had two teachers at the best. Though Sub-paragraph 3(d) of Paragraph 8 of the Sixth Schedule authorises the Mizo District Council to levy and collect taxes on the maintenance of schools, dispensaries or roads, most of the Primary Schools were understaffed due to paucity funds at the disposal of the District Council. This indicates that the quality of elementary education at the grassroots level greatly depends on the performance of Rural Local Governments at the district level.

What is amply clear from this point is that the District Councils of today should be able to make better performance if taxes and fees are honestly levied and collected by the officials from the tax-payers for meeting expenditure required for the improvement of elementary education within their respective jurisdictions.

Recruitment

The Mizo District Council framed Service Rules for the appointment of officers and other staff for District Administration. Sometimes, the Service Rules, though framed by the Council, virtually lost their relevance under the pressure of nepotism and favouritism. In fact, this type of appointment could pull down the efficiency of other officers and other staff recruited based on merits and, above all, the entire office management. In addition, most of the lower primary school teachers appointed by the District Council were only Class VI qualifiers. When appointments were made based on political patronage, serious consideration was not always given to the financial position of the District Council. As a result, the inflated expenditure of the Mizo District Council on establishment due to overstaffing could have serious adverse effects on the development funds for building socio-economic overheads.

Therefore, recruitment of their officers and staff should be made by the District Councils strictly on the basis of merit as far as possible. It not, no improvement in the good work culture of their employees could be expected by the Councils. As long as establishment and maintenance of elementary schools falls within the purview of the District Councils for uplifting their own people from educational backwardness, the District Councils should not use them for dumping local uneducated unemployed candidates. So, in order to lift up their school going children people up to standard, they should recruit only those qualified candidates having genuine interests in teaching profession.

District Council Court and the Subordinate District Councils

Mizo District Council Court located at Aizawl and the two Subordinate District Councils located at Aizawl and Lunglei (previously spelled as Lungleh) were sometimes manned by politicians earlier rejected in the elections or persons without having any judicial background or training in their past track records. During its life-time of almost twenty years, the Mizo District Council could not codify customary laws although codification of the customary laws was considered to be essential for the preservation of the Mizo customary way of life.

It is, therefore, suggested that District Council Courts and Subordinate District Courts in other Sixth Scheduled areas should be manned at least by Law graduates having an in-depth knowledge of the customs and traditions of the tribal people living within the jurisdiction of their District Councils.

District Development Planning

The Mizo District Council had a District Planning Board to formulate district development plans for implementation. Unfortunately, district Development Board was ever in need of expert inputs in developmental matters. Apart from lack of expert contribution, the Mizo District Council was considered as not serious enough in the formulation of plans, schemes and their monitoring for sustainable development in the district. For instance, when *Mautam (Melocanna Baccifera)* famine swept the length and breadth of Mizo Hills in 1959, no proper planning for combating impending famine was in place although Members of the District Council knew well in advance based on some signs from nature that it was going to occur.

In the light of the experience of the Mizo District Council, it may be suggested that the District Planning Boards should be manned by experts in the field of socio-economic planning who can practically formulate sustainable development plans, schemes and projects for their districts. Hence, District Planning Boards should not be used for accommodating unsuccessful politicians who never had any experience in one of the branches of planning.

No proper Land Use for economic Benefits

During the traditional period in Mizoram, lands belonged to the Local Self-Governments run by the traditional Chiefs who always made proper use of their respective village lands with a sense of belonging. Under their administration, there was practically no room for private ownership of lands. But, after the birth of Autonomous District Council in Mizoram as one of district level Local Governments of Assam, the traditional Local Governments and their respective Chiefs lost their existence and their village lands had passed into the hands of the Mizo District Council which used Village Councils as its Agents to carry out land administration at the grassroots level. Though the Village Councils were empowered to carefully allot some parts of their village lands for house sites and gardens, they sparingly utilised their village lands for cultivation and never gave or sold their village lands to the outsiders. However, after the elevation of the Mizo District to a Union territory (UT) status, the existing Mizo District Council got abolished and the power to control lands had been transferred to the UT Government in 1972 and the State Government since 1987 which have been using Village Councils as their Agents only for protecting village lands against man-made fire but without empowering them to effectively control improper land use. Though the Village Councils were set up under the Sixth Schedule, they are no more authorised to retain their powers over village lands by the concerned authorities after the loss of their Sixth Scheduled status by the undivided Aizawl Sub-Division together with the undivided Lunglei Sub-Division. As a consequence, large scale private ownership of land has emerged not for the economic benefits of the people but for serving the vested interests of the well-to-do-individuals in Mizoram.

In the light of Mizoram experience, it may be suggested that the existing Autonomous District Councils in other parts of the country should place village lands under the stringent control of village communities with the condition that they should always take utmost care of their village lands as theirs. Only then, greedy individuals will not be given an opportunity to grab village lands for their personal gains at the cost of common interest of the village community.

Inadequate Tax Efforts leading to over-dependence on the State

As stated under financial functions of the District Council earlier, the Mizo District Council had powers to assess and levy taxes, fees and tolls on building and land, animals, boats, entry of goods into the area, roads, ferries, bridges, employment and income and general taxes for the maintenance of schools and roads. In addition, the District Council could share motor vehicle tax and royalties from minerals with the Government of Assam State in a given proportion. Under Article 275 of the Constitution of India, the Mizo District Council was also entitled to Grants-in Aid from the Government of Assam. In spite of all these sources of tax and non-tax revenue sources, the performance of the Mizo District Council in collecting tax and non-tax revenues from the citizens was inadequate that it had to depend more and more on the State Government for Grants-in-Aid and other shared taxes. However, too much dependence of the District Council on State Government for financial grants and allotments slowly and steadily tightened the autonomy of the former.

In the absence of any clear-cut guideline for the release of funds from the State Government to the Mizo District, leaders of the Mizo District Council occasionally charged the State Government as intentionally delaying the release of funds to the Council authorities. The District Councillors were of the opinion that such delays were done by the State Government of Assam on political considerations to tarnish their images before their own people. For example, one of the root causes of outbreak of Mizo National Front's movement for independence from India was the inordinate delay of the State Government in releasing aids to the Mizo District during *Mautam* famine in 1959.

It is, therefore, suggested that, in order to lessen over-dependence of the District Councils on the State Government for funds, the former should be made more responsible for raising funds from those sources under the Sixth Schedule to the Constitution of India. In order to augment Grants-in-Aid received from the State Government, the District Councils should try to explore other sources of revenue for meeting their expenditure for the development of their respective districts. Simultaneously, anew provision may be made for mandatory release of Grants-in-Aid and other funds at the right time to the District Councils by the State Governments.

Lack of Proper Financial Management

Under Paragraph 7 of the sixth Schedule to the Constitution of India, the Mizo District Council constituted District Fund to which all the moneys received by the Council in the course of the administration were credited. The Governor of Assam was empowered to make detailed rules for the management of District Council's finances, taxes etc. The District Council was to keep its account in the format prescribed by the Comptroller and Auditor-General of India. In spite of the allegation from some right-thinking citizens that the District Council was not efficient in managing the public funds, the system of audit was lately introduced by the Comptroller and Auditor-General in 1969. Since that year onward, the Auditors from Office of Accountant General in Shillong carried out audit of Mizo District Council's Account. However, a provision remained absent for the Government of Assam to audit the accounts of the Mizo District Council pertaining to the Grants-in-Aid that it received from the State Government.

Suggestion may be made in this connection that a new provision may be inserted in the Sixth Schedule to the Constitution of India for empowering the Audit agencies of the State Government to carry out internal audit of the Accounts of the District Councils so that better discipline in financial management must be ensured. Besides, it should be made compulsory for the District Councils to make timely submission of their utilisation certificates for the Grants-in-Aid they had received from the latter.

Absence of Institutional Arrangement for Coordination between the State Government and the District Council

Though Mizo District Council was virtually a Rural Local Government at the district level within the composite State of Assam, there was neither permanent nor *ad hoc* institutional arrangement for proper coordination between the two. The Sixth Schedule to the Constitution of India did not give the State Government any power to review or assess the working of the District Council which received Grants-in-aid from the former. Indirect coordination has seldom taken place through the Governor of Assam who was to approve their legislations and to sanction loans and grants for development schemes. This absence of proper channel of coordination enabled the District Council to retain the unspent balances of the grants and transfer the unspent amounts for other purposes without proper sanction from the State Government.

It may be suggested that the Sixth Schedule may be amended to incorporate a provision for arranging coordination between the District Councils and the State Governments through meetings without any infringement of the autonomy of the former by the latter.

(B) Rural Local Governments at the Grassroots Level-Village Councils

At the beginning, Village Councils as Rural Local Governments at the grassroots level were empowered to carry out their executive, legislative and judicial functions without undue political interference from above. In spite of the absence of fund allocation from the District Council, Village Councils had done many good things for their subjects. However, some of their powers and functions were silently taken away in favour of the Headquarters through amendments of the Mizo District (Village Councils) Act 1953 particularly after the elevation of the Mizo District Council to the Union Territory status. Let us look into some of the striking features of Village Councils in Mizoram with a view to finding out the scope for empowering and strengthening them.

Village Councils with numerous functions but without real powers and authority

The Village Councils are used by most of the departments of the State Government as an indispensable instrument for implementing their policies and development programmes in the rural areas. Though the State Government, on many occasions, could not successfully carry out its rural development schemes/programmes without the support and co-operation of the Village Councils, it finds it difficult to decentralise more powers to the Village Councils in the rural areas. Not to speak of their empowerment, the State Government has taken away some of their original powers whenever revision of the Village Council Act took place. According to the original Village Council Act of 1953, the Village Councils were previously empowered to distribute some portions of their village lands to the villagers for settled cultivation. Unfortunately, the Village Councils of today in the rural areas are devoid of this authority as the State Government has taken this power away from them some time back.

Village Councils are not made competent to initiate Village Development plans and Schemes

Village Councils were to know the ground situation far better than the officials of the State Government. But, the State Government of Assam hardly consulted Village Councils at the time of preparing socio-economic development programmes for the people at the grass root level. When Community Development Projects were prepared and implemented in the then Mizo Hills, the Village Councils functioning as Rural Local Government were not consulted.

It is, therefore, proper for the State Government to consult the Village Councils when it prepares rural development programmes. If possible, keeping in view the specific needs of each of the villages, the State Government should give some responsibility to the Village Councils to initiate the preparation of the development programmes. If the Government does so, it will instil a sense of belonging in the minds of those members of the different Village Councils.

Village Councils with limited functional Autonomy

A Village Council enjoys some measure of functioning autonomy while discharging its multifarious functions for the development of the people within its jurisdiction. However, the State Government or the three District Councils within the State can, at any time, propose lands within the jurisdiction of any village as reserved on ground of public interest. Besides, the State Government can, at any time, dissolve the Village Councils on flimsy ground. Similarly, each of the three District Councils in the southern part of Mizoram can initiate dissolution of Village Councils falling within their respective jurisdictions on the same ground. It will not be an exaggeration to maintain that a change of hands either at the State or the District levels has frequently been followed by the dissolution of the Village Council(s). This is a clear indication of total absence of functional autonomy for the Village Councils.

No Specific Source of Development Funds for the Village Councils

With the exception of financial allocation made by the Department of Local Administration (LAD) as honoraria for the Village Councillors, the State Government hardly made any specific allocation of funds to the Village Councils for the execution of development programmes in their respective jurisdictions. Apart from this, the State Government never gave any contingency funds to the Village Councils to meet their unforeseen expenses due to any untoward incidents in their respective villages. Thus, the only sources of funds available to the Village Councils are: fines realised from the losers of the cases tried by the Village Council Courts, fines imposed on the violators of orders issued by the Village Councils for public interests, proceeds from the sale of dry timbers in the forests and the money paid by some villagers who cannot take part in community work.

Performance of the Treasurer's role by the President inappropriate

In the beginning of establishment of the Village Councils in the Mizo Hills, the President of the Village Council was to act as its Treasurer as well. Although the Village Council of today has a separate Treasurer, the 'Local Fund' of the Village Council remains in the custody of the President and the Treasurer is to act only as the custodian of the 'Development Fund.' It is, therefore, suggested that the State Government should review the handling process of fund by making the Treasurer in charge of all the funds, both the Local and the Development Funds, operated by the Village Council. However, a provision should be made for keeping a limited contingency fund by the President.

Conclusion

To conclude, democratisation of the traditional polity which ultimately led to the abolition of indigenous institutions of Rural Government manned by the hereditary Chiefs paved the way for the birth of two tier democratic Rural Local Governments one after another in Mizoram- *first*, District Council at the district level and *second*, Village Councils the grassroots level. It is significant to note that the Constitutional foundation for the birth of these democratic institutions of Rural Local Government was laid by the Sixth Schedule to the Constitution of India. The fundamental objective of the Sixth Schedule as recommended by the Bordoloi Sub-Committee in its Report was to give a set-up of administration to the Mizos and other tribals in excluded areas of Assam based on the concept of regional autonomy in all matters affecting their customs, traditions, forest, etc. So, keeping in mind the need for democratisation of their autocratic Chieftainship on the one hand and preservation their customs and traditions on the other, the Sixth Schedule had given executive, legislative, financial and judicial powers and functions to the erstwhile Mizo District Council. By exercising its legislative powers, the District Council passed 'The Lushai Hills (Village Councils) Act, 1953" which was assented to by the Governor of Assam. In fact, the legislation made by the District Council laid essential foundation for democratisation of the polity at the grassroots level. When democratic institutions of Village Council were set up to supplant the institution of chieftainship, the formers derived their powers and functions from the Sixth Schedule to the Constitution of India.

At the initial stage of formation of the Mizo District Council, the people felt empowered as they were emancipated from the rule of their hereditary Chiefs capturing their rural Local Governments. Likewise, even those local politicians running the District Council as people's representatives felt empowered and did not precisely know whether their powers and functions were deficient or not. They seemed to be contented with the powers and functions given to them by the Sixth Schedule to the Constitution of India. But, the proposed imposition of Assamese as the State official language of Assam and the subsequent outbreak of *Mautam* famine in the Mizo Hills in 1959 had shown the seeds of doubt in the minds of the Mizos in general and Members of the Mizo District Council about the Constitutional status of their land. Those who were at the helm of affairs in district administration found their Rural Local Government at the district level as ineffectual to solve their socio-economic problems for uplifting or improving the well-being of the unprivileged rural people from the clutches of poverty.

If the critics argue that the District Council did not effectively function due to its constant over-dependence on the State Government for financial support, they are not wrong in making such argument. Truly speaking, the Mizo District Council was not active enough to discharge its assigned functions to levy and collect taxes on profession, trade, callings and employments, animals, vehicles and boats to meet the necessary expenses for easing the plight of the people within the jurisdiction of the Mizo district. So, in the light of the deficiencies and weakness of the existing Districts Councils as well as various Institutions of Village Governance in North East India, it may be suggested that the Sixth Schedule to the Constitution of India may suitably be strengthened with those relevant powers and functions given to their counterparts by the 73rd Constitution Amendment Act. 1992. It significant to note that the Sixth Schedule under which the premier District Councils and Village Councils were set up in many parts of North East India was as old as our Indian Constitution and hence the abolition or overhauling of these democratic Local Governments with indigenous characters may not be acceptable to the tribals in North East India.

Notes

1. '*Khawper*' means a hamlet and one Chief could have more than one hamlet from hismain Village.
2. 'The Lushai Hills District' was changed to 'The Mizo District,' Vide 'The Lushai Hills District (Change of Name) Act, 1954,' 29th April 1954.
3. "The Lushai Hills District (Village Councils) Act, 1953 published in the *AssamGazette*, dated the 9th December, 1953.
4. "The Assam Lushai Hills District (Acquisition of Chiefs' Rights) Act of 1954" was passed by the Assam Legislative Assembly which received the Assent of the President of India on 26th June 1954 and was published in the *Assam Gazette*, dated the 30th June 1954.
5. '*Hnatlang*' means community works.
6. '*Siallu*,' '*thilthek*,' '*laisawral*,' are big leaves in the jungle used for roofing typical Mizo houses.
7. '*Ram*,' in English, means land.

8. '*Ngawidawh* 'means construction of a trap or device in the river by the villagers for trapping and collecting fishes.
9. '*Khamkhuai'* in English means bees found in the cliff whose honey used to be extracted by the Mizos.

References

- Aggarawala Om Prakash and Aiyar S.K. (1950): The Constitution of India, First Edition, Rajkamal Publications Ltd., New Delhi.
- Baveja, J.D. (1970): The Land Where the Bamboo Flowers, Assam Publication Board, Gauhati.
- Chaltuahkhuma (1981): Political History of Mizoram (1920-1980), Chaltuahkhuma & Sons, L.B. Press, Aizawl.
- Chaube, S.K. (1973): Hill Politics in North-East India, Orient Longman Ltd., Calcutta.
- Government of India (2005) : The Constitution of India (As on the 26th January, 2005), Ministry of Law and Justice, New Delhi.
- Government of India (2020): The India Penal Code 1860 (Bare Act with Illustrations), Law Literature Publication, Shubham Vihar, Dwarka, Mangla, New Delhi.
- Government of India (1966): Report of the Pataskar Commission on the Hill Areas of Assam, 1965-66, Ministry of Home Affairs, New Delhi.
- Government of Mizoram (1953): The Lushai Hills District (Village Council) Act 1953 (Amended from time to time).
- _______The Lushai Hills Autonomous District (Administration of Justice) Rules, 1953(Amended from time to time.
- _______Records maintained by the Local Administration Department (LAD).
- McCall, A.G.(1949): Lushai Chrysalis, Luzac & Co., London.
- Memorandum of Mizo Union, submitted through the Advisory Sub-Committee to His Majesty's Government, Government of India and its Constituent Assembly, dated 24.4.1947.
- Pakem, B. (ed.)(1981): "The Changing Power Structure of the Political Institution of Chieftainship in Mizoram" in The Journal of the North-East India Council for Social Science Research, Vol. V, No. 11, Shillong, October.
- Poonte, B. (1965): Zoram Thlirna, (Deputy Commissioner, Mizo District, Aizawl
- Ray, A.C. (1982): Mizoram: Dynamics of Change, Pearl Publishers, Calcutta.
- Reid, Robert (1978): The Lushai Hills, (Firma KLM Pvt. Ltd., Calcutta, Reprint.
- Report of the North-East Frontiers (Assam) Tribal and Excluded Areas Sub Committee (Bordoloi Sub-Committee), 1947, Manager Publications, Delhi, 1950.
- Sangkima, (1992): Mizos: Society and Social Change,Spectrum Publications, Guwahati: Delhi.
- Thanga, L.B. (1978): The Mizos: A Study in Racial Personality, United Publishers, Gauhati.
- Thanhlira, (1951): Demi-Official Letter sent to Subramanian, 18 September.

- Vanlawma, R. (1972): Ka Ram Leh Kei, (My Country and I), Zalen Printing House, Aizawl.
- Zoram Hriattirna(1953): Lushai Hills District Council (Village Council Act, 1953.

8

Governing Urban Areas in India (Administrative Challenges)

— V. Gnaneshwar

Introduction

Apart from general population growth, India has been witnessing an unprecedented urbanization as all superlatives of growth are gravitating towards urban areas. The result has been a consistent shift of population from rural areas to cities and towns. The contribution of urban population which was less that 10 percent a century back increased to over 31 percent by 2011. This may look better compared to other large developing countries like China (45 per cent), Indonesia (54 per cent), Mexico (78 percent) and Brazil (87 percent). But, the most disturbing aspect is the population numbers which stood at 377 million in 2011 and projected to increase to 473 million by 2021, 600 million by 2031 and 820 million by 2051 adding about 100 million every decade.[17] The census reports and other studies bring-out that the larger cities of over one million populations are witnessing faster growth and expansion compared to the core municipal cities and towns leading to metropolitanization. The current urbanization debate, therefore, is not about rural-urban divide but how to integrate the interests of the urban areas with the rural areas and; core areas with the peri-urban areas in the metropolitan city regions where the faster growth has been occurring in recent decades in India. The Indian urban thinktank should focus on options for accommodating population in municipal and beyond municipal boundaries while providing housing, jobs, transport and infrastructure, that is, nurturing metropolitan economies in the words of the World Bank. At the other spectrum, environmentalists are cautioning about impending climatic change threats due to metro centered and unregulated urbanization; and are advocating for sustainable habitat development. The rising urban poverty especially, in the developing countries, is another dimension demanding the attention of policy makers and administrators. These challenges put tremendous burden on the capabilities of administrative authorities at the central, state and local levels to address the emerging problems and to meet the developmental needs in urban areas satisfactorily. In this context, India faces critical challenge of putting in place effective governance structures and strong politico-administrative commitment to bring desirable urban transformation in terms of urban form, infrastructure and development in cities and towns in the twenty first century, the first urban millennium in history.

The administrative perspective reveals that the developmental demands have necessitated creation of several sectoral agencies - autonomous as well as line agencies, beside the traditional local government institutions. Further, involvement of the central and state government agencies, private sector and civil society organization in the urban development process has made urban governance complex and fragmented going much beyond the ambit of the traditional municipalities. The fast-emerging urban governance scenario in India is rather harshly termed as complicated, chaotic and myopic by the scholars. Apart from this harsh terminology, the fact remains that it is a great challenge to the capabilities of administrative authorities as they must deal with. A humble attempt is made here to map-out the urban scenario in its multi-dimensional form.

Urban Local Bodies

The system of urban local bodies which exists in India is a British legacy. The basic legal, functional and financial structure of the Urban Local Bodies (ULBs) inherited from the British period remains broadly same after Independence. Though there have been certain changes in the composition of the municipal councils like representation to the weaker sections, committee system, personnel policies, involvement of the local communities and financial management, the core functions and the financial resource base remained static.

Decentralization has been the proclaimed philosophy of governance in India. In the governance parlance, decentralization entails building democratic governing institutional structures with adequate functions, resources and powers at the local and grassroots levels. The urban local government system needs to be examined in this perspective.

Even after Independence, the Indian Constitution did not accord an autonomous status to the ULBs in its federal structure. The subject of local government falls within the jurisdiction of the state governments. That is why they are considered as creatures of the states. The urban local bodies are called municipal corporations, municipalities and *nagar*/town panchayats. Their entire functional and financial powers, therefore, emanate from the statutes of the state governments. Unfortunately, state governments in general preferred to strengthen their own arms rather than promoting ULBs as self-governing institutions. As a result, there has been a continuous trend towards centralization of powers and unwarranted state government interference in the local affairs and issues over time. At the other end, the Central government has been playing critical role in sponsoring development schemes in the urban areas. Urban slum improvement, housing, water supply and sanitation, urban infrastructure development and urban poverty alleviation are some of the prominent areas where central financial assistance has been flowing into urban areas. This, interestingly, has led to indirect Central government control over the ULBs. Many a time, the state governments are resisting this trend and wanting to retain total control over the ULBs. This tussle continues in India affecting the state-local relations.

There has been, however, rethinking and reinforcement of the principle of decentralization in the governance of urban areas especially, during the last two decades. The report of the National Commission on Urbanization in August, 1988 paved way for a number of reform initiatives. The Urbanization Commission report is a comprehensive document covering a range of areas like strategies for the development of cities and towns, urban poverty, housing, transport, energy, water and sanitation, and financing and governing. The recommendations of the Urbanization Commission were discussed widely in various fora viz., the Conference of Housing Ministers and Ministers of Urban Development (December,1988), the Meeting of the Central Council of Local Government and Urban Development and the Executive Committee of All India Council of Mayors (1989). Several reform initiatives took place based on these discussions. One landmark reform relates to municipal government reform.

The 74th Constitution Amendment Act, 1992

The most significant step has been the in the area of decentralization and strengthening of municipal bodies as self-governing institutions. The 74th Constitution Amendment Act (CAA), 1992, considered as a milestone in the evolution of local self-government in India, primarily focuses on democratic and decentralized governance and development. This has provided constitutional status to municipal bodies making them integral parts of the Indian federation. Main objectives of the 74th CAA are:

- Endowing the Urban Local Bodies with such powers and authority as may be necessary to enable them to function as institutions of local self-government; and
- Providing for adequate devolution of powers and finances to the urban local bodies to perform the functions entrusted including those listed in the Twelfth Schedule.

The 74th mandates certain provisions to achieve the above objectives. The main Major features are:

- While dispensing with confused and multiple nomenclatures of urban local bodies prevailing in different states, the Amendment provided for three main categories of ULBs: *nagar panchayats* for transitional urban areas; municipal councils for smaller urban areas; and corporations for larger urban areas.
- The democratic spirit of the municipal bodies was totally undermined by the state governments by keeping them under suspension for years and decades together. In order to reestablish the local democracy, constitutional provisions were made to constitute State Election Commissions on the lines of the Central Election Commission to conduct municipal elections regularly while making municipal elections mandatory limiting the State Power to do away with the democratically elected local bodies.
- Providing for constitution of ward committees at the municipal level has been another important step toward democratic decentralization at the grass-root level in urban areas. These ward committees consisting of the elected councillors from the respective wards are expected to focus on resolving the ground level problems with people's participation.
- The weaker section representation in the municipal elected bodies was rationalized based on their proportionate population to SCs and STs. Quota based women representation has been the most important feature of the 74th CAA. One-third of the elected seats irrespective of their population were reserved for women. It is heartening to note that the quota in many states has been increased to 50 percent recently. This measure is a booster for improving women participation in municipal government and finally leading to women political empowerment.
- The fiscal base of the urban local bodies remained fixed since Independence in India leading to steady financial decline of the urban local bodies over a period. The state governments in general were not interested in improving the resource base of the urban local bodies putting them at the mercy of the state governments for assistance. This has been a significant handicap for urban development in India. In order to overcome this constraint, the 74th CAA provided for constituting State Finance Commission in each state. These Commissions constituted every five years are expected to study the status of the local bodies-rural and urban and suggest measures to improve the financial status of local bodies. Another important measure has been enlarging the mandate of the

National Finance Commission under Article 280 to include the aspect of local government finance and the issues related. This also makes the Central Finance Commission to make provisions for financial assistance to local bodies from the Central Government.

- In order to democratize the urban planning process, the constitution of the District Planning Committees and the Metropolitan Planning Committees to prepare draft development plans at the district and metropolitan levels respectively was provided.
- Another important feature of the 74th CAA is providing 12th Schedule in the Constitution which listed 18 functions for municipal bodies. These functions are expected to be entrusted to the municipal bodies. The list is as below:
    - (i) Urban planning including town planning;
    - (ii) Regulation of land use and construction of buildings;
    - (iii) Planning for economic and social development;
    - (iv) Roads and bridges;
    - (v) Water supply for domestic, industrial and commercial purposes;
    - (vi) Public health, sanitation, conservancy and solid waste management;
    - (vii) Fire services;
    - (viii) Urban forestry, protection of the environment and promotion of ecological aspects;
    - (ix) Safeguarding the interests of weaker sections of society, including the handicapped and mentally retarded;
    - (x) Slum improvement and upgradation;
    - (xi) Urban poverty alleviation;
    - (xii) Provision of urban amenities and facilities such as parks, gardens and play-grounds;
    - (xiii) Promotion of cultural, educational and aesthetic aspects;
    - (xiv) Burials and burial grounds; cremations, cremation grounds and electric crematoriums;
    - (xv) Cattle ponds, prevention of cruelty to animals;
    - (xvi) Vital statistics including registration of births and deaths;
    - (xvii) Public amenities including street lighting, parking lots, bus stops and public conveniences; and
    - (xviii) Regulation of slaughterhouses and tanneries.

The 74th CAA doesn't alter the basic structure of the municipal bodies but only provided certain protective measures to strengthen democratic, functional and financial status. The state governments have already enacted the conformity legislations to implement the provisions of the 74th CAA. Without disturbing the existing federal structure of India, the Constitution 74th Amendment provided for a three-tier federalism wherein the central, state and local governments operate with specified functional and financial jurisdiction. A framework is provided for the devolution of functions and finance, regular conduct of the elections and empowerment of weaker sections in municipal governance. The 74th CAA is not a panacea for all the ills of the Urban Local Bodies. It propelled certain positive trends and reform initiatives especially, in the areas like local government autonomy both, financial and functional, democratic local governance and decentralized development. Some of the visible changes emerging in the country are:

- Regular conduct of local body elections.
- Review of the local government functions in the light of the 12th Schedule of the 74th CAA.
- Extensive survey and analysis of municipal revenue and expenditure patterns and the entire gamut of municipal financial administration including the legal provisions.
- Search for alternative strategies and mechanisms to bridge the fiscal gaps at the municipal government level.
- A sound and comprehensive statutory base for urban governance.
- Integrated planning and administration of urban development through District/Metropolitan Planning Committees.
- Administrative decentralization at the local levels through Ward Committees.
- A re-look at the governance and management of the municipal affairs.

Though the 74th CAA has provided a constitutional base for improving the municipal governments, the subsequent implementation measures are not forthcoming from the state governments. Several measures remain in the statute books of the states. Even if mandatory provisions are carried-out, their implementation suffers. As a result, the functional domain of the urban local bodies remain same as important functions like planning, water supply and sewerage, etc. still remain with the either with the state agencies or the autonomous agencies. The extent of functional devolution has been discouraging. The working of the State Election Commissions has been far from satisfactory. Their recommendations are not taken seriously and implemented. The metropolitan planning committees are not constituted while the district planning committees remain de jure bodies.

Devolution of Functions and Powers to Urban Local Bodies

Urban local bodies have been created to undertake functions of civic and regulatory nature. Civic functions include provision of water supply, streetlights, roads, sanitation, etc. The regulatory functions relate to building regulations, implementation of master plan, etc. Overtime, they began to undertake socio-economic planning and development functions like poverty alleviation and slum improvement in addition to civic functions.

True democratic decentralization depends on the level of functional and financial powers entrusted to the urban local bodies. The functions listed in the Twelfth Schedule represent broad areas, most of which are already being performed by the Municipalities. Some of the functions like protection of the environment, tanneries, fire services and economic planning are being performed by state level agencies, which need to be devolved on the Municipalities. In fact, the functions like poverty alleviation, protection of the environment and economic planning are very broad in nature performance of which need involvement of the state and local governments, even the central government in some respects. Part of these functions could be devolved on the Municipalities. Therefore, the question is not whether the list of functions is adequate or not, but it is the extent of functional responsibilities devolved on the Municipalities.

The Twelfth Schedule incorporated in the 74th CAA provided a list of functions for devolution to the Municipalities and it is left to the discretion of the state government concerned to decide on the matter. There is no point in prescribing a list of broad general functions and blaming either the local governments for non-performance or the state governments for their reluctance to devolve the functions. In the constraining circumstances mentioned above, the municipal functions should be defined in specific terms rather prescribing generalized functions like town planning, economic planning, poverty alleviation and environmental protection, and it should be made mandatory to devolve such specifically defined functions to the Municipalities along with the necessary authority, powers, expertise and finances. This appears to be essential in the context of complex nature of the process of urban development and the need for involving various agencies on partnership basis to achieve the goals of urban development at various levels.

The ULBs are subjected to many controls and limitations by the state governments in the administration of taxes and non-taxes and, implementation of various works and programmes. They should follow the prescribed rules, regulations and government orders. Various exemptions granted under tax laws result in loss of revenue to the urban local bodies. The limits on administrative and technical sanctioning powers may lead to delays and cost escalation. Many legal and administrative constraints have not been addressed and the ULBs continue to remain in the same status of dependence syndrome on the state governments in the post-74th period also.

It is true that the state governments in general show reluctance to transfer functional responsibilities to the Municipalities unless there are compulsions. Growth of special purpose agencies to carryout local functions in India demonstrates this tendency. It is also argued that when the municipal bodies are not able to carry-out the existing functions either due to lack of manpower or financial resources, additional devolution has no meaning unless functional devolution is accompanied by the necessary financial and manpower support. This view has also been expressed by some State Finance Commissions while discussing the issue of financial devolution to the Municipalities. Strengthening of the Municipalities is, therefore, related more to the extent of authority, powers and finances devolved rather than just providing a list of functions in the Municipal Acts. General feeling at the municipal level has been that they lack adequate authority, powers and finances to perform their functions effectively. They depend on the state authorities for various sanctions, expertise and finances. This point, in fact, has been raised and discussed at various forums and conferences.

The following measures are essential to make the ULBs stronger enough to meet the emerging challenges of urban development and to deal with the problems being encountered:

- A clearly specified list of local functions and financial sources for the local bodies is required. A national level consensus should be achieved on this aspect and an amendment to the Constitution, if possible, should be brought-out which is desirable to achieve uniformity across the states.
- The functional and financial roles and responsibilities of state governments and the local bodies must be clearly defined to avoid confusion and ambiguities that breed ad hoc decisions.
- Once the functional and financial responsibilities are clearly specified, the devolution of the necessary authority and powers must be made mandatory at the state level.
- There should not be undesirable interference by the state authorities in the functioning of the local bodies once the roles and responsibilities are specified.
- The State Finance Commissions (SFC) must be strengthened in terms of their status, composition and expertise.
- There should be a timeframe fixed for constitution of the SFC, submission of the reports by the SFC, placing the report before the State Legislature along with the action report and the implementation of the recommendations of the SFC reports by the state governments. The period of SFC recommendations must be made coincide with the Central Finance Commission.

Urban Development Challenge and Roles of the Central and State Governments

In the Indian federation, the local bodies-rural and urban are created and administered by the state government concerned. The powers, functions and resources of the local bodies are provided according to the state legislations. The entire legal and administrative framework of the urban local bodies is installed by the state governments according to the local situations. No doubt, the Constitution 74th Amendment discussed above has streamlined and strengthened the status of urban local bodies; its implementation however was not as the goals of the amendment. In this situation, the central government guidance and monitoring became essential to realize the objectives of the Constitution Amendment.

As the Central government can not interfere in the state affairs, the necessary support and guidance is being provided by the central government to the state authorities and urban local bodies. The Central government has been providing policy and technical support, development support through various urban projects, financial devolution of central funds to local bodies through the Central Finance Commission mechanism and bringing-out various urban reforms to manage the urban development effectively.

With the increasing rate of urbanization, the cities and towns across the country have been growing and expanding at alarming rate. This rapid growth has put tremendous strain on the institutions responsible for providing civic infrastructure and services leading to urban crisis in India. If the haphazard growth reflects the inability of the urban local bodies and planning agencies to regulate growth properly, acute basic service deficiencies and other social facilities is making life miserable to urban dwellers. The growth of slums decline of service system and amenities and mindboggling urban congestion and pollution are few of the problems confronting the urban areas. Meeting this urban challenge necessitated a partnership approach between the central and state governments and its administrative authorities. The central government has taken several legal, administrative and financial measures to extend the necessary support to the state governments and urban local bodies.

(a) Central Government Initiatives: In the context of growing urban problems and failure of the civic administration, the central government has taken several initiatives to improve the status. Based on several commission and committee reports which studied problems in depth, the Government of India realized that bringing constitutional amendment to revive the urban local bodies was essential. The 74th CAA was brought-out to strengthen the urban local government system. This exercise was done with full-fledged vigour during 1990s. Apart from this governing reform, several strategic interventions were initiated by the Central Government.

The major areas include policy and institutional support, introduction of some reforms in the areas like accounting, public-private partnerships, property tax, intergovernmental financial support, service level benchmarking of municipal services, etc. These initiatives are made to improve the status of urban infrastructure and service levels in urban areas as urban areas have become major nodes for national development. These initiatives are further discussed here.

(i) Institutional Development: The Urban Development plays key role in extending support to the state and local bodies the needed support. In India, though there is no national urbanization policy as such, the national government has initiated steps to devise some sectoral policies to solve the key urban problems. Based on the National Commission on Urbanization and reports of several commissions and committees at the national level, the Government had taken certain steps. Two national level organizations namely, Town and Country Planning Organization and the Central Public Health & Environmental Engineering Organization (CPHEEO) were set-up to prepare standard norms for town planners and the public health engineers to help in their respective areas namely, town planning and urban public health services like waste management and water supply and sewerage.

After implementing the 74th CAA, it was thought necessary to prepare a Model Municipal Legislation to guide the state governments in bringing-out comprehensive legislations to govern urban areas in the respective states as the existing laws have become complex and dated in the changing urban context. The Model Municipal Law is a comprehensive legal frame providing for simplification of municipal laws, enhancing borrowing by ULBs, allowing the entry of private sector and authorizing concessionaires to penalize users for non-payment of tariffs. In brief, this initiative aims not only to enhance the capacities of ULBs to leverage public funds for development of urban sector but also will help in creating an environment in which urban local bodies can play their role more effectively and ensure better service - delivery. The state governments need not copy this legislation but use it as a framework to formulate municipal laws by adopting it suitably to the state specific needs.

The states like Kerala and Tamil Nadu had formulated the municipal legislations in an integrated manner in line with the 74th CAA. The Kerala has redrafted the municipal laws making a unified law for municipalities and corporations while incorporating the provisions of the 74th CAA. Tamil Nadu also did such an exercise. Unfortunately, many of the states did not accord importance to this aspect.

(ii) Urban Policy Initiatives: On the policy front, the policy initiatives concerning urban services relate to urban land, housing and sanitation. The

National Urban Housing and Habitat Policy, 2007, National Urban Sanitation Policy, 2008, National Urban Street Vendors' Policy, 2009 and National Slum Policy, 1999 are major policies devised in recent decades. The National Urban Housing and Habitat Policy, 2007 aims the following:

- Urban Planning: Regional planning to promote symbiotic development of rural and urban areas.
- Affordable Housing: Promoting development of cost-effective, quality approved building materials and technologies with a view to bringing down the cost of EWS/LIG houses.
- Increasing flow of Funds: Promoting larger flow of funds from governmental and private sources; suitable fiscal concessions; access to tenure, land, finance and technology; and shifting to a demand driven approach and from subsidy based housing schemes to cost recovery-cum-subsidy schemes for housing.
- Spatial Incentives: Relaxation of Floor Area Ratio for ensuring 20-25 percent of the FAR are reserved for EWS / LIG.
- Increased supply of land: Facilitating accessibility to serviced land and housing with focus on economically weaker sections and low-income group categories.
- Special provision for SC/ST/OBC/Minorities/Disabled
- Special Provision for Women: Catering to women's needs.
- Employment Generation: Up-gradation of construction skills and giving an impetus to employment generation
- Public-Private Partnerships: Forging strong partnerships between public, private and cooperative sectors.
- Management Information System: Developing information and data base on housing.
- Healthy Environment: Encouraging use of renewable energy resources and ensuring effective solid waste management and protecting cultural heritage and architecture.

The goal of the National Urban Sanitation Policy, 2008 is to transform Urban India into community-driven, totally sanitized, healthy and livable cities and towns. The specific goals are:[18]

(a) **Awareness Generation and Behaviour Change:** Generating awareness about sanitation and its linkages with public and environmental health amongst communities and institutions; and promoting mechanisms to bring about and sustain behavioral changes aimed at adoption of healthy sanitation practices.

(b) **Achieving Open Defecation Free Cities:** All urban dwellers will have access to and use safe and hygienic sanitation facilities and arrangements so that no one defecates in the open.

(c) **Re-orienting Institutions and Mainstreaming Sanitation toward city wide approach :** Mainstream thinking, planning and implementing measures related to sanitation in all sectors and departmental domains as a cross-cutting issue, especially in all urban management endeavors; strengthening national, state, city and local institutions (public, private and community) to accord priority to sanitation provision, including planning, implementation and O&M management; and extending access to proper sanitation facilities for poor communities and other un-served settlements.

(d) **Sanitary and Safe Disposal:** 100 percent of human excreta and liquid wastes from all sanitation facilities including toilets must be disposed of safely.

The Ministry of Housing and Urban Affairs has formulated the National Policy on Urban Street Vendors, 2009. The Street Vendor Policy aims to foster a congenial environment for the urban street vendors to carry out their activities. It is conceived as part of the national urban poverty alleviation strategy. The primary objective of this Policy is to provide for and promote a supportive environment for the vast mass of the urban street vendors to carry out their vocation, at the same time, ensuring that their vending activities do not lead too overcrowding and unsanitary conditions in public spaces and streets.[19]

The National Slum Policy, 1999 while recognizing the slums as integral part of the urban areas, suggested that the slum development initiatives should basically focus on: creating awareness amongst the public and Government of the underlying principles that guide the process of slum development and improvement and the options that are available for bringing about the integration of these settlements and the communities residing within them into the urban area as a whole; strengthening the legal and policy framework to facilitate the process of slum development and improvement on a sustainable basis; and establishing a framework for involving all stakeholders for the efficient and smooth implementation of Policy objectives.[20]

These national level policy initiatives led follow-up reforms in various at the central and state levels. In the housing sector, the Urban Land Ceiling Act was abolished; the Land Acquisition and Rent Control Acts are being suitably amended to promote urban housing. The state town planning legislations have also been modified to simplify the building permissions, adopt new building techniques, and more importantly acquire the lands for housing by devising innovative land development schemes like land pooling with active peoples' involvement. Community involvement in slum up-gradation and development is pursued. In the housing sector, Public-Private Partnerships are being promoted.

(iii) Initiatives in the Finance Sector: In the financial sector, major initiatives relate to preparation of National Accounting Manual for Municipalities and the scheme of Inter-governmental financial transfers. The accounting practices of the urban local bodies have become outdated as they are based on single entry and non-accrual basis. The funding agencies like World Bank and Asian Development Bank have been insisting for adoption of the double entry accrual-based system to manage the finances of the urban local bodies. Even the Supreme Court of India also suggested for reforming the municipal accounting to bring-out financial accountability of the urban local bodies. The state governments have taken measures to adopt the National Accounting Manual features in their state manuals.

The Government of India has been funding several urban development schemes in the country. As this support is based on partnership basis with the state governments, the financial status of the urban local bodies remained critical in the absence adequate resource mobilization at the local level. Through the 74th CAA, the mechanism of State Finance Commission was provided to focus on finances of urban local bodies. Still, the situation demanded further help from the Centre. The Government of India has entrusted an additional responsibility of providing financial support to the local bodies to the existing Central Finance Commission. The Central Finance Commission funds have become significant to-day to the local bodies including urban local bodies. Interestingly, performance-based grant is also being provided to improve the performance levels of the urban local bodies.

Apart from these major initiatives, the Government of India has also introduced the tax incentives for raising funds for urban development through municipal bonds. Further, national guidelines were also issued to reform the property tax which is the main resource for urban local bodies in India. The reform suggested is to make the assessment system more rational, tax-payer friendly and at the same time increasing revenues from the property tax. Several state governments like Andhra Pradesh, Tamil Nadu, Karnataka, Uttar Pradesh, Bihar, Jharkhand and the urban local bodies have reformed the property tax administration. A state level facility like state property tax board is also being set-up to help the urban local bodies in this respect. New concepts like land monetization are emerging on the urban scene which are expected to yield much needed income through land development initiatives. In fact, several urban development authorities in the have started auctioning the developed plots to fetch more income in the light of the real estate boom in cities like Hyderabad, Bangalore, Kanpur, Lucknow etc. For instance, the Hyderabad Metropolitan Development Authority generated over Rs 300/- crores through land sales recently.

(iv) Improving Urban Service Levels: The status of civic services in core areas like water supply, sewerage, solid waste management, street lighting, etc., has been declining rapidly in urban areas. The scheme called Service Level Benchmarks for Urban Local Bodies has been devised by the Government of India. The scheme aims to improve the basic civic services as per the national standards. A state and local level information system is devised to monitor the service levels every year. This exercise not only helps in improving the service levels as per targets but also develops a competitive spirit among the urban local bodies across the country as the national level assessment is made by the Ministry of Urban Development.

All these reforms were initiated by the Government of India. In order to promote their implementation by the state governments, reform based urban development funding mechanism has been adopted by the Central Government. The major urban funding scheme called *Jawarlal Nehru* National Urban Mission (JnNURM) makes it binding on the part of state governments to implement the national reform agenda prepared by the Central Government to avail assistance under the scheme.

As a result of all these central government initiatives, the states have been moving though slowly to implement various reform measures. The reforms like redressal of citizen grievances, public-private partnerships, property tax and accounting reform, computerization and digitalization of municipal operations and records, and focus on resource mobilization to fund urban infrastructure have gained significance at the state as well as the ULB level. Several innovative methods are being adopted by the states and the ULBs to carry-forward these urban governance reforms.

(v) Municipal E-Governance: Information and communications technology are transforming the way of life in modern times. In fact, it has become a global movement. If the private sector has taken major steps in this direction, the not for profit and public sectors are also moving steadily in that direction. Information Technology is all about connectivity. Connectivity brings proximity which makes the delivery of services offered by governments nearer to people. In this respect, the IT has major role in governance process. Apart from the central and state governments, the ULBs deserve maximum attention as they are at the cutting edge of communities and it has immense potential to affect the lives of the citizens. The term 'e-governance' means the use of a range of modern information and communication technologies such as internet, local area networks, mobiles etc. by government to facilitate effective and efficient delivery of services and to promote democracy. The primary advantages of e-governance are greater attention to improve service delivery mechanism; enhancing the efficiency of production; and emphasis upon the wider access of information.

In India, the Government of India framed following principles for adoption of e-governance in urban local areas.

- As Information Technology rests on connectivity, a stand-alone computer can offer only minimal utility, and networking therefore would be essential to maximize the gains;
- The larger goal is to maximize citizen satisfaction about the delivery of civic services and the design of the system would therefore keep citizens as the centre-point and every process would be designed keeping them in view;
- The design of the system would be such that it is amenable to web enabling as web offers the easiest method of citizens gaining access to information they need;
- To the extent possible, the project may be designed on a public-private partnership model that would involve cost and revenue sharing with the private sector; and
- The insiders possessing computer skills be encouraged to develop the model for the computerized system.

The Government of India has formulated the National e-Governance Plan (NEGP), part of which includes a National Mission Mode Programme (NMMP) for e-Governance in Municipalities. This NMMP intends to roll out e-governance in ULBs on a nation-wide basis and has now been included as part of the *Jn*NURM scheme. The NMMP on e-Governance in Municipalities envisages covering Urban Local Bodies (ULBs) in 35 mission cities identified in the first phase.[21] Following goals are expected from this exercise.

(i) Focus on clearly identified list of citizen services that would be covered with clearly laid down service levels and outcomes that would be achieved;

(ii) Improve efficiency and effectiveness in interaction between local-government and its citizens and other stakeholders (i.e. Non-governmental organizations (NGOs), community-based organizations (CBOs), resident welfare associations (RWAs), private sector, etc.);

(iii) Improve quality of internal local-government operations to support and stimulate good governance;

(iv) Bring about transparency and accountability in the governance of urban local bodies;

(v) Enhance interface between urban local bodies and citizens; and

(vi) Help improve delivery of services to citizens.

The activities such as registration, births/ deaths certification, management of utilities that come under the ULBs, property tax administration, redressal of citizen grievances, building approval process, e-procurement and monitoring of projects, local works, health programmes, licensing, municipal accounting and personnel management. In recent years, the Government of India has expanded the programme and initiated a separate development project named Smart City Mission. In this programme, the IT applications in city administration have been widened covering various organizations involved in the city administration.

The concept of Smart City is not uniform across the countries. Each country can have its smart city definition based on its level of technological innovation and economic development. But, a broader idea of smart city has been devising smart solutions for all-round development of urban economies and urban life. Smart solutions include application of IT solutions in dissemination of public information, citizen grievances resolution, electronic service delivery, video crime monitoring, installation of smart meters, smart parking, intelligent traffic management, tele-medicine, tele-education, and in several other urban services. The purpose of the Smart Cities Mission launched in India is to drive economic growth and improve the quality of life of people by enabling local area development and harnessing technology, especially technology that leads to Smart outcomes. Area- based development will transform existing areas (retrofit and redevelop), including slums, into better planned ones, thereby improving livability of the whole City. New areas (green field) will be developed around cities to accommodate the expanding population in urban areas. Application of Smart Solutions will enable cities to use technology, information and data to improve infrastructure and services. Comprehensive development in this way will improve quality of life, create employment and enhance incomes for all, especially the poor and the disadvantaged, leading to inclusive Cities.[22]

The Smart City Mission aims to achieve development of urban infrastructure and services in urban areas which could be replicated. Further, the project emphasizes convergence with the other urban projects to avoid duplication and wastage. Inclusiveness and convergence are the main features of the Mission. Achieving these objectives entails applying smart solutions including IT solutions. This makes city administration too smart, accessible, responsive and efficient- smartness in solutions, accessible to the communities, responsive to the needs of the people and efficiency in solving the problems. In the process, urban governance can become good governance.

Recently, the IMD World Competitiveness Centre described the smart city as an urban setting that applies technology to enhance the benefits and diminish the shortcomings of urbanization. The IMD Centre in collaboration with the Singapore University of Technology and Design, has done an international survey 102 cities and ranked them on certain criteria covering five key areas: health and safety (basic sanitation in poorest areas, recycling services, public safety, air pollution and medical services), mobility (traffic congestion and public transport), activities (green spaces and cultural activities), opportunities (employment finding services, access to good school for most children, lifelong learning services by local institutions, creating new jobs and welcome to minorities), and governance (information accessibility on local government decisions, corruption of city officials, resident contribution to local government decision making and resident feedback on local government projects).[23]

The survey was based on perceptions of the people who are living and working in the respective cities. According to the digital smart city index arrived at, the city of Singapore occupied top position followed by Zurich and Oslo. Some Indian cities were also covered in the survey. The Indian City rankings are - Hyderabad (67), New Delhi (68), Mumbai (78) and Bangalore (79). The Indian ranking has been the result recent urban initiatives taken by the central, state and city level governments.

(vi) Urban Governance

The term 'governance' in broader sense is concerned with the system of exercising political and administrative power. In simple terms it relates to the process of governing by the modern governments. The concept has assumed complex dimensions in recent times. The aggressive privatization trend and involvement of the civil society organizations in the governance necessitated by pressing developmental demands call for an inclusive system of governance to manage the interfaces across the stakeholders. This has virtually displaced the traditional system of regulation and control based of administration. Further, administrative specialization became essential to pursue the developmental goals in various sectors. Emergence of autonomous organizations on the other hand led to coordination issues. In this context, search for better concept on governance is needed to understand the governance dynamics. Rhodes feels,[24] governance refers to self-organizing, inter-governmental networks characterized by interdependence, resource-exchange, rules of the game, and significant autonomy from the state. As the new actors enter the scene, complementary networks of inter-relationships become essential to accommodate and synchronize diverse ideas, interests, approaches and motives toward achieving the common goals. The United Nations defines governance as 'the exercise of political, economic and administrative authority in the management of a country's affairs all levels. It comprises the mechanisms, processes and institutions through which citizens and groups articulate their interests, exercise their legal rights, meet their obligations and mediate their differences'. In this perspective, governance is not government and it is a broader concept which recognizes that power exists inside as well as outside the formal authority and institutions.[25]

Traditionally, urban governance was mainly focused on the urban local bodies. But, with increasing urbanization, cities have assumed global significance and are being called global cities in terms of development. As a result, developmental demands have put tremendous pressure on the administrative capabilities of urban bodies. With the emerging urban demands and pressures, governing of urban areas has become complex and challenging in India. The mindboggling challenges have often led the urban life into chaotic and deplorable conditions. The central and state governments have undertaken several policy and administrative reforms to meet the emerging urban demands effectively.

The scope of urban governance therefore covers several institutions namely, municipal governments, autonomous organizations or parastatals, central and state government departments and non-governmental organizations. Urban governance, to-day, has become complex because of institutional and functional interfaces of all these organizations as each institution has its own laws, structures, powers, finances, plans, programmes and working style. The functional framework of urban governance appears fragmented and myopic with the existence of several laws and regulations governing a plethora of institutions.

In urban areas, if the urban local bodies are the core governing institutions, the autonomous agencies like water supply and sewerage boards, housing boards, urban development authorities, pollution control boards, industrial townships, etc., are the other institutions which function in the urban areas attending to some sectoral functions.

Good Urban Governance in India

The concept of good governance has gained currency in recent years in the context of citizen-government interface. In public domain, governance involves a process that goes much beyond government and its institutions integrating the governing institutions and the governed that is, the people at large. In democracies, governments are formed by the people to realize their common needs. If the governments ignore people's needs, such governments cannot survive and sustain. The governments, therefore, should evolve such processes through which people realize their objectives. Urban governance is not dissimilar and should follow this fundamental principle. Urban governance in simple terms means the process through which the urban local governments strive to meet the common needs of the people living in urban areas. It implies that the policies, programmes and activities of the governments must be people- centered meeting their needs. The UN Habitat identified following principles for achieving the aims of good governance.[26]

- Participation
- Respect for the law
- Transparency in decision making and information
- Responsiveness in implementing decisions and meeting needs
- Consensus orientation
- Promoting equity and inclusiveness
- Effective results
- Accountability

In compliance with the UN Habitat ideology and Global Campaign for Good Urban Governance, the Government of India commenced the National Action Plan for Good Urban Governance to realize the objective "inclusive city", which provides space and voice to all its stakeholders. Good urban governance involves improving the quality of life in cities through improved local governance by reinventing a city as an inclusive city. Such a city provides space and voice to all its stakeholders through inclusive decision-making. The inclusive city allows full flow to women's thoughts and initiatives, since women are one of the biggest levers of positive change in the society.

In urban context, good governance entails four basic elements namely, decentralization, transparency, social accountability and civic engagement and social integration of the poor. The main action points in these broad areas are out-lined here.[27]

- **Decentralization:** Decentralization is essential for participatory governance in democracies. In the urban governance too devolution of functional and financial powers to urban local bodies is recommended. In this respect, defining state-municipal relationship is specific terms is important. This should be followed by necessary transfer of powers to the elected representatives but coupled with right to recall so that the elected representatives act responsibly.
- **Integration of Poor and Marginalized:** Citizen Integration with the government is another important area. The poor, differently able, women, children-all disadvantaged citizens should be mainstreamed and integrated. Some important action steps include following.

  (a) Shelter for all

  (b) Promoting better understanding among all stakeholders.

(c) City-wide action plan to integrate the poor and marginalized population into the city with special attention to land tenure, basic services, housing and employment needs, including support for informal enterprise of the poor, particularly women.

(d) Partnership with non-government and community-based organizations.

(e) Ensuring access to education, health and other social services.

- **Transparency and Civic Engagement:** Transparency entails the conduct of public business in a manner that affords stakeholders wide accessibility to the decision-making process and the ability to effectively influence it. Some important steps needed to achieve this are as below:

  (a) Identifying major bottlenecks through consultative processes.

  (b) Discretionary powers in favor of classes rather than individually.

  (c) Code of conduct for municipal executives and elected representatives.

  (d) Public-private partnership.

  (e) Networking.

  (f) Transparent engagement of private sector.

  (g) Right to information on all matters pertaining to local government.

- **Social Accountability:** The ULBs should adopt adequate social accountability measures to ensure that the citizens' problems are solved fulfilling their needs. Important steps needed here include implementing citizen charters, providing grievance redressal mechanisms and Introducing measures like social audit.

Looking Forward

While the cities are becoming important territorial nodes in the face of globalization, there is also an increasing trend of fragmentation in terms of their communities, economy, politics and administration. Added to this paradoxical trend, city governance, to-day, has become a complex process involving multiple stakeholders, inter-dependent resources and actions, shared purposes and blurred boundaries between private and public, formal and informal and state and civil society sectors demanding coordination, negotiation and consensus. Urban governance, therefore, must address three key tasks: coordinating a fragmented governance landscape; steering inter-dependent activities; and integrating and managing diverse networks.

This process makes urban governance a complex and challenging task for the administrators as the process is beyond the traditional administrative ethos involving hierarchy, span of control, supervision, control, etc. The tasks which are confined to a single organization become inadequate in the multi-organizational context. In the development context, devising city-wide mega goals and binding all the stakeholders to these goals is vital. Ensuring this binding is difficult as each organization has its own regulatory framework, objectives and workstyles. For instance, the working environment of municipal governments differs from the autonomous organization working in different sectors. The authorities concerned are struggling to coordinate them. In fact, the urban areas in India are criticized most for the utter inabilities and failures of coordination. Failed coordination has been leading to delays in works and waste of scarce resources due to delay costs and duplication.

Another important dimension in city administration is working-out effective public-private partnerships. This is essential in the context of privatization of public works. Partnerships across non-governmental organizations and private sector institutions are needed become important. Building partnerships with non-governmental organizations differ from private sector as the former is mostly not-for-profit organization; the later is profit motive organization. Different styles are needed to succeed in partnerships in this situation.

The application of e-governance facilities lost in developing interfaces with the stakeholders-communities, beneficiaries, aggrieved people, etc. The city administration and citizen interface become faceless avoiding personal interactions and consequential corruption issues. The process is time consuming as it needs change in the mindsets of the people as well as the authorities. The transparent administration could build win citizen confidence which in turn help in getting needed cooperation from the people. Peoples' cooperation is essential for the successful implementation of development programmes. It could be inferred that the ease of interacting with administration makes people more productive and less dissatisfied.

Several administrative initiatives in recent years have raised high hopes among the urban dwellers. Realizing the hopes of stakeholders and people in urban areas depends on how effectively and smartly these initiatives are carried-out on the ground. If it is done successfully, it will be a paradigm shift re-defining public administration-its domain, organization and working. The recent trend of period assessment of performance levels of cities at the national and international levels is a good sign which could promote competitiveness among cities thereby fulfilling the needs and aspirations of the urban communities.

References

1. Planning Commission, 12th Five Year Plan (VOL. II), p 318, HPEC, 2011, National Urban Transport Policy, Ministry of Urban Development and The World Bank, Urbanization beyond Municipal Boundaries: Nurturing Metropolitan Economics and Connecting Peri-Urban Areas in India, 2013, Washington, p. 77.
2. Ministry of Urban Development, Government of India, National Urban Sanitation Policy, 2008, pp. 8-9.
3. Government of India, Ministry of Housing and Urban Poverty Alleviation, National Policy on Urban Street Vendors, 2009, pp. 2-5.
4. National Slum Policy (Draft for discussion), April 1999, Ministry of Urban Affairs and Employment, Government of India, New Delhi.
5. Ministry of Urban Development, Government of India, Smart City – Mission Statement and Guidelines, June, 2015, pp. 6-7.
6. IMD World Competitiveness Centre and SCO Smart City Observatory, Singapore University of Technology and Design, Smart City Index.
7. Anne Mette Kjaer, Governance, Polity Press, 2004, p. 3.
8. UNDP, Governance for Sustainable Human Development, New York, 1997, pp. 2-3.
9. What is Good Governance? United Nations Economic and Social Commission for Asia and the Pacific, www.unescap.org/huset/gg/governance. htm
10. UN Habitat, Action Plan for Good Urban Governance-Recommendations for National Action Plan for Good Governance, www.UNhabitatg/ 2105_30168_ India_ Plan_recommendations.doc

9

Empowering And Strengthening of Local Governments – Issues and Challenges

— *S. Vijay Kumar*

Introduction

Local Governments or local bodies are institutions of the local self-governance, which look after the administration of an area or small community such as villages, towns or cities. The local bodies in India are broadly classified into two categories. The local bodies constituted for local planning, development and administration in the rural areas are referred as Rural Local Bodies known as Panchayats and the local bodies, which are constituted for local planning, development and administration in the urban areas, are referred as Urban Local Bodies, known as Municipalities. Mahatma Gandhi advocated Panchayati Raj as the foundation of India's political system, his term for such a vision was ***"Gram Swaraj"*** or ***"Village Self-governance"***, a decentralized form of government in which each village would be responsible for its own affairs.Instead, India developed a highly centralized form of government.However, this has been moderated by the delegation of several administrative functions to the local level, empowering elected gram panchayats. There are significant differences between the traditional Panchayati Raj system that was envisioned by Gandhi and the system formalized in India in 1992.

Brief History of Local Governments in India

Local self-government implies the transfer of the power to rule to the lowest level of the political order. It is a form of democratic decentralization where the participation of even the grass root level of the society is ensured in the process of administration. The shape of the present local self-government in India was laid by the Panchayati Raj System (1992). But, the history of Panchayati Raj starts from the self-sufficient and self-governing village communities. In the time of the Rig - Veda (1700 BC), evidence suggests that self-governing village bodies called 'Sabhas' existed. With the passage of time, these bodies became panchayats.The existence of local bodies in ancient India is evident from the decentralization of power in the kingdoms of the Maurya and the Gupta period. Panchayats were functional institutions of grassroots governance in almost every village. The village panchayat, as a system of administration, began in the British days, as their offer to satisfy the demands for local autonomy. They opened up the governance of the lowest levels to the citizens. The Government India Act, 1935 also authorises the provisions to enact legislations. Even though such minor forms of local governance was evident in India, the framers of the Constitutions, unsatisfied with the existing provisions, included Article 40 among the "Directive Principles", whereby: *"The state shall take steps to organize village panchayats and endow them with such powers and authority as may be necessary to enable them to function as units of self-government."* Later, the conceptualization of the system of local self-government in India took place through the formation and effort of four important committees from the year 1957 to 1986. Panchayati Raj is included in the State List of the Seventh Schedule of the Constitution. It is the States that have been charged with the responsibility for devolution of powers to the Panchayats. It will be helpful to us, if we take a quick look at the various committees and the important recommendations that were put forth by them.

Balwant Ray Mehta Committee (1957)

Appointed by the Government of India to examine the working of two of its earlier programmes, the committee submitted its report in November 1957, in which the term "Democratic Decentralization" first appears.The important recommendations are:

- Establishment of a three-tier Panchayati Raj system – Gram Panchayat at village level (Direct election), Panchayat Samiti at the Block level (Mandal) and Zilla Parishad or Zilla Praja Parishad at the district level (Indirect Election).
- District Collector to be the Chairman of Zilla Parishad or Zilla Praja Parishad.
- Transfer of resources and power to these bodies to be ensured.

The existent National Development Council accepted the recommendations. However, it did not insist on a single, definite pattern to be followed in the establishment of these institutions. Rather, it allowed the states to devise their own patterns, while the broad fundamentals were to be the same throughout the country. Rajasthan (1959) adopted the system first, followed by Andhra Pradesh in the same year. Some states even went ahead to create four-tier systems including Nyaya Panchayats, which served as judicial bodies.

Ashok Mehta Committee (1977 – 1978)

This Committee was constituted by the Janta Government to study the Panchayati Raj Institutions in our country. Out of a total of 132 recommendations made by it, the most important ones are:

- Three-tier system to be replaced by a two-tier system.
- Political parties should participate at all levels in the elections.
- Compulsory powers of taxation to be given to these institutions.
- Zilla Parishad to be made responsible for planning at the district level.
- A minister for Panchayati Raj to be appointed by the State Council of Ministers.
- Constitutional recognition to be given to Panchayati Raj institutions.

Unfortunately, the Janta Government collapsed before action could be initiated on these recommendations.

GVK Rao Committee (1985)

Appointed by the Planning Commission of India, this Committee concluded that the developmental procedures were gradually being taken away from the local self-government institutions, resulting in a system comparable to 'grass without roots'. Their major recommendations are:

- Zilla Parishad to be given prime importance and all developmental programmes at that level to be handed to it.
- Post of DDC (District Development Commissioner) to be created acting as the chief executive officer of the Zilla Parishad.
- Regular elections to be held.

LM Singhvi Committee (1986)

Constituted by the Rajiv Gandhi Government on 'Revitalization of Panchayati Raj Institutions for Democracy and Development', its important recommendations are:

- Constitutional recognition for PRI institutions.
- Nyaya Panchayats to be established for clusters of villages.

Rajiv Gandhi presented the 64th and 65th Amendments to the Constitution in the Lok Sabha on 15 May 1989 itself, but Rajya Sabha opposed it. It was only during the P. V. Narasimha Rao Government's term that the idea finally became a reality in the form of the 72rd and 73th Constitutional Amendment Bills, Their number was changed to 73rd and 74th respectively after the approval of the President of India. The Amendments came into force on 24 April 1993 (Rural) and 1st June, 1993(Urban) respectively.

Panchayati Raj System under 73rd and 74th Constitution Amendment Acts, 1992

In the history of Panchayati Raj, in India, on 24 April 1993, the Constitutional (73rd Amendment) Act 1992 came into force to provide constitutional status to the Panchayati Raj institutions. This Amendment was extended to Panchayats in the tribal areas of eight states, namely: Andhra Pradesh, Gujarat, Himachal Pradesh, Maharashtra, Madya Pradesh, Odisha, and Rajasthan beginning on 24 December 1996. This amendment contains provision for devolution of powers and responsibilities to the panchayats, both for the preparation of economic development plans and social justice, as well as for implementation in relation to 29 subjects listed in the Eleventh Schedule of the Constitution, and the ability to levy and collect appropriate taxes, duties, tolls and fees. The Act aims to provide a three-tier systems of Panchayati Raj for all states having a population of over 2 million; to hold Panchayat elections regularly every five years; to provide seats reserved for SCs, STs and women; to appoint a State Finance Commission to make recommendations regarding the financial powers of the Panchayats and to constitute a District Planning Committee.

The Acts of 1992 added two new parts IX (The Panchayats) and IX-A (The Municipalities) to the Constitution. It also added two new Schedules– 11 and 12 which contain the lists of functional items of Panchayats and Municipalities.

Panchayats and Municipalities

- Panchayat and Municipality are the generic terms for the governing body at the local level. Both exist as three tier systems – at the lower, intermediate and upper levels.
- The 73rd Constitution Amendment Act provides for a *Gram Sabha* as the foundation of the Panchayati Raj System. It is essentially a Village Assembly consisting of all the registered voters in the area of the Panchayat. The State has the power to determine what kind of powers it can exercise, and what functions it has to perform at the village level.
- The 74th Constitution Amendment act provides three types of Municipalities:
    1. *Nagar* Panchayat for a transitional area between a rural and urban area.
    2. Municipal Council for a small urban area.
    3. Municipal Corporation for a large urban area.
- Municipalities represent urban local self-government.

- Most of the provisions of the two acts are parallel, differing only in the fact that they are being applied to either a Panchayat or a Municipality respectively.
- Each *Gram Sabha* is the meeting of a particular constituency called Ward.
- Each Ward has a representative chosen from among the people themselves by Direct Election.
- The Chairperson of the *Panchayats* at the intermediate and district level are elected from among these representatives at the immediately lower level by Indirect Election.

Types of Urban Local Government

There are mainly following types of urban local governments currently existing in India:

1. Municipal Corporation
2. Municipality Council
3. Notified Area Committee/*Town Panchayat/Nagar Panchayat*
4. Cantonment Board
5. Industrial Township

Elections Procedure in the Local Government Bodies

- All seats of representatives of local bodies are filled by people chosen through Direct Elections.
- The conduct of elections is vested in the hands of the State Election Commission.
- At all levels, the Chairperson shall be elected in a mode defined by the State Legislature.
- Seats are reserved for SCs and STs in proportion to their population.
- Out of these reserved seats, not less than one-third shall be further reserved for women.
- There should be a blanket reservation of one-third seats for women in all the constituencies taken together too (which can include the already reserved seats for SCs and STs).

Qualifications Required to become a Member of the *Panchayat* or Municipality

Any person who is qualified to be a member of the State Legislature is eligible to be a member of the *Panchayat* or Municipality. "But he shall not be disqualified on the ground that he is less than 25 years of age if he has attained the age of 21 years". This means that unlike the, State Legislature a person needs to attain only 21 years of age to be a member of *Panchayat*/Municipality.

Duration of the Local Government Bodies

- The local governing bodies are elected for a term of Five Years.
- Fresh elections should be conducted before the expiry of the five-year term.
- If the *Panchayat*/Municipality is dissolved before the expiry of its term, elections shall be conducted within six months and the new *Panchayat*/Municipality will hold office for the remainder of the term if the term has more than six months duration.
- And for another five years if the remaining term is less than six months.

Powers of Local Government Units Bodies

- The powers of local bodies are not exclusively defined. They can be tailor-fitted by the state governments according to the environment of the States. In general, the State Governments can assign powers to *Panchayats* and Municipalities that may enable them to prepare plans for economic development and social justice. They may also be authorized to levy, collect, or appropriate taxes.

Issues & Challenges of Local Bodies in India

The following are the issues and challenges of local bodies in India:

(a) **Scarcity of Financial Resources:** Generally, their sources of income are inadequate as compared to their functions. The taxes collected by the local bodies are not sufficient to cover the expenses of the services provided. Though, they can impose certain new taxes, the elected members of these bodies hesitate in doing so for fear of displeasing their electorate. The administrative machinery, at the disposal of these local bodies, is insufficient and ineffective. The staff, which is often underpaid, indulges in corrupt practices which lead to loss of income. Quite often, failure in collecting taxes leads to accumulation of arrears running into crores of rupees. As a result, many local bodies are on the brink of bankruptcy.

(b) **Audit Objections Unattended:** In various municipalities, audit objections remain pending for many years and, in some, even audit is not conducted regularly. It is sometimes revealed by audit that the funds borrowed at a high rate of interest lie unutilized. Action is not taken on the audit report on time, with the result that, with the passage of time, no action can be taken.

(c) **Funds Crunch:** Because of inadequate finances, the local bodies have not been able to fulfill their obligatory functions. As a result, they suffer a constant outcry from the public as well as the government. The most basic necessity, water is not supplied properly, drainage facilities do not cover the entire city, unplanned colonies and slums develop fast, menace of stray cattle on the roads continues, traffic is hazardous, roads are not properly maintained and unsafe buildings are allowed to continue to exist despite the obvious threat to the inmates and the inhabitants of the area. In short, poor sanitation, poor hygiene and shortage of basic necessities make cities and villages unsafe.

(d) **Excessive State Control:** The excessive control exercised by the State Government over local bodies is another issue. To ensure proper performance of their functions, the state government exercises legislative, administrative, financial and judicial control. This proves to be more of a curse than a boon, because, instead of providing guidance and support through the control mechanism, the control turns out to be negative, restricting the functioning of these bodies. The Constitution 74th Amendment Act has taken away the power to supersede or suspend the municipal body from the state government. However, the state government can dissolve them. The financial control over the urban bodies has also been so rigid that they have virtually no autonomy left. When the control becomes too oppressive, the relationship of the state government with the urban bodies would naturally be strained.

(e) **Postponement of Elections:** Elections to the local bodies have suffered constant postponement for indefinite time, for long after the term of an local body has expired, the state governments does not announce fresh elections and extensions are granted to the same body. The state government feels it safer and easier to deal with bureaucracy placed at the helm of the civic administration than with the popularly elected councillors. The Constitution 74th Amendment has prescribed strict conditions in this regard with a view to ensuring regularity of elections.

(f) **Lack of Adequate Training Facilities & Scarcity of Staff:** The need for adequate training of the staff has not received due emphasis. Several vacancies are not filled for years; corruption, favoritism and nepotism are rampant.

(g) **Unplanned Urbanisation:** It is generally observed that the urban bodies have failed to perform their primary duty, that is, to check the problems and complications created by rapid urbanisation. The shifting of a vast number of the rural population towards cities has led to several problems such as the unplanned growth of towns and cities. In the absence of proper planning, judicious use of land is not being made, colonies are set up without proper facilities such as schools, parks and hospitals, the growth of slums is not checked, there is a shortage of houses, traffic congestion is rampant and hardly any effective steps are taken to check urban poverty and unemployment.

(h) **Civic Responsibility is Poor:** Most of the citizens in cities and towns are least bothered event to cast their vote in municipal elections. They are also very careless with regard to the maintenance of neatness at home and on roads.

(i) **Low Level of Public Participation:** Due to lack of civic consciousness, public participation in local bodies has been negligible. When compared with village, population in cities is of heterogeneous groups and they are alienated from one another. Most of the city population was once rural and, even now, it looks at the city merely as a place to earn a livelihood and has little attachment with it. Despite, a relatively higher level of literacy and educational standards, city-dwellers do not take adequate interest in the functioning of the urban government bodies. It is ironical that the urban population has rarely, if ever, raised its voice against cases of prolonged supersession of democratic municipal bodies. The urban leadership also fails to inspire any confidence among the people and, once elected, they hardly visit their wards to learn about the gravity of the problems in their constituencies. Moreover, the urban bodies do not have proper public relations machinery, through which the achievements of the urban bodies can be communicated to the people.

(j) Elected representatives at the city- level are rendered powerless by making them subservient to the State Government.

(k) In most municipal corporations, while the mayor is the ceremonial head, the executive powers of the corporation are vested with the State government appointed commissioner.

(l) Municipal corporations are further denied their political role by the continued operation of various parastatal agencies created by the State government. These may take the form of urban development authorities (which build infrastructure) and public corporations (which provide services such as water, electricity and transportation). These agencies, which function with a certain autonomy, are accountable only to the State government, not the local government.

(m) Even urban planning and land- use regulation (globally a quintessential local government function) is with State Government--controlled development authorities or town planning bodies.

(n) Central government programmes such as the Smart Cities Mission seek to guarantee that funds allocated will not be spent on any other projects from local government.

(o) The creation of parallel institutions that disempower the elected local government.

(p) Even for performing functions that are within its purview (such as levying local taxes or undertaking civic projects above a certain budget) the local government requires State government permissions.

(q) Failure of States to implement the provisions of the 74th Amendment in its totality as per spirit of the supreme law of the land.

(r) Failure in implementation og programmes and functions. Local governments are financially constrained and do not have the administrative capacity to carry out its functions.

(s) Many of its (74th amendment) key provisions are not mandatory for the State government, hence poor or no implementation.

(t) Massive corruption in local bodies.

(u) The audit of local bodies is a sham.

(v) District administration with overlapping functions.

(w) Misutilisation of funds.

(x) Domination of senior political leaders in local body process.

Suggestions for Empowerment and Strengthening of Local Governments

The landmark 73rd and 74th Amendments to the Constitution empower the rural and urban local bodies, respectively. The Amendment Acts give them taxation powers and powers to finance basic services that the populace needed. But have they really transformed governance in India? We should look into this aspect very seriously. We need the following measures for strengthening and empowerment of local bodies in India:

Local governments should have functional autonomy

They should have financial autonomy and should aim to be financially viable

Parastatals should not be allowed to undermine the authority of ULBs

Need to establish a dedicated and a specialized trained cadre to serve and cater to the complex needs of local bodies governance

Creating an enabling framework for public-private-people partnerships, privatization and out-sourcing, where beneficial and feasible

- Mobilization of resources is an acute problem of the local bodies. In this context, Raja Chelliah Taxation Expert Committee advocates that the hands of urban authorities should be adequately strengthened to mobilize resources, take independent investment decisions and exercise a high degree of self-discipline
- Political and administrative autonomy to local bodies
- Devolution of revenues to local bodies and empowering them to levy taxes to fund part of their expenditure
- Periodic local body elections. Reservation of seats on local bodies for weaker social sections
- Creation of local database on administration
- Local voluntary and private sector organizations collaborate with local governments in addressing development issues
- Build local human capacities through improved access to health care, education and productive assets to ensure that decentralization empowers the poor
- Fixing user charge for a service to equate the cost of its provision at the margin as far as possible, for example: Water Supply
- Adopting "beneficiaries pay" and "polluters pay" principles; fiscal instruments to address both direct and indirect beneficiaries
- Reforming budgeting, accounting and auditing procedures so as to promote accountability
- Enabling preparation of city perspective, development and annual action plans, capital investment plan and capital budget and making a clear distinction between capital and revenue budgets
- Developing a transparent system of accountability and disclosure to the public and the higher levels of government through laws and regulations
- Developing laws and guidelines on information gathering, dissemination, budgeting, accounting, financial reporting, contracts, dispute settlement, design of user charges and grants, audit evaluation, etc., to fully inform the public about the consequences of decisions taken by the concerned local body
- Enabling the public to have free information and full knowledge of the role of the service providers, the cost of the services, the sources of their financing and the distribution of responsibilities, keeping in view the Freedom of Information Act
- Defining state-municipal administrative and fiscal relationships clearly on the principle of local autonomy without ambiguity and providing for state intervention in municipal affairs only in exceptional cases

Clarity of vision, objectives and commitment to address the overall challenges of urban sector at the highest authority levels

For improving efficiency of the municipal organization there is a need for decentralization of authority and a greater decision-making capability at the grassroots levels

Financial management of a large public agency like a municipal organization deserves integrated direction by managers with a professional training and commitment. Financial viability based on vigorous exploitation of the local revenue base and sound financial management cannot be compromised

Improving technical competence in the choice, design and execution of investment in infrastructure, and in its operation and maintenance

Improving human resources through training, process consultation, action research methods and role workshop

Improving responsiveness to the needs arising from urban growth, with the ability to plan development of the city and its services ahead of, or at least in pace with demand

Sensitivity to the needs of the urban poor, and a weighting of public interventions to promote their access to shelter, basic services, employment and concern for environmental protection, through public service provision and regulation of the private sector

Leadership and teamwork are essential

Keeping tax rates low and emphasizing enforcement and compliance will lead to significant increases in the property tax collection

Services like education, health care and social security, the public distribution system and old-age pension are inadequately provided to the urban poor. While designated agencies exist in rural India to address these issues, urban local bodies have not oriented themselves to ensuring that these universal services reach the urban poor. The Ministry of Housing and Urban Affairs has to work to ensure that basic services are indeed provided to the urban poor

Timely elections

Public participation especially of women should increase in Gram Sabha meetings

Women headed panchayats should increase so that social evils like child marriage, liquor ban etc. will reduce

Women raising their voice in Panchayats should increase, so that it will impact gender elections positively

Though, some studies in Tamil Nadu, Gujarat, Joint Andhra revealed a significant contribution of PRI's to boosting agriculture production, but in some States like Karnataka, several schemes were transferred to PRIs from the departments such as Agriculture, Animal Husbandry etc. and as a consequence the schemes suffered due to lack of technical guidance. Hence, this problem should be addressed

The biggest impact has been political. In most States PRI's have appointed committees to address weaker section concern but the Parji, Guj & Sadik Ali Committee of Rajasthan have concluded by and large PRI's have underperformed with regard to weaker sections issues. Hence, weaker sections concerns should be addressed

In many states, Primary and Secondary education has been transferred to PRI's but, progress is not up to the mark. Hence, measures to be taken in this regard

A comprehensive exercise should be done for broadening and deepening the revenue base of local bodies

State Governments should concentrate and prepare appropriate plans for rapid urban development and strengthen the Urban Local Bodies in view of the following:

By 2021, 41 percent of the population would be in urban areas

Presently, urban areas contribute 65 percent of GDP

Review of Property Tax

High cost of administration

The following Basic Problems of Urban Local Governments should be addressed.

Rising levels of unplanned urbanization

Overcrowding of cities and crippling infrastructure in increasing slums and poverty

Increasing health related problems

Public health issues

Pollution of all kinds- garbage, vehicular, industrial

Power and water shortages

Rising levels of crime particularly against women

Traffic congestion – strengthening of public transport system

Separate track for pedestrians

Hiking number of parking places

Fast-track property tax reforms

Cost of local tax collection and compliance should be reduced. Ceiling on profession tax under Art. 276 should be revised periodically

Enhance the fines for civic offenses – spitting on roads, littering etc.

Incentivize revenue collection by local bodies by linking it with State Government grants

Encourage municipalities to run municipal enterprises such as municipal bus service

Municipalities should be encouraged to access capital markets through instruments like municipal bonds

Conclusion

To conclude, local self-government is one of the most innovative governance change processes our country has gone through. The noble idea of taking the government of a country into the hands of the grass root level is indeed praiseworthy. However, like any system, this system has also some lacunae like problems of maladministration and recurring misappropriation of funds. But this shall not stand in the way of efficient governance; and if these ill practices are rooted out, the local governments in our country will be successful in all respects.

References

- Anirban Kashyap (1989): Panchaytiraj, Views of founding fathers and recommendation of different committees, New Delhi, Lancer Books.
- Bandyopadhyay, D., Ghosh, S. K., Ghosh, B. (2003, September 20–26): Dependency versus autonomy–identity crisis of India's panchayats. Economic & Political Weekly.
- The Local Government System in India": Commonwealth Local Government Forum.
- Mahoj Rai et al.: The state of Panchayats – A participatory perspective, New Delhi, Smscriti, 2001.
- Mohinder, S., Kumar, V.: (2005, April–June). State control over Panchayati Raj institutions. The Indian Journal of Political Science, 66(2), 221–232.
- Ramnath Jha & Sayli Udas-Mankikar: India's Urban Challenges: Recommendations for the new government (2019-2024).
- Reddy, G. (2013):Status of Decentralized Bodies: Post-73rd Amendment Scenario; Economic & Political Weekly, 38(12, 13), 1290.
- Singh, H. (1994): Constitutional base for Panchayati Raj in India: The 73rd Amendment Act; Asian Survey, 34(9), 818.

10

Financial Empowerment of Urban Local Bodies

— Chaganti Nagaraja Rao & M.A. Hussein

Introduction

The Constitution (74th) Amendment Act, 1992 envisages a bigger role for the Urban Local Bodies in the administration of cities and towns. By this Amendment 18 functions are transferred to the exclusive domain of the Urban Local Bodies (ULB) but the transfer of responsibilities is not accompanied by devolution of adequate finances to the ULBs to perform their newly assigned tasks. 'How to make cities better governed' is now the question before the municipal functionaries.

The quick pace of urbanisation brings with it several new challenges like infrastructure deficiency for the burgeoning urban population and expanding urban areas. While urbanisation is a positive economic aspect since it contributes more and more to the country's Gross Domestic Product, it also creates several problems for which adequate finances are required. Since the resource-raising capacity or Urban Local Bodies is limited there is the need for devolution of funds from higher levels of government for efficient management of urban basic services, since the increase of revenues of the ULBs has not kept pace with the increase in expenditure. The main reason for the sorry state of finances of the ULBs is that the broad based taxes are with the higher levels of government while the brunt of expenditure functions is with the ULBs. This situation necessitates the transfer of funds from higher levels of government to ULBs to offset the fiscal disabilities of the ULBs.

The problem of urban finance is that the fiscal role of the ULBs in Indian economic framework has never been systematically assessed with the result that the finances of the ULBs have always been in doldrums. The Constitution Amendment points towards a larger role for the ULBs in the country's development affairs and suggests a larger fiscal space for them. The Act has not improved the financial position of the ULBs but exacerbated the problem by the addition of new functions. This necessitates the sound financial management of the ULBs based on vigorous exploitation of local resources which is essentially required for the provision of civic infrastructure and efficient urban management. Hence augmentation of local revenues is a must to meet the maintenance cost of essential services.

According to P.K. Mohanty (2014: 152), "The share of own revenue sources in most ULBs was only about 1 percent of city income," and hence he suggests that "equipping them with suitable revenue instruments could raise their own resources in the range of 6-7 percent of city income." Revenue locally generated by ULBs fall short of revenue expenditure in all states in India, except Maharashtra and Punjab. The ULBs have, therefore, to plug loopholes in levy, assessment and collection of local taxes and non-taxes in order to improve their financial base to improve their revenue and expenditure performance since provision of better infrastructure and service delivery efficiency depend on the availability of financial resources. In most of the ULBs there is a wide gap between the requirement of revenue and actual receipt which will hamper the growth potential of the urban areas. The increasing demand for improved services is pressing hard against the limited resources and poor administrative capacity of the ULBs to cope with the problems of inadequate distribution and inequitable access to urban basic services. The ULBs have, therefore, to exploit the full potential of revenue under each source, since the standard of civic amenities provided is directly influenced by the availability of finances from all sources.

Internal Sources of Revenue to Urban Local Bodies

The major sources of income for ULBs can be broadly divided into five sources: (i) Taxes (ii) Non-Taxes (iii) Assigned Revenues (iv) Non-Plan Grants and (v) Plan Grants. While taxes and non-taxes are internal resources which are levied, assessed and collected by the ULBs themselves, assigned revenues are collected by other government departments and allotted a share of it to the local bodies. Plan and Non-plan Grants are sanctioned by the Governments-Central and State.

Mobilisation of resources by the ULBs is a Herculean task for most of the cities and towns in India. Resources are to be mobilised not only for enabling Urban Local Bodies to function efficiently and effectively but also to tide over the inadequacy of governmental assistance. There are possibilities for mobilising additional revenues at the local level both through taxation and through charging for services. ULBs should have built-in mechanism for promoting local resource mobilisation and better financial performance.

Taxes

Property Tax

Property tax is a major source of income for the ULBs but its tremendous potential is not fully exploited. That is why property tax revenues decline in real terms in many states particularly because of improper valuation. Property tax is assessed based on the annual or monthly rental value and the capital value. The significant problem of municipal property taxation is the basis of taxation. The shift from rental-value based taxation to capital-value based system improves the yield of tax since the capital value of buildings increases faster than their rental value. Further, it obviates the necessity of arriving at hypothetical rental value. But this system abnormally increases the tax with the result that protests from cash-poor and property-rich rate payers are unavoidable.

The only alternative available for the ULBs is to take up a periodical revision of rental values of the entire city and to revise property tax on buildings from time to time whenever there is a change in its occupation, change of use, change of tenant or additions or improvements made. Non-detection of these changes or delay in revising property tax on all buildings which attract revision due to the change of occupancy or use of the buildings result in loss of revenue to the ULBs. The municipal authorities should, therefore, keep a continuous watch on all the changes that occur in properties within the city or town and bring about the revision so that the financial position of the ULB will rise from year to year.

Advertisement Tax

The increasing commercial activity in urban areas would quite naturally lead to increasing advertising of their products. The increasing publicity and advertising has become another major source of income to the ULBs if all the advertisements in the urban area are properly taxed. But it is observed that most of the ULBs have not booked all the advertisements in the town thereby incurring heavy loss of revenue from this important source. When the assessment and collection of advertisement tax is privatised in certain cities there was a tremendous increase in income to the municipal corporation from this head. The only reason is the collection efficiency of advertisement tax by the private agency. The demand kept on increasing from year to year due to privatisation of collection of advertisement tax through tender-cum-auction. It is, therefore, desirable to privatise the assessment and collection of advertisement tax to fully exploit the potential under this source of income.

Vacant Land Tax

Vacant Land Tax is levied to discourage owners of lands to keep them vacant to avoid their misuse, and to encourage housing activity. There has been an unearned increase in land values in cities from year to year. But the ULBs are unable to tap even a fraction of it. Further, vacant land is taxed at a rate much higher than land with built-up property with the result that evasion of tax by vacant landowners has become the routine rather than the exception. In most cases it is difficult to locate the owners of vacant land in cities. If vacant land tax is collected only as a onetime assessment and collection it will yield sufficient demand under this source of income.

Non-Taxes

A city government of an Urban Local Body can be defined as State-Government writ small in that it has all the branches of a State Government. It consists of Revenue Section, Health Section, Engineering Section, and Town Planning Section besides the establishment section. Each section has certain sources of income called the Non-Taxes which are not properly exploited in most of the city governments.

The Revenue Section has to collect (i) Market Fee; (ii) Slaughter House Fee; (iii) Rent from Shopping Complexes; (iv) Rent from Municipal Quarters; (v) Parking Fee; (vi) Mutation Fee; and (vii) Sale of Forms etc.

The Health Section is responsible for (i) Contribution to Water Supply; (ii) Fee on Birth and Death Certificates; (iii) State Proceeds of Swept Material and Compost; (iv) Burial Ground Charges; (v) Fee for Issue of No Objection Certificates for various purposes etc.

The Engineering Section collects (i) Contribution for sanction of to Water Supply Connections; (ii) Water charges for non-domestic supply of water; (iii) Sewerage Connections; (iv) Monthly sewerage connection charges; (v) Road cutting charges for laying private lines for various purposes.

The Town Planning Section is authorised for collecting (i) Building Licence fee; (ii) Layout fee; (iii) Development Charges; (iv) Betterment charges; (v) Compounding (on unauthorised building constructions); (vi) Encroachment fee; (vii) Other town planning receipts.

Measures for Improvement of Finances under Non-Taxes

The expenditure on provision of civic services like piped water, sewers, drains, roads, electricity, garbage collection, transport, health care and education has gone high up. The cost-effectiveness of infrastructure is significantly reduced due to the widening gulf between the expenditure incurred on provision of these services and income derived from the recipients.

Inadequate finances or bankruptcy of Urban Local Bodies disable them to effectively address issues relating to slums, poverty, pollution, congestion, environmental degradation, crime, social unrest and the like. Hence, additional sources of revenue are to be searched to meet the ever-increasing cost of infrastructure and maintenance of essential services. Efficient collection of non-tax revenue will, therefore, is of utmost importance to solve these problems at least to some extent. The most important non-tax sources in which ULBs show slackness are discussed here.

Water Charges: In almost all ULBs in India including the Metropolitan cities water charges are collected on flat rate basis irrespective of the quantity of water consumed by the consumers. As a result there is a heavy loss of revenue in respect of charges collected for the supply of protected water. In no single ULB the income derived from water supply is equal to the expenditure incurred for supplying protected water to the consumers. The best alternative is to collect water charges on metered basis. But there is a wide protest from the public against collection of water charges on the basis of metered system. The deficit is, therefore, to be met from other sources. Thus, protected water supplied in cities is heavily subsidised. This gap increases from year to year resulting in escalation in the cost of supply of water. Besides the loss of revenue there is heavy loss of safe drinking water due to unauthorised water tap connections given to the public by the field level functionaries who are interested in illegal earnings. The mismanagement of water supply system by the field level functionaries is largely responsible for the heavy financial deficit in the ULBs.

When a survey of civic amenities available and required to the citizens was conducted in certain cities, about one-third of the total water supply connections in the cities were found to be unauthorised ones. When they were regularised duly collecting the penal fee it had brought adequate revenue to the city governments. This example emphasises the need to take up similar measures in other cities to avoid loss of revenue from water supply as well as saving non-revenue water. The best way of realising this is by serving an integrated notice for both house tax and water supply charges which would enable the ULBs to improve their revenue as well as timely collection of house taxes and water charges. Another important measure is to collect water charges from no-domestic users on metered system.

Drainage Cess

Drainage cess is levied from building owners as a component of property tax but not separately for each drainage connection provided to the building. Towns/cities which have this system must concentrate on providing drainage connections and by assessing drainage cess separately and not as a component of property tax as this source will fetch considerable income if each connection is assessed separately.

Market Fees and Shop Room Rents

This is one of the important sources of income for all ULBs in the country which is being paid scant attention and the loss from which is not properly watched. Enquiries have revealed that the ULBs incur recurring loss of revenue from this source of income due to neglect of municipal authorities.

Every ULB has to grant market fee collection rights every year and the lessee is bound to pay the lease on monthly basis. Whenever the lessee defaults to pay the monthly lease it is the bounden duty of the municipal authorities to take timely legal action against the defaulter, to realise the lease. But it was observed that most of the ULBs have not shown proper attention to it within the stipulated time with the result the ULBs have incurred heavy loss of revenue every year.

While that is the case with regard to market fee collection lease rights, the shop rooms owned by ULBs are let out without watching the rents to be collected from tenants, besides not renewing the rent at revised rates as per the Gazette Notification. In certain ULBs the rents were not revised for a decade resulting in heavy loss of revenue. Timely collection of shop room rents from the rented municipal shop rooms as well as revising the rents from time to time is the bounden duty of municipal authorities to protect their finances in public interest. This is an area which should be kept watch on.

Encroachment Fees

Trades carried on in municipal road margins fetch heavy profits to the traders while the fee collected from them is nominal. Encroachment fees fetch considerable income to the ULBs if properly assessed leaving no single trade without assessing and collecting encroachment fee. Most of the municipal sites and road margins are encroached upon by small traders who make abnormal profits since investment is less and profit is more on these trades. But the ULBs pay scant attention to it. In respect of all unobjectionable encroachments, fee can be levied and collected from encroachers of municipal lands to realise adequate revenue.

Building Licence Fees

Construction activity is very fast in all cities and towns of India. Building licence fee assessed and collected for according licence to construct building is a major source of income to ULBs. But it is observed that there is heavy leakage of revenue from this major source due to mismanagement of the Town Planning staff of the ULBs who wrongly calculate the fee to promote their vested interests that result in heavy loss of revenue to the ULBs. Even the Vigilance and Enforcement Department had to poke its nose into the serious irregularities that have kept into the collection of building licence fee in certain ULBs in certain states. A keen watch on the construction activity and the income generated from the Town Planning Section will remarkably improve the income to the ULBs. The Governments should evolve a stringent system to avoid evasion of licence fee so that loss of revenue can be minimised.

Parking Fees

Parking fee collected in most of the cities including metropolitan cities is very low. This is another important source of revenue to the ULBs, particularly in big cities but the potential is not fully exploited with the result that development of parking spaces is stunted. Improper maintenance of parking spaces results in traffic congestion on roads and traffic problems. Reasonable enhancement of parking fee from time to keeping in view the maintenance costs is not treated as a burden by the users of parking space since it is essential for them to safely park their vehicles. Fast growing cities can generate substantial revenue if parking places are privatised, particularly in congested and busy commercial localities of towns and cities.

Trade Licence Fees

Licence fee for running shops and business establishments are another important source of income for the Health Section of the ULBs. It has been observed that most of the small trades are not levied the trade licence fee that results in heavy loss of revenue. Govinda Rao and Richard Bird (2014:214) say that "the present system of issuing licences and the common flouting of regulations by shops and establishments provide erroneous and highly undesirable rent-seeking opportunities for local officials." It is observed in certain cities that the number of trades levied and assessed to licence fees is not even five percent of the actual number of trades functioning. Thus, there is heavy loss of revenue from this source due to non-booking of trades for granting licence. If income from this source is not adequate, it is due to the non-listing of trades for collection of licence fees from the trades by the licensing authorities and awful corruption among the field level functionaries of the ULBs.

Trade licence must be collected from all trades without leaving a single trade unassisted to avoid loss of income from this important source of income. The trade licence fee is very small in each individual case but the total demand from this source is huge. The number of trades in a city can approximately be the number of non-residential property tax assessments. Preparation of an inventory of the existing trades in every urban area by a private agency will considerably improve income to the ULBs from this source and minimise mismanagement by licensing officials.

Tax vs. Charges

Urban Local Bodies in India have been faced with endemic problems of poor cost recovery and low quality of services. Certain essential services are not cost-effective, for example, protected water supply. In most of the cities the expenditure incurred for supply of protected water is double the income derived from sale of water, with the result that the ULBs have to meet the additional expenditure from its general funds. Thus water supply is heavily subsidised beyond the financial capacity of most of the ULBs. It is, therefore, suggested that where the service can be measured and beneficiaries can be identified (like water supply, garbage collection etc) user charges are the best financing instrument. Where services cannot be measured and beneficiaries cannot be identified (street lighting, traffic control etc) the best way of financing them is through taxation on local residents; in respect of development of infrastructure like roads, public utility services etc, the appropriate source is through grants from higher level of government.

Economic Self-sufficiency of the ULBs

The ULBs have to financially strengthen themselves with their own resources of revenue at least to meet the maintenance cost of essential services. Unless the services provided are cost-effective, financial self-sufficiency of ULBs cannot be achieved. In most of the ULBs of India, less than 10 percent of the cost of services is recovered through user charges, and in a few others cost recovery is between 10 to 20 percent. There are hardly three or four ULBs in India in which the cost recovery ranges from 50 to 75 percent. User charges are grossly underexploited while property tax, which constitutes the primary source of local tax revenue to ULBs is regarded as an unbearable burden by the tax payers. Even after all taxes and non-taxes are assessed and collected to the fullest extent there remains a wide gap between the cost of the services provided by the ULBs and the income generated through all sources of revenue locally. As P.K. Mohanty (2014: 149) rightly says, "The share of tax revenues in total municipal revenues has dwindled, eroding local fiscal autonomy. User charges are yet to dominate the municipal scene." ULBs have, therefore, to focus their attention on user charges and cost recovery to meet the O&M charges of water supply. There are certain services like protected water supply, excess water usage, clearance of bulk garbage from bulk garbage generating units, sewerage etc which can be measured and for which the beneficiaries can be identified and can be financed through direct user charges so that the service would be cost-effective and the quality of services can be maintained at a reasonable level. Cost recovery of certain important services is an important measure of the municipal finances for retaining the self-sustainability of the service. Low cost recovery results in poor service quality. Since the resource-raising capacity of ULBs is limited by statutes, Governments (State and Central) should give serious thought of this issue, failing which the ULBs cannot discharge the larger responsibilities assigned to them by the Constitution.

Certain suggestions in this regard are: Government should enhance the taxation and revenue raising powers of the ULBs; create special infrastructure development fund; make provision of statutory payment to local bodies at fixed percentage of recurrent revenues of central and state government departments' budget as grants, thus giving ULBs more flexibility to meet local needs and demands. The Government of Tamil Nadu has created such a fund which could be utilised exclusively for creating infrastructure facilities in urban areas. All other states do better by emulating this example.

Additional resource mobilisation for infrastructure development is not only inevitable in the present situation for meeting the challenges of fast urban growth but also due to the fact that in the absence of such development of infrastructure, the quality of urban life deteriorates; and it ultimately hampers the positive aspects of urbanisation, that is, economic and human development.

Devolution of Funds

At present the city governments are unable to respond to the increasing infrastructure demands of the citizens owing to poor financial position of the ULBs and the lack of revenue-raising powers of the ULBs to improve their own resources, inevitably necessitating the devolution of funds from the central and state governments to ULBs to meet the increasing expenditure on provision of urban basic services. International economic competition is linked to cities and as such city governance should be improved in all aspects. The increasing urban infrastructure deficiency in fast growing cities is a hindrance for economic development of the country since cities are places of innovation and development. But the inadequate finances of city governments will not enable them to provide the infrastructure needed for burgeoning urban population and expanding cities. Financial assistance from central and state governments is, therefore, inevitable and essential for urban infrastructure development. It is high time Governments at all levels had addressed this issue seriously to sustain the quality of urban life.

The CAA points towards a larger role for the ULBs in the country's development affairs and suggests a larger fiscal role for them. The problem of urban finance is that the fiscal role in India's economic framework has never been systematically assessed with the result that the finances of the

ULBs have always been in doldrums except in a few states. Though the CAA provides for a review of financial position of the ULBs once every five years and provides for revenue-sharing arrangement between the ULBs and state governments, the assignment of responsibilities to the ULBs has not been matched with devolution of funds to enable the ULBs perform their tasks efficiently. Unless the finances of the ULBs are improved through devolution of finds from the state and central governments, mere transfer of functions from central government to ULBs serves no useful purpose. The CAA has not improved the financial position of the ULBs but exacerbated the problem by adding new functions. There is a need to mobilise additional resources to cover the increasing financial requirements of the ULBs for service provision and fulfil the constitutional obligations ordained on the ULBs by the CAA.

In regard to devolution of finds from the governments to the ULBs there should be a systematic method of transfer of state resources to support the development activities of the ULBs, particularly the development of infrastructure like weaker section housing, augmentation of protected water supply, development of parks and open spaces, provision of thoroughfares, sewerage treatment plants, solid waste recycling units etc. At present new infrastructure projects are funded through budgetary support from the central and state governments laid down in the five-year plans and annual plans which is inadequate. In order to fill the gap between supply and demand of urban infrastructure services the government has no alternative but to increase the allocation of resources for the most required basic services.

The need for devolution of additional finances to the ULBs is further necessitated by the dissatisfaction with the quality of urban infrastructure services which is constantly pushing investment out of the fringes of prominent urban agglomerations. The State Finance Commissions constituted under Article 243Y of the Constitution must review the financial position of the ULBs and make recommendations to the government as to the measures needed to improve their financial position in such way that the fiscal gap is filled. In order to fill the gap there should be a good intergovernmental transfer of revenues which should be at a pre-determined percentage of sales tax, other shared taxes or general state revenues. Urban infrastructure projects must be financed by centre and states each project wise and leave the maintenance part to the ULBs.

The best criteria to be adopted for devolution of funds from states to the ULBs is the per capita own resources as the most feasible summary indicator of a city's vulnerability to volatility. There is the need for a formula-based regular devolution of funds to provide better infrastructure, improve governance and to build a modern urban India that is economically productive, socially just and environmentally sustainable, since the future of Indian economy wholly depends on urban India. The formula for such devolution of funds to the ULBs should be the difference between the total annual income of the ULB and the total annual expenditure, both capital and maintenance. The devolution of funds from the centre to the ULBs should be equitable between regions, and should be so designed as to provide correct incentives to urban local bodies to mobilise local revenues and to pursue appropriate policies. The other alternative is to fill the fiscal gap through plan grants, that is, grants for specific purposes.

References

- Mohanty, P.K. (2014): Cities & Public Policy: An Agenda for India, Sage, India.
- Rao, Govinda and Bird, Richard (2014): Urbanisation in India, Sage, New Delhi.

11

Administrative Responsiveness with Respect to Public Service Delivery in India: A Study of E-Disha Centres in Haryana

— *Rajbir Singh Dalal*

Introduction

India is the largest democracy of the world having over 125 crore population which is 18 percent of the world whereas it owns just 2 percent of the total land. Moreover, India has the highest youth population in the world. So far the economic development and growth is concerned, it is the fastest growing economy of the world during 2012-2016 (with 7.5 percent GDP) which was more than 5 percent in 2019-20. It has acquired the status of fifth largest economy of the world with volume or size of 2.68 trillion dollar (3.27 percent of world economy) and surpassed even the economies of Britain (2.62 trillion dollar) and France (2.58 trillion dollar) by December, 2019.[1]

Simultaneously, India is the biggest consumer market of the world and in the era of Liberalisation, Privatisation and Globalisation (LPG), the quality of administration prevailing in the country is of great significance to the public in general and the marginalized and deprived sections in particular. The LPG process has widened the gap of the rich and the poor. The irony of the Indian economy is that on one hand, the quantum and number of the riches is incessantly increasing in the country and 200 millionaire persons are owning more than 500 million dollar property (each) in 2017 and on the other hand, about one third of its population is still forced to live on one dollar per head per day.[2] Simultaneously, the debt on India is 2.5 percent of the world total debt which is far less than that of the USA (31.8 percent), Japan (18.8 percent) and China (7.9 percent). Thus the Indian economy has shown rapid growth during the last one and half decades (2000-2015).

No doubt, in the era of LPG, the sphere of state activities has diminished but still in India public sector is vital and over 1.5 crore personnel are employed therein. The developmental and welfare activities carried out by state are important for the public in general and the weaker sections in particular. But equally important is the issue of quality of services rendered by the state.

In the entire human history, states have been classified good or bad on the basis of their services to the citizens both in quantum and quickness. However, in independent India there is an overhaul change in the nature and role of state as compared to its colonial rule. Accordingly, a number of administrative reforms have been incorporated in public administration to make it more and more effective, efficient, people oriented and responsive, yet the public delivery system in the country is not up to the mark and a number of challenges are there. E-*Disha*/ E-District project is meant for electronic delivery of high volume citizen centric services at district and *tehsil* levels which comprises of 170 State Government to Citizens (G2C) e-services of 24 Departments and 90 Business to Citizens (B2C) and 12 (G2C) services of Government of India[4]. These services comprise of various types of certificates such as Birth and Death Certificates, Caste and Income Certificates, *Aadhar* and EPIC cards, Marriage registration, Domicile and Vehicle registration, Driving License, Property sale, purchase and deed, Land registration certificates etc.[3] The ICT initiatives taken up by the state government under this project are: CM Window, e-*Disha*, e-*Girdavari*, e-*Mausam Krishi Sewa*, e-*HARLIS* etc.

Therefore, in the present write up a modest attempt has been made to define the concept of administrative responsiveness, assess its impact in terms of public service delivery in Haryana in context of e-*Disha* centres. Simultaneously, the constraints and remedies of public service delivery through e-*Disha* centres have been highlighted.

E-*Disha*: Concept

Administrative responsiveness refers to the ability of administration to react quickly or responding with emotions to the public cause. In other words, it refers to the quality of administration reacting to public needs and causes, quickly and positively. According to Cambridge Advanced Learner Dictionary, "Administrative responsiveness is the quality of having a reaction to public cause or affairs by administration specially a quicker and positive reaction". Administrative sensitiveness and sensitization are its synonyms. The term 'Administrative Responsibility' is more frequently used for administrative responsiveness. However, both have minute difference. The word 'responsiveness' has some ethical, moral and emotional values whereas responsibility owns legal bindings. The former is intrinsic in nature whereas the latter is extrinsic one. How the administration responds to the citizen grievances, needs, queries and concern along with their resolution and remedies. It is the government concern to the citizens. Administrative responsiveness is the extension of administrative accountability which has raised frustration among people owing to poor or mal-administration. The services rendered by the State should be to the satisfaction of the consumers or people. It is also referred to as cutting edge administration. It is a problem solving administration which is citizen-centric, democratic and participatory in nature or it is a sort of representative administration. It is a question of administrative attitude or concerned with administrative culture which focus on providing efficient, cost effective and quick services to the citizens.

In India, since 1996 during the conference of the Chief Secretaries, the need of administrative responsiveness was felt which was further taken up in the meeting of the Chief Ministers. The use of Information Communication Technology (ICT) has enhanced the objectivity, quickness and efficiency in administration multifold. That's why the e-governance concept has made the government around the clock (24x7) and it is everywhere and anywhere.

The e-*Disha* centres are the specially created sites or offices in the Haryana state at District and *Tehsil* levels where most of the public services are rendered and the beneficiary/ client has not to move from one place or office to another for getting different types of services from the administration. Thus it is an attempt to harness the need of administrative responsiveness through these centres.

Attempts towards Administrative Responsiveness

Various committees and commissions including Paul H. Apple by Committee (1950), Gorewala Committee (1951), K. Santhanam Committee (1964), first Administrative Reforms Commission (1967-70) and second Administrative Reforms Commission (2004-07) etc. have given detailed and specific reports for administrative reforms in the country. The emergence of the concept of good governance in 1992 and introduction of computers and ICT in public sector are vital in this regard. Democratic decentralization provisions (73rd and 74th CAAs, 1992), the Citizens Charter Act, 1998, Anti-Corruption Laws, 1988, Central Vigilance Commission Act, 2003, Establishment of *Lokpal* and *Lokayukta* institutions through different Central and provincial legislations, *Lok Adalats*, Regulatory Authorities Acts like IRDA, TRAI, RERA etc., Right to Information Act, 2005 and Right to Service Act, 2014 are considered as the significant initiatives in ascertaining Administrative responsiveness in the country, in general and, in the state of Haryana, in particular. The concepts of Public Grievance Redressal Committee which meets monthly and chaired by a State Government's minister and well attended by the top bureaucracy of the district as well as the C. M. Window which is monitored at the highest level, are very effective measures to ascertain administrative responsiveness in public administration.

The e-*Disha* centre scheme was introduced by Haryana Government to provide hassle free and efficient services to the people with utmost transparency and objectivity in the administration under the Right to Services Act, 2014. This Act has made the public services as a right of citizens and developed a network of it with punitive provisions in case of failure. Now the different types of services are made in time-bound manner and that too in a single building or centre.

Constraints

No doubt, the use of e- governance equipments like ICT, biometric machines, CCTV camera, token system etc. in e- *Disha* centers has enhanced the administrative responsiveness to a greater extent. Still the centres are not full proof. There are some obstacles faced by these centres in the form of lack of regular staff, poorly motivated, untrained and poorly paid staff. Majority of them are outsourced or contractual who have always the apprehension or fear of discontinuity of their services or concern for job security. Lack of adequate resources and their proper maintenance, poor infrastructure like building, equipments, electricity, internet connectivity etc. are the other obstacles in smooth functioning of these centres. The overburdened key officials like the Deputy Commissioner, Sub-Divisional Magistrate, *Tehsildar,* etc. who are the controlling, supervisory and commanding officers, also put a negative effect on their performance on one hand and provides space to the petty officials to work as per their whims and desires, discretion and other considerations.

It has also been observed that a nexus or mafia comprising of typists, tickets or stamp vendors and the official in e-*Disha* centers remains active in these centres which adversely affect their objective and impartial functioning. The unaware, illiterate and poor people or clients have limited options to escape from the clutches of aforementioned mafia or hawks. They are usually duped by them. Sometimes resourceful clients promote the trends of out of turn benefits or not to follow the instructions and prescribed procedure which paves way to make the mafia active. The cases or complaints taken up in the meetings of Public Grievances Committee are very limited and decided well in advance; hardly any complaint is taken up out of the box or on the spot. Similarly, the fake and revengeful complaints are floating the C. M, Window which has made it almost useless or irrelevant. Owing to these fictitious complaints, the genuine complaints are overlooked.

Conclusion

Despite all efforts, like use of token system, CCTV camera, photography of each beneficiary, biometric entries etc., the e-*Disha* Centres are working and performing to a variety of degree depending upon the quality of personnel's engaged in rendering the services, supervision and control of key officials, awareness and vigilance of beneficiary etc. to get the services. Though more than 200 State services of 29 State departments and 25 Central Services are covered under these centres which are time-bound and even provisions of penalty are there if the designated officers fail to provide service within the stipulated period. The client or service seeker can file first and second appeals against the decision or lapses of designate officers. These services are covered under the Right to Service Act, 2014 and this Act even makes provision for establishment of Haryana Right to Service Commission, a statutory and quasi-judicial body.

Thus these centres have contributed a lot in ascertaining transparency, accountability and openers in public administration, hence paved way for administrative responsiveness. Moreover, the proper training, supervision, control and motivation of the personnel concerned will help in developing a healthy environment and administrative culture in the state. The consumers or service seekers are also a vital component in this entire process and their awareness, sincerity and honesty will strengthen the notion of administrative responsiveness.

References

1. cia.gov, census.gov
2. https: howmuch.net/articles/the-ultra-wealthy-by country.
3. http: e-Disha/Haryana.gov.in url 4-4-2020 at 3:00 P.M.
4. Govt. of Haryana, Chandigarh, No. 7/31/2014-3AR dated 15.02.2016

12

Role of Digital Technology in Governance for the Local Development: Issues in Local Government Administration of Upcoming Smart Cities in India: A Case Study of Nagpur District

— Neelima Deshmukh

Introduction

Digital India is a latest flagship programme of Government of India to transform India into complete digitally empowered as well as IT enabled and knowledge economy of the world. The main aim of this brainchild of PM Narendra Modiji is to provide Indian citizens electronic government services by reducing the paper work and reducing the corruption and red tapism saving the manpower and time. No doubt it is a very good technique of good governance which was launched on 1st July 2015 to ensure that the government services are made available to the citizens electronically by improving online infrastructure and internet connectivity. The digital India provides intensified impetus for further momentum and the progress for e-governance and would promote inclusive growth that covers electronic services, products, devices manufacturing and the job opportunities. The main aim is to reform governance through technology. This three dimensional vision of this programme is to provide digital utility to every citizen Governance and Services on demand and Digital empowerment of the citizens.

E-Governance, Good Governance & Smart Governance

In the present electronic era, the Governance, Good Governance, Smart Governance, or e-Governance, are the ways forward in every field including administration or management in particular to make citizen's life decent and better. Fully based on digitalization, thorough advanced technologies makes it a basic very essential factor, but taking it to a grass root level through local governments amongst the public is a very difficult and challenging task. Hence topmost priority is being given by the government to strengthen the process of digitalization at all levels. The need for this was identified and given a definite shape in 2015. This becomes all the more must in the states in which one or more cities have been selected under the Smart City Mission for the development. There are many problems and intricacies are involved which are ultimately having their impact and influence on the efficiency and the success of the implementation of the ambitious project that calls for intense study and analysis the various dimensions involved there in.

The practice of good governance has been widely facilitated with the use Information & Communication Technology (ICT) It. is globally used to deliver services to its citizens in most effective, efficient and transparent manner. India being a land of diversity spanning across culture, traditions, languages and uneven economic conditions needs effective governance as a tool particularly for the rural population for all round development of Rural Society. It is no more technological innovation available only to few elites, but it is a need of hour and has become vital necessity for efficient, transparent and democratic governance and public service delivery too. India too has been successfully incorporating e-governance techniques for service delivery and building citizen-centric administration but still there is a need to develop more holistic, easily accessible participative approach to e-governance. The issues of equality and development in socio-economic fields still remains farfetched but equality, empowerment, participation and transformation seems to be achievable through virtual world of internet which has become a powerful tool of shaping the public opinion as well as good governance through the use of digital and ICT tools leading to real empowerment of the people. All the more its importance increases many fold when it aims at development at grass-roots levels of the local bodies which are committed to the public empowerment in letter and spirits for its face-lifting.

Thus e-governance in its essence is application of Information Technology to government functioning in order to create Simple, Moral, Accountable, Responsive, and Transparent (SMART) Governance. While e-governance is defined as mere a delivery of government services and information to public using electronic means, e-governance allows for direct participation of the constituents in government activities. E-governance is the development, deployment and enforcement of the policies, laws, and regulations necessary to support the functioning of knowledge society as well as e-governance. Application of e-governance in the recent past have demonstrated surprising results in terms of quality services, data bank creation, tracking and monitoring system, interacting with departments and related organizations. If the attributes of good governance are transparency, efficiency, responsiveness and accountability, e-governance is the means to attain these attributes through application of technology.

Importance of Good Governance

Good Governance conceptualized in the past as ideal state of *Ram Rajya* has suddenly entered into the vocabulary of Public Administration since 1990s. Traditionally, the governance refers to the form of political system and the manner in which the power is exercised in utilizing country's economic and social resources for the development. Good governance is associated with efficient and effective administration in a democratic framework. It is purposive and the development oriented administration which is committed to the improvement of the quality of life of the people. It implies high level of organisational effectiveness and also relates to the capacity of centre of power of political and administrative system to cope with the emerging challenges of the society. It refers to the adoption of new values of governance to establish the efficiency, legitimacy and credibility of the system. In simple terms good governance can be considered as citizen friendly, citizen caring and responsive administration.

Good and humane governance is the most important issue faced by the country today which is tottering under the weight of political and bureaucratic corruption. Good governance implies gearing up of the government machinery and administrative structure to provide responsive, transparent, clean, and people friendly administration. Further it is also considered as an act or manner of governing the way of control. It is linked up with the role of the state what it can do or cannot do matching its capacity and the resources to undertake the task assigned for it.

Good Governance from the Systems Perspectives

Administration *vis*-a-*vis* does not function in isolation. It has to respond to the changing situation every now and then responding to the public demands and the call of nation and need of the hour effectively and the governance operates under the fluctuating scenario of currents, undercurrents, cross currents etc, coping up with the constant change hence needs to be seen from the systems perspectives facing various problems and challenges from various aspects for delivering the goods and services to the public as an end product.

E Governance & SMART Governance

With the global advent of Good Governance, Structural Adjustment Programme introducing New Economic Policies, in 1991 India was facing a new challenges of Liberalization, Privatization and Globalization, posed a challenges to respond to the process of development which was governed by market as a principal factor across the international borders inviting attention of the scholars, policy makers, administrators to the struggle for existence and the survival of fittest. In this process extremely technocracy situation aroused which was effectively contributing to handling the change successfully. In order to respond to the tenets of New Public Management (NPM) philosophy to ensure the speedy delivery of the results latest technology oriented computer era emerged on the scene giving rise to e-Governance system which was totally a new concept and venture for the Indian society to adopt but there was no choice other than to respond to this challenge particularly in the rural development background as majority of Indian population hails from the rural background.

Smart Cities

The ambitious project of Smart Cities in India came into an existence on 15th August 2015 when the Prime Minister Shri Narendra Modi made this announcement from the Red Fort on the historical occasion. The objectives of the Smart Cities Mission is to promote cities that provide core infrastructure and give a decent quality of life to its citizens, a clean and sustainable environment and applications of the smart solutions. The focus is on the sustainable environment and inclusive development. The idea is to look at compact areas, create a replicable model which will act like a light house to other aspiring cities. Smart Cities Mission of Government of India is a bold initiative meant to set the examples that can be replicated both within and outside the Smart City catalyzing the creation of similar Smart Cities in various regions and the part of the country.

Accordingly, the purpose of Smart Cities Mission is to drive economic growth and improve the quality life of the people by enabling the local area development and harnessing the technology that leads to the smart outcomes. Area based development will transform the existing areas (retrofit and redevelop) including the slums into the better planned ones, thereby improving the livability of the whole city. New areas Greenfield would be developed around the cities in order to accommodate the expanding population in urban areas; application of the smart solutions will enable the cities to use technology information and the data to improve infrastructure and services. Comprehensive development in this way will improve the quality of life, create employment and enhance the incomes for all, especially the poor and disadvantaged leading to inclusive cities. Comprehensive development in this way will improve the quality of life, create employment and enhance the incomes for all, especially the poor and disadvantaged leading to inclusive cities.

According to the Ministry of Housing & Urban Affairs, till now 97 Special Purpose Vehicles (SVPs) have been constituted to execute the Projects selected under Smart Cities Mission. Tenders have been issued for 1686 Projects worth Rs. 63,000 crores in various Smart cities while 1200 projects more than Rs. 38000 crores are under the implementation.[1] Smart Cities Mission is the largest mission with citizen consultations ever undertaken and has a long incubation programme. Every city took about 12-15 months to establish SVPs and identify Project Management Consultants (PMC), but now with 97 Special Purpose Vehicles and 82 PMCs in place the mission is going well and truly on its way (Ministry Tweeted). Each smart city will have an SVP headed by full time CEO and have nominees of Central Government, State Government and Urban Local Bodies on its Board. Additionally in order to provide safety and better services to the citizens, 11 State of the Art Command and Control Centres have been operationalised, and another 17 Centres are on their way. Tenders have been called for additional 31 Centers across the Country.[2] Under the Mission cities propose to take up various projects including smart roads, rejuvenation of water bodies, cycle tracks, walking paths, smart classrooms, skill development centres, upgrading health facilities and Pan city project like integrated command and control centre.

Nagpur Smart City

E-governance issues assumes greater importance in the context of Nagpur district as it is one of the 100 cities included in the list of smart cities aimed at the all-round development throughout the country and it is emerging very fast as a not only as Metro city but also the smart city working for its holistic development on war footing for meeting the parameters of global standards, with huge infrastructure coming up to cater to needs of the globalization and the citizen of this new era. With the advent of international ambitious project of MIHAN (The Multi-modal International Hub Airport at Nagpur.

In order to attract the foreign investors all the plans, programmes and strategies are being implemented through local institutions such as Nagpur Municipal Corporation, Nagpur Improvement Trust, *Zilla Parishad* and other Panchayat Raj Institutions effectively and efficiently. Further due to the continuous migration of people from neighboring and other various areas, the population has grown up to the large extended and the city limits have been extended to the additional radius of 25 kms., including 721 villages. Naturally the existing set up of local government institutions is finding it difficult to cope up with the situation and are facing the problems of various nature such as administrative, financial, legal, social which are hindering the process of development. Nagpur being the seat of political power, with committed leadership, and tremendous support from ruling party, is expected to deliver the results in effective and measurable terms but the various factors are hampering the growth and the development of this sub capital of Maharashtra. One needs to study what are those factors.

Nagpur District: The Evolving Metro Region of Vidarbha

Nagpur is the third largest city of Maharashtra and is sub-capital of state. It is the 13th largest urban agglomeration in India and the largest city in Vidarbha Region which comprises of 11 districts. It has one of the highest literacy rate of 91.92 percent among all the urban agglomerations in India, and one of the proposed Smart Cities from Maharashtra.[3]

Since1990s the agglomeration of the city has rapidly expanded beyond the municipal boundaries. The unplanned growth has posed certain challenges for the future growth of the city and its fringes in an organized manner. With a view to achieve balanced development within the region, the Nagpur Improvement Trust (NIT) has been notified as the Special Planning Authority (SPA) for the Nagpur Metropolitan Area (NMA) and entrusted with preparation of a Statutory Development Plan as per provisions of the MRTP Act, 1966. The notified NMA comprises areas outside the Nagpur city and includes 721 villages under 9 tehsils of the Nagpur District spreading across an area of 3,567 km^2.

In 1999, the government of Maharashtra declared that the Nagpur Metropolitan Area shall comprise all of Nagpur city, Nagpur *gramin* (rural areas near Nagpur), Hingna, Parseoni, Mauda and Kamptee Taluka and parts of Savner, Kalmeshwar, Umred and Kuhi. The boundaries of the "Metro region" around the municipal corporation limits of the city have been defined as per the notification with the addition of almost 721villages around the city.

In 2002, the government extended the jurisdiction of the Nagpur Improvement Trust (NIT) by 25 to 40 kms. This new area was defined under clause 1(2) of NIT Act-1936 as "Nagpur Metropolitan Area".[4]

Nagpur Metro Rail

The Nagpur Metro Rail project is announced by the state government of Maharashtra for the city with the expenses of 4,400 cr and 3,800 cr rupees for its two phases of 25 km (from Sitabuldi to MIHAN and Butibori via Airport) and 20 km (Sitabuldi to Automotive Square in Kamptee) respectively.

The site inspection has already begun in March 2012 with the initiatives from Nagpur Improvement Trust. The project will be executed by a new company called Nagpur Metro Rail Co. Ltd (NMRCL) formed under the NIT. In July 2015, the project has been approved by government of

Maharashtra and has been given "In Principle" nod by MoUD of Government of India. The *Bhoomipujan* for Metro rail work has been performed on 21 August 2014 at the hands of Prime Minister Shri Narendra Modi.

The Multi-modal International Hub Airport at Nagpur (MIHAN)

MIHAN is a project for the Dr. Babasaheb Ambedkar International Airport, Nagpur. It is the biggest economic development project currently underway in India in terms of investments. The project aims to exploit the central location of Nagpur and convert the airport into a major cargo hub with integrated road and rail connectivity. This project consists of two parts:

- An international airport to act as a cargo hub and
- A Special Economic Zone (SEZ) with residential zone covering an area of 40.25 km^2 on the southern end of Nagpur.

The government of Maharashtra formed a special purpose entity, Maharashtra Airport Development Company, for the development of MIHAN. The project is financed by Indian banks with a loan of INR 3,000 million along with investment from the state government and Airports Authority of India. With a projected target of serving 14 million passengers and handling 0.87 million tons of cargo, this is one of the largest aviation projects in India. The estimated capital cost of the project is INR 2581 crores (by the year 2035) and it is supposed to generate revenues INR 5280 crores.

With the growing challenges of modernization and the expected response of the government to meet those, the government of Maharshtra has its commitment for the development it has undertaken two ambitious programmes for world wide connectivity for free trade according to new terms of globalisation providing facilities for its economic activities from local to global level raising not only the standards of living of a common man but bettering the job opportunities and achieving the international standards. Since India has adopted the model of Britain for its entire practical purposes this evolving metro city is expected to be more or less on the line of London city. Needless to say that it is a Herculean task creating a landmark in the Indian history facilitating the very fast transition of development phase which was a day dream for all of us. India being a signatory to Millennium Development Programme along with the newly introduced Happiness Index, creation of infrastructural facilities as a way bridge to respond to the achievement of developed state is its established priority.

Nagpur Metropolitan Area comprises of all Nagpur city and the rural area including 721 villages under the 9 *tehsils* of the district. Therefore e-governance as an instrument to the local to global level development and coping up of the challenges of LPG the local government has face many challenges and overcome the problems and the issues of administration responding to change of paradigm of New Public Management. Also while launching such an extra big venture it would be appropriate to visualize its prospects as well to have clear picture and blue print of the committed vision and mission. Therefore this topic has been of immense importance with its practical relevance and the need of the hour from the from the systems perspectives. If very thing goes as per plans the Nagpur city located at zero mile distance would be seeing the new modern era meeting the needs of new generation with a sustainable development, Although the crucial role of digital technology cannot be undermined at any point of time in the context of smart governance it is a very tough proposal to implement the same on the gigantic level of building Smart Cities of international standards with a progressive vision on account various administrative, financial, technical, legal, and social issues which are intermingling with each other from the Systems Perspective in deed. Out of the many few problem areas are enumerated as follows:

Issues and the Problem Areas

Rural -Urban Divide: A lop sided Development

The infrastructural development work like constructions of roads, flyovers, bridges, commencement of Metro Mono Rail project, facilities and development of facilities for attracting the international companies through its MIHAN project is going on in its full swing throughout the city is creating lot of inconveniences to the citizens in terms of distorted traffic at times leading to the loss of lives agreed it's all part of the game, to By now the Nagpurians are used to this life, true to the slogan today's pain is tomorrows again. But there is a huge discrepancy observed while delivering the performances, the urban area /city is coming up very fast but at the same time the rural area seems to be neglected and devoid of any mentionable work, so the rift urban–rural continues to grow instead of bridging the gap.

NMC's e-Governance Modules are Not in Working Conditions

Since most of the work is focused in city area, mainly Nagpur Municipal Corporation is playing pivotal role in supplying the very basic amenities to the citizen of upcoming smart city, But it is observed that contrary to the expectations NMC's e-Governance modules are not in working conditions proving the sheer negligence of officers of NMC around 90 percent modules are not in working conditions.[5] NMC conferred with the national level "Skoch gold award 2014 for introducing comprehensive e-Governance programme has failed in its implementation of modules. The civic body has spent Rs. 17 crore on the development of those e government modules. E Government Foundation TCS and *Aryansh* Company had developed 64 different modules for the paperless and transparent system which were reduced to 37 for its convenience later on. Further it is also learnt that senior level officers are not user friendly with the on-line system as they have not undergone any type of training to handle the operations. Recently the NMC has decided to engage Project Management Unit (PMU) to manage its e-governance system which will comprise of one Principle Consultant, Senior Consultant and Consultants. These experts will be hired from Deloitte, Ernest and Young, Grant Thornton, PWC, KPMG and Wipro. However this decision is long pending and the file is not cleared by the Municipal Commissioner who is on leave for more than one month. The leave is just an eyewash but in reality the non-cordial relations between the officials and non-officials are the underlying cause for this delay. On account of this situation property tax department is most affected due to the failure of e-Governance system as a data of more than 2 lakhs properties is not uploaded in the system which is ultimately leading to the non- collection of revenue to the desired levels. The modules like Birth & Death Management System, Works Management System, Property Tax Grievances, PWD Contractor License Management System, Finance Management System, Fire Services and Emergency Departments, Marriage Registration Document Management System, City Web Portal, and Hospital Management System are in working conditions. As far as building permission is concerned the, the Town Planning Department has moved on Maharashtra Governments system to grant permission to building plans, sanitation and the drainage system is also not working as NMC is using Fleet Vigil System, while in the Education Department its using *Ahalarath* System of the State Government. Trade License Management System, Hospital License Management System, Veterinary License Management System and the Electrical Contractor License Management Systems are not in use due to various other reasons. The Systems are vulnerable to huge corruption and the department is not ready to mark the System transparent has been the allegations of the contractors whose huge outstanding dues are long pending and the NMC is not paying much attention and seriousness to it.

In addition, other departments like Land and Estate, and Market Management System, Social Welfare, Library, Legal Case Management System, Garden Records, Slums, Workshop, Roads, Quality Control System, Hot Mix plant, Cattle Pond Committee, Sports and Cultural Committee, Special Desk Office, Pench and other major Projects, Dashboard and Enforcement Departments are not functioning on e-Government modules. No doubt the local body is implementing several innovative ideas to improve the system. However officers and employees do not want to use it for their own convenience and the vested interest making the mockery of pro- people concept of the government.

Shortage of funds and strained relations of officials and non-officials

With multiple huge developmental on-going activities in the city, the due and legitimate payments for the various tenders executed on behalf of the local bodies, are unpaid for years together and the contractors are not getting their bills and payments released on time to continue further stages of their assigned project works. There is too much of discontent over the issues, and they have formed a chain, all of them together refusing to undertake any work with the NMC. Majority of the construction work has been outsourced to outsider vendors who have been engaging the local petty contractors for minor work. Even for the regular work of NMC the same situation continues as there is always a paucity of funds and the proportionate quantum of funds are never available. Due to the non-functioning of e-governance modules, the targeted revenue from the taxation has not been raised and NMC is struggling with the poor financial conditions of cash strapped NMC, the Municipal Commissioner has issued a directive to clip the wings of corporators and the officers of the local bodies. As per the directions, now every corporator will get Rs. 1.25 lakhs per month for the development work in his/her ward, meaning Rs. 20 lakhs per month to every zone for the development,[6] as per the directives of the Corporator which is a very meager amount to talk about. This has triggered resentment amongst the public representatives who are planning to undertake various developmental works in their *prabhag*. The Commissioner has also applied brakes over the distribution of the funds from Additional Municipal Commissioner to Assistant Municipal Commissioner levels.

It may also be mentioned here that the chairman of Standing Committee presented a 2018-19 budget of Rs. 2900 crores before the general body which didn't match the targets.[7] Therefore the Commissioner took this strong decision to maintain a balance between committed and development expenditure. Previous Municipal Commissioners have also applied such measure to maintain the financial balance in the local body. The Commissioner has further fixed financial and administrative approval limits of Rs. 50 lakhs per month for the subordinate officers and Rs. 20 lakhs for the Assistant Municipal Commissioner and departmental heads per month. Four Deputy Municipal Commissioners will be having the powers to sanction works up to Rs. 40 lakhs. Total financial powers delegated to the officers is up to six crores per annum and the Assistant Municipal Commissioner will spend Rs. 2.40 crores per annum. This curtailing of financial powers have irked the elected representatives who were very enthusiastic about starting new projects in their area before 2019 elections, which has led to the confrontation between officials and non-officials powers leading to chaos and non-cooperation leading to the stranded and tardy growth of development when the city has been included in the ambitious project of Smart Cities Mission deserves much more than this.

Sanction of Special Grants of Rs. 150 crores by the State Govt.

After the hue and cry, followed by the threats of the civil, electrical contractors, and the bus operators have issued the warning to NMC to release their funds immediately or face the stir, totally stopping ongoing development work. The government of Maharashtra on the initiative of the chief minister intervened into the matter as a result of which a special grant of Rs. 150 crores was sanctioned and released immediately to meet the requirement of stalled payments of ongoing work of the city. Be it mentioned here that the Urban Development Department in its order stated that the earlier government had released Rs. 15 crores per annum from 1995-2000 for the special development of second capital of Maharashtra which latter on was not released by the successive governments. Now the present BJP lead government with their strong political lobby headed by the chief minister Shri Devendra Fadnavis has revived the pattern and decided to release this special fund of Rs. 150 Crores for undertaking the special development of orange city. Further considering its financial crises, the Finance department of NMC suggested to the local body to request the government to release the special grants of Rs. 325 crores to suffice the requirement for undertaking the developmental work. Since the Corporation doesn't have its own resources to continue with the development work at this pace therefore they need special financial assistance justifying their demand for the special grants.

The committed expenditure of the local body over the salary, pension grants, electricity, raw water bill, payment to orange city water body, petrol, diesel, telephone bills, security, repayment of loan, garbage lifting etc. is around Rs. 92 crores. [7] In addition to this abolition of octroi and Local Body Tax (LBT) the civic body is receiving only Rs. 52 crores against Goods and Service Tax (GST) from the state government which is very meagre as compared to income generated from the octroi in the past. In addition to these constraints, the recovery from the property tax is also very poor mainly due to failure of ineffective performance of e-Governance module aimed at smooth paperless, transparent and smart governance in the institution. Therefore the civic body is facing many difficulties in contributing towards the development work as well as to maintain public transport system efficiently.

Collection of Goods and Services Taxes from the contractors: Additional Revenue

Focusing attention to the financial crunch of the civic body the strict measures to collect 2 percent GST from the contractors as tax deducted at source from the bills of the contractors and suppliers were adopted from October 2018.Till now this TDS was not deducted at source for last

15 months. According to the directions issued by the government under section 51 of GST Act 2017, to deduct 2 percent TDS against GST from the bills of the contractors and suppliers for the due payment of more than Rs. 250,000. The local body will have to issue the TDS certificate within 5 days of crediting the amount to the government treasury .In case of failure to make the payment before due date then 18 percent per annum interest will be charged, delay in filing TDS will also attract the penalty. Earlier local body deducted value added tax (VAT) from the bills of contractor and suppliers but after the enforcement of GST the government deferred the deduction of GST from the bills of the contractor. This strict vigilance and the measure adopted proved effective because of which the revenue to the tune of Rs. 52 crores was raised additionally.[8]

State Government relaxes the condition for the utilization of Rs. 150 Crores Special fund

It was with in the span of one week the government of Maharashtra issued two government resolutions, which is a very rare phenomenon otherwise. It permits NMC to release outstanding payments of the development work. As per the directive of the earlier GR dated December 12, 2017, imposed the condition to spend money only for the new work which created hurdles for the Municipal Corporation to release the payments to the contractors and the ongoing development work which has already been done.[9] Ultimately the ruling party pleaded with the Chief Minister to revise the said GR and remove this condition in the interest of the prevailing situation. The new GR was issued immediately relaxing the earlier conditions and authorized Nagpur Municipal Corporation to spend the released fund of Rs. 150 crores as per its requirement and priority. So as on today the civic body has more than Rs. 200 crores in their treasury to carry on the development works in full swing[10]. The State Government in its order clearly mentioned that Nagpur is a second capital of Maharashtra therefore the government has released special financial assistance to the civic body off course because of its status as the upcoming metro city of the state.

Conclusion

Laying emphasis on universal digital literacy, and availability of the digital resources /services in Indian language, which would facilitate to meet the challenges of LPG era, upcoming smart cities, metro cities, and other infrastructural development of the nation, would be at world class level. It assumes greater relevance and importance in the context of Smart City where in every household and the individual will be digitally empowered having the thrust on IT the great enabler for empowerment, equity and efficiency. Its focuses on the broad banding villages, participative governance, digital learning, tele medicine, mobile health care, e-learning tools, skills development, jobs creation, open source and open standards, e-*bhasha* and others.

This time bound project is to be completed by 2019. Today till November 2019 there is no visible movement and impact of the programme and hardly only few elites know about it and the ordinary common man is totally ignorant and unaware about his programme for which it is meant. But looking at the grimed picture, administrative issues, other complexities, very slow and tardy growth of this upcoming Smart City of Nagpur there is an acute need to create awareness and sensitize public to accept, welcome and handle this change in their progressive life. But at this moment it is very disheartening and disappointing to witness performance of the local government institutions at zero development rate, very slow non-noticeable at grass root level the needs to be expedited at multiple levels with the corrective measure to overcome the lacunae to improve the present scenario.

More precise, perfect, electronic instruments, equipments and logistics along with high precision trouble free citizen-friendly computerisation, digitalization procedure should be developed and adopted for the easy access.

With the effective and strong powerful ruling *Bhartiya Janata Party's* existence from local to central level (except at state level) headed by its committed strong willed leadership for the nations development, the administration is running smoothly streamlining its objectives, and overcoming all hurdles, difficulties, and the constraints thereby delivering the desired visible results to the last man of this city leading to the Vidarbha's holistic development.

References

1. https://enwikipedia.org/wiki/ smart_city.
2. Ministry of Housing and Urban Affairs: Tweet, quoted by "The Hitvada, Nagpur" dated August 24, 2018.
3. Ibid.
4. https://enwikipedia.org/wiki/Nagpur#citi _note 15.
5. https://enwikipedia.org/wiki/Nagpur#citinoteMetroRegion88.
6. The Hitvada ,Nagpur Dated City line page No. 5, dated 08 July 2018.
7. The Hitvada ,Nagpur Dated page No 1 City line .2Nd Aug. 2018.
8. Ibid page 1 City Line. 23 oct. 2018.
9. Ibid page 1 City Line. 25 Oct. 2018.
10. Ibid page 1 City Line. 30 Oct. 2018.
11. Ibid page 1 City Line. 2 Nov. 2018.

13

Disaster Risk Reduction and Resilience Management in Smart Cities: A Proposition for State Governments in India

— Krishna Pratap Singh & Abhinav Sharma

Introduction

Rapid urbanization in this global setting is a major challenge for all the countries. Even India is not immune to this challenge. India is the second-largest in population and fifth highly valued economy in the world. Thirty percent (30 percent) population of India lives in cities that contribute approximately 60 percent in the Gross Domestic Product (GDP) of India (Census of India, 2011). It is estimated that probably urban population in the country may reach to eighty crores in 2050 that would be 50 percent of the total population of India (Census of India, 2011). There has always been debate on planned and unplanned urbanization, but the possibility of the entire socio-economic system being on the ebb cannot be disagreed. The cities in India are already faced with the issues of basic amenities, poverty, hunger, and unemployment; now challenged more by disasters — both manmade as well as natural. In order to overcome the challenges and makes our cities more livable and sustainable, the Government has been promoting the idea of smart cities. To what an extent this Information Communication Techonology (ICT) enabled concept could provide solutions and assist in disaster management shall be highlighted in this paper.

Smart Cities in India: An Introduction

Today's India is not free from the challenges of urbanization, hence the Government of India announced Smart City Mission in 2015 to deal it in a structured and systematic way. But what is the standard of a Smart City? What is the definition of Smart City? Which type of events would be accepted? These are some important questions.The meaning of a Smart City varies in different situations;there is no universal definition present for Smart City and its planning (Government of India, Smart City Mission Plan, 2015). There are nevertheless some common goals that seem to guide this choice: local economic development, promotion of environmental sustainability, improvement in the quality of life of citizen through better service, innovation in governance structure and processes and adoption of information and communication technologies (ICT) to support service delivery (Nesti : 2018). One of the most cited definitions of the smart city is, '…believe a city to be smart when investments in human and social capital and traditional (transport) and modern (ICT) communication infrastructure fuel sustainable economic growth and high quality of life, with a wise management of natural resources, through participatory governance' (Caragliu, Del Bo, and Nijkamp: 2012).

In the imagination of any city dweller in India, the picture of a smart city contains a wish list of infrastructure and services that describes his or her level of aspiration. To provide for the aspirations and needs of the citizens, urban planners ideally aim at developing the entire urban eco-system, which is represented by the four pillars of comprehensive development-institutional, physical, social and economic infrastructure (www.smartcities.gov.in). But their development would be done based on keeping in mind that, "Development that meets the needs of the present without compromising the ability of future generation to meet their own needs" (WCED: 1987). Hence smart cities would be developed according to sustainable development goals.

Component of Smart Cities—Indian Perspective

Since it is difficult to universally define smart city, the Indian government has taken the approach of focus on its different components. This is highlighted by Figure-1:

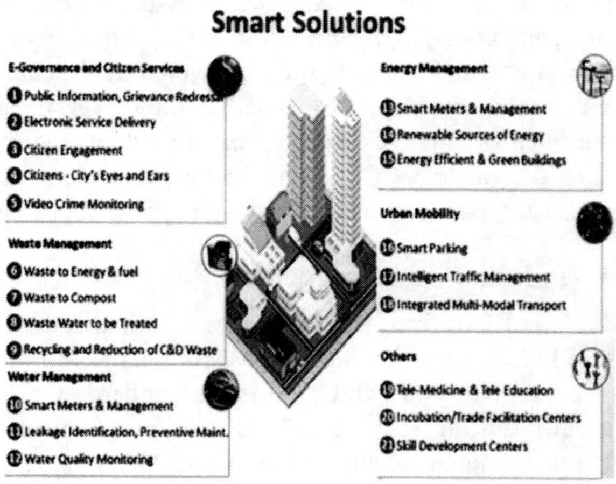

Source: http://smartcities.gov.in/content/innerpage/what-is-smart-city.php (retrieved online April 10, 2020)

Figure-1

To complete the Smart City Mission (www.smartcities.gov.in) successfully, the strategies of development are divided mainly into three parts, which implemented in Smart City Mission.

(1) City Improvement (Retrofitting): Existing developed areas will be well reconnected with the help of local government (Municipalities), other service provider agencies, and citizens which will affect the lives of people qualitatively.

(2) City Renewal (Redevelopment): Under this goal, there will be a focus on redeveloping of 50 acres of land.

(3) City Extension (Greenfield development): Under this goal, 250 acres of land, in the precinct of local government, will be developed to meet the demand of growing population so that this area will be equipped with smart solutions and as a convenience technical services, will be available, due to which social-economic and psychological development of public will be better.

Further, a fourth part has been also later on added by the Union Government to make it more inclusive through avenue of civic engagement.

(4) Pan-city Development: A special type of smart solutions will be incorporated so that the local people (citizen) generate a sense of inclusion between them and the concept of a smart city. Apart from this, urban areas would more be inclusive. (www.smartcities.gov.in)

Urban Local Bodies: The Foundation of Smart Cities in India

The formation of local urban self-government was completed on 1 June 1993 by the 74th CAA with a view to the concept of democratic decentralization. It is divided into Municipal Corporations, Municipal Council, and *Nagar Panchayat* respectively by population. The basic unit of any urban local self-government exists as a ward. (Areas, where there is no presence of urban self-governance or there, is no presence of ward committees for disaster management, such areas can be divided into units through the coordination between the administration and civil society after assessing the vulnerability of the disaster, that the benefits of all activities conducted for the disaster management should be reached the affected people, which will make disaster management inclusive). These urban bodies are the third and important component of Indian governance. The services of local urban administration are described in Schedule 12 of the Constitution. But if it is said in a broad sense, then the urban bodies (local self-government) execute almost all the functions which directly or indirectly affect human life. The services of these bodies range from maternity, maternity assistance, birth certificate to the crematorium, and issuing of the death certificate (from cradle to grave).Almost all the programmes and schemes related to urban body development and public welfare are related to the town planning, described in the Twelfth Schedule, planning for socio-economic development, poverty alleviation (urban), slum area improvement, roads and bridges, public health, sanitation, safe drinking water supply, etc. Apart from promoting cultural and educational works, cremation, and proper arrangement of electric crematoriums are also the responsibility of the urban bodies.

Role of urban local bodies and frontline worker in smart cities

Co-ordination between all the parts of the organization is indispensable for any organization to succeed, but the workers of the front line in the organization are the organs on which the responsibility of successful or unsuccessful implementation of any system depends. The more responsible, transparent and accountability of the system is, the better it will prove to be. At present, when the system is radically shifting away from other than the traditional system to the "government to governance", there is a need for change in the management of the administration as well, the task of making the management of any system successful is always with the frontline workers who we say are street-level bureaucracy (SLB, Lipsky:1980). Who are street-level bureaucrats? Street-level bureaucrats are 'public service workers who interact with citizens in the course of their jobs, and who have substantial discretion in the execution of their work' (Lipsky: 1980: 3). Or the other way, what are street-level bureaucrats? First, 'street-level' means they are working in direct contact with individual citizens. The latter include consumers, clients, pupils, and their parents, and patients as well as car drivers, etc. Second, 'bureaucrats' implies that they are doing their work while in public service. They work directly with individual citizens, but may, in some cases, be employed by commercial corporations, such as private hospitals. Even then, however, it is decided that they fulfill public tasks on behalf of the common good. Third, street-level bureaucrats have a specific occupation for which they have been trained in a sustained way. Because of these joint characteristics, street-level bureaucrats, by implication, have inherent discretion while functioning as policy co-makers. (Nielsen: 2006: 864). Municipal personnel, police, health workers, etc., play an important role as SLB in all the challenges and developmental tasks facing the smart city. It is impossible to make any system of Smart City Mission successful without the role of Municipality. It is necessary to have mutual coordination among all stakeholders to make the smart city mission a grand success.

In disaster management, local governments are the principal actors who formulate disaster management policies and administer their implementation. In particular, although existing disaster management has focused on central government-led orders and controls, recent disaster management has changed to governance based on communication and collaboration between central government and local governments (Jung: 2016).The present era is working on the concept of "less government, more governance", beyond the traditional method that "everything is government". Therefore, if the government shares common thoughts, ideas with local bodies, police system, health workers, disaster managers, community-based organizations and civil society on which the planning strategy, the process is based, then it will be very easy to make decisions which will also reduce the burden from the shoulders of the government. It will also realize the concept of governance network, where the public sector, businesses, NGOs, and civil society work in tandem for the betterment of society.

Disaster: Meaning and Nature

The Oxford English Dictionary (OED) states that the word "DISASTER" derives from the 16th-century French word "DESASTRE". The OED goes to define disaster as "Anything that befalls of ruinous or distressing nature, a sudden or great misfortune, mishap or misadventure; a calamity". Internationally, the generally accepted definition is "Disaster means any accident occurred or critical incident happened in any region, which is caused by any natural phenomena or by human carelessness, therefore this results in huge loss to the environment and large population be affected as well."

Type of Disasters

Basically, disasters categories in two parts-

Natural Disasters

Physical: This includes originating from the geological process.

Aquatic: Incidents/Events due to change in forest cycle, flood, landslides, etc.

Seasonal: This includes cyclone, tornado and heavy rain, etc., that happened only when the radical change in atmosphere.

Climatic: This type of disaster occurs due to continuous change in climate (mainly adverse). This includes drought, wildfire, bush fire, intense cold or heat wave, melting of glaciers.

Biological: In this group, such type of disasters is included which are related to microbe structures as virus, bacteria, parasites, fungus.

Man-made Disaster

The main cause of man-made disasters is urbanization and industrialization. In this classification mainly industrial accident (Bhopal gas tragedy, Chernobyl power plant accident), traffic accidents, building collapse or construction works, fire, oil spill, use of nuclear bombs are included.

The Reason for Manmade Disasters

We have to face many problems due to working in the structure of untrained personnel: road accidents caused by an untrained driver.

The presence of institutional infrastructure is also a cause: rail accident due to fault in the signal, rail accident at unmanned railway crossings, working for personnel without training, all increase the vulnerability of disaster.

Disaster Management: Concept and Dimensions

There is growing need and demand throughout the world to plan, prepare, and respond to disasters caused either by natural or manmade reasons. The Red Cross and Red Crescent societies define disaster management as the organization and management of resources and responsibilities for dealing with all humanitarian aspects of emergencies, in particular preparedness, response and recovery in order to lessen the impact of disasters.

In the UK, the Civil Contingencies Act, 2004 is the legislation governing the preparation for and response to disasters. In the Civil Contingencies Act, the definition of 'emergency' is very broad, applying to any event that 'threatens serious damage' to human welfare, the environment or 'the security of the United Kingdom'. An event threatens 'human welfare' if it threatens to cause loss of life or injury, but also if it causes 'homelessness' or the disruption of various essential services. Local authorities are required to provide guidance to the public on how to prepare for emergencies and how to make business continuity arrangements. Part 2 of the Act deals with the response to an emergency. It empowers Her Majesty 'by Order in Council' to make urgent emergency regulations to deal with any urgent emergency. If the matter is so urgent that even taking the time necessary to arrange for an Order in Council is not practicable, then a 'senior Minister of the Crown' may make urgent emergency regulations.

In the US, the federal emergency management legislation is the Robert T. Stafford Disaster Relief and Emergency Assistance Act. This Act doesn't govern the response by the states but it does govern, and empower the President to manage emergency management programs across the whole PPRR spectrum. With respect to prevention or mitigation, the Stafford Act provides for the establishment of federal disaster preparedness programmes and the provision of technical and financial assistance to the states to allow them to develop programmes and maintain emergency management plans. It requires the President to 'ensure that all appropriate Federal agencies are prepared to issue warnings of disasters to State and local officials. It further allows the federal government to disperse funds from the National Pre-disaster Mitigation Fund to state and local governments to provide up to 75 percent of the cost of hazard mitigation projects (or 90 percent for 'small impoverished communities'). A federal interagency taskforce is normally established by the federal government for the purpose of coordinating the implementation of pre-disaster hazard mitigation programmes.

Disaster Management Strategies by the Government of India

On 23 December 2005, the Government of India (GoI) took a defining step by enacting the Disaster Management Act, 2005which envisaged the creation of the National Disaster Management Authority (NDMA), headed by the Prime Minister, State Disaster Management Authorities (SDMAs) headed by the Chief Ministers, and District Disaster Management Authorities (DDMAs) headed by the District Collector or District Magistrate or Deputy Commissioner as the case may be, to spearhead and adopt a holistic and integrated approach to disaster management (DM). DM involves a continuous and integrated process of planning, organizing, coordinating and implementing measures which are necessary or expedient for:

- Prevention of danger or threat of any disaster.
- Mitigation or reduction of risk of any disaster or its severity or consequences.
- Capacity building including research and knowledge management.
- Preparedness to deal with any disaster.
- Prompt response to any threatening disaster situation or disaster.
- Assessing the severity or magnitude of effects of any disaster.
- Evacuation, rescue and relief.
- Rehabilitation and reconstruction.

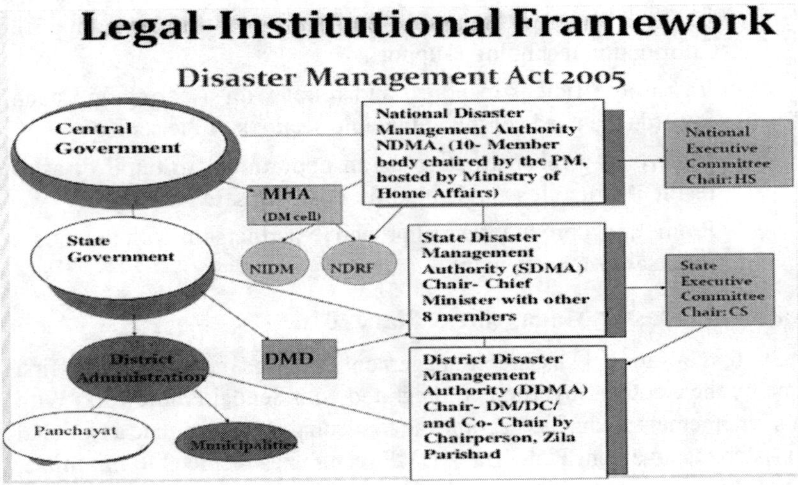

Source: ndma.gov.in

Figure: Structure of NDMA (2005)

National Policy on Disaster Management, 2009

In its review of better and effective implementation of the NDMA, the GoI introduced a National policy on DM in 2009. It was to have a holistic and integrated approach that will be evolved towards disaster management with emphasis on building strategic partnerships at various levels. The themes underpinning the policy were:

- Community based DM, including last mile integration of the policy, plans and execution.
- Capacity development in all spheres.
- Consolidation of past initiatives and best practices.
- Cooperation with agencies at National and International levels.
- Multi-sectoral synergy.

Its declared objectives were as follows:

- Promoting a culture of prevention, preparedness and resilience at all levels through knowledge, innovation and education.
- Encouraging mitigation measures based on technology, traditional wisdom and environmental sustainability.
- Mainstreaming disaster management into the developmental planning process.
- Establishing institutional and techno-legal frameworks to create an enabling regulatory environment and a compliance regime.
- Ensuring efficient mechanism for identification, assessment and monitoring of disaster risks.
- Developing contemporary forecasting and early warning systems backed by responsive and fail-safe communication with information technology support.
- Ensuring efficient response and relief with a caring approach towards the needs of the vulnerable sections of the society.
- Undertaking reconstruction as an opportunity to build disaster resilient structures and habitat for ensuring safe reliving.
- Promoting a productive and proactive partnership with the media for disaster management

National Disaster Management Plan, 2016

In 2016, the National Disaster Management Plan was prepared for the first time by the Central Government integrated with Sendai Framework. With this arrangement, India has become the first country to formulate a National Disaster Management Plan. The NDMP recognizes the need to minimize, if not eliminate, any ambiguity in the responsibility framework. It, therefore, specifies who is responsible for what at different stages of managing disasters. It is meant to be implemented in a flexible and scalable manner in all phases of disaster management: (a) Mitigation (prevention and risk reduction), (b) Preparedness, (c) Response and (d) Recovery (immediate restoration and build -back better). While the names of ministries/ departments of the Centre and State/UT having specific roles and responsibilities are mentioned in the Plan, in the spirit of the DM Act 2005 and the exigencies of humanitarian response, every ministry/ department and agency is expected to contribute to DM going beyond their normal rules of business.

The objective of this scheme is to make India disaster resilient and making the loss negligible to the wildlife and the property as well. The scheme is based on four points of the Sendai Framework:

(1) To study the level or standard of disaster risk.

(2) Improving Disaster Risk Management.

(3) Investing in structural and non-structural measures to reduce disaster risk.

(4) It includes pre-preparedness, prior information and better rehabilitation after a disaster to face the disaster situation.

The goal of the Sendai Framework has been largely incorporated by the Government of India in formulating the Disaster Management Plan. Along with this, provision has been made for all types of integration of agencies between different government institutions and departments in all the stages (prevention, risk reduction, response, and restoration) of disaster management. The plan mentions mutual coordination between role and responsibility at every government level, including *Panchayats* and urban bodies. The inclusion of local self-government in the plan will not only improve efficient disaster management but will also be beneficial for development planning. Structured information, preparedness will also play an important role in post-disaster rehabilitation and restoration (NDMP: 2016).Special emphasis has been laid on information, educational communicative activities to make communities better equipped to counter disaster.

National Disaster Management Plan (NDMP), 2019

The NDMP, in a sense, can be said to have five main pillars:

(i) Conforming to the national legal mandates – the DM Act 2005 and the NPDM 2009.

(ii) Participating proactively to realise the global goals as per agreements to which India is a signatory – Sendai Framework for Disaster Risk Reduction (SFDRR), Sustainable Development Goals (SDGs) and Paris Agreement on Climate Change – consistent with the international consensus for achieving mutual reinforcement and coherence of these framework

(iii) Prime Minister's Ten Point Agenda for DRR articulating contemporary national priories

(iv) Social inclusion as a ubiquitous and cross-cutting principle

(v) Mainstreaming DRR as an integral feature

Smart City and Disaster Management

For disaster management in urban planning, disaster resilience approach and disaster risk reduction management will also have to be focused. Who can establish coordination for disaster management (before, during and post the disaster) between public and private agencies at the ground level? During the three phases of the disaster (before, during and after) the mentality of the community is of the victim, which is entirely dependent on the system. Apart from providing the humanitarian assistance of disaster-struck community from public and private administration withal, people should also be trained in mitigation, capacity building, and pre-disaster preparedness at ground level. so that during the recurrence of upcoming problem or disaster they will be alert for the help of the people and society at the local level with the help of proper coordination of technologically equipped (through online tracing app, food delivery app or web, essential service delivery chain and immunization, etc.) community organizations and civil societies along with reducing the intensity of disaster, this step will limit the loss of the immense public wealth and lives.

To make any arrangement successful, coordination of all the organs of the organization is inevitable. Better coordination is necessary for disaster management between the preparations for the three stages of the disaster (before, during, and after the disaster), In the case of smart city, it can be much better through the command center, which should be based on knowledge, determined by skill, and operated by techniques, respectively. We get to know what to do, how to do it, which technology to do it, which reduces the risk of the problem and intensity of the disaster. Therefore, to deal with the intensity of the disaster, it can be done better than the traditional methods through modern Technological Attitude, Knowledge, and Smart Skills (principle of TASK).

Role of Smart city (through TASK) in Disaster Management

The TASK approach used through smart city should focus on the disaster management cycle that has been illustrated in Figure-3.

As depicted in the Figure-3, there are four main stages: Response begins directly after a disaster, identified by a focus on tasks such as search and rescue, provision of medical attention and construction of temporary housing. Following the response phase, recovery begins when individuals, communities and organisations start the rebuilding process. Ideally, reconstruction involves measures that will thwart the impact of future events (i.e., prevention and mitigation) including, for example, the implementation of hazard resistant building codes and appropriate land-use planning (Smith, and Petley: 2009)

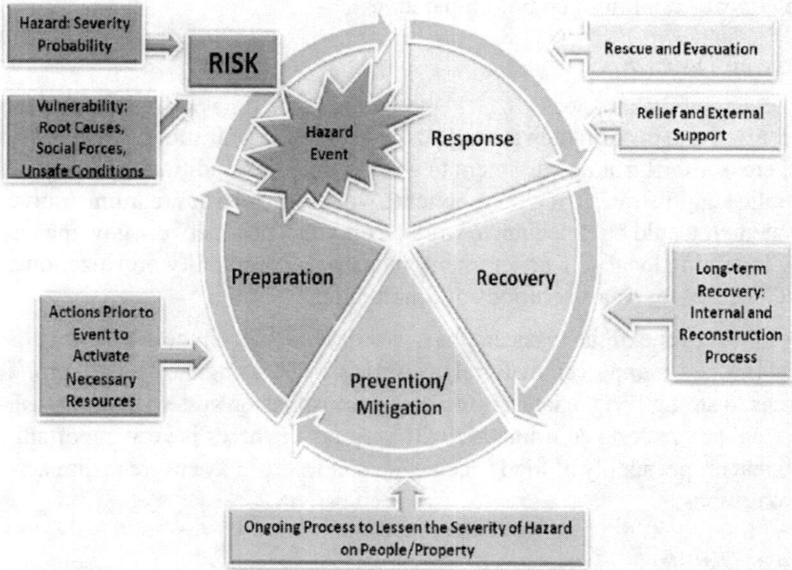

Source: https://www.researchgate.net/figure/Disaster-Management-Cycle_fig3_258343662 (*Lisa J. Wood, Bryan J. Boruff and Helen M. Smith, 2013*)

Figure - 3

For efficient and effective disaster management there is a need to highlight the three phases of the disaster management (pre, during, and after).

Disaster: (Mitigation & Preparedness)

By creating a standard of better coordination between the smart city and local self-government, a common platform can be developed between the stakeholders of various sectors such as industries, private establishments, and various educational institutions. The quality of this type of platform is that the burden of work is traditionally not only on the shoulders of the government, but all the stakeholders are divided mutually according to their capacity, in this system, the result can be achieved on the common platform by sharing the Idea of resources, opinions, and challenges with other stakeholders other than a public-private partnership.

This system is called a form of governance networks, through this system, (which includes private establishments, industries, businesses, etc. with the government) pre-disaster preparation can be done in a very strategic way. In which better work can be done keeping political, economic, social, and technical issues in mind.

Apart from this, initiatives like community awareness through local self-government and education related to disaster management should be arranged in school colleges, so that the impact of the disaster can be reduced to a great extent through pre-preparedness.

During Disaster

The main thing that needs to be kept in mind at the time of disaster is inter-departmental coordination among all the working organizations. Apart from, (there is a shift from government to governance) this traditional concept of public administration, it will be better to work through a new administrative system. It would be expedient to work on the concept of network governance by involving local self-government, industries, community organizations, NGOs, etc. for smart solutions of Smart cities.

At the time of the disaster, it is necessary to focus on the availability of 3M (money, manpower, material) as well as by focusing the disaster-prone areas to strengthen the latest information transmission system and warning system and making coordination with responsive forces is very important. So that proper supply of food vaccine, medicine, etc. may ensure in disaster-prone areas.

Post- Disaster

Disaster and poverty are inversely proportional. Disasters affect the poor, marginalized, and socially deprived sections more. This class is more vulnerable to disaster, so while determining the post-disaster arrangement and rehabilitation, it is expedient to determine the needs and requirements of these sections. Disasters are a hindrance to sustainable socio-economic development; it also harms the environment.

Under the National Disaster Management Plan (NDMP) issued by the government, from the central level to the *Panchayati Raj* system has been added. So, while developing the three major tasks ((i) Retrofitting, (ii) Re-Development, (iii) Greenfield area development) under the Smart City Mission, it is necessary to check the urban condition and disaster vulnerability. Under smart solutions such as Geographic Information System (GIS) and soil testing, it is possible to collect information about the natural disaster proneness of that area and it can also be arranged to prevent as well as prevent the promotion of much industrialization in such areas.

The most pressing problem after the disaster is of livelihood, in which poverty-stricken communities, beggars who pick up garbage (rag pickers), etc. suffer more. The local self-government institutions are responsible for the rehabilitation and livelihood of street vendors etc. Therefore, how can local self-government institutions rehabilitate these vulnerable groups through a smart city is a common question. To provide basic physical infrastructure along with food, life support medicine to vulnerable groups and other groups affected by the disaster, the front-line workers, non-governmental organization (NGO), voluntary organization (VO), community based organizations (CBO) can be engaged by training who will help in the rehabilitation of such groups or communities. The supply of essential commodities to the needy can be made through drone surveillance, GIS, and a good communication system. Traditional and regional knowledge and methods should also be adapted to deal with the disaster. For example, a language (BOO) in the Andaman and Nicobar island that had measures to deal or avoid tsunamis, Therefore, none of the tribal have been affected by the tsunami casualties in the Andaman and Nicobar. Under the National Disaster Plan, various ministries have been entrusted with the responsibility according to the nature and level of the disaster at the time of various disasters. Therefore, smart city and local self-government can ensure rehabilitation and livelihood through various technical community groups, NGOs, citizen groups under the direction of district administration. Restoring basic services immediately after a disaster is a major challenge in which this step plays an important role.

Disaster management through Smart solutions

Tele surveillance— through the command center of smart city, all areas are divided according to disaster proneness and intensity of threat (e.g. categorize in the cluster, zone, etc.) and tele-surveillance can be done by citizens through a particular app and operating mobile network, mobile data through which the necessary action can be taken.

Strong and secure Closed-Circuit Television (CCTV) and drone surveillance- video monitoring can be done by connecting the smart city command center with CCTVs to all major areas of the city square, intersections, crossings so that the actual location of the area can be ascertained. Apart from this, the drone system can also be used in many cases due to which drug supply can be made easy and the pesticides can be sprayed at the time of or pandemic, etc. if needed.

Structured information system— information is the biggest weapon of the modern era. The most important role at the time of a disaster is the information system, so timely rescue or supplies of essentials during a disaster can also be fulfilled only after getting proper information. For proper and positive information during a disaster, you can get clear information by using the internet, Radio Frequency Identification (RFID), radio Ham, GIS, real-time data, which can reduce disaster damage. It will be appropriate to engage the information system with an accountable response team so that coordination between responsibility and accountability will be maintained; e.g., national migrants information system (NMIS) developed by national disaster management authority (NDMA). It has been developed to ensure information related to migrants and their safe movement in other states. It will maintain the central repository of migrant workers.

Telemedicine— during or after a disaster, physical conditions are mostly unfavorable, in such a situation, 'telemedicine' is a highly effective tool for the advice of experts for life-saving medicines. This is also known as 'healing by wire'.The distinguished doctor of the city is assisted by a remote person through ICT technology. Efforts can be used in times of disaster as per the requirements of the city with the shared help of Smart City or Municipal Corporation. For example: India is working with the telemedicine application "SANJIVANI" in 2005 and "SEHAT" in 2015. Covid-19 National tele consultants and center (CON-TEC)- It has been established by AIIMS New Delhi, through which doctors from different fields will be available 24x7 who will treat people through audio-video conversation.

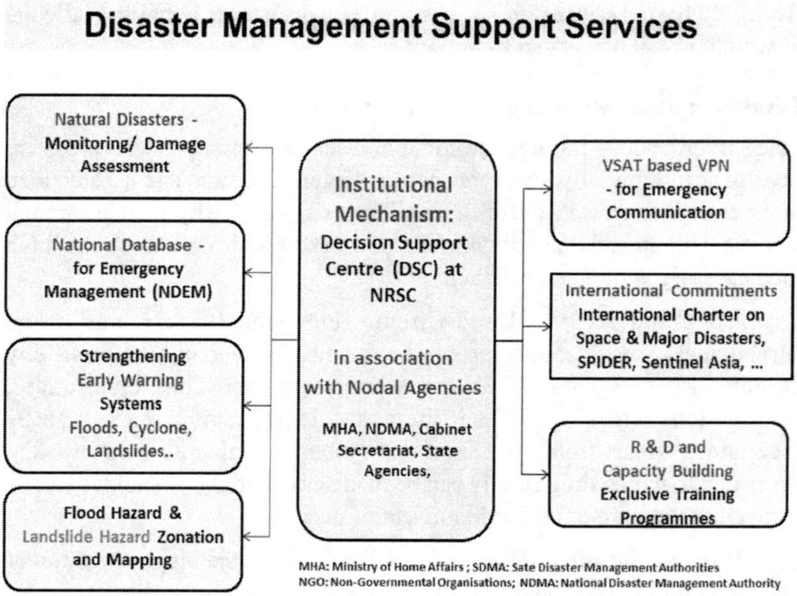

Source: https://www.nrsc.gov.in/EO_Objective_dmss

Figure - 4

Internet of Things (IoT), Artificial Intelligence (AI) based app: in the era of modern artificial intelligence, it can manage the mitigation and revival or rehabilitation of any disaster with various applications and IoT tools. Artificial intelligence works on the concepts of purely reactive, limited memory, brain theory, and self-conscience. For example, Arogya Setu app launched by the Government of India; Aayush kavach app launched by the Government of the U.P.

Remote Sensing Tech— the contribution of remote sensing technology is important in reducing the impact of any disaster and in its management. Through this technique, risk analysis, mapping, disaster recurrence, and the status of unaffected areas can be detected. The compensation of disaster is possible through risk analysis and GIS. Apart from this, this technique also plays an important role in proper location management, basic service supply restoration, for disaster rehabilitation.

National Remote Sensing Center is an institution that plays important in the field of multi-dimensional development of the country as well as in disaster management. The decision support centers of the National Remote Sensing Center are connected to several nodal agencies (Ministry of Home Affairs, NDMA, Central and State Agencies) of the Government of India through its institutional mechanism. Through the satellite system, this organization strengthens the pre-disaster Early warning system, such as where the cyclone is forming and which area will be affected the most. A flood can also be estimated through it, which can save people from the flood before the runoff area is submerged. Also, construction development should be banned in such areas that fall in the river runoff area (which includes pre-disaster planning in disaster management goals and SDGs). So that excessive use of time can be ensured in the pre-disaster preparation and mitigation so that more loss can be avoided during the disaster. Information and communication technology plays an important role during disaster management, without which many challenges come in rescue and relief work. Therefore, when all sources of information and communication are destroyed during a disaster, then the emergency communication can be established through VSAT (Very Small Aperture Terminal) based VPN (virtual private network), which will make disaster management even better and stronger.

E- Supply chain— the biggest catastrophe of any disaster is a livelihood crisis, which is mainly affected only when the gap creates between demand and supply or interrupted completely. Therefore, to avoid this situation, platforms like the e-National Agriculture Market (e-NAM) should be added with the help of the command center and basic supply should be ensured by dividing urban areas into units (like- cluster, zone). This work will prove to be highly effective in the concept of network governance with the help of various stakeholders.

Loudspeaker— information about various relief works such as supplies, medicines, rehabilitation, etc. must be made available among the public so that people's trust should remain in the government.

Strong cyber security cell—as the world moves from regionalism to globalization and the method of its working is changing from traditional to modern, challenges are becoming increasingly complex, A cyber security cell is needed to strengthen the security of smart solution-based systems apart from incidents related to human- theft, snatching. All the disaster management and developmental aspects can be failed by hacking the command center database, which is a significant challenge in itself. Therefore, to avoid this kind of rigging and irregularity and to protect the country from socio-economic collapse, the need for cyber security cell and its trained personnel is first. For example, Nature of cybercrime, confidential information leaked from ministries, theft from bank account issued for disaster management funds (UPI, Payment gateway), and transmission of wrong information through the command center of smart cities.

Grievance Redressal Mechanism—apart from all these things, it is very important to have an effective grievance redressal mechanism under Smart City. Information disposal must be done online to ensure transparency.

Challenges to the Smart City and Disaster Management Relationship

The development of proper communication systems and a good network to disaster-affected people poses a challenge as the problem of rescue and rehabilitation will remain without a clear communication system, so it is necessary to make the communication/information system reliable and strong.

The involvement of frontline workers in all smart solutions of the smart city is necessary, proper implementation is almost impossible without personnel but lack of awareness, training, and sensitivity among personnel is also an important challenge. Technology for employees is easy and common, it is necessary.

As India's level of literacy rate does not match with the current digital system, coordination between the systematic technology system and public participation is a significant challenge because the smart city and its other components (smart solutions) are impossible without a smart citizen.

Since India is a country with a democratic system, whose accountability to the common people at the level of the administrative structure (street-level bureaucracy, front line workers, and network governance) indicates a major problem. Since there is mutual coordination between responsibility and answerability in the administration, it is necessary to ensure the answerability in such a situation which is a major challenge.

In disaster management, the role of grievance redressal mechanism during and after the disaster is very important. What is the level of complaint? Who is responsible? This is a very important point to determine.

The cyber security system is an important aspect of the security of smart solutions because, in case of database hacking, complete preparation can prove to be meaningless or in vain at any moment. Hence cyber security is an important step in a smart city.

The municipal capacity of a city plays an important role in the development of that city. Therefore, the challenge of trained personnel, incomplete management of finance system (just 1percent of Indian budget), and lack of finance hinders many developments works. Apart from Municipal Corporation, the need for the cooperation of the Municipal Development Authority, Water Authority, Transport Corporation, Metro Rail, Police, Fire Services, and Residential Authority is also important.

Conclusion

A better plan is the one that is ready to deal with all the challenges and crises. Proper training, good skills along with the proper infrastructure to cope with natural and man-made disasters are also inevitable. Two percent of India's GDP is wasted due to disasters (UNISDR: 2016). Therefore, to fully realize the vision of the smart city, it is necessary to periodically strengthen and train administrative skills through technical competence (IoT, AI, Block chain, remote sensing) at the level of the city keeping in view the national policy programs of the government as well. The achievement of the Smart City Mission is incomplete without local self-government: the third pillar of democracy. Therefore, a visionary experiment of a smart city can be made successful only by mutual coordination among local self-government, civil society, and administration, which will also keep environmental development alive, keeping in view socio-economic outlook. This smart city will deal with any disaster crisis and determine the potential of human life which will also be compatible with the Sustainable Development Goals. "A city always contains more than any inhabitant can know and a great city always makes the unknown and the possible spurs to the imagination" (Rebecca Solnit.)

References

- Asthana, V. (2014): Disaster Risk Management: Shifting Paradigm. Economic and Political Weekly, 49(39), 17-20. Retrieved April 10, 2020, from www.jstor.org/stable/24480727
- Brodkin, E. (2012): Reflections on Street-Level Bureaucracy: Past, Present, and Future. Public Administration Review, 72(6), 940-949. Retrieved April 10, 2020, from www.jstor.org/stable/41688028

- Butler R &Lachow I (2016): Smart city partnerships: Smart cities & internet of things: Benefit, risk & options (pp. 1-16). New America. Retrieved April 10, 2020 from https://www.newamerica.org/cybersecurity-initiative/policy-papers/smart-city-partnerships/
- Caragliu, A., C. Del Bo, and P. Nijkamp(2012): "Smart Cities in Europe." JournalofUrbanTechnology18(2): 65–82. Retrieved April 10, 2020 from https://www.tandfonline.com/doi/full/10.1080/10630732.2011.601117
- Dae Woong Lee (2019): Local government's disaster management capacity and disaster resilience, Local Government Studies, 45:6, 803-826, DOI: 10.1080/03003930.2019.1653284
- Depoorter, B. (2006): Horizontal Political Externalities: The Supply and Demand of Disaster Management. Duke Law Journal, 56(1), 101-125. Retrieved April 10, 2020, from www.jstor.org/stable/40040541
- Hayat, P. (2016): Smart Cities: A Global Perspective. India Quarterly, 72(2), 177-191. Retrieved April 10, 2020, DOI:10.2307/48505495
- Johanna I. Höffken & Agnes Limmer, (2019): Smart and eco-cities in India and China, Local Environment, 24:7, 646-661, Retrieved April 10, 2020, DOI: 10.1080/13549839.2019.1628730
- Jung, K. (2016): "Disaster Resilience in Self-Organized Inter-organizational Networks: Theoretical Perspectives and Assessment." Journal of Contemporary Eastern Asia 15: 1. doi:10.17477/jcea.2016.15.1.098.
- Kyte R, https://blogs.worldbank.org/climatechange/sustainable-development-gains-require-greater-climate-and-disaster-resilience Retrieved MAY 10, 2020
- Kyte R, https://blogs.worldbank.org/voices/23-million-lives-lost-we-need-a-culture-of-resilienceRetrieved MAY 18, 2020
- Lisa J. Wood, Bryan J. Boruff and Helen M. Smith When Disaster Strikes…How Communities Cope and Adapt: A Social Capital Perspective, In: Social Capital: Theory, Measurement and Outcomes ISBN: 978-1-62417-822-1 Editor: C. Douglas Johnson © 2013 Nova Science Publishers, Inc. Retrieved April 10, 2020 https://www.researchgate.net/publication/ 258343662_ When_Disaster_Strikes_how_communities_cope_and_adapt_a_social_capital_perspective/figures?lo=1
- Lipsky, M. (1980): Street-level bureaucracy: the dilemmas of the individual in public services. New York: Russell Sage Foundation
- Nielsen, V. L. (2006): Are street-level bureaucrats compelled or enticed to cope? Public Administration Vol. 84, No. 4, pp.861–889, Retrieved May 10, 2020, https://doi.org/10.1111/j.1467-9299.2006.00616.x
- Nesti, G. (2018): Trasformazioni urbane. Le cittàintelligentitrasfide e opportunità. Roma: Carocci editor
- Piyoosh Rautela & R. K. Pande (2005): Traditional inputs in disaster management: the case of Amparav, North India, International Journal of Environmental Studies, 62:5, 505-515, DOI: 10.1080/00207230500034586
- Russell M. Smith, Prasad Avinash Pathak & Girish Agrawal (2019): India's "smart" cities mission: A preliminary examination into India's newest urban development policy, Journal of Urban Affairs, 41:4, 518-534, Retrieved April 10, 2020 DOI: 10.1080/07352166.2018.1468221

- Sharma M & Ghosh A (2015): What does India think (pp71-76 rep) (Godement.F. Ed) European council on foreign relations?
- Sheshadri Chatterjee, Arpan Kumar Kar & Syed Ziaul Mustafa (2019): Securing IoT devices in smart cities of India: from ethical and enterprise information system management perspective, Enterprise Information Systems, Retrieved April 10, 2020, DOI: 10.1080/17517575.2019.1654617
- Sinha, P.C. (ed.) (1998): Encyclopedia of disaster management, vol-1, New Delhi: Anmol Publication.
- Smith, K., and Petley, D. N. (2009): Environmental Hazards: Assessing risk and reducing disaster (fifth edition). London: Routledge
- Tali Hatuka, Issachar Rosen-Zvi, Michael Birnhack, Eran Toch &Hadas Zur (2018): The Political Premises of Contemporary Urban Concepts: The Global City, the Sustainable City, the Resilient City, the Creative City, and the Smart City, Planning Theory & Practice, 19:2, 160-179, DOI: 10.1080/ 14649357.2018.1455216
- Triparna Vasavada (2013): Managing Disaster Networks in India, Public Management Review, 15:3, 363-382, DOI: 10.1080/ 14719037. 2013. 769854
- Tyagi, A. (2010): Need for a paradigm shift in approach to disaster management. The Indian Journal of Political Science, 71(1), 9-23. Retrieved April 10, 2020,
- https://censusindia.gov.in/Census_And_You/migrations.aspx Retrieved April 10,2020
- https://ndma.gov.in/en/irs-training.htmlRetrieved April 10, 2020
- http://smartcities.gov.in/content/innerpage/strategy.php Retrieved April 10, 2020
- http://smartcities.gov.in/content/innerpage/what-is-smart-city.php Retrieved April 10, 2020
- https://www.gfdrr.org/en/feature-story/how-can-we-finance-resilient-cities-future Retrieved May 14, 2020
- https://pib.gov.in/PressReleseDetailm.aspx?PRID=1577944 Retrieved May 14, 2020
- https://ndma.gov.in/images/policyplan/dmplan/National%20Disaster%20Management%20Plan%20May%202016.pdfRetrieved May 14, 2020
- https://www.nrsc.gov.in/EO_Objective. Retrieved May 18, 2020

14

Urbanization in India: Challenges and Solutions

— *C. N. Rao*

Urban Scenario

We are living in a fast urbanizing world. India is one of the fast urbanizing countries in the world and is no exception to this socio-economic change. The definition of urbanization differs from country to country. Urbanization in India can be defined as the spatial concentration of people and economic activity. It is a socio-economic transformation in the history of civilization. Urbanization is a global phenomenon. The pace of urbanization varies from one country to another and one region to another. In this respect, India is one of the fastest urbanizing countries in the world with 377.1 million (census, 2011) people living in urban areas. The percentage of urbanization in India is 31.67 percent as per 2011 census. As most of the villages are gradually increasing both in area and population owing to increasing commercial activity and occupation of people in non-agricultural professions, the governments are left with no alternative to constitute them as Municipalities bringing them within the purview of the Urban Governance.

Urbanization is a positive economic force since it contributes increasingly to Gross Domestic Product (GDP). Urban areas contribute 63 percent to Gross Domestic Product as on date which is likely to increase to 75 percent mark in the coming two decades. Besides its positive contribution, the quick pace of urbanization brings with it several new challenges which, if not properly addressed, will vitiate the positive role of urbanization. Since urbanization cannot be stopped it is for the urban managers to cope with greater numbers, improve the quality of urban life through provision of basic amenities and development of infrastructure commensurate with the growing needs and demands of cities. In view of the growing importance of urban governance and the complexities of Urban Local Governments (ULGs), urban governance experts have to bring about reforms needed for the improvement of governance in the functioning of the Urban Local Governments.

While the quick pace of urbanization cannot be stopped, it should be welcomed by Governments and people duly coping with the challenges of fast urbanization, since it is a positive economic force, and hence a desirable phenomenon since urbanization is pivotal to growing wealth of nations and reduction in absolute levels of poverty. Urbanization brings about great and desirable changes in people's lives through their life styles, employment, welfare, social structures and institutions.

Cities are the foundation of modern civilization, the engines of economic growth and the centres of culture, innovation, knowledge, development and creation of jobs. An estimated 120,000 people are added every day to the urban population of Asian cities, requiring the provision of more than 20,000 new dwellings, 250 kilo meters of new roads, and additional infrastructure to supply six mega liters of safe drinking water.

Urbanization has also its negative impact. Large expanses of productive agriculture land is lost daily to generally poor-quality forms of urban development. Further, the urban environment is polluted by ever-increasing traffic and traffic congestion, pollution due to emission of affluences from industries etc which make city life vulnerable. Inadequate infrastructure to growing urban population is an increasing social problem. All these factors swamp urban governance. As urbanization continues, quality of urban life deteriorates. Governments have, therefore, to concentrate on provision of improved infrastructure commensurate with the increasing needs of urban areas in order to ensure that urbanization continues to be a positive economic force. Economic growth is associated with urbanization, but urbanization also leads to several problems like mushrooming of slums, traffic problems, congestion, inadequacy of water, shelter for slum dwellers etc. The social, economic, political, and environmental transformation of unprecedented magnitude associated with urbanization brings with it unpredictability and chaos.

These urban challenges are addressed haphazardly and inefficiently with the result that the challenges of urbanization are slowing down the improvements in living standards and reducing the potential benefits of urbanization and further they undermine the economic, social and environmental sustainability in all Indian cities. If urban challenges are addressed efficiently and effectively, it increases the benefits of urbanization by diminishing constraints on economic productivity and raises the standard of living of the urbanites. This is possible through improvement in governance through efficient organization of the municipalities and adequate investment in infrastructure development.

The present deterioration of the sustainability of cities and the gradual erosion of the quality of life in all urban areas of the country are attributable to the organizational incapacity of the ULGs to meet the growing urban challenges and inadequate investment in urban infrastructure. If urbanites are to be insulated against the adverse effects of urbanization, investment in urban infrastructure provision and improvement must be increased both from the public and private sector. Public and private sector investment in the provision of services will improve the sustainability of cities and the quality of life of their inhabitants. Active private sector participation in infrastructure development depends on the capacity of ULGs and their management to plan, implement, and finance infrastructure provision and service delivery through partnership with private sector.

The growing urban problems are due to scant attention from governments at all levels all these decades. It is very late by the time government has fully geared up itself to pay adequate attention to urban renewal through schemes like *Jawaharlal Nehru* National Urban Renewal Mission (JnNURM) in 2013 and its modified form of AMRUT in 2015. Urbanization is to be given the same level in the national policy debate on par with political, economic and defence concerns. The political, economic and environmental costs of urban development in India are on a critical threshold. All urban development programmes should be planned in such a way that they result in major improvements in economic productivity and welfare, creation of jobs and reduction poverty.

Governments have put in too little effort into developing the enabling environment in the country for affecting local government operation and strengthening urban local governance and local capacity building. This has resulted in ineffective and incapacitated local governance, provision of services and for their operation and maintenance. Governments have to evince renewed interest in urbanization and spatial dimensions of development, since the social, economic and environment challenges associated with cities cannot be ignored any longer and which are to be addressed efficiently and effectively through local policies and through decentralization of powers and functions which yield political and financial benefits besides improving governance.

Huge capital, improved city planning, and management are required to address the growing needs of health, sanitation, water supply, shelter and transportation. The Urban Local Governments, starved of funds and capacity to address these issues, need support from higher levels of government. The prevailing urban scenario in India calls for large scale urban environmental improvement programmes and for strengthening urban local governance and the capacity of municipalities to plan, implement and finance infrastructure provision and ensure better service delivery. This will be possible only if the local governments are enabled to meet the challenges of urbanization through appropriate national administrative and financial arrangements, to match their service obligations with their financial resources.

Strengthening city governance to fulfil the new constitutional obligations entrusted to the ULGs and improving local resource mobilization have engaged the attention of urban governance experts for quite some time but not with much success in respect of results. These two important issues involve several complex problems and it will be a time consuming process to achieve. As a measure of improving the functioning of the municipalities decentralization of powers and functions from national to state and state to local governments has been in the process. But transfer of powers and functions, unaccompanied by devolution of adequate funds for provision and maintenance of services is of no avail. ULGs need "substantial investment in strategic planning, institutional development and capacity building, and management and financing systems development to achieve these goals, as Brian Roberts and Trevor Kanaley (2006) rightly observe, since ULGs are starved of funds for investment in infrastructure required for burgeoning urban population and expanding urban areas, adequate funds must be devolved from the higher levels of government according to a pre-evolved formula.

Human resource development is an important issue in strengthening urban governance. City governments have to partner with community groups and leverage capital and resources with the private sector to deliver services to the level of expectation of urbanites. ULGs in India have to create and build networks and information systems to disseminate and share knowledge and ideas about good practices in urban management and provision of infrastructure.

Urban development and management involve multiple stakeholders and has a complexity of issues. Emulation of best practices which proved successful elsewhere goes a long way in improving governance and development and maintenance of infrastructure. "Planning operational practices that have proven successful in particular circumstances. Best practices are used to demonstrate what works and what does not and to accumulate and apply knowledge about how and why they work in different situations and contexts," is the general definition of best practice, as developed by United Nations (UNDP: 2006).

While urbanization in India is very fast urban development is very slow, owing to weak governance structures, appalling environmental conditions, and the short falls of infrastructure and services which disclose that urban areas cannot meet the needs of urban dwellers on their own, unassisted financially by state and central governments. The challenges the urban areas are facing in the country are no doubt enormous, but at the same time they are not insurmountable, if governments at all levels prepare urban development plans meticulously, execute them carefully in a time-bound manner and financed by central government through devolution of adequate funds.

Urban Housing

Housing for urbanites is an important issue for all Indian cities. More than 40 percent of urban population in India lives in substandard housing. Most of the dwelling units are overcrowded with hardly 50 square meters per unit. Most of the dwelling units are shacks and shanties prone to vicissitudes of climate. Besides insecurity in the temporary structures they live in, they face other acute problems like poor sanitation, lack of access to safe drinking water and electricity. Added to it, the slum dwellers have no secure title and very often face problems like fire accidents, periodic flooding, vulnerability due to risks like natural hazards, political vendettas etc. The demand for low cost housing for slum dwellers exacerbate from time to time. There is, therefore, the need for increasing investments in housing and subsidiary infrastructure and services. There is also the need for replacement of the shacks and shanties by permanent houses.

Urban Infrastructure

The most challenging problem for ULGs is meeting the demand for urban infrastructure to provide access to good quality, affordable, and improved basic services. Inadequate investment in urban infrastructure undermines economic growth, private sector development, and the achievement of poverty reduction goals. Failure to meet the demand for infrastructure will stunt economic growth, employment generation, standards of living and poverty reduction. Thus, there is an urgent need for improving services like sanitation, road access, water supply, efficient solid waste management, electricity and transport. Adequate investment in road development and transport will connect cities and enable the flow of goods and services and thus it is vital for urban growth.

Inadequate infrastructure investment in Indian cities is not only due to the fact they have long-term benefit flows and financial and maintenance implications but also due to lack of sophisticated, well-coordinated governance arrangements in the ULGs and their technical capabilities. Large infrastructure investments are difficult for ULGs whose fiscal position is stretched by poorly controlled expenditure and underperforming tax bases and user charges. It should, therefore, be concluded that if infrastructure is to be provided and maintained successfully, projects must be cost-effective and technically and financially viable.

Private sector participation in the provision of urban infrastructure is invited to fill the investment gap and reduce financial pressures on ULGs and to achieve improved project financial performance.

Urban Poverty

Despite the major inroads economic growth and urbanization have made into the incidence of poverty, urban poverty still remains a major problem in all Indian cities and remains a critical issue. Unemployment, lack of skills, and unequal access to infrastructure services are contributory factors to urban poverty. The urban poor mostly live in low-quality housing in squalid settlements on the periphery of cities or overcrowded slums, where minimum basic needs are not available. Urban poverty is a potentially explosive issue. Genuine efforts to prevent large scale migration of rural poor to urban areas in search of livelihood could not be prevented by lopsided rural development. Addressing urban poverty is, therefore, is an important issue for ULGs for which the ULGs have to adopt targeted poverty reduction policies and programs to address urban poverty in order to keep pace with the *rural poverty push and urban prosperity pull.*

Urban Finance

Augmentation of finances of ULGs is an urgent need to address a wide range of problems of urban growth and to achieve more sustainable development outcomes in Indian cities, since funds-starved ULGs cannot cope with fast urbanization. Huge funds are required to finance infrastructure and service provision for expanding urban areas and burgeoning urban population. The ULGs have to gear up their financial systems and arrangements required to mobilize additional funds and ensure their effective use. Investment requirement is increasing from year to year. ULGs have to increase resource-raising activity to finance this investment. The present funding short falls are not due to unwillingness of tax payers in urban areas to pay for services, but due to the inability of ULGs to mobilise adequate resources through exploitation of existing resources to the fullest potential and search for additional as well as non-conventional sources of revenue to meet the investment requirements. Governments have to create an enabling environment for ULGs to overcome the structural weaknesses in urban local governments. Unless the ULGs remove the institutional weaknesses and capacity constraints in the local governments, generation of adequate financial resources is not possible. ULGs with inadequate financial sources and weak governance structures cannot access to loan funds and capital markets. The central and state governments in India have not properly addressed the structural and viability problems of ULGs with the result that the private sector is not actively coming forward in infrastructure and service provision. Mere transfer of powers through Constitution (74th) Amendment Act, 1992 from central and state governments to the ULGs have not given any positive results and the ULGs are not capable of financing, planning, delivery and management of infrastructure development and urban services. In the prevailing financial situation of the ULGs in the country, central and state governments have to fund urban development, leaving the maintenance part to the urban local governments.

The revenue base of ULGs in India is very weak, with weak administrative structures and inadequate revenue-raising powers. Coupled with this lacuna, the ULGs are unable to exploit their limited tax base and user charges to the fullest extent. Governments have to initiate reforms to broaden the tax base, to align the responsibilities, nay, the constitutional obligations, with the revenue base and should introduce systems and processes to improve local revenue more efficiently and effectively so that the increase of revenues of ULGs keep pace with the increasing responsibilities.

Most of the services rendered by ULGs, particularly protected water supply are not cost-effective and are heavily subsidized, which is the main reason for the bankruptcy of most of the ULGs in India. Ineffective billing of services coupled with poor recovery has miserably failed the pricing structure of public utilities. The users of services are quite naturally reluctant to pay for poor quality services. Another aspect that ULGs utterly neglect is asset management. Most of the ULGs in India have not maintained register of assets, such as public lands, and they have no idea of the holdings they own or their market value. ULGs have not adopted modern financial management practices, such as performance-based budgeting and double entry accrual based accounting system which gives way to cash flow and financial mismanagement problems. This results in inordinate delay in the implementation of projects and programmes, because of poor cash flow management and increasing the overall costs of the projects.

Urban Governance

Efficient and effective urban governance is central to the performance of urban local governments. The economic growth of cities depends on efficient urban governance. Urban governance has to play a key role in the sustainability and amenity of cities through the provision of improved infrastructure and services and the management of urban development required for fast growing cities. In order to achieve efficacy of development, urban local governments have to develop participatory mechanisms to allow the involvement of local communities and civil society in local decision-making, so that governance becomes more transparent and accountable.

The existing governance structures of ULGs are very complex with poorly coordinated administrative systems. This complexity encourages overlapping of functions and shifting of responsibilities. ULGs do not have the capacity to design, finance, and implement urban development policies and programmes, owing to inadequate revenue-raising powers and technical capabilities. The systems and processes of urban local governance are often poorly developed with the result that they are not able to provide a transparent, accountable, corruption-free administration. While these inherent problems adversely affect the efficiency and effectiveness of urban governance the rapid growth of cities further exacerbate them. It is, therefore, imperative for ULGs to strengthen their capacities for improving their performance. Unless the performance of ULGs improves, the sustainability of cities will further deteriorate and the economic development of cities will stifle and the living standards in cities will further decline. Rapid population growth strains urban local governance and service provision. It is needless to elaborate that urban governance in India has been swamped by fast urban growth without proportional increase in urban development and service provision. It, therefore, necessitates that governance should be improved to continue the economic growth of cities.

In regard to local government finances, the national and state governments in India have not given a serious thought of either to devolve adequate funds to the ULGs to meet the development expenditure or to strengthen their finances by enhancing their financial base and revenue-raising powers. The present weak, fragmented governance arrangements of ULGs in India are due to inadequate administrative capacity and insufficient financial resources. The national and state governments in India are reluctant to cede taxation powers to ULGs commensurate with their service-delivery functions. In view of the new role the ULGs have to play as independent local self-government units, they should be first made financially viable institutions. Mere decentralization of functions and responsibilities will give no efficacy unless the higher controls are balanced with local level decision-making responsibilities and appropriate resources if the benefits of decentralization are to be achieved.

The legal, financial and administrative arrangements in ULGs are important matters of concern, since cities have to accommodate additional population every year in future. The magnitude of ever-increasing urban challenges is too great with the result that cities will experience crises and collapse. Governments at all levels have to realize these facts and should initiate steps to reverse these trends to make urban life qualitative one and make cities sustainable and liveable. Urban governance experts should take an optimistic view of urbanization and take all steps required to exploit the benefits of urbanization to the fullest extent. The cities in India are dynamic, vibrant and vital. City governments have to improve the quality of their urban services and environments. City governance should be improved to the best satisfaction of urbanites through strategic planning, institutional strengthening, management and capacity enhancement.

Housing the Slum Dwellers

While cities in India play a major role in the country's economy, as they are the epicentre of human development, growth and sustainability and provide opportunities for social equity, economic equity, economic growth and innovation, city life is deteriorating day by day owing to scant attention that urban areas received. Since Indian economy was mainly agricultural until two decades ago, planning mainly aimed at rural development for the first four decades after independence. Now that there is a shift of economy from agriculture to industry, erstwhile villages have now become towns and towns have become cities. Urban areas, therefore, need a firm place in the national agenda in the fast changing urban scenario.

One of the adverse aspects of urbanization, as far as India is concerned, is the growth of urban slums and urban slum population. Fast urbanization is inevitably linked with fast growth of slums. The immediate requirements of urban areas are housing for all and minimum basic needs for slum dwellers. Since migrants from rural areas in search of livelihood opportunities in urban areas cannot afford to live in well-developed localities they seek shelter in slums by erecting shacks and shanties. Thus, slums grow fast along with urbanization and slum population grows in proportion to urban population growth. Urban areas need both skilled and unskilled labour since urban life cannot be sustained without their supporting services, and the labour need livelihood in the unorganized sector in urban areas. Instead of taking up lopsided rural development programmes to prevent the rural migrants to urban areas, up-gradation of urban slums and improving the living conditions of urban slum dwellers is a better solution to meet the challenges of urbanization and to cope with the rural push and urban pull, in search of better living conditions, education for children, medical facilities and more particularly livelihood opportunities in the unorganized sector.

All fast growing cities in India experience problems like excessive concentration of population particularly in slums, congestion, shortage of housing, transportation bottlenecks and inadequate basic amenities, all of which lead to unprecedented demand for infrastructure, services and basic amenities. Addressing these challenges is the immediate need of ULGs to sustain urban life. Municipalities in India are plagued not only with capacity gap but also with poor fiscal health.

Realizing the need for slum improvement and housing, the Government of India has taken up a massive housing programme called Housing for All

(Urban) by 2022, which aims to provide every family a permanent house with water connection, toilet facilities and 24×7 electricity supply by the time the Nation completes 75 years of its Independence. The Government of India has further initiated an ambitious programme called the Atal Mission for Rejuvenation and Urban Transformation (AMRUT) with the principal objective of bringing about comprehensive sustainable urban development in all cities and towns of India with a population of 100,000 and more.

Slum Development Fund (SDF)

Since the future of the world, including India, is inescapably urban it is found necessary to constitute Slum Development Fund which should be exclusively utilized for provision of minimum basic needs in all urban slums.

Need of New Towns

All metropolitan cities in India have reached a saturation point and the infrastructure available in these cities clearly indicates that they cannot afford to grow any further and cannot accommodate any further migrants. This situation necessitates the development of satellite cities in the peripheries of mega cities. Migrants from rural to urban areas cannot be ignored while planning the development of urban areas. Urban challenges must be addressed with meticulous planning by a multi-level governmental approach, for otherwise, it will lead to further deterioration of urban life in the years immediately ahead. Hence, instead of allowing slums to grow in urban areas and then taking up slum up-gradation and weaker section housing to accommodate the rural migrant labour it is desirable to plan the outskirts of mega cities in such a way that they continue to attract the labour into their expanding fold unabated.

References

- Brian Roberts and Trevor Kanaley (2006): Urbanization and Sustainability in Asia, ADB, Philippines, p. 5.
- UNDP: 2006

15

Women Empowerment and Engendering Development in Urban Administration: A Study of Bihar

—A. K. Singh

Introduction

Women are significant contributors to India's economy and important constituent of development. Their empowerment is essential for distributive justice for the nation's growth. Engendering national development plans is imperative for gender mainstreaming and their empowerment. Engendered development plans would include a gender dimension in all macro policies and budgetary support for their implementation. Engendering public policy and gender budgeting are the major gender commitments by Government of India. Gender budgeting has three basic dimensions. One, the empowerment has to be holistic and it should cover political, social and economic implications for women. It should be universal in terms of equal opportunities. The second dimension is that it should be participative and inclusive (Singh and Singh: 2018). This requires that planning, policy and implementation process should have a bottom-up approach, where women have a voice from the gross roots to the highest echelons of power. The third dimension of gender budgeting is the need for convergence. Women's needs are multi-dimensional – access to health and nutrition, water and sanitation, asset based marketing, credit, technology, education and skills, political participation etc. Thus, convergence of development policies, programmes, schemes and institutional resources is imperative for engendering and inclusive development. There is also the need for revision in existing urban development schemes and programmes so that gender issues may be incorporated and their concerns are effectively addressed.

Gender equality is central to the realization of Sustainable Development Goals (SDGs). Gender equality, leading to increased work opportunities, enhanced capacities for livelihood developments, enhanced social protection and overall increasing voice may enable women to participate equally in productive employment, contributing to women's development leading to economic growth of the nation. No nation can afford development without considering women who constitute about half of the stock of human resources. Thus, engendering growth has been internationally recognized instrument of development by incorporating gender perspective and concerns at all levels and stages of development planning, policy, programmes and delivery mechanisms. The issue of engendering development and women empowerment has been in the centre stage with the shifting of paradigm of development and governance. Gender budgeting has emerged as an important instrument for gender mainstreaming and empowering women. Gender budgeting refers to the systematic examination of the budget programmes and policies for the impact on women. Studies show that programmes and policies designed to improve women's economic opportunities lead to higher rates of economic growth. Gender budgeting has thus gained prominence in the policy circles in the recent years.

Gender equality and women empowerment are the key terms that defined and determined the direction of diverse discourses on women, nationally and globally. The Beijing Conference was the most significant milestone in journey towards ensuring gender equality and enriching pragmatic insights into the issues concerning women empowerment (Singh & Srivastava: 2001). However, gender discrimination across the life cycle is still prevalent in most of the countries across the globe. In India too, gender discrimination is prevalent in its socio-cultural setup. Gender discrimination is pervasive while the degree and forms of inequality may vary; women and girls are deprived of equal access to resources, opportunities and political power in every region of the world. The oppression of girls and women can include the preference for sons over daughters, limited personnel and professional choices for girls and women, the denial of basic human rights and outright gender based violence (UNICEF: 2007).

There has been paradigm shift from a welfare orientation to an empowerment approach. This has further led to the emerging concept of engendering development in order to ensure gender equity, gender mainstreaming and women-centric governance. Though, India is among the most complex democracy in the world, with a long history of commitments to women's welfare and empowerment through constitutional provisions, legislation, policies and plans even while deep levels of structural gender bias persists within families, societies and economies. There are formidable opportunities and challenges, including continued high rate of economic growth in the phase of declining sex ratio, decreasing energy and natural resources, increasing income inequality and an urban rural divide.

Thus, gender equality has become a core prerequisite for sustainable and equitable economic growth (National Alliance of Women: 2008). Women are major contributors to the India's economy and therefore empowerment of women is essential for distributive justice and national growth. Engendering growth model and development plans may create opportunities for women in their mainstreaming in development process and governance. The growth models and development planning requires the suitable mechanism which is able to address the gender concerns at all stages and policy commitments along with budgetary support for them.

Mainstreaming Gender Equality

The term 'gender mainstreaming' came into wide spread use with the adoption of the Platform for Action at the 1995 UN World Conference on Women held in Beijing. The 189 governments represented in Beijing unanimously affirmed that the advancement of women and the achievement of equality with men are matters of fundamental human rights and therefore a prerequisite for social justice. Mainstreaming gender equality tries to ensure that women's as well as men's concerns and experiences are integral to the design, implementation, monitoring and evaluation of all projects so that gender inequality is not perpetuated. It attempts to overcome the common problem of 'policy evaluations in the implementation due to which impact of development projects fails to reflect policy commitments (Helan: 2001). In the late 1990s, donor-supported development shifted away from discrete project interventions to general poverty elimination, which potentially provides an ideal context for gender mainstreaming. Attention is only just beginning to be paid to the gender dimensions of poverty alleviation (Narayan & Petesch: 2002).

The Millennium Declaration signed at the United Nations Millennium Summit in 2000 set out the United Nations Goals for the next decade. These goals stormed from the resolutions of the various world conferences organized by the United Nations during the 1990s (UNDP: 2003). The Beijing Platform for Action prioritized gender mainstreaming as the mechanism to achieve gender equality. Mainstreaming a gender perspective is the process of assessing the implications for women and men of any planned action including legislation, policies or programmes, in all areas and at all levels (Moser and Moser: 2006). Empowerment of all women and girls is to be realized through sustainable development. Sustainable development depends on an equitable distribution of resources and it cannot be achieved without gender equality. Gender equality is the process of allocating resources, programmes, and decision making fairly to both males and females without any sort of gender discrimination and addressing any imbalances in the benefits available to males and females. Sustainable development cannot be achieved without gender equality (Development

Alternatives: 2015). Hence, the following targets have been included among the SDGs to attain gender equality and empowerment (U N. Women: 2015):

- End all forms of discrimination against all women and girls at all places;
- To abolish all forms of violence against women and girls in the public and private spheres, including trafficking, sexual abuse and other types of exploitation;
- Eliminate all harmful traditional practices, such as child marriages, early and forced and female genital mutilation;
- Value the unpaid care and domestic work through the provision of public services, infrastructure and social protection policies/ schemes and the promotion of shared responsibility within the household and the family;
- To ensure that women practice full and effective participation and equal opportunities for leadership at all levels of decision-making in political, economic and public realms of life;
- To assure universal access to sexual and reproductive health and rights.

Engendering Development

The Eleventh Five Year Plan was aimed at inclusive development. Its vision envisaged that every woman in the country should be able to develop to her full potential and share the benefits of economic growth and prosperity. The approach adopted was to empower women and to make them partners in their own development. This it sought to do by mainstreaming gender in all sectors as well as by undertaking targeted interventions. The Plan period witnessed the introduction of many new schemes and programmes aiming at addressing specific issues. The Eleventh Five Year Plan referred to gender budgeting and gender outcome assessment and underlined the importance of gender audits of public expenditure, programmes and policies at national, state and district levels. The Plan envisaged the strengthening of the Gender Budget Cells set up in the various Ministries and Departments. During the 12th Five Year Plan a Working Group on 'Women's Agency and Empowerment' was established which viewed that development is a process of expanding freedoms equally for all individuals, and considered gender equality as a core development goal in itself. It adopted an expanded definition of women's empowerment by looking at it as a process, which enables women to have a notion of dignity and self worth, bodily integrity, freedom from coercion and control over resources. In order to ensure women are empowered, the **government and the public sector** need to play important roles to enable their welfare in various sectors. Whether it's providing free cooking gas and education schemes or enabling women to leverage technology, a slew of schemes have been launched in recent years to empower women to be independent in their lives. *Beti Bachao Beti Padhao Yojana* was launched in **2015, in Panipat, Haryana.** It is a joint initiative of the Ministry of Women and Child Development, Ministry of Health and Family Welfare, and Ministry of Human Resource Development. Under the Ministry of Women and Child Development, the government launched *Mahila-E-Haat* in 2016. It is a bilingual online marketing platform that leverages technology to help aspiring women entrepreneurs, self-help groups, and NGOs to showcase their products and services. Among the many services provided by *Mahila-E-Haat* is facilitating direct contact between the vendors and buyers, sensitisation, advocacy, training on packaging and soft intervention workshops, and offering a web-based approach. The government established *Mahila Shakti Kendra* in 2017 to empower rural women with opportunities for skill development, employment, digital literacy, health and nutrition. The *Mahila Shakti Kendras* are expected to work through community engagement through student volunteers in the 115 most backward districts. Each *Mahila Shakti Kendra* will provide an interface for rural women to approach the government to avail of their entitlements through training and capacity building One Stop Centre Scheme, popularly known as *Sakhi*, was implemented in 2015 with the 'Nirbhaya' fund. The One Stop Centres are established at various locations in India for providing shelter, police desk, legal, medical and counselling services to victims of violence under one roof integrated with a 24-hour Helpline. The *Nari Shakti Puruskars* are national level awards recognizing the efforts made by women and institutions in rendering distinguished services for the cause of women, especially vulnerable and marginalized women,,for pregnant women and lactating mothers has achieved a significan milestone by crossing one crore beneficiaries.

Urbanization in Bihar

India as a country has witnessed steady growth in its urbanization process, but not at a very accelerated pace. The rate of urbanization was recorded 25.5 percent in 1991 which rose to 27.2 percent in 2001 and further to 31.2 percent in 2011. The state of Bihar has recorded relatively high rate of economic growth in the last few years, however, it has a very low urbanization rate. The pattern of urbanization in Bihar is lopsided with South Bihar considerably more urbanized than the North Bihar, and urbanization overwhelmingly concentrated in large cities. Bihar is one of the lowest urbanized states of India. The scope of urban development in state is enormous due to its regional backwardness in the state. There are 9 Regional Administrative Divisions in Bihar namely Patna, Tirhut, Saran, Darbhanga, Kosi, Purnia, Bhagalpur, Munger and Magadh. Patna and Tirhut divisions comprise of 6 districts each. Bhagalpur division comprises of only 2 districts.

Patna Division has reported the highest urbanization (22.27 per cent) followed by Munger (22.27 per cent) and Bhagalpur (22.27 per cent). Kosi and Saran Divisions have registered the lowest urbanization. According to Census, 2011, 57 percent urban population of Bihar is concentrated in 26 class towns. One of the most exclusive features of urbanization in Bihar has been the exceptional growth of Patna. In fact, more than 95 percent urban population is concentrated in 130 larger towns. Class I towns (with more than one lakh population) accounted for about 59.3 percent of the total urban population of the state in 2001. This share declined slightly to 57.5 percent by 2011. In 2001, class II (population between 50,000-<100000) and class III (population between 20000-<50000) towns accounted for about 37 percent of the population. The rest of the towns accounted for only around 3.5 percent of the total urban population. The distribution of population shares among the different size-class of towns has not changed substantially in 2011, with Class II and Class III towns accounting for 37.2 percent of the urban population and the smaller towns accounting for just above 5 percent. The Class IV towns (population between 10,000 -19,999) accounted for 2.8 percent of urban population while Class V (population between 5000-9999) recorded population of just 2.2 percent. Thus, the number of all classes of towns has increased during the decade, and there is a remarkable increase in the number of class V towns from 3 in 2001 to 38 in 2011. Bihar urban development policy requires more attention towards process of urbanization, urban governance and infrastructure, if the state really wants to keep its urban centres as engine of growth. The challenges of development in Bihar are enormous due to persistent poverty, complex social stratification, unsatisfactory infrastructure and weak governance, problems that are known but not well understood (Singh:2019).

Governance Framework

Population growth of cities makes the scale and complexity of urban problems very daunting. It requires efficient and effective governance framework. Urban governance refers to the management of civic affairs by institutions to improve the quality of life in an inclusive, transparent, equitable and accountable manner. The 'good urban governance' is characterized by equity, efficiency, transparency, accountability, civic engagement and security of people as well as environment. This is the urban governance that enhances cities competitiveness and contributes to sustainability. The Seventy-Fourth Constitution Amendment Act, 1992 had envisaged creation of local self-governments for urban area population and accordingly the Municipalities were accorded constitutional status for governance. The States were required to entrust Municipalities with powers, functions and responsibilities to enable them to function as institutions of local self-government and carry out the responsibilities conferred upon them including 18 subjects listed in Twelfth Schedule of the Constitution. Accordingly, the Government of Bihar enacted the Bihar Municipal Act, 2007 by repealing the Bihar and Orissa Municipal Act, 1922 and framed Bihar Municipal Accounts Rules, 2014, the Bihar Municipal Accounting Manual and the Bihar Municipal Budget Manual. As of March 2016, there were 141 Urban Local Bodies (ULBs) in the State with 3,320 councillors.

Sections 7 and 20 of the Bihar Municipal Act, 2007 lay down the criteria for classification of municipal area by Government of Bihar. Municipal area of the state was divided into a number of wards on the basis of population which were determined and notified by the State Government. There were minimum 10 wards and maximum 75 wards across different classes of Municipalities in the state. As of March 2016, there were 3,320 wards in the state .The ULBs are under administrative control of Urban Development and Housing Department, Government of Bihar and headed by the Principal Secretary. The Municipal Commissioner is the executive head of the Municipal Corporation while Municipal Council and *Nagar Panchayat* are headed by the Executive Officers appointed by the State Government. City Manager is appointed on contractual basis in ULBs to assist the Executive Officer. The ULBs have an Empowered Standing Committee (ESC) comprising councillors elected by the people and headed by the Mayor (for Municipal Corporations), the Chairman (for Municipal Councils) and the Municipal President (for *Nagar Panchayats*) elected among members who preside over the meetings of the ESC. The Bihar Municipal Act, 2007 entrusts the State Government with certain powers so as to enable it to monitor proper functioning of the ULBs. The ULBs have some powers in delivery of some functions, but decision on all key issues rests largely with the State Government. The Seventy-Fourth Constitution Amendment Act (74th CAA) enables the ULBs to perform functions related to 18 subjects listed in the Twelfth Schedule of the Constitution. Accordingly, Government of Bihar made provisions in Bihar Municipal Act, 2007 for functions relating to 17 subjects (except fire services) to be carried out by the ULBs. Section 21 and 22 of Bihar Municipal Act, 2007 provide that in every Municipality, there shall be an Empowered Standing Committee (ESC) and the executive powers of a Municipality shall vest in ESC. The Chief Councillor shall exercise such powers and functions as are delegated to him by the ESC. The ESC is collectively responsible to the Municipal Corporation, the Municipal Council and the *Nagar Panchayat* as the case may be.

Article 243ZD of the Constitution envisages formation of a District Planning Committee (DPC) to consolidate the plans prepared by both the *Panchayats* and the Municipalities in the district and to prepare a Draft Development Plan (DDP) for the district as a whole. Accordingly, government framed Conduct of Business Rules, 2006. Section 275 of Bihar Municipal Act, 2007 also provides that all development plan to be executed by the

ULBs should be included in the DDP of the district consolidated by the DPCs and approved by the State Government. It was, however noticed that the development works executed up to 2015-16 by the ULBs from their own sources and civic amenities heads were not included in the DDPs of the district.

Women's Participation in Local Government

Women constitute half the world as well as in urban population. Despite their large numbers they have a very limited role to play in urban governance—policy and decision making as they are not sufficiently and properly represented in the Urban Local Bodies (ULBs). Though the functions and working of ULBs affect every man and woman, the latter has no or very minimal role as they are under-represented in leadership positions in local government institutions until recently. They do not have a role to influence local decisions resulting in insufficient access to services. This necessitates measures to provide equal representation in the municipal councils. As the ULBs are closest to the community they are the best places to involve women in local policy and decision-making so as to enable them to contribute in the policies and decisions that impact provision of civic services and quality of life. Several factors including discrimination, family burdens, financial constraints to contest to local governments, cultural factors, etc., come in the way of women participation. The political empowerment requires transformation of existing political structures and processes that are more responsive to women.

As the World Declaration on Women in Local Governance, 1998 noted that the problems and challenges facing humanity are global but occur and have to be dealt with at the local level. Women have the equal right to freedom from poverty, discrimination and insecurity. To fight these problems and to meet the challenges of sustainable human development, it is critical that women are empowered and participated in local governments as decision-makers, planners and managers. The 74th Constitution Amendment Act, 1992 for the first time widened the base to provide representation to hitherto under represented or unrepresented categories of the community, including women, in urban local self-government institutions. This has raised the question as to what key role women could play in urban governance. The 74th Constitution Amendment Act, 1992 provided one-third reservation for women. Based on the experience gained over two decades, the Government of India proposed 50 percent reservation for women in urban local bodies. The reservation for women in the local bodies is aimed at securing their active involvement and support in socio-economic development. Reservations became very important as in the normal process women were reluctant to contest the elections either because of murkiness and violence that often characterize electoral politics (Prasad: 2014).

The 74th Constitution Amendment Act, 1992 has laid foundations for the emergence of strong bottom up women leadership who could climb the ladder to occupy positions of power at the state and national levels. The 74th Constitution Amendment Act, 1992 which provided a constitutional status for ULBs in the country and considered a revolutionary and radical legislation, provided reservation of one-third of the strength of the council to women and also extended the same principle of reservation to women in other categories like SCs, STs apart from General category. The 74th Constitution Amendment Act, 1992 entrusts, through the 12th Schedule, important development functions to ULBs viz., urban planning, planning for socio-economic development, slum improvement, urban poverty alleviation, provision of basic amenities like roads, water supply, public health and sanitation, protection of the environment, safeguarding the interests of the weaker sections, etc., which have a major bearing on the development of women and children. The ability of the local bodies to undertake these functions, particularly those relating to poverty alleviation, safeguarding the interests of the weaker sections would, to a great extent, depend on the composition of the members of the councils who influence the local decision-making process (Prasad: 2014).

Role of Women in Urban Governance

Municipal Acts governing their organization and working specify the functions of municipalities and municipal corporations. Experience reveals that the chairpersons or councillors, whether they are men or women, have broadly four important roles to play in ULBs viz., policy, developmental, political and administrative.

Policy Role

Formulate development policies, prepare town development plans, take decisions regarding the integration of spatial development planning with economic development planning, lay down broad parameters for the future growth of the towns, mobilize resources to undertake both obligatory and discretionary functions, undertake measures for assisting the weaker sections, etc.

Development Role

Formulation, implementation and monitoring of development plans, including those for the weaker sections, women, etc. is their responsibility. Both national and state governments have articulated a number of development programmes. Formulation of city action plans under these schemes and ensuring their proper and effective implementation is a part of their development role. They have also to mobilize their share of the resources, to implement various plans and programmes wherever necessary.

Political Role

As peoples' representatives, the elected councillors are to be in constant touch with their constituents to reflect their aspirations, needs and perspectives in the articulation of town's development policies and plans. They are the links between the electors and the urban local body. Apart from this, as representatives of political parties they also have to undertake political activities. Mayors, chairpersons and councillors are constantly approached by their constituents with complaints or grievances relating to the municipal functioning. Being people's representatives, they have to attend to their day-to-day problems and continuously establish rapport with the community.

Administrative Role

Mayors, chairpersons and the chairpersons of standing and special committees play important role in civic governance. Supervising the functions of municipal officials in the implementation of development plans, monitoring their progress, ensuring the proper implementation of municipal laws and regulations, administrative coordination and convergence within the municipality and with external agencies, liaisoning with non-governmental organizations, resolutions of conflicts in the management of municipal affairs between the groups and communities, effective utilization of resources both internal and external, etc. are some of their administrative roles. The mayors and chairpersons, who are directly elected and have a term co-terminus with that of the council, will tend to have more of these responsibilities.

The 73rd and 74th Amendments (1992) to the Indian Constitution have served as a major breakthrough towards ensuring women's equal access and increased participation in political power structure. There are about one million elected women representatives in *Panchayats* and municipal bodies in India. It is estimated that elected women in all the three categories of ULBs account for 22622. However, a few states like Bihar, Madhya Pradesh and Rajasthan have declared to provide 50 percent reservation to women in ULBs elections. Thus, the number of elected women representatives is likely to increase (Table 1).

Table 1: Women Representation in ULBs of Selected States

State	*No. of ULBs*	*Total No. of Elected Representatives in ULBs*	*Total No. of Male Councillors*	*Total No. of Women Councillors*	*Percentage of Women Councillors*
Uttar Pradesh	653	12161	7266	4895	40.25
Chhattisgarh	168	3385	2257	1128	33.32
Madhya Pradesh	378	6706	3362	3344	49.87
Bihar	143	3358	1673	1658	49.37
Jharkhand	51	1061	513	547	51.56
Manipur	27	305	156	149	48.85
Uttarakhand	92	1150	694	456	39.65

Source: RCUES, Lucknow, 2019.

The Constitution Amendment Acts also ensured the provision of reservation of women in local governments. One-third seats were reserved in urban local bodies also. A few states such as Bihar, M.P. and Rajasthan have made provision for 50 percent reservation for women in local governments. Thus the gender mainstreaming in decentralized governance has been initiated. Moreover, women's share in policy perspective and resources allocation in urban sector has been reported to be very low. Gender mainstreaming is getting momentum. Smart City Mission, AMRUT, *Swachh Bharat* Mission, and reforms agenda seek to improve the effectiveness, accountability, efficiency, sustainability and service equity in cities. It also aims to reduce class and gender fragmentation by making socio-political-economic institutions, processes and resource allocations more equitable. Thus, gender based urban development is about promoting cities that respond, equally to men and women. Urban women experience cities differently and thus meeting their needs becomes critical for promoting sustainable and equitable urban development (Singh: 2013). The 74th Amendment to the Indian Constitution, 1992 has served as a major breakthrough towards women's equal access and increased participation in local government. The Constitution Amendment Act aims at constitutional guarantees to safeguard the interests of urban local government to enable them to function as effective and self governing institutions at grassroots level. This Amendment provides for reservation of 33 percent of elected seats for women at local government level in urban areas. There is also one-third reservation for women of posts of chairpersons for these local bodies. Involvement of women in the political arena and in decision making process is an important tool for empowerment as well as monitoring standards of political performance at local level.

Policy, Programmes and Schemes

Urban development schemes, programmes and projects target to infrastructure development, delivery of services, and strengthening of local governments. Sanitation has significant health costs and untreated sewage from cities is the single biggest source of water resource pollution in India. This indicates both the scale of the challenge ahead of the Indian cities and the huge costs incurred from not addressing them.

Swachh Bharat Mission

The *Swachh Bharat Mission* with the aim of elimination of open defecation, eradication of manual scavenging, modern and scientific municipal solid waste management, effect behavioral change regarding healthy sanitation practices, creation of awareness about sanitation and its linkage with public health, capacity augmentation for ULB's, and creating an enabling environment for private sector participation was launched in 2014. All statutory towns were covered under the Mission.

AMRUT (Atal Mission for Rejuvenation and Urban Transformation)

In the urban sector, the provision of amenities and basic services, viz., water supply, sewerage and urban transport in cities which improve the quality of life for all, and especially the poor and the disadvantaged is a national priority. It is considered that along with infrastructure creation, the last mile connectivity such as providing taps and toilet connections to all households would have a direct impact on the real needs of the people. AMRUT is aimed at transforming 500 cities and towns into efficient urban living spaces over a period of five years. AMRUT Mission was launched in June 2015, the AMRUT Mission focuses on provision of basic services - water supply; sewerage; storm water drainage; pedestrian, non-motorized and public transport facilities; development of parks and open spaces. The purpose of the Mission is to ensure that every household has access to a tap with assured supply of water and a sewerage connection; increase the amenity value of cities by developing greenery and well maintained open spaces; and reducing pollution by switching to public transport or constructing facilities for non-motorized transport. Overall, 500 cities/ towns in India have been selected while in Bihar state 26 towns have been selected for the AMRUT Mission. Access to piped water supply has been given the first priority in the state. Out of 26 project cities under AMRUT, first priority has been given to those towns whose DPRs are ready and can be executed immediately after approval. These 14 cities include those 4 cities where sewerage projects are likely to be completed in this year or early next year and therefore, water supply is the utmost priority. To make the urban towns green and environmentally healthy and livable, second priority has been given to the component "Development of Parks & Open Spaces". Although water supply is the first priority of the urban towns of the state, third priority has been given to water supply projects of other 7 towns of which DPRs are under preparation. Water supply project for Bhagalpur city is already being funded by the ADB, hence, the project has not been included in the SAAP.

Smart City Mission

Under the Smart Cities Mission, the objective is to promote cities that provide core infrastructure and give a decent quality of life to its citizens, a clean and sustainable environment and application of 'Smart' Solutions. The focus is on sustainable and inclusive development and the idea is to look at compact areas, create a replicable model which will act like a light house to other aspiring cities. The Smart Cities Mission of the Government is a bold, new initiative. It is meant to set examples that can be replicated both within and outside the Smart City, catalyzing the creation of similar

Smart Cities in various regions and parts of the country. Accordingly, the purpose of the Smart Cities Mission is to drive economic growth and improve the quality of life of people by enabling local area development and harnessing technology, especially technology that leads to Smart outcomes. Area-based development will transform existing areas (retrofit and redevelop), including slums, into better planned ones, thereby improving liveability of the whole City. New areas (Greenfield) will be developed around cities in order to accommodate the expanding population in urban areas. Application of Smart Solutions will enable cities to use technology, information and data to improve infrastructure and services. Comprehensive development in this way will improve quality of life, create employment and enhance incomes for all, especially the poor and the disadvantaged, leading to inclusive cities. The Mission will cover 100 cities and its duration will be five years (2015-16 to 2019- 20).

Muzzafarpur, Bihar Sharif, Patna and Bhagalpur have been selected under the Mission in Bihar state. The strategic components of Area-based development in the Smart Cities Mission are city improvement (retrofitting), city renewal (redevelopment) and city extension (Greenfield development) plus a Pan-city initiative in which Smart Solutions are applied covering larger parts of the city. Below are given the descriptions of the three models of Area-based Smart City Development. The Smart City Mission will be operated as a Centrally Sponsored Scheme (CSS) and the Central Government proposes to give financial support to the Mission to the extent of Rs. 48,000 crores over five years i.e. on an average Rs. 100 crore per city per year. An equal amount, on a matching basis, will have to be contributed by the State/ULB; therefore, nearly Rupees one lakh crore of Government/ULB funds will be available for Smart Cities Development.

Prime Minister's Awas Yojna-Housing for All

"Housing for All" Mission for urban area is being implemented since 2015 to provide central assistance for implementing agencies through states and UTs for providing houses to all eligible families/beneficiaries by 2022. All 4041 statutory towns as per Census 2011 with focus on 500 Class I cities would be covered in three phases as follows:

- Phase I (April 2015 - March 2017) to cover 100 Cities selected from States/UTs as per their willingness.
- Phase II (April 2017 - March 2019) to cover additional 200 Cities
- Phase III (April 2019 - March 2022) to cover all other remaining Cities

The Mission will be implemented through four verticals giving option to beneficiaries, ULBs and State Governments. These four verticals viz. slum re-development; affordable housing through credit linked subsidy;

affordable housing in partnership; and subsidy for beneficiary led housing. A Beneficiary will be eligible for availing only a single benefit under any of the existing op-tions i.e. slum redevelopment with private partner, credit link subsidy, direct subsidy to individual beneficiary and affordable housing in partnership. It will be the responsibility of State/UT Government to ensure that the beneficiary is not given benefit under more than one component of the Mission.

HRIDAY (National Heritage City Development and Augmentation Yojna)

The HRIDAY Scheme offers tremendous opportunity towards an integrated, inclusive and sustainable development of some heritage in India. The main objective of HRIDAY is to preserve the character and soul of the heritage city and facilitate inclusive heritage linked urban development by exploring various avenues including involving private sector HRIDAY offers a paradigm shift in India's approach to city development, bringing together urban planning/economic growth and heritage conservation in an inclusive and integrated manner with focus on livelihoods, skills, cleanliness, security, accessibility and service delivery. The scheme will support civic infrastructure development projects linking heritage facilities with trunk infrastructure of the city. The broad approach for implementation will be programme based rather than project based and accordingly the scheme will not bind it or create conditionality on proposed activities but should be based on the need and demand from the city. HRIDAY scheme focuses on development of twelve heritage cities viz Ajmer, Amravati, Amritsar, Badami, Dwarka, Gaya, Kanchipuram, Mathura, Puri, Varanasi, Velankanni and Warangal.

Gaya city has been selected from Bihar under the scheme. It is a central sector scheme with 100 percent funding coming from Central Government. Cities will be required to prepare City HRIDAY Plan for the city and develop DPRs for identified projects for availing assistance under the scheme.

DAY-NULM (Deendayal Upadhyay-National Urban Livelihood Mission)

The objective of the DAY- NULM is to reduce poverty and vulnerability of the urban poor households by enabling them to access gainful self-employment and skilled wage employment opportunities, resulting in an appreciable improvement in their livelihoods on a sustainable basis, through building strong grassroots level institutions of the poor. The main objective of the Mission is to reduce poverty among the urban poor through promotion of diversified and gainful self-employment and wage employment opportunities, leading to increased income on a sustainable basis. The components of the Mission include (i) social mobilization and institutional development; (ii) capacity building and training; (iii) employment through skill training and placement; (iv) self-employment programme; (v) support to urban street vendors and (vi) scheme of shelter for the urban homeless. The Mission emphasizes on building community institutions – SHGs and their federations, universal financial inclusion, revolving fund support to SHGs and their federations, capacity building and training, employment generation through skill training and placement activity, micro enterprise development, credit support for enterprise development and strengthening of livelihood centres/service centres at city/town level. In view of the gender inclusive policy approach, Government of India, under the Mission has made mandatory provision for reservation of women up to 30 percent in the beneficiaries of the scheme besides formation, strengthening, bank linkages and credit support to women SHGs. Credit support with the provision of interest subsidy for women has also been incorporated in the component of self-employment programme of the Mission. There are 13 towns/ cities from Bihar viz. Chapra, Bhagalpur, Munger, Patna, Arrah, Fatwah, Barh, Sultanganj, Barhya, Buxar, Mokama, Kahelgaon, and Hazipur.

Namami Gange Yojna

The aims and objectives of NMCG is to accomplish the mandate of National Ganga River Basin Authority (NGRBA) to ensure effective abatement of pollution and rejuvenation of the river Ganga by adopting a river basin approach to promote inter-sectoral co-ordination for comprehensive planning and management; and to maintain minimum ecological flows in the river Ganga with the aim of ensuring water quality and environmentally sustainable development. National Ganga River Basin Authority (NGRBA) has so far sanctioned a total 83 projects in 49 towns in Ganga States costing Rs.5918.56 crore under NGRBA Programme including Externally Aided Projects (EAP) component with the assistance of Japan International Agency (JICA) and the World Bank of Rs.4387.31 crore. These include projects of Rs. 1702.06 crore in Bihar for lying of sewage networks, treatment plants, development of river fronts, etc.

Slum Development

Bihar State Slum Policy, 2011 has been developed within the framework of the National Slum Policy and is to guide the state and local governments in addressing slum specific issues. All ULBs in the state shall endeavor to take up the work of up-gradation of slums, which are listed as tenable. 'Up-gradation' would mean facilitating housing, provision of basic services i.e. water supply, sewerage, toilets, street-lighting, street-paving, storm water drainage, collection and disposal of solid waste. Up-gradation would also include facilitating provision of social services such as health, education, income generation activities, and electric connections.

Managing Street Vendors

Bihar State Street Vendors (Protection of Livelihood and Regulation of Trade) Act, 2012 has been enacted to create suitable environment for urban street vendor and protecting their livelihoods. The state of Bihar has more than 41 percent of its population living below poverty line and it is not possible to provide employment opportunities to all of them in public sector thus it is imperative to find ways and means to earn their livelihood lawfully. The urban poor are unable to find suitable place for carrying out their trade and business at affordable price in urban areas and consequently are forced to take up street vending to earn their living. The urban street vendors form an important segment of the workforce in the unorganized sector. The street vendors' trade or business does conflict with the right of other citizens and requires regulation on certain principles so as to ensure free flow of traffic, smooth movement of pedestrians, maintenance of cleanliness and hygiene in public places; and protect the interest of street vendors to earn their modest living. It is considered expedient to give due recognition to the vital role played by the street vendors in the urban economy, legalize their status, promote a supportive environment for their activities and protect their livelihoods. The provisions under the Act have made for creation of vending zones, registration of vendors and constitution and functioning of Town Vending Committees.

State Development Mission

The Government of Bihar has constituted the Bihar *Vikas* Mission, registered under the provisions of Societies Registration Act, 1860 to ensure the implementation in mission mode, fixation of priorities, monitoring of achievements against the targets of programmes and other resolutions for development of Bihar under the programme of Good Governance 2015-2020. These resolutions include urban water supply, concretization of drains and streets in urban areas. These resolutions have been integrated in the existing centrally sponsored schemes of the state.

Girl Child Development

The state government envisions girls' education as a strategic pathway for women's economic empowerment and it has invested heavily in education programmes. Girls' access to quality formal schooling is being enhanced through several schemes such as the *Mukhya Mantri Balika Cycle Yojana, Mukhya Mantri Akshar Aanchal Yojana* and the *Mukhya Mantri Kanya Uthan Yojana*. Further, a plethora of skilling initiatives under the Bihar Skills Development Mission are being implemented to prepare young women to enter the workplace (Gender Report Card: 2019). The state government has also taken on the mantle to increase women's work participation in Bihar. Through landmark policies like 35 percent reservation for women in government jobs, and the focus on women's collectives under *JEEViKA*, it is hoped that women and girls in Bihar will be able to achieve their potential and fulfill their aspirations. Women's decision making ability and agency has intrinsic relevance for their individual well-being and quality of life, and is required if women are to play an active role in transforming institutions, social norms, and the well-being of their communities (Kabeer: 1999).

Skill India Mission, *Deen Dayal Upadhyay Grameen Kaushalya Yojana* (DDU-GKY), *Pradhan Mantri Kaushal Vikas Yojana*, Green Skill Development Programme have been initiated. The Government of Bihar's commitment to skilling is also evident; the Bihar Skill Development Mission provides for training to women and men through the *Kushal Yuva Programme* and Domain Skilling Centres. Entrepreneurship is a promising area for growing women's work participation, as it can offer opportunities for women from diverse contexts and with different capacities, within prevailing social norms. In the last decade, Bihar has taken several forward strides to improve governance, strengthen infrastructure, stimulate the economy, and advance social development through gains in education and health, especially for women and girls (Gender Report Card: 2019).

Gender Needs in Urban Development

Urban development in India is in need of a gender perspective because women and men experience cities in different ways. Research has shown that women and men experience and use the urban environment in different ways, and have different priorities in terms of municipal services and infrastructure (Beall: 1996). Women's interests and needs have been underrepresented in urban policy and development, largely due to a gender-blind approach, conventionally used in India. In order to promote sustainable and equitable urban development, it is critical to integrate women's needs in the design of programmes, infrastructure and services. Urban poverty is an unfortunate consequence of urbanization, with adverse impact on women and girls (Khoshala, 2009). Gender planning and tools of gender audit integrate these priorities into the urban development agenda, lay policy priorities, develop programmes, decide budget allocation priorities and create institutional mechanisms to ensure appropriate expenditures thereby providing significant opportunities for women's empowerment.

Water affects a range of issues that have serious impacts on quality of life for women, including health. Lack of adequate water infrastructure and services has different implications for women and men and particularly the most vulnerable women and households. Lack or inadequacy of basic sanitation services and infrastructure bears a disproportionate impact on women, particularly with regards to their time and security. Lack of safe and clean toilets has an adverse effect on women's health, physical security and exposure to violence. Housing provides multiple benefits to households. Housing security is important for the following reasons: it addresses the question of multi-dimensional poverty, ranging from reducing shelter deprivation to improving health status to providing space for home-based workers, etc. Transport and mobility have an important role to play not only in helping to meet women's practical needs such as access to maternal healthcare, but also in contributing to the strategic empowerment of women through promoting access to employment and socio-political upliftment The provision of safe, well-lit and accessible footpaths may be seen as a gender-specific priority. Difficulty in accessing safe and reliable transportation and footpaths is a form of social exclusion which restricts movement of women, and is particularly restrictive in regards to potential economic output.

Gender Approaches in Urban Administration

Gender-responsive urban planning can contribute to gender equity and women's empowerment in significant ways through the provision of: (i) accessible and affordable infrastructure and services for water supply and sanitation, waste disposal, electricity, transport, and housing; (ii) security of tenure; (iii) employment and income-generating opportunities through formal and informal labor markets; and (iv) safety and security for all citizens in growing urban neighborhoods. Gender inclusive infrastructure and service delivery approach will include (a) developing mechanisms for involving women in the planning, design, management, operation, and maintenance of urban infrastructure and services; (b) involving women in site planning and design; (c) considering gender-responsive physical design of urban infrastructure—vendor markets, bus and train terminals, municipal buildings, and separate male and female toilets in public spaces and buildings; (d) considering redesign of service technology and equipment (e.g., easy-to-handle water taps and lighter garbage bins, containers, user interface etc.; and (e) ensuring accessibility and affordability of basic services such as water supply and sanitation, electricity, waste disposal, transport, and health care.

A gender-and socially-inclusive city promotes equitable rights and provides opportunities and support for all residents to participate in urban life. Although there are encouraging urban initiatives in various cities in South Asia (UN-HABITAT: 2008), there is not yet a consolidated approach to inclusive urban policy and governance (Brown and Kristiansen: 2009). It is important for urban planners to look at what factors undermine women's capacity to participate in public decisions, for example the burden of multiple responsibilities, safety concerns, literacy, or lack of confidence / skills. Gender-sensitive urban governance involves more than simply increasing women's participation in urban planning, Addressing urban planning in a gender-sensitive way involves looking at how women and men access and benefit from the different aspects of urban life, for example municipal services, employment and livelihoods, housing, transport, and safety. Transportation systems are the key to urban life, enabling women to access healthcare, education, and employment opportunities. However, far too long, women have been ignored in urban transport planning and design (GTZ: 2007).

Research suggests that women are more likely to: walk or use less expensive transportation means; use off-peak and peripheral public transport routes; and feel unsafe and be at risk of violence while using urban public transport. There is a need for a new planning and governance approach to gender-balanced urban transport management, including capacity building and a new toolkit of measures and policies (John: 2011). The research finds that improving women's safety and security involves action in three key policy areas: (i) urban infrastructure, particularly street lighting, public toilets and public transport; (ii) urban planning, for example zoning to promote mixed-use developments, permanent traders and diverse activities, can improve women's sense of safety; (iii) police response to crime, for example: recruiting more women police; introducing a special police force to work proactively towards the protection of women especially in crowded places; creating a safe space in each police station for counseling; and training to sensitize key urban actors, including bus and auto drivers (Lama-Remal: 2011).

Gender Budgeting

Gender budgeting refers to the systematic examination of the budget programmes and policies for the impact on women. Studies show that programmes and policies design to improve women's economic opportunities lead to higher rates of economic growth. Gender budgeting has gained prominence in the policy circles in the recent years. Gender budgeting has gained prominence in the policy circles in the recent years. In view of the growing importance of the gender budgeting, the present study purports to critically review the plans, policies, programmes and schemes and also to examine union budgets through gender lens. In 1984, Australia first introduced the gender budget. Taking budgets as essential instruments for promoting gender equality, pioneering analysis of the impact of public budgets on gender relations was carried out. Since then, more than 90 countries have adopted gender budgeting as a tool for women empowerment and engendering development. In India too, many states, local governments, corporate houses and private agencies have initiated gender budgeting and have introduced specific policies, programmes and schemes for gender mainstreaming.

There are three major sources of income for ULBs. These are state and central governments allocation, state and centrally sponsored schemes; revenue obtained through local taxes, fees and user charges; and funds devolved by Central and State Finance Commissions. Besides international donor agencies like World Bank, Asian Development Bank, Japan Bank for International Cooperation, DFID etc. also provide financial support to municipalities for specific development projects in urban areas. Gender Sensitive Budgets demand reprioritization of financial allocations by the ULBs in favour of (Singh: 2019) as under:

- Working Women's Hostel, Crèches, Restaurant, Food Points, Public Toilets,
- Subsidized and low cost housing for single/deserted/divorced/ widow and female headed households,
- Skill training centres for women,
- A safe efficient and cheap public transport system,
- Safe drinking water,
- Waste Management Technological up-gradation,
- Multipurpose community centres,
- Proper electrification,
- Delivery of health and nutritional services.

Budgetary allocation for social services expenditure for capacity building, reduction of domestic drudgery and better quality of life for women is need of hour. Education, health, crèche, working women's hostel, housing, nutrition, water supply, drainage, sanitation, public toilets, fuel and energy, waste management and public transport are some of the major areas of social services expenditure by which women are likely to get more benefits. Women also need SHG based credit for self-employment. Similarly, training programmes, vocational and skill improvement training in prospective areas like bio-technology, IT etc. will create employment opportunities to women. Marketing facilities for women entrepreneurs and the implementation of National Street Vendor Policy will provide additional benefits to women for promoting self-employment ventures. Thus, it is imperative to create Women Development Cell in each urban local body for gender responsive budgeting and gender based profiling of municipal expenditure. This cell is also likely to address the gender issues and concerns in urban areas.

Gender Budgeting as a tool is used for achieving gender equality and particularly correct the planning and investment distortions within government spending. Gender Budgeting is likely to help to (i) balanced gender needs through appropriate budget in financial systems; (ii) ensure pro-poor urban expenditure in areas such as water supply, sanitation-provision of sewerage and toilets, infrastructure development, storm water drainage, solid waste management; provision of low cost public transport, development of roads, provision of economic infrastructure etc.; (iii) provide for human specific urban expenditure that are targeted to include women's requirements in the provision of housing, markets, buses, parks and recreation centers. Gender auditing tools have been developed by UNDP that recommend a participative process for gender budgeting and for development of gender sensitive urban expenditure policy and guidelines.

A toolkit has also been developed USAID for identifying gender needs in planning the successfully tested mechanism for gender based planning. The tools for gender inclusion in budgeting and urban planning process include: (a) spatial maps to asses women's access to physical, social, economic, infrastructure to help develop a mix of macro and micro level plans; (b) gender profiling a public expenditure, with impact assessment studies to understand gender based spending and (c) gender based auditing and beneficiary assessments.

Gender Budgeting in Bihar

During the last decade, improvement in various socio-economic indicators demonstrates that Bihar is steadily moving upward in the development ladder. Presently, Bihar is one of the fastest growing states in India. Bihar's recent growth rate is greater than the national average. Higher economic growth has been translated into higher expenditure in the social services, viz. health, education, housing, water & sanitation, social security, etc., which, in turn, led to substantial poverty reduction and improvements in various development indicators in Bihar. Introduction of Gender Budgeting is a good initiative from the Government of Bihar. At the same time, it should be noted that at present, there are a large number of programmes/ schemes for the welfare of women and children run by the central and state governments. Many of these programmes/schemes cannot be segregated exclusively for women and children as welfare of women and children are intertwined. Over the years, the scale of operation of these programmes is also expanding which is reflected in the increasing size of annual budget (Oxfam: 2017). The achievement of human development is heavily dependent and empowerment of the 4.9 million women and girls in Bihar who, as per Census, 2011 is 47.8 percent of total population of the state. These women and girls not only comprise a large part of the valuable human resource of the state, they are also individual in their own right and their socio-economic development sets the foundation for sustainable growth of the economy and society as a whole (Gender Resource Centre: 2018).

Bihar has been pioneer in launching the gender report card in 2019. Gender report card is a vital measure of transformational approaches being undertaken in the state of Bihar in order to achieve equitable socio-economic development and gender equality. This provides vital information on health, education, water and sanitation, social, economic and political empowerment of women and girls in the state. The state has evolved indicators for measuring the progress in social and economic sector particularly empowerment of women. The state has launched State Policy for Empowerment of Women with the vision of equitable access by women irrespective of class, caste and race to economic, education and health resources by addressing structural and institutional barriers and ensuring that gender equality and to ensure that equity transcends across all sectors of development. In view of Sustainable Development Goals and ensuring gender equality, the state has fixed targets for ending all forms of discriminations against women and girls; eliminating harmful practices, forms of violence; recognizing and value unpaid care and domestic work; ensuring women's full and effective participation and equal opportunities for leadership; ensuring universal access to sexual and reproductive health; undertaking reforms for equal rights to economic resources; enhancing the use of enabling technology; and adopting and strengthening policies and legislations for promotion of gender equality.

The schemes, programmes and projects have been classified in three broad categories in terms of expenditure viz. (i) women specific expenditure-: those schemes, programmes and projects which have 100 percent targets for women; (ii) pro women expenditure- those schemes, projects and programmes which have target upto 30 percent women; and (iii) gender neutral expenditure - those schemes, programmes and projects which targets less than 30 percent women. The gross gender budget comprises of expenditure under category one and category two. Gross gender budget in Bihar is shown in Table 2. Gross gender budget was amounted Rs. 5970.44 crores in 2011-12 which increased to Rs. 25573.80 crores during 2018-19. The gross gender budget has increased by more than 4 times during the period. Out of total gross gender budget, gross gender budget under

Table-2: Gross Gender Budget in Bihar

(Rs. Crores)

Year	*Category-A*	*Category-B*	*Total*
2011-12	2005.04	3965.40	5970.44
2012-13	1907.51	5933.89	7841.40
2013-14	1864.20	6152.42	8016.62
2014-15	3484.97	5899.26	9380.24
2015-16	3189.96	8267.97	11457.92
2016-17	6039.46	8476.11	14515.57
CAGR	24.5	14.5	17.8
2017-18 (RE)	9810.08	12491.15	22301.23
2018-19 (BE)	11307.83	14265.97	25573.80

Source: Department of Finance, Government of Bihar, Patna.

category-A accounted for 33.58 percent in 2011-12 while it was recorded 44.22 percent in 2018-19. During the period 2011-12 to 2016-17, gross gender budget increased by 17.8 percent per annum while it was recorded as high as 24.5 percent per annum in gross gender budget under category-A.

Percentage of gender budget to total budget and GSDP in the state is shown in Table 3 Gender budget accounted for 5.8 percent to state budget during 2008-09 which increased to 11.5 percent in 2016-17. Gender budget constituted 1.9 percent of GSDP in 2008-09 which increased to 4.3 percent in 2016-17.

Table 3: Percentage of Gender Budget to Total Budget and GSDP

Year	*Percentage of State Budget*	*Percentage of GSDP*
2008-09	5.8	1.9
2009-10	7.1	2.6
2010-11	8.7	2.8
2011-12	10.1	2.9
2012-13	11.3	2.7
2013-14	12.1	2.8
2014-15	13.3	2.1
2015-16	9.4	2.4
2016-17	11.5	4.3

Source: Department of Finance, Government of Bihar, Patna.

Expenditure of gross gender budget in the state is shown in Table 4. Establishment expenditure accounted for 15.64 percent in 2011-12 which decreased to 9 percent in 2018-19. Thus, more than 90 percent expenditure under gender budget was reported under various schemes.

Table 4: Expenditure on Gross Gender Budget in Bihar

(Rs. crore)

Year	***Establishment***	***Schemes***	***Total***
2011-12	934.07	5036.37	5970.44
2012-13	1256.73	6584.68	7841.40
2013-14	1434.67	6581.95	8016.62
2014-15	1490.47	7889.77	9380.24
2015-16	1535.22	9922.71	11457.92
2016-17	1419.09	13096.48	14515.57
CAGR	8.1	19.3	17.8
2017-18 (RE)	1928.41	20372.82	22301.23
2018-19 (BE)	2312.61	23261.19	25573.80

Source: Department of Finance, Government of Bihar, Patna.

Department-wise expenditure for women in the state is shown in Table 5. Bihar initiated the gender budgeting process way back in 2008-09. During 2013-14, 9 departments indicated Rs. 272267.96 lakh for women specific schemes while 14 departments indicated Rs. 687969.2 lakh as pro-women allocations. Presently, 28 Departments of the state have constituted Gender Cell and have introduced gender budget analysis. The 19 departments which allocated budget for women during 2015-16 and 2016-17 as shown in Table 4 demonstrated that gender budget constituted 41.44 percent of total budgetary allocation of these departments in 2016-17. It has shown an increase of 5.56 percentage points from previous year. The Department of Revenue and Land Reforms, Information and Technology, Department of Health and Department of Rural Development and Urban Development and Housing Department allocated more than half of the budget for women in 2016-17. During 2015-16, proportion of women expenditure against total budgetary allocation was /recorded high for Department of Revenue and Land Reforms, Department of Rural Development, Department of Labour Resources, Department of Social Welfare and Department of Urban Development Housing (Table-5).

Table-5: Department-wise Expenditure for Women in Bihar

(Rs. Crores)

Departments	*2015-16*		*2016-17 (BE)*	
	Expenditure	*Percentage*	*Expenditure*	*Percentage*
Social Welfare	1907.09	51.59	2362.38	49.66
SC/ST Welfare	413.61	28.96	465.51	29.67
PHED	329.94	29.99	397/91	29.99
Minority Welfare	50.25	30.87	18.26	32.48
Education	4537.66	33.06	4732.25	30.28
Health	85.12	13.63	1890.14	89.29
Rural Development	2605.67	62.24	3540.7	69.98
Urban Development and Housing	1.61	50.16	6.08	50.04
Panchayati Raj	112.29	49.99	167.5	50.0
Labour Resources	4.02	56.62	5.62	47.63
Planning and Development	269.63	30.0	0.0	0.0
BC and EBC Welfare	593.58	30.35	593.59	30.38
Revenue and Land Reforms	26.25	100.0	20.75	100.0
Art, Culture and Youth	13.71	29.99	11.62	29.99
Industry	29.73	11.32	63.87	30.0
Agriculture	56.09	2.99	646.92	29.99
Information and Technology	0.43	27.04	1.88	89.52
Building Construction	90.28	30.67	77.23	28.45
Home	0.0	0.0	61.48	40.45
Total	**11126.96**	**35.88**	**15063.68**	**41.44**

Source: Department of Finance, Government of Bihar, Patna.

Conclusion

Gender inclusive urban planning and development is gaining momentum in the context of economic liberalization, globalization and new policy regime. Government of India under various mission mode schemes has also provided massive investment for urban infrastructure development and delivery of municipal services. Many pro-poor policies and programmes have been initiated by the Central and state governments besides the provision of urban reforms for strengthening urban local governments to improve their functioning and thus bettering basic services to the urban poor. The issue of engendering development and women empowerment has been in the central stage with the shifting of paradigm of development and governance at the global level and particularly in India. Gender budgeting has emerged as an important instrument for gender mainstream and women empowerment across the globe. It has been well recognized by the policy makers and feminist economists that gender budgeting is imperative for gender equality and engendering development planning. Gender budgeting refers to the systematic examination of the budget programmes and policies for the impact on women. Studies show that programmes and policies designed to improve women's economic opportunities lead to higher rates of economic growth. Gender budgeting has gained prominence in the policy circles in the recent years.

Here are some suggestions to effectivise the gender budgeting:

- The gender disaggregated database has to be created and strengthened in the local governments including parastatal agencies, which will enable better analysis and more effective monitoring of targets and achievements for men and women. The Gender Report Card is vital for social transformation and ensuring gender equality. However, gender disaggregated data from each department/ organization will be required.
- The role of women in decision making process and urban planning must be enhanced besides, ensuring participatory budgeting in local bodies. Political and administrative will power is required for gender mainstreaming in urban development and governance. The women councillors need training for their active participation in decentralized governance.
- Construction of toilets, night shelters, rest houses, etc. for women has to be ensured at the major bus stations, railway stations and public places besides ensuring proper street lighting in isolated places, fruits and vegetable markets, hospitals, nursing homes, religious places, etc.
- The vulnerable and marginalized cannot be painted with a broad brush. The needs of those women who are marginalized may not

be the same as those of people on the verge of rising above it or to those who have just crossed this threshold but are still short of achieving a minimum standard of living. Understanding these different faces of deprivation can shed light on the most critical needs confronting each segment of women who struggle below empowerment line. Thus, hunger, poverty, health care, drinking water, sanitation is key issues. Besides deprivation, discrimination, exclusion among socio religious groups and disparities among gender and geographical regions are to be addressed through development planning and enhancing budgetary allocations.

- Special emphasis should be given to promote the employment opportunities for women in those sectors of economy which have been leading the economic growth in the country such as information technology, telecommunication, bio-technology, street vending, domestic help, nursing, teaching, etc.
- The state governments must produce outcome budget while the performance report must contain the quality and authentic information. The state governments should provide statement on gender budget allocation from all the departments. All departments must provide data about allocation and expenditure for women's specific schemes along with the fiscal and financial achievements.
- There is a strong need to monitor the gender specific impact of budgetary policies and expenditure and reprioritize policies to reduce the bias against women in the benefit incidence of the budget.
- Gender responsive budget approach is a tool and not necessarily a standalone exercise. Unless the necessary resources are allocated, gender sensitive policies and programmes will not succeed. The prerequisite of gender budgeting are political will, accountability, human and financial resources, coordination, gender disaggregated data, transparency and partnership and cooperation. Thus, there is need to establish linkages and cordial relations for ensuring the achievements of the prerequisite for promoting gender budgeting exercises.

References

- Beall, J (1996): 'Urban Governance: Why Gender Matters', Gender in Development Monograph Series No 1, UNDP, New York.
- Brown, A. and Kristiansen, A.(2009): 'Urban Policies and the Right to the City: Rights, Responsibilities and Citizenship', MOST-2 Policy Papers series, UNESCO/UN-HABITAT.
- Development Alternatives (2015): Achieving The Sustainable Development Goals in India : A Study of Financial requirements and Gaps, development Alternatives, New Delhi.

- Gender Resource Centre (2018): Status Report on Gender Budgeting in Bihar, Gender Resource Centre, Women Development Corporation, Deptt. of Social Welfare, Government of Bihar, Patna.
- Government of Bihar (2019): Women & Girls in Bihar Taking Stock, Looking Ahead Gender Report Card – 2019, Deptt. of Social Welfare, Government of Bihar.
- GTZ, (2007): 'Gender and Urban Transport: Fashionable and Affordable', Module 7a, Sustainable Transport: A Sourcebook for Policy Makers in Developing Countries, GTZ, Eschborn.
- Helan, D. (2001): General Manual: A Practical Guide for Development Policy Makers and Practitioners, DFID, London.
- John, J. (2011): 'Gender Inclusive Urban Transport: Issues and Initiatives', Prepared for Regional Seminar, Gender, Urban Development and Water Supply and Sanitation, 14-16 November 2011, Vientiane, Lao PDR.
- Kabeer, Naila. (1999): Resources, Agency and Achievements: Reflections on the Measurement of Women's Empowerment. Development and Change 30 (3): 35–64.
- Khoshala, Renu (2009): Addressing Gender Concerns in India's Urban Renewal Mission, UNDP, New Delhi.
- Lama-Rewal, S.T. (2011): 'Women's Rights to the City: From Safety to CItizenship', in UNESCO (ed). Urban Policies and the Right to the City in India: Rights, Responsibilities and Citizenship, pp. 31-38.
- Narayan, D. & Petesch, P. (Ed.) (2002): Voices of the Poor from Many Lands, Oxford University Press, New York.
- National Alliance of Women (2008): Engendering 11th Five Year Plan: Removing Obstacles, Creating Opportunities, National Alliance of Women, New Delhi.
- Oxfam (2017): Development in Bihar: Some Policy Prescriptions From Gender Lens, Oxfam India, Policy Brief, 24, July, New Delhi.
- Prasad, D. Ravindra (2014): Women Empowerment in Urban Governance in India, Indian Journal of Public Administration, Vol. LX-3, July-September.
- Singh, A. K. (2019): Gender Inclusive Urban Development in Bihar, Anveshan, Volume 9, Number 2, July- December.
- Singh, A. K. and Singh, A. P (2018): Mainstreaming Gender: A Study of Urban Women Street Vendors of women's Markets in Manipur, Journal of Social Work Education, Research and Action, Volume 4, issue 1, January- April.
- Singh, A.K. (2013): Gender Mainstreaming in Urban Administration, IN Empowerment of Women Through Gender Budgeting, Edited by Mita Ashish Shah, Aviskar Publishers, Jaipur.
- Singh, S. & Srivastava, S.P. (2001): Gender Equality Through Women Empowerment, Bharat Book Centre, Lucknow.
- UN Women (2015): Women and Sustainable Goal, UN Women, Nairobi, Kenya
- UNDP (2003): Human Development Report, UNDP, Washington.
- UN-HABITAT (2008): 'Gender Mainstreaming in Local Authorities: Best Practices,' UN-HABITAT, Nairobi.

- UNICEF (2007): Women and Children: The Double Dividend of Gender Equality, UNICEF, New York.
- UNIFEM (2013): Locating Gender in the 12th Five Year Plan Approach: Issues Emerging from a Gendered Analysis, UNIFEM, New Delhi.

16

Tourism Administration and Infrastructure in Meghalaya and Mizoram

— Jyoti Bikash Chakma & NVR Jyoti Kumar

Introduction

The tourism and hospitality industry is currently one of the most important industries worldwide. Tourism being a multi sectoral activity has the capacity to stimulate different sectors of the economy. It is evident from highly developed countries that tourism opens up immense opportunities for economic development, poverty reduction and income generation. Considered as one of the world's most diverse regions, the bio-diversity of Northeast India (NEI) is quite amazing. The land is a blend of wild life, flora and fauna, tribal and non-tribal populations with unique cultural identity, colourful festivals and arts and crafts. In fact, the region is a kaleidoscope of cultural extravaganza with enormous natural delights (Rizal and Asokan: 2013).

Though considered remote and isolated as compared to other parts of the country, tourism holds high potential in the select states of NEI, viz. Meghalaya and Mizoram because of their natural assets, ethnic diversity and the societal ethos. Tourism has one of the greatest potentials for generating income and employment opportunities in these two states as they are exceptionally rich in tourism resources. The select states are endowed with beautiful treks, charming caves, wildlife sanctuaries, scenic lakes, waterfalls, picturesque villages and so much more. The turbulent rivers, green forests, mountains, hills and cliffs of higher altitude offer thrilling adventure sports of trekking, mountaineering, river rafting, rock climbing, cave exploring, etc. The unique cultures of the beautiful tribes through their festivals with folk songs, dances, food and crafts, etc. reflect the cultural richness of these two states. One may wonder by seeing the abundance of tourism resources in these states which are still to be explored.

The paper aims to study the tourism administration in Meghalaya and Mizoram and to explore the tourism infrastructure available in these two states. The efficiency and efficacy of state administration reflect in the pace of development of tourism infrastructure in these states. The administration in these states seems to be committed to unleash the potential of so far untapped tourism therein.

Emergence of Tourism in Select States

The history of tourism industry in Northeast India (NEI) including the select states, i.e. Meghalaya and Mizoram is quite new. However, with the introduction of tourism as an industry, it has emerged as one of the prospective sectors in the region recently.

The initiative of the Government of Meghalaya towards tourism promotion started with the establishment of the Directorate of Tourism in the year 1972. The objectives of the Directorate of Tourism are firstly to promote tourism and take steps for creation of proper infrastructure for tourism development in the state. The Meghalaya Tourism Development Corporation Ltd. (MTDC) was subsequently set up in January, 1977. In fact, Meghalaya was the first state in Northeast India and also one of the pioneer states in India to launch a tourism development corporation (Bhattacharjee: 2001). Before the establishment of Tourism Department in the state, tourist information centres were already established at New Delhi and Kolkata, in the year 1970. Other tourist information centres at Tura, Guwahati, Baghmara and Jowai were established during 1975, 1978 and 2001 respectively.

In Mizoram, the Tourism Department had a subordinate status prior to 1987 when it was a part of the Department of Information and Public Relations. The tourism promotion activities in Mizoram were actually started following its emergence as the 23rd state of Indian Union in 1987, when the state government set up the Directorate of Tourism. The Directorate is having its head office at Aizawl but has no district office in the state. In addition, the state government has five Liaison Houses situated outside the state. These five offices are at New Delhi, Kolkata, Guwahati, Shillong and Silchar. These offices, apart from the issuance of inner-line permits (a permit needed while visiting the state) to domestic tourists provide necessary information about the state.

Organisational Structure

Meghalaya tourism

The Department of Tourism, Meghalaya is the administrative department responsible to oversee and co-ordinate the function of the Directorate of

Tourism and the Meghalaya Tourism Development Corporation Ltd., (MTDC) so as to ensure uniform implementation of governmental procedures. The department is a part of the State Secretariat that normally confines itself to general policies - direction, legislation, assembly business, inter-departmental matters and review assessment of execution of policy and scheme.

At present, the Directorate of Tourism is headquartered in Shillong and its main aim is to provide tourist amenities like accommodation, transport, etc. and place Meghalaya on the world tourist map. The initiative of the directorate is to provide adequate services and infrastructural facilities for enhancing tourist traffic and generate revenue for the state. It is taking steps to upgrade the tourist infrastructure, identify new tourist spots and improve the existing ones. The directorate promotes tourism in the state and implements various schemes for the benefit of the visiting tourists. With this in view, a technical cell has been created recently to monitor various tourism projects. Promotional activities are being organised in the form of festivals, participation in fairs, exhibitions, marts, holding of awareness programmes and publicity campaigns through advertisements in the print and electronic media. The main functions of Department of Tourism in Meghalaya are identified as the following:

(i) Policy matters on development of tourism in the state,

(ii) Preparation and approval of schemes for the development and promotion of tourism and tourism infrastructure,

(iii) Promotion and marketing of tourism products of the state,

(iv) Financial assistance for creation of home-stays and resorts, and

(v) Building skill and capacity in the hospitality sector of the state by providing relevant training.

The MTDC was established in 1977 under the patronage of the Government of Meghalaya. The main objective was to promote tourism in the state and to expand the infrastructure facilities for the tourists. The corporation started its activities from 1st July, 1984. The aims and objectives of the corporation as spelt out in its Memorandum of Association are briefly described as follows:

(i) Manage existing hotels, restaurant, cafes and transport in efficient manner,

(ii) Produce, distribute, design, print and publish publicity materials for providing publicity,

(iii) Provide entertainment by way of cultural shows, dances, music concerts etc.,

(iv) Provide shopping facilities to tourists, and

(v) Promote tourism by all ways and means and to adopt such methods and devices desirable and necessary to attract tourists.

The management of the corporation is vested in the Board of Directors appointed by the state government, which includes a Chairman and Vice Chairman. The Managing Director is the Chief Executive of the corporation and is assisted by officers both at the head office in different divisions as well as managers of units. At the corporate office, the distribution of responsibilities is divided into the different divisions.

Mizoram tourism

The Department of Tourism in Mizoram was established by bifurcating from the Department of Information and Public Relations in the year 1987. The department was created to act as a nodal agency for development and promotion of tourism in the state. Since then it has been making endless efforts to promote tourism in the state by utilizing the available resources, building new tourist infrastructures, promoting rural tourism, focusing on human resource development and by promoting fairs and festivals. At present, it is headquartered at Aizawl and has no other offices in the districts.

The vision of the department is "to develop tourism in a sustainable and integrated manner so as to make Mizoram a major national and international tourism destination, catalyzing growth and economic development". The main objectives of the department are:

(i) Promotion of tourism industry with a comprehensive approach and which will not be in conflict with the social, religious and cultural values of the host community,

(ii) To create conducive environment for growth of tourism industry by imparting awareness of the scope and the positive impacts of tourism to both urban and rural population,

(iii) To actively promote ecotourism and nature based tourism,

(iv) To upgrade and develop manpower skills with a view to providing requisite expertise to the youth so as to render them fit for employment in this industry,

(v) To promote public private partnership in development and management of tourist infrastructures in the state,

(vi) To enhance and monitor the growth of tourism by way of registration and formulation of guidelines for the tourism sector, and

(vii) To encourage private sector participation for creation of quality tourism infrastructure and to ensure better management of tourism projects.

The department has a Directorate but has no district offices in the state. The Directorate, headed by a Director, is the implementing agency of the Department of Tourism. Its main function has been the development of tourism and its allied activities and building basic infrastructure for tourists. Other than the Tourism Department, two agencies namely Mizoram Tourism Development Authority (MTDA) and Mizoram Tourism Development Board (MTDB) were also created for smooth functioning of tourism developmental activities in the state.

The MTDA is a society formed in the year 2008 and is chaired by the Minister of Tourism, Government of Mizoram with members drawn from officers of Tourism Department, Government of Mizoram and representatives of tourism service providers in the state. The main aim and objective of the society is to assist the efforts of the Central Government and the State Government in respect of development of tourism in the State. MTDA has been the main agency for implementing projects and other developmental works assigned to it by the Tourism Department.

The Mizoram Tourism Development Board (MTDB) under the chairmanship of the Hon'ble Chief Minister, Government of Mizoram was created on 8th June, 2010 by the Government of Mizoram for promotion and development of Tourism in Mizoram. The chief function of the MTDB is to identify and recommend strategies/ policies for development of tourism industry in Mizoram.

Tourism Infrastructure

Tourism provides direct benefits to the local community and businesses. The infrastructure required by tourism includes transport, communications, water supply and health services (Yes Bank: 2014). The status of the basic tourism infrastructure in NEI is much below the minimum standards. Over the years attempts have been made by various tourism organizations for improving tourism infrastructure in the region in the areas of transport, communication, power, water supply, etc. but quantum is quite limited. Besides, such infrastructural improvement generally polarized in pockets of the region which were explored and campaigned under conventional 'circuit specific strategy' of tourism planning adopted by govt. of India and subsequently by the concerned states of the region (Bhattacharya: 2008).

(1) **Connectivity:** Connectivity acts as a bridge between places of tourist origin and destinations. Tourism becomes more attractive if a region has all possible types of alternative connectivity facilities like transportation and communication, and accessibility to different tourism destinations. A tourist requires not just an access to a tourism destination but also an easy access in terms of cost, time and level of comforts.

(a) Connectivity of Meghalaya

(i) *Roads:* Meghalaya is well connected by a network of roads with all important cities of NEI. There are two major National Highways (NH) pass through Shillong, the state capital. One is NH-40 that connects to Guwahati and the other is NH-44 that connects the state with Tripura and Mizoram. Private bus operators as well as state transport buses from other states ply to and from Shillong daily. Maxi cabs and taxi services are also available to various destinations like Guwahati, Agartala, Dimapur and other important towns and cities of NEI.

(ii) *Airways:* Meghalaya is connected to the rest of India by airways too. The state has an airport located at Umroi, a small township 30 km away from Shillong. Guwahati is the nearest international airport from where Shillong can be reached by bus or car. Pawan Hans Helicopters Ltd., under the aegis of the Government of Meghalaya, has commenced regular helicopter flights connecting Shillong and Tura to Guwahati.

(iii) *Railways:* The state does not have any railway service. The nearest railhead of Meghalaya is at Guwahati (Assam), which is well connected to major cities in India via an extensive rail network. Taxis, maxi cabs, bus services are available for travel between Shillong and Guwahati at regular intervals.

(iv) *Waterways:* The Parliamentary Standing Committee declared four rivers of Meghalaya, Jinjiram, Kynshi, Simsang, Umngot (Dawki), as national waterways on August 12, 2015 to enhance trade and commerce with Bangladesh. The matter came into prominence during Prime Minister Narendra Modi's visit to Bangladesh where India and Bangladesh inked the agreement on Coastal Shipping for two-way trade through ports. According to the MoU, two Bangladesh ports, i.e. Chittagong and Mongla Ports can be used by India to ship goods to landlocked states in the Northeast which includes to Agartala (Tripura), Dawki (Meghalaya) and Sutarkandi (Assam).

(b) Connectivity of Mizoram

(i) *Roads:* Mizoram is connected to the Indian road network through NH-54. Another highway, NH-150 connects the state with Selling (Mizoram) to Imphal (Manipur) and NH-40A links the state with Tripura. A road between Champhai (Mizoram) and Tiddim (Myanmar) has been proposed but the Myanmarese authorities are unwilling to complete the link. Aizawl, the capital city is connected from Shillong and Guwahati by buses and maxi cabs through Silchar through NH-54.

(ii) *Airways:* Mizoram has an airport at Lengpui, a small town about 32 kms from Aizawl city. It is thoroughly connected by flights from major cities like Kolkata, Guwahati and Imphal. Mizoram can also be reached from Kolkata via Silchar Airport, which is about 180 km (about 6 hour by road) from Aizawl. However, many times due to inclement weather conditions certain times flights get delayed or even cancelled.

(iii) *Railways:* In Mizoram, there is a rail link at Bairabi station but it is primarily for goods, that also still in a non-functional state till recently. Hence, the nearest practical railway station for Mizoram is at Silchar in Assam.

(iv) *Waterways:* Mizoram is in the process of developing waterways with the port of Akyab, Sittwe in Myanmar along Chhimtuipui River. India is investing $ 103 million to develop the Sittwe port on Myanmar's northern coast, about 160 km from Mizoram. The Myanmar government has committed $10 million for the venture, which is part of the Kaladan Multi-Model Project (Joshi: 2011). This joint venture has been the focal point of the popular "Act East Policy" of Government of India. Mizoram has a potential of developing waterways with Bangladesh too, as Bangladesh can be approached by a ferry through the river Khawthlangtuipui near Tlabung.

(2) Tourism Circuits: Tourism circuit has become a very popular concept in the tourism sector today. Developing tourism circuits make tours and travel more economical for both tourists and tourism departments. As noted earlier, both Meghalaya and Mizoram are rich in varied tourism attractions, some of which are unmatched in terms of attractiveness and pull factor. However, due to lack of proper tourism circuits in whole NEI, these tourism products do not get well marketed. Thus, it is important to develop tourism circuits, so that these tourism destinations get good tourist visitation and developed.

(a) Tourism circuits in Meghalaya: Barring Sikkim and Assam, tourism circuits of Meghalaya are relatively advanced than other states of NEI. Shillong, the state's capital forms an integral part of the most visited tourism circuits (other than Sikkim circuit) of NEI. Some of the important intra-state tourism circuits in Meghalaya are highlighted in Table 1:

Table-1: Tourism Circuits in Meghalaya

Sl. No.	*Intra-state tourism circuit*
1.	Shillong (Day Trip)
2.	Shillong-Barapani-Shillong (Day Trip)
3.	Shillong-Sohra-Shillong (Day Trip)
4.	Shillong-Sohra-Laitkynsew-Shillong (Day Trip)
5.	Shillong-Mawphlang-Mawsynram-Shillong (Day Trip)
6.	Shillong-Smit-Thadlaskein-Nartiang-Shillong (Day Trip)
7.	Jowai-Nartiang-Syndai-Jowai (Day Trip)
8.	Tura-Babadam-Nokrek-Tura (Day Trip or a 3 day trek)
9.	Tura-Siju-Balpakram-Baghmara-Tura (Approximately a week)

Source: Department of Tourism, Meghalaya.

Beside these, the Meghalaya Tourism Development Corporation (MTDC) organizes the following local and conducted tours:

(i) *Shillong package*: Elephant Falls, Shillong Peak, Lady Hydari Park, Laitumkhrah Cathedral, Wards Lake, Golf Course and State Museum.

(ii) *Shillong-Barapani package:* The tour covers the following places of tourist interest: Elephant Falls, Shillong Peak, Lady Hydari Park, Laitumkhrah Cathedral, Wards Lake, Golf Course, State Museum, Bishop Beadon Falls and Barapani Lake.

(iii) *Sohra (Cherrapunjee) package:* Mawkdok Valley, Ramkrishna Mission, Nohkalikai Falls. Mawsmai Caves, Eco Park, Nohsngithiang Falls, Thangkharang Park and Motrop (giant conical rock).

Mawsynram package: Mawjyngbuin Cave, Khreng Khreng (cracked rock), Rit Mawksir (view point) and Jakrem (hot-water spring).

(iv) *Nartiang package:* Durga Mandir, Shiv Mandir, Monolith Park, Thadlaskein Lake and Thadlaskein Resort.

(b) Tourism circuits in Mizoram: There are no specific inter-state tourism circuits identified in the context of Mizoram state. Intra-state circuits may also not be so required considering the fact that this is a small state in terms of spread. However there is potential to have key inter-state circuits, which could be worked out with careful planning and support system, even at the present situation. Meanwhile, the state's tourism department provides the tourists the itinerary to some intra-state tourism circuits, which are presented in Table 2:

Table 2: Tourism Circuits in Mizoram

Circuit	*Duration*	*Highlights*	*Destinations*	*Operated By*
Exploring Indo-Myanmar	6 Nights & 7 Days	Nature exploration, Border Trade Centre, Soft Trekking	Aizawl, Champhai, Zokhawthar and Rih Dil (Lake)	**Evergreen Tours & Travels**
Mystic Mountains	3 Nights & 4 Days	Trekking, Nature exploration, experience Mizo rural life.	Aizawl, Hmuifang and Reiek Mountain.	Evergreen Tours & Travels
Blue Mountain Treks (Highest Peak in Mizoram)	6 Nights & 7 Days	Trekking & Camping, Nature exploration, Bird watching, Rock climbing.	Highest Peak in Mizoram	Evergreen Tours & Travels
A Glimpse of History	8 days & 7 nights	Visits to historical places	Aizawl, Kawlkulh, Chawngtlai, Zokhawthar, Rih Dil, Tam Dil and Reiek.	Omega Tours & Travels
Panoramic Reiek Peak	4 days & 3 nights	Nature exploration, experience Mizo rural life	Aizawl and Reiek	Omega Tours & Travels
Mizoram Delight	5 days & 4 nights	Local sightseeing, music/culture, visits to traditional villages and jhums, hiking, bird watching, etc.	In and around Aizawl, Falkawn and Hmuifang	Chawngvawr Ecotours

Source: Department of Tourism, Mizoram.

(3) Tour Operators/Travel Agencies: Tour operators and travel agencies are such organisations which play crucial roles in the entire process of developing and promoting tourism of a region. They are the ones who package and process all the various attractions of a region and present them to the tourists. In the context of Mizoram, there is a dire need to encourage more tour operators/travel agencies by the state government to sell the different tourism products available in the state.

(a) ***Tour operators/ travel agencies in Meghalaya:*** Some of the important tour operators and travel agents authorized by Tourism Department, Meghalaya are presented in Table 3.

Table 3: Tour Operators and Travel Agents in Meghalaya

Sl. No.	*Tour Operators*	*Name of Travel Agents*
1.	Tourist Information Centre, Meghalaya Tourism Development Corporation	Van Rap Tours & Travels
2.	Van Rap Tours & Travels	Sheba Travels
3.	Cultural Pursuits Adventures	Jais Travels
4.	Meghalaya Adventure Tours (Cave Tourism)	Global Tours & Travels
5.	Natural Ways - Adventure Tour Garo Hills	Indrani Tours & Travels
6.	Nakliar Tourist Info Centre & Travels	Just Trippin'

(Contd...)

7.	Tower Tours & Travels	Nongbri Travels
8.	Meghalaya Road Runner Tours	Sophia Tours & Travels
9.	Walk With Nine Lives	Travel City
10.	Quest Holidays	Natasha Travels
11.	New Horizon Travel & Tours	Towers Tours & Travels
12.	Pioneer Adventure Tours	Nakliar Tours
13.	Campfire	Golden Arrow

Source: Department of Tourism, Meghalaya.

(b) *Tour operators/ travel agencies in Mizoram:* In Mizoram, the tour operators/travel agents have been identified under two categories, viz. government-recognized and private/others. Following are the tour operators/travel agents identified to be operating their businesses in the state:

Table 4: Tour Operators/Travel Agents in Mizoram

Sl. No.	*Private/Others*	*Sl. No.*	*Government-recognized*
1	City Car Bazar & Rentals,	1	Ever Green Tours & Travels,
2	Quality Tour & Travels,	2	Omega Travels,
3	Skyline,	3	Zoram Tours
4	Aizawl City Bus Owner Association (ACBOA)	4	CMS Holidays,
5	Vandygo		
6	Blue Bell Tour and Travels		
7	Paradise Tours and Travels		
8	Alpha Travels,		
9	TBC Car Rental,		

Source: Department of Tourism, Mizoram.

(4) Accommodation/ Hotels: Accommodation or lodging is, by a long way, the largest and most ubiquitous sub-sector within the tourism economy (Cooper et al: 2008). In other words, accommodation is a matrix of tourism, and therefore, appropriate choice of accommodation is required in order to expand and develop the tourism industry (Saxena: 2008.) Therefore, it is logical that development of accommodation should be a fundamental element of the overall planning process of a tourism destination.

(a) Accommodation/hotels in Meghalaya: Meghalaya has many great budget hotels and *'Bed and Breakfast'* places that offer good service and amenities to the prospective tourists. Widely known as the rock capital of India, Shillong is a bustling city with a wide range of accommodation options. One can opt for accommodation ranging from economy to deluxe status. The important and popular accommodation facilities recognized by the Tourism Department, Meghalaya is presented in Table 5:

Table 5: List of hotels and guest houses (govt. and private) recognized

Sl. No.	*Hotels* / *Location: Shillong*	*Sl. No.*	*Guest Houses* / *Location: Shillong*
1.	Hotel Pinewood	1	Summit Guest House
2.	Hotel Orchid	2	Bonnie Guest House
3.	Royal Heritage-Tripura Castle	3	Hilltop Chateau
4.	Hotel Centre Point	4	Highwinds
5.	Hotel Polo Towers	5	Pine Brook Guest House
6.	Shillong Club	6	Apsara Guest House
7.	Hotel Poinisuk	7	Best Holiday Inn
8.	M crown Hotel	8	Aesthetics Guest House
9.	Blueberry Inn	9	White Orchid – The Guesthouse
10.	Hotel Heiga	10	Aerodene Cottage
11.	Hotel Gateway	11	Na-I-Mei Guest House
12.	Hotel Orchid Annex	12	Rosaville Guest House
13.	Hotel Alpine Continental	13	Dew Drop In
14.	Hotel Pegasus Crown	14	Eldorado Guest House
15.	The Majestic Hotel	15	Tranquil Inn
16.	The Eee Cee Hotel	16	Sunrise Guest House
17.	Ashutosh Inn	17	Meghalaya Housing Co-operative Guest House
18.	Hotel Yalana	18	Aibans Guest House
19.	Hotel J. K. International	19	Lachumiere House
20.	Hotel Boulevard	20	Stay-Inn Guest House
21.	Hotel Micasa	21	Nalgre Guest House
22.	Hotel Broadway	22	Woodland Hill Stay
23.	Eden Residency	23	Winnie's Lodge
24.	Hotel Rainbow	24	Shillong Hills Guest House
25.	Hotel Lake View Inn	25	Ha Sharing Guest House
26.	Hotel Knight Inn		Location: *Sohra*
27.	Ladybird Hotel	26	Sa-I-Mika
28.	The Habitat Shillong	27	Eco – Park Guest House
29.	Hotel Embassy	28	Nalgre Restaurant & Guest House
30.	Hotel Pine Borough		Location: *Mawphlang*
31.	Hotel Blue Mount NX-1	29	Keanean Guest House
	Location: *Sohra*		Location: *Ri Bhoi*
32.	Cherrapunjee Holiday Resort	30	RI Kanaan Guest House
33.	Coniferous Resort	31	Da-Wan-Ki Farm Homestay
34.	Sohra Plaza	32	Erbatemon Homestay
	Location: *Ri Bhoi*		State Government Guest Houses *Shillong*
35.	Orchid Lake Resort		
36.	Ri Kynjai Resort		
37.	Breeze-Dale Tourist Resort	(i)	Meghalaya Government Circuit House
38.	Star Valley Tourist Resort	(ii)	Meghalaya Housing Co-operative Guest House
39.	Sanctuary Song Resort	(iii)	Assam House
40.	Sunshine Farms and Resort	(iv)	Nagaland House
	Location: *Jowai*	(v)	Arunachal Pradesh Bhavan
		(vi)	Mizoram House
41.	Orchid Inn	Sl. No.	Bed & Breakfast *(Shillong)*
	Location: *Tura*	1.	Café Shillong Bed & Breakfast
42.	Orchid Lodge	2.	Travellers Bed & Breakfast
43.	Hotel Rikman Continental	3.	Pine Hill Homestay
44.	Hotel Sundare	4.	Traveler's Nest
	Location: *Williamnagar*	5.	Sanctum B & B
45.	Williamnagar Tourist Lodge	6.	Kaizun (Bed & Breakfast)
	Location: *Baghmara*	7.	Golf View Bed & Breakfast
46.	Baghmara Tourist Lodge	8.	Pine Air Bed & Breakfast

(*Contd...*)

34.	Sohra Plaza	32	Erbatemon Homestay
	Location: *Ri Bhoi*	State Government Guest Houses *Shillong*	
35.	Orchid Lake Resort		
36.	Ri Kynjai Resort		
37.	Breeze-Dale Tourist Resort	(i)	Meghalaya Government Circuit House
38.	Star Valley Tourist Resort	(ii)	Meghalaya Housing Co-operative Guest House
39.	Sanctuary Song Resort	(iii)	Assam House
40.	Sunshine Farms and Resort	(iv)	Nagaland House
	Location: *Jowai*	(v)	Arunachal Pradesh Bhavan
		(vi)	Mizoram House
41.	Orchid Inn	Sl. No.	Bed & Breakfast *(Shillong)*
	Location: *Tura*	1.	Café Shillong Bed & Breakfast
42.	Orchid Lodge	2.	Travellers Bed & Breakfast
43.	Hotel Rikman Continental	3.	Pine Hill Homestay
44.	Hotel Sundare	4.	Traveler's Nest
	Location: *Williamnagar*	5.	Sanctum B & B
45.	Williamnagar Tourist Lodge	6.	Kaizun (Bed & Breakfast)
	Location: *Baghmara*	7.	Golf View Bed & Breakfast
46.	Baghmara Tourist Lodge	8.	Pine Air Bed & Breakfast
47.	Siju Tourist Lodge	9.	The Pear Tree Bed & Breakfast

Source: Department of Tourism, Meghalaya.

(b) Accommodation/hotels in Mizoram: The tourism department of Mizoram has been running various tourist lodges and highway restaurants in the state, meeting the demands of the government as well as the general public and the tourists visiting the state. The department has now 49 tourist/accommodation facilities (tourist lodges/highway restaurants/wayside amenities etc), under its management at present. Table 6 presents the number of accommodation facilities provided and managed by the Department of Tourism, Mizoram.

Table 6: Number of tourist facilities (hotels, lodges, resorts, restaurants, etc.

Sl. No.	*Tourist Facility*	*Sl. No.*	*Tourist Facility*
1	Berawtlang Tourist Complex	26	New Laty Tourist Lodge
2	Bualpui NG Tourist Lodge	27	Ngopa Tourist Lodge
3	Chakheitla Tourist Lodge	28	Niawhtlang Tourist Lodge
4	Chaltlang Tourist Lodge	29	Pangzawl Tourist Lodge
5	Champhai Tourist Lodge	30	Phura Tourist Lodge
6	Changsil Tourist Lodge	31	Reiek Tourist Resort
7	Chawngte Tourist Lodge	32	S. Vanlaiphai Tourist Lodge
8	Chhiahtlang Highway Restaurant	33	Saichho Tourist Lodge
9	Darlawn Tourist Lodge	34	Siaha Tourist Lodge
10	Darzo Tourist Lodge	35	Saipum Tourist Lodge
11	E. Lungdar Tourist Lodge	36	Saitual Tourist Lodge
12	Farkawn Tourist Lodge	37	Sangau Tourist Lodge
13	Hmuifang Tourist Lodge	38	Serchhip Tourist Lodge
14	Hnahlan Tourist Lodge	39	Serkawr Tourist Lodge
15	Hnahthial Highway Restaurant	40	Serlui Tourist Lodge
16	Hrangchalkawn Tourist Lodge	41	Tamdil Picnic Spot
17	Kanhmun Tourist Lodge	42	Tawipui 'S' Highway Restaurant

(Contd...)

18	Kawlkulh Tourist Lodge	43	Thenzawl Tourist Lodge
19	Kolasib Tourist Lodge	44	Tlabung Tourist Lodge
20	Lawngtlai Tourist Lodge	45	Tlangnuam Viewing Gallery
21	Lengpui Tourist Resort	46	Vawmbuk Tourist Lodge
22	Lunglei Tourist Lodge	47	W. Phaileng Tourist Lodge
23	Mamit Tourist Lodge	48	Zawngling Tourist Lodge
24	N. Maubawk Tourist Lodge	49	Zokhawthar Tourist Lodge
25	N. Vanlaiphai Tourist Lodge		

Source: Department of Tourism, Mizoram.

Beside these government-run accommodations, a number of private hotels/ accommodation facilities have been mushrooming in Aizawl, the capital city. Among them, important ones are Hotel Regency, Hotel Flora, Hotel Arini, David's Clover Hotel and many others.

Conclusion

Today, NEI is virtually a landlocked region in India having a distinct identity of its own. The region has been isolated by the partition of Indian Union in 1947 leaving only a narrow strip of land of 22-37 km wide, called the Siluguri Corridor, or the Chicken's Neck that connects Northeast India with the rest of India. This partition has been the reason for severe connectivity infrastructure constraints in the region till date. Hence, there is a need to open up this region to the rest of the country by developing efficient transportation and connectivity networks.

The present status of tourism in NEI is shrouded in mystery with immense tourism potential not yet fully utilized. Its diversity, uniqueness and richness in tourism resources are yet unexplored. Meghalaya and Mizoram are quite unique in terms of potentiality of various kinds of tourism. The two states are well endowed with natural beauty that can attract a mass volume of tourists. Needless to mention, the two states are trying hard to market its tourism products. But, the present level of promotional activities that have been undertaken is not much effective to attract tourists throughout the year to sustain the sectoral economy. Inadequate tourism infrastructures such as absence of rail connectivity, considered as the cheapest mode of transportation is virtually absent in these two states. Meanwhile, communication networks like internet connectivity, well connected roads, hygienic eateries and hotels, instant banking and exchange facilities, etc. are some sorts of efforts that need to be addressed at the earliest possible, if the two states are to enjoy the fruits of tourism boom.

The process of infrastructure development has been rather slow in the region for many reasons. Amongst them, the rugged topography of hilly and mountainous terrains of NEI covering most of the states including Meghalaya and Mizoram is one that hampers the rapid growth of infrastructure development. To develop tourism sector in the select states it will heavily depend upon the immediate improvement of infrastructure within the next few years. However, this will require a total revolutionary thinking. Interstate connectivity must be planned on a priority basis and up-gradation of road transportation, railways and existing airports should be done at regular intervals.

Although the two select states have tremendous tourism potential, the tourism industry is still miles away to go to exploit its full potential. There is need for proper tourism marketing strategy for these states. Tourist information centres must be established at most of the important tourism circuits in NEI. Trainings on tourism and hospitality should be imparted to all the stakeholders who are directly involved in the tourism sector of these states. Further, the marketers need to address the negative perceptions of the people in general about different tourism destinations through proper brand positioning.

References

- Bhattacharya, P. (2008): Changing Recreational Demand, Developmental Challenges and Issues associated with Sustainability, European Bulletin of Himalayan Research, 32, pp. 143-161, http://himalaya.socanth.cam.ac.uk/collections/journals/ebhr/pdf/EBHR_32_07.pdf accessed on 5th September 2016.
- Bhattacharjee, S. (2001): Tourism Marketing in North-East India: A Study of the Promotional Strategy and Marketing Practice of the State Level Tourism Promotion Organisations, PhD thesis submitted to the Department of Commerce, Assam University, Silchar.
- Cooper, C., Fletcher, J., Fyall, A., Gilbert, D. and Stephen, W. (2008): Tourism Principle and Practice, (4th ed.), Prentice Hall, Harlow, England.
- Joshi, S.C. (2011): Splendid North-East! Tourism Perspective & Prospects, Vol. II, Akansha Publishing House, New Delhi.
- Rizal, P. and Asokan, R. (2013): A Comparative Study of Tourism Industry in North-Eastern States of India, IOSR Journal of Business and Management, Vol. 12, Issue 4, pp. 56-62.
- Saxena, A. (2008): New Trends in Tourism and Hotel Industry, http://site.ebrary.com/lib/cop/docDetail.action?docID=10416183&page=198 accessed on 26.01.2008.
- Yes Bank (2014): Tourism in North East & Eastern India, Focus East: Tourism Driving the Next Phase of Socio-Economic Growth, Public and Social Policies Management, Yes Bank and Indian Chamber of Commerce.
- http://megtourism.gov.in
- https://tourism.mizoram.gov.in
- http://meghalaya.gov.in/megportal/department/45
- http://theshillongtimes.com/2015/11/21/4-state-rivers-to-fall-under-natl-waterways/

17

Government Initiatives for Skills Development of Youth in Mizoram

— *C. Devendiran*

Introduction

Youth is a significant segment of any country and also an important stage of human life. The United Nations Report (2014) mentioned that India has the world's largest youth population with 356 million between the age group 10-24 years despite having a smaller population than China with 269 million. It is also stated that the world is home to 1.8 billion young people out of which 28 percent of India's population (The Economic Times, 2014). India is recognised as one of the youngest nations of the world with over 50 percent of the population below the age of 30 years by 2020; India is in a position to become the world's youngest country with 64 percent of its population in the working-age group. The total youth population in the N.E. region is about 4 percent of the total youth population of the country which is about 20, 22,527 youths in the age group of 15 to 35 years. The total population of the Mizoram is 10, 91,014.

The youth population is facing a lot of issues and challenges due to poverty, illiteracy, unemployment, and changing family structure and lifestyle in this digital era. The recent studies show that this enormous youth potential force is facing challenges due to the impact of mass media factors along with peer pressure which leads youth to indulge in risk-taking behaviours like smoking, consumption of alcohol, tobacco chewing and indulgence of substance abuse in the North East. The consumption of tobacco and alcohol consumption is very much prevalent among the youth of the northeast. In general, the North-Eastern states of India, drug abuse among young people, have become a major problem threatening the social fabric and structures of the society because of the golden triangle. At the same time, they are facing long term challenge of huge unemployment among youth due to lack of skills and poverty in India. Due to these issues, they prone to vulnerable and they need desperate professional care and guidance and also life coping and supporting skills for gainful employment.

The main aim of this paper is to analyse the government programmes on skill development for youth, opportunities and challenges of skill development in Mizoram. The present paper is attempted to critically examine the skill gap. The paper emphasises how serious it is for the government and other stakeholders to come together and work together to create a skilled workforce to break the skill gap and boost economic growth.

Issues and challenges of Youth in Mizoram

Taking into consideration of the above issues the Government of India has taken different initiatives to address the above mentioned issues related to youth development in terms of skills. Skills and knowledge are the driving forces of economic growth and social development. Mizoram is one of the most literate states of India (91.33 percent as per 2011 census). State's GDP growing at the rate of 8.5percent annually between2005-2014. Despite this, unemployment, particularly among the educated youth of the state, is becoming an increasing concern for the state administration. This high literacy rate has to be appropriately translated into gainful employment for their survival. Mizoram is a skill deficit state and the penetrated on vocational education in the state has been quite low. Only 45 per 1000 persons reported any kind of vocational education. It is low in comparison to the national average of 68 per 1000, which is also low when compared internationally.

The skill misalignments and aspirations of the present workforce to engage themselves in some of the available jobs leaves unfulfilled demand gap in the labour market. There is weak institutional and physical infrastructure, lack of training facilities and quality trainers, absence of accredited vocational training programmes are the major constraints to the skills development to youth in the state of Mizoram. Moreover, there are a number of factors responsible for this situation, one of the major challenges being the public perception on skilling which is viewed as the last option meant for those who have not been able to progress or opted out of the formal academic system. A vast majority of students in Mizoram pursuing higher education opts for Arts and Humanities as a discipline followed by Science and Commerce. Professional and vocational courses are opted by the least number of students. Such choices are unlikely to align job seekers to labour market needs. Moreover, most of the vocational training programmes are not aligned with the requirements of the industry. There are also mismatches between qualification/types of skills and job roles among those employed.

Formal, mainstream higher education alone does not empower youth to succeed in the employment market. The lack of awareness among students and their parents (who open influence the career choices of students), their Socio-cultural orientation, as well as lack of other opinions that can provide vertical mobility, channelize the youth into higher education open with subjects that are not in demand by the industry. These results in skills mismatch and about one-third of the graduates and post-graduates remain unemployed.

Government Initiatives for Youth

Government initiated to collect data by adopting several rounds of fieldwork conducted in India in the field of Skills Development to Youth; Reframing the National System of Skills Development, India has become serious about skills development to youth introducing a series of education and training reforms. In the 11th Five Year Plan (2007—2012) focused on skills development as a priority area of concern for the first time.

The Prime Minister's Independence Day speech of 2006 emphasized the need for a vocational education mission. In his Independence Day speech of 2007, he announced 1,600 new ITIs and polytechnics, 10,000 new vocational schools and 50,000 new skill development centres would be established to provide access to vocational training for more than 10 million students.

Apart from this, in his budget speech of 2007, the Finance Minister described the emerging shortages of skilled workforce in many sectors. These political commitments from the top leadership of the Central government have raised awareness among the line ministries that they must expand vocational and entrepreneurship training programs "to take advantage of the demographic dividend of the country and to fulfill the aspirations and right of the youth to gainful employment and contribute to national productivity".

These speeches have generated momentum for skills development, and a strong sense of urgency among government officials, industry, and educationalists. In the year 2009, Union government announced its first skills development policy and set up a new institutional framework involving close coordination among government, industry, and training institutions to facilitate skills development efforts at the central level.

For the first time, the Prime Minister's National Skills Development Council came into existence to coordinate various schemes provided by various ministries. The Office of the Advisor to Prime Minister for Skills Development serves as an apex coordinating body and as a secretariat for Skills Development for Youth in India.

Then, the National Skills Development Board was set up under the Planning Commission to coordinate 17 relevant ministries. Subsequently, National Skill Development Corporation was created, operating as a public-private partnership involving industry associations and industry representatives to upgrade training institutions and deliver vocational training. Thereafter, sector Skills Councils have been set up for about two dozen sub-sectors involving various interested industrial associations to identify skills gaps and enhance skills training in each sub-sector. These organizations are responsible for developing policies, setting priorities and strategies, and overseeing and coordinating the various stakeholder initiatives and efforts. In the 12th Five-year Plan (2012—2017), the government emphasized skills development even more ambitiously as a priority agenda item. Projecting that by 2022, India's working-age population will reach 700 million, of whom, 500 million will need to be skilled, the government set a national target of skilling 500 million people by then, allocating increased budgets for skills development. Thus, it ambitiously plans to increase the capacity of training institutions to 15 million (currently 2.5 million), by setting up more ITIs, encouraging the private sector to engage in vocational training, and expanding tertiary education.

Accordingly, Government of India has initiated two programmes, Skill India and Make in India to create a framework for skill development and entrepreneurship activities in the country. Skill India's primary objective is to ensure a well-established infrastructure for skill development and focus on professional skills and employment-oriented training to create a skilled labour workforce. Young Indians must be prepared not just for domestic markets but also for the international labour markets which are in line with the PM's vision of Make in India, the skill capital of the world.

The Government of India structured the National Policy for Skill Development and Entrepreneurship 2015. The primary objective of the policy is to meet the challenge of skilling at scale with speed, standard (quality) and sustainability. Skills development is the shared responsibility of the key stakeholders namely government, the entire spectrum of the corporate sector, community-based organizations, those outstanding, highly qualified and dedicated individuals who have been working in the skilling and entrepreneurship space for many years, industry and trade organizations and other stakeholders. The policy links skills development to improved employability and productivity in paving the way forward for inclusive growth in the country. The skill strategy is harmonized by specific efforts to promote entrepreneurship to create sufficient opportunities for the skilled workforce.

Growth Sectors in Mizoram

Various studies have identified the following sectors as critical growth sectors in which Mizoram can intensify its skilling efforts:-

- Agriculture & Allied Sector (Horticulture, Animal Husbandry, Floriculture & Sericulture), Food & Meat Processing Sector, Apparel & Fashion Sector, IT & ITES Sector, Forest-Based Industries Sector, Handloom & Handicrafts Sector, BFSI Sector, Education & Training, Health & Allied Sector, Construction Sector.
- Handloom, Handicraft, Horticulture, Fruit Processing, Hospitality, IT/ITES, Healthcare, Education, Motor Repair, Beauty Culture, Construction, Forest-based/Bamboo.

Table 1: List of Technical and Vocational Education &Training (TVET) Institutions

Sl. No.	*Name of Institute*	*Trade/Job Roles*	*Capacity*
A. it is			
1.	Government ITI, Aizawl	Electrician, Wireman, Motor Mechanic, Mechanic (Diesel), Mechanic (Auto Electricals & Electronics), Mechanic (R & AC), Fitter, Welder, Sheet Metal Worker, Electronic Mechanic, Carpentry, Plumber, Draughtsman, Radio & TV Mechanic, diesel, IT & ESM, Surveyor, Mason, COPA, Hair & Skin Care, Cutting & Sewing, Computer Hardware Mechanic, Bakery & Confectionery, Stenography	512
2.	Government ITI, Lunglei	Carpentry, Mechanic (MV), wireman, Electronic Mechanic, Dressmaking, COPA	92
3.	Government ITI, Saiha	Electronic Mechanic (MV), IT & ESM, Hair & Skin Care, COPA	108
B. Polytechnics			
4	Mizoram Polytechnic, Lunglei	Civil Engineering, Electric Engineering, Mechanical Engineering, Computer Science &Engineering	110
5.	Women's Polytechnic Aizawl	Modern Office Practice, Electronic & Telecom Engineering, Garment Technology, Beauty Culture & Cosmetology	100
C. Schools/Colleges			
6.	Higher Secondary Schools under School Education 15 nos.	Computer Technique & Computer Software, Automobile Engineering Technology, Automobile Engineering Technology, Medical Laboratory Technology (MLT), Commercial Designing & Making; Horticulture Sericulture	762
7.	Secondary Schools under RMSA-10 nos	IT & ITES Healthcare, Automobile	550

(Contd...)

D. Private VTPS			
8.	Centres in Mizoram -24	ICT, Beauty Culture & Hair /Dressing, Garment Making, Hospitality, Medical & Nursing, Plastic, Processing, Security, Soft Skill, Travel & Tourism, Business & Commerce, Spa Therapy, Masonry, Carpentry, Plumbing, House Wiring, Surveyor, Draughtsman (Civil) etc.	
9.	Centres outside State -31		

Source: Mizoram State Policy on Skill and Entrepreneurship Development, Government of Mizoram (2018).

At least 14 Departments have implemented Central or State Schemes for Skill Development in the state as shown in the table below:

Table 2: Skilling initiatives of the Central and State Government in the State

Sl. No.	*Name of the Department*	*Name of Programmes/ Schemes/ Institutes*	*Training Types*
1.	Agriculture	*Krishi Vigyan Kendras* (KVKs), Integrated Training Centres (ITCs)	Farmer Field School, Agri-Clinic & Agri-Business Centres, Basic Agriculture & Allied
2.	AH & Vety	AI Training Centres, Integrated Vety & AH Training Institute	Training in Artificial Insemination in Cattle & Pig. Elementary Science in Vety & AH
3.	Commerce & Industries	State Plan Scheme Integrated Skill Development Scheme, Block Level Handloom Clusters	Knitting & Tailoring, Weaving, Cane & Bamboo, Computer Foundation Course O level, Designing & Dyeing
4.	Health & Family Welfare	Paramedic & Nursing Institutes, ASHA training	Diploma, Certificates & short-term courses
5.	Higher & Technical Education	Community College Scheme	Vocational subjects in Schools & Colleges
6.	Horticulture	Extension Services, MIDH	Cultivation of Vegetables & Fruit crops, Flower Arrangement, Food Processing
7.	LESDE	CIS, SDIS, PMKVY, (MYC & MBOCWWB)	National/State Trade Certificates, Short term courses
8.	MEDMOC, Planning &Programme Implementation	Entrepreneurship Development Scheme under NEDP	Entrepreneurship Awareness, Skills cum Entrepreneurship Development Programme, Maters Trainer Programme, Business Plan Competition, Micro Start-Up Competition, Entrepreneurship Knowledge Centre, etc.
9.	Rural Development (MzSRLM)	DDU-GKY, RSETL, BADP	Livelihood related skill training under IWMP
10.	School Education	Vocationalisation of School Education	Vocational subjects in Secondary & Higher Secondary Schools
11.	Sericulture	Sericulture Training Institute (STI)	Silkworm rearing, Seeds Farms
12.	Social Welfare	Residential Institute & Training Centre (RITC), Vocational Training Centres (VTCs), Handicapped Training Centres, Anganwadi Worker's Training Centre	ICT, Beauty & Wellness, Garment Making Hotel management, Electrician, Electronics, Plumbing, Tailoring, Shoe Making, Training Anganwadi Workers & Helpers
13.	Tourism	In-house, Internal & Departmental Trainings	Food Crafting & Cooking

(Contd...)

14.	UD &PA	DAY-NULM	Apparel, Automobile, Beauty & Wellness, Construction, Electronics & Hardware, Healthcare, IT&ITES, security, Telecom, Tourism & Hospitality, Handloom & Handicrafts, Media & Entertainment, Food Processing, Knitting, Flower Making, Hair Cutting, Candle Making, Shoe Repair, Metal Work

Source: Mizoram State Policy on Skill and Entrepreneurship Development, Government of Mizoram (2018).

International Labour Organisation study has identified the following top eight sectors as having high hiring plan by the Industry: Automobile, Bamboo / Timber based Products, Light Fabrication, Furniture, Handloom, Beauty& Wellness, Construction, and Food/Fruit Processing. The following new possibilities areas were also identified: Leather & Hide Industry, Media &Film Industry, Food Processing Industry, and International Trade.

Mizoram Industrial Development Policy 2012 also identified the following thrust sectors industries based on value addition of locally available resources: forest based, food processing, handloom, handicrafts, plantain fibre and hill brooms tea/rubber/coffee & plantation-based, textile related, animal & poultry feed, entertainment/music, packaging.

The New Economic Development Policy has identified the following sectors as potential key growth drivers of the State economy:

(a) Agriculture & Allied Sector: Rice, Vegetables, Fruits, Floriculture, Animal Husbandry, Dairy, Fishery;

(b) Industry-Manufacturing Sector: Forest-based Industry

(c) Infrastructure Development: Roads, Energy, Water Supply, ICT, Sanitation & Sewerage;

(d) Service Sector: Tourism & Hospitality, Sports & Recreation, Education, Health Care, ICT, Transport, Services.

State Authorities for Skill Development Programmes in Mizoram

Skill Development Authorities in Mizoram are as follows:-

(i) Mizoram State Council for Technical Education

(ii) Mizoram State Council for Vocational Training

(iii) State Council for Educational Research and Training

(iv) Mizoram Board of School Education

(v) Mizoram Nursing Council

(vi) Others (Department and Private Establishments)

At present the Department/Agencies working in the field of Skill Development are as follows:

(a) LE & IT Department
(b) Rural Development Department
(c) Mizoram Skill Development Society
(d) Mizoram Youth Commission

List of Different Schemes under LE & IT

(i) Up-gradation of 1396 Govt. ITI through PPP. This project looks after the ITIs are at Lunglei and Saiha. Govt. of India gave an interest-free loan of Rs. 500 lakhs which is in progress.
(ii) Vocational Training Improvement Project
(iii) Vocational Training Providers (VTP)

There are a number of Training Institutes under this scheme which imparted training to the youth of different trade in their area. These VTP students can avail assistance depending on the strength of the students. At present the VTP under this department are:

(i) Zoram Avry Commerce Institute, Zodin Square, Aizawl
(ii) Society for Information Technology (SITD), Zarkawt, Aizawl
(iii) AessInfotser (Pvt) Limited, Lower Chanmari, Aizawl
(iv) CD Tailoring, Chhinga Veng, Aizawl
(v) St. Mary Tailoring Industry & Dispensary, Champai
(vi) Mission Foundation Movement, Bawngkawn, Aizawl
(vii) Integrated Development & Environment Awareness Society (IDEAS), Aizawl
(viii) Zorin Computer Graphics Printing and Paper Works, Treasury Square, Aizawl
(ix) Medsys Solution, Tuikhuahtlang, Aizawl
(x) Mizoram Agro & Allied Products, Near Youth Hostel, Luangmual, Aizawl

Recently, the author has done some case studies with the Department/ Agencies working in the field of Skill Development in Aizawl with the LE&IT department, DIC-Aizawl, Rural Development Department and Mizoram Youth Commission. From the case studies, it was found out that some of the challenges faced by the LE & IT department.

The DIC-Aizawl is offering trades such as automobile mechanic, wireman, carpentry, turner, blacksmith and tinsmith. These trades are offered right from the inception but there is up-gradation of new trades so far. They want to upgrade the new trades like AC- mechanic, computer hardware and mobile repairing, aluminum works but they could implement due to various reasons like recruitment, infrastructure, trainees etc.

Ministry of Labour & Employment, Government of India and Mizoram Youth Commission conducted skills development training for youth under Skill Development Initiative Scheme.The following are the trades and courses:-

Beauty, Hair & Spa Therapy, Makeup, Beauty Therapy, Aviation, Hospitality Management, Retail Management, ICT, BPO, Tourism, Commerce & Accountancy, Banking & Finance, Plastic Processing, Aviation, Soft Skills & Hospitality, Hospitality & Food Production.

In spite of all these efforts taken by Government of India as well as State Government of Mizoram, still youths are facing lot of problems, issues and challenge to skill themselves which are discussed below.

Challenges

- There are lack of infrastructure facilities such as laboratory facilities, tools and equipment is often outdated and modernize and upgrade laboratory, tools, equipment and teaching aids: NSDC has predicted an incremental requirement of 347 million skilled personnel in India by 2022 but the country is faced with a significant skill development challenges for the years and every year approximately 12 million people are expected to join the workforce. In contrast, the country has a total training capacity of around 4.3 million, thus depriving every year around 64 newcomers of the opportunity of the skill development training. It is a major challenge of devising such a huge infrastructure set up to bridge the gap.
- An Industry-interface is very essential for any education/training institute as it helps in the assessment of demand for skills in the local area/region and thus updating of course content. Industry linkages have an important role in helping an educational/training institute to build a strong image in the minds of the students as it ensures them that the course curriculum is in relevance with the practical industry requirements. Most of the training institutes have low industry interface as a result of which the performance of the skill development sector is poor in terms of placement records and salaries offered.
- The enrolment in skill institutes like ITIs, and polytechnics, remains low as compared to their enrolment capacity. The main reason for this problem is the student mobilization to get trained due to orthodox thinking, reluctant to migrate and low salaries at entry-level. Vocational training is not considered desirable by the students and they prefer a regular degree because it is more valued than a certificate, other things being equal. One of the major causes of the low quality of training is the low frequency of pre-assessment

or entrance tests before admitting students to the skill training institutes. Arbitrarily chosen training courses may lead to a mismatch between the interests and the abilities of the students as a result of which students are unable to cope with the course requirements and thus drop-outs occur.

- There is no standardization of the course curriculum or training delivery systems due to which it is not possible to compare courses across different training institutes which also creates confusion among the student about skills which will be imparted under a particular course at some training institute. There is a lack of a standardized approach for measuring and evaluating the competence outcomes.
- The course curriculum of some of the courses of skill training institutes does not provide training as per the requirement of the industry requirements. Therefore, outdated and inflexible curriculum leads to some training programs completely redundant leading to the supply of specific skills exceeding their demand.
- There is no clear cut proper career guidance to the youth due to the inadequate placement data and inadequate industry linkages of the training institutes because institutes are set up in rural areas but the jobs offered to the trainees are in urban areas. The absence of information of the job leads to uninformed skill oriented choices.

Suggestions

Based on the analysis, the following suggestions are made to improve the quality of training and bridge the skill gap in Mizoram:-

- There is an urgent need to provide quality training to the youth to enhance their employability. When National Skill Development Corporation provides grants to training institutes, they should also develop some evaluation techniques to evaluate the performance of such institutes and motivate them to perform well. May be a kind of incentives should be given to the training institutes based on their performance and also they can be evaluated based on certain criteria.
- Youths should be made aware of the existing training institutes, courses offered and career opportunities after course completion. Such information can be made available through newspapers, magazines or centralized portals highlighting the list of all the recognized institutes, courses offered and placement records along with the institute ranking. These initiatives will help the youths to choose the right institute and course based on their interests and demand in the market.

- Training for the informal sector needs to be strengthened and upgraded.
- The need of the hour is to make vocational education aspiration and make it a matter of choice for the youths of Mizoram. To enable this, it must provide vertical growth pathways, be associated with growth and sustainable livelihood corridors and, have a causal relationship with increased income for a skilled workforce.
- The extensive campaign must be organized to create awareness and mobilization. Information and electronic communication kits and packages should be developed and standardized Audio-Visual/Print/Social media should be utilized and Educational Institutions, Private Training Providers and Community Organizations should be involved in the campaign.
- Skilling would be integrated with formal education by making general education provided in schools an integral part of skill development initiatives by improving the quality and learning outcomes of school education and make skill development more aspiration to the youths than what it is today.
- Skilling would also be increasingly integrated with higher education with the introduction of NSQF aligned vocational courses at appropriate levels.
- The ITIs and Polytechnics should be modernized with courses and curriculum that are aligned to competency-based demand in the market.
- The Government should promote the use of certified-skilled man-power for its works and projects. Recruitments rules shall be amended with clear and precise eligibility criteria for various positions in terms of NSQF levels, wherever suitable. The industry would be the courage to follow suit.
- The proposed Central government initiatives such as National Skill Awards, Skill Development Fellow schemes, etc. shall be adapted, promoted and replicated.
- The Government may make extensive provisions for career counseling to different categories of the population. Counseling and Capacity Building Centre may be set up in the LESDE Department. Infrastructure shall be set up for information dissemination to all on a robust online platform.

Conclusion

When the Government of India is hugely investing in skill development initiatives for the future, there is widespread concern among the industry and academia that the efforts may not be sufficient to avoid a skill scarcity in the future. The opportunity for Mizoram largely lies with skilling the youth in the country. Hence there is a need to align the efforts of the Government with the Industry that will pave the way to the successful implementation of the programmes, thereby enabling the skilled manpower for the nation. The PM has approved the country's first integrated national policy for skill development and entrepreneurship. In his own words, skill development in India should envision the "Creation of an ecosystem of empowerment by skilling on a large scale at speed with high standards and promote a culture of innovation based entrepreneurship generating wealth and employment and ensuring sustainable livelihoods for all."

The study highlights that Mizoram will face a major challenge of bridging the skill gap over the years. Even though Government of Mizoram has identified the need for a well-defined framework for skill development accordingly state government has created many organisations to take responsibility for skill development, but still, there is need to take much more efforts to develop skill culture in the context of Mizoram. Otherwise, the skill gap can lead to a serious impact, not only on the employees but also on the economy as a whole. The major concerns of today are the loss of productivity and income because many of the jobs have remained vacant for many years due to the lack of skilled labour.

Overcoming the problem of unemployment in the state of Mizoram, particularly that of the educated unemployed is reaching an alarming rate which needs immediately focused and coordinated attention with new policy initiatives, sound institutional arrangements and effective operational strategies for creating employment opportunities and enhancing employability of all youth in the state of Mizoram.

The youth organizations like YMCA, YWCA, YMA (Young Mizo Association), NYK, VYK may be involved actively in the existing local branches along with various Departments, Government of Mizoram for promoting skill development programmes at different levels.

References

- Central Statistics Office, Ministry of Statistics and Programme Implementation, Government of India (Social Statistics Division) (2017), New Delhi. Retrieved on -2-06-2020
- Chaturvedi, S. (2013): Skill Development for the Youth: A Global Quest, AISECT University Journal Vol.2:4
- Directorate of Labour Employment and Industrial Training, GOI, Mizoram, Citizens' Charter 2013-14
- District Industrial Centre, (2015), Aizawl
- Empowering Youth, (2017) Yojana, New Delhi

- Government of India, Census Report-(2011). New Delhi: Government of India Publications
- Jha, A.K. (2014): Promoting Entrepreneurship in North East India, Employment News, Vol.38:36, 56 December 2013- 3 January 2014
- Ministry of Skill Development and Entrepreneurship,(2015)GOI.
- Mizoram Industrial Policy,(2012), Govt. of Mizoram, Industries Department
- Mizoram State Policy on Skill and Entrepreneurship Development, (2018), Labour, Employment, Skill Development and Entrepreneurship Department, Government of Mizoram.
- Mizoram Youth Commission, (2015), Govt. of Mizoram
- National Youth Policy, (2014)M: Ministry of Youth Affairs & Sports, GOI. Retrieved from yas.nic.in/sites/default/files/National-Youth-Policy-Document%20.pdf 15062020
- Okada, A. (2012): Skills Development for Youth in India: Challenges and Opportunities, Journal of International Cooperation in Education, Vol.15 2:pp169-193. Accessed on 01072020
- Rajamani Singha,A, (2015): Skilling of Youth Bettering the Employability Status The Bharamputra Rhythm of the Promises, Vol.9: 1 Pg.8-10
- Report of the Working Group on Skill Development and Training set up for preparation of XI Plan, GOI, Planning Commission New Delhi, Accessed on 01-08-2020
- Roy, A.D and Rajat Bhattacharjee, (2014): Entrepreneurship Development in North Eastern Region with Special Reference to IIE, Guwahati. International Journal of Scientific Research, Vol3:1 January 2014, ISSN No. 2277-8179
- The Economic Times, Retrieved on 1st July 2020
- World Youth Report, (2014), New York: UN Publications

18

Role of Women Representatives in Urban Governance in Himanchal Pradesh

(A Study of Shimla Municipal Corporation)

— *Pawan Kumar Banta*

Introduction

The Constitution (74th) Amendment Act, 1992 mandates at least one-third of seats among elected representatives to women belonging to SCs, STs and general castes. Many state governments in the country have gone up to fifty percent and also to the OBCs. This move facilitates women's participation in decision making in urban governance. More than one-fourth of a century has elapsed in this historical step. It is imperative now to analyse the situation from women's point of view. Elected representatives have a crucial role to play in ensuring effective local governance. What is the role that elected representatives play in today's urban governance scenario in Himachal Pradesh in Municipal Corporation, Shimla. Do they and are they able to function as links between municipal administration and the people? Does the voice of the common citizen get reflected in urban governance in the local bodies of the state through their elected representatives particularly women? In order to find the answer to these questions, we undertook a questionnaire-based survey among elected women representatives in the Municipal Corporation, Shimla. The prime objective of the survey was to know their opinion about the present structure and functioning of the institutions they were a part of, the problems and difficulties they faced while working in Municipal Corporation, Shimla the gaps and lacunae the needed to be addressed to strengthen urban governance.

Women's Status - a General View

A generally accepted connotation given to status is that it refers to a position in a social system or sub--system which is distinguishable from and at the same time related to other positions through its designated rights and obligations. Each status is expressed in terms of a role. As Ralph Linton, an eminent social anthropologist observed that “The individual is socially assigned to a status and occupies it with relation to other statuses. When he puts the rights and duties, which constitute the status to effect, he is performing a role. Role and status are quite inseparable, and the distinction between them is only of academic interest.”

Status is of two types, ascribed status and achieved status. Ascribed status is assigned to individuals by birth without reference to any innate abilities, but it is often ascribed on the basis of sex, age, family relationships, and birth in a particular social group; on the other hand, achieved status requires social qualities gained through competition and individual effort. It can be based on education, occupation and marital status.

Women’s status is a complex phenomenon, and has to be studied as an integral part of the socio-economic structure in which women had been and are living. In the course of Indian history through the rise and fall of civilizations, women’s position has also been fluctuating. A five-dimensional categorization based on specific, historical periods is made to discuss the transitions in the status of women in India as follows:

- Vedic period;
- Buddhist period;
- Mughal period;
- British period; and
- Post-Independence era.

Women in the Vedic Period

Women enjoyed a high status and equal freedom with their Aryan men folk who desired full co-operation of their women in every matter. As early as the eighth century, the acceptance of equality between men and women was discussed at the time of Shankaracharya. There is a famous story about this: Once a female ascetic sent a messenger to the great Shankaracharya requesting audience. Absorbed his meditations the Master snapped: “ I have better things to do than talk to a woman.” The woman sent back this reply: “Tell the Master, I did not know there were any males in the universe outside of God. Compared to him, are we not all women.” Shankaracharya smiled and said, “Bring her to me.”

Reference in the Vedic literature is found of a ritual mainly recommended for ensuring the birth of a scholarly daughter. During this period, women had full freedom in their marriage matters, i.e. to marry early or in a mature age or to choose their life-partners. “A wife was the husband’s companion in weal and woe, mistress of the household, and partner in all his activities temporal or spiritual." Equality of status and freedom encouraged women to develop extra-curricular activities and provided them with the opportunity for creative literary activities. A few of them participated in philosophical discussions and contributed to Indian thought by their works. "Some of the Vedic hymns have been ascribed to Lopamudra, Gargi, Apala Maitreyi- distinguished women scholars. There are references of women being employed as armed bodyguards by Chandragupta Maurya in his palace. "There is a sculpture at Bharhut of about the 2nd century B.C., which represents a woman carrying a standard on horseback as belonging to the vanguard of the cavalry."

But during the later Vedic period women's status slided down by the authoritative order of Manu (the law-giver on whom rested the fabric of Hindu Society). He believed that there is a vital structural difference between man and woman. The two, according to him, "are different from each other from top to toe and suited for different types of work, e.g., man is intended by nature to do all rough and hard work for earning bread, while woman is designed for household affairs." "He was against the freedom of women in any matter because of his interest in merging the wife's individuality in that of her husband, while recommending strict seclusion for women and rigorous discipline for widows, but he allowed all freedom to women in the household affairs." Manu observes that by a girl, by a young woman, or even by an aged one, nothing must be - done independently even in her own house. In childhood, she must be subjected to her father, in youth to her husband, and in old age to her sons, when her lord is dead. But along with these conservative views, he had some reserved importance for women. He points out clearly that man cannot make any progress if there be no woman standing by his side ready to co-operate with him in all his activities. Man's powers lie dormant so long as they are not touched by the spark of a woman's love and affection. The wheel of the world cannot move in her absence.

While concluding the position of women, during this period, it can be mentioned without any hesitation that though Manu's concept of women was prevalent in that period, women's presence was not ignored totally, and they enjoyed an enviable status, which was exclusively reserved for them.

Women in the Buddhist Period

During this period, women were assigned an honourable place in social life. They were allowed to participate in the religious order, to join *Bhikshu-sanghas*, the order of nuns, which opened to them avenues of culture, social service and opportunities for public life. Some of the women of that period achieved great fame in literature and philosophy. But these were not accepted as equals of male ascetics because their entry into the order was not favoured by the Indian society. There was a reaction produced in society by maidens joining the Buddhist and Jain *Bhikshu-sangha* without a genuine spiritual urge or without a free and spontaneous permission to their big ideals and the public furiously commented upon their lapses. Social thinkers began feeling that it would be better to prevent such abuses by making marriage obligatory for all girls.

The consequences of this reaction were that the position of women deteriorated in the post-Vedic-Buddhist period, as it was then thought that the honourable place of women was in the family. Early marriages were adopted in the whole country and the education of women hybernated behind a long eclipse. "Women, who soon became the least educated in society with few rights and privileges left to them, blindly followed these dictal and rules laid down by the exponents of *puranic* literature and they no longer thought for themselves, nor attempted to exercise their individual judgment, nor fought for their lost status and position.

Women during the Mughal Period

From the eleventh century onwards, when muslims invaded India, women's fortunes dwindled. The Hindu society's attitude towards women became somewhat rigid and the conditions prevalent compelled Hindus to restrict the freedom of their women and to marry them at an early age, as powerful muslims resorted to marrying or eloping with Hindu girls forcibly. The *Purdah* system also originated during this period as it was considered essential to keep women in the secluded apartments, because of the constant invasions, as the men folks were often too busy in the outside home activities. "At the same time, the constant political strife created an atmosphere of uncertainty and insecurity among people and protection of young girls became a problem for the parents. Due to the practice of polygamy, unequal marriages took place, which denied women the right to choose their life-partners, and infanticide among girls. The fate of widows, under strict moral sanctions, became particularly miserable."

On the other hand, many instances are found of brilliant women among the Muslim ruling families as well as Hindu families. Princess Razia of Delhi, a great scholar, Chand Sultana, an exceptional woman given to many talents, Gulbadan Begum, Salima Sultana and Nurjahan from Muslim ruling families and Maharani Rudrama Devi who ruled Orugallu and modern Warangal in Andhra Pradesh, Mirabai, a great and reputed poetess, Molla and Avvoyar, noted poetess and philosophers from Hindu families.

To sum up the position of women; it may be pointed out that women remained between the two portrayals, with no education, no special privileges, but simplicity, patience, perseverance, endurance, understanding, immense love for the home and children and intense religiousness adorned them.

Women during the British Period

When the Britishers anchored in India, women's position was a subjugated one and they were considered as 'dump driven cattle.' The most common evil was infanticide, which prevailed in the country especially in Rajasthan, Punjab, Gujarat and Uttar Pradesh. Girls were usually married before they attained puberty and if by any chance parents failed to find a suitable match with in the age limitation of 6 to 10 years they suffered religious and social disgrace. And it was the custom of infanticide, through which parents could maintain their respect in the society. "The best method to kill the girls was either by strangulation or by smearing opium on the breast of the mother before she fed the baby." Raja Rammohan Roy, Ishwarchandar Vidyasagar, Swami Dayanand Saraswati, Rabindranath Tagore, Swami Vivekananda, Gopal Krishna Gokhale and Mahatma Gandhi, were the eminent leaders who fought for the cause of women and devoted full attention to the problems, which Indian women faced and firmly believed that general progress and development of society is not possible without the betterment of women. And it was all due to the efforts and hard work of these social reformers that Indian women played a great and leading role in freedom struggle and it was Mahatma Gandhi, the great Indian Nationalist, who advocated women's rights and urged women to come forth and fight for their independence and the upliftment of the poor and the unfortunate. It was the call given by Mahatma Gandhi, which ignited women with the spark of nationalism so much so out of their secluded that they left their centuries-old seclusion and in large numbers joined the freedom movement.

On the basis of the various legal provisions enacted to improve and secure the status of women, it can be pointed out that during the British Raj, women achieved a high degree of consciousness about their status due to the impact of western thoughts and the efforts put in by the social reformers and leaders of both the sexes, and they enjoyed a good status with a certain degree of freedom.

After having discussed the general status of women from Vedic period to pre-independence period, it is essential to search out the history of women's status in administration. Though legally women were not allowed to compete for the administrative services, there have been many successful women administrators from the very birth of civilization. Many instances are available when women showed their efficiency and administrative skills with enough courage and the power of initiation. "As early as the second Century B.C., there was a queen named Nayanika who was the head of the administration of the extensive Satavahana Empire of the Deccan during the minority of her son. After that in the fourth century A.D., when the king Lalithabharanadeva and his son died, the widowed queen ascended the lion-throne… till the birth of a grandson."

Women after Independence

As soon as India achieved its freedom, its first task was to formulate its Constitution, which was enforced on 26th January 1950. The document confers equal rights on all its citizens, and is pillared on the four directions by Justice, Liberty, Equality and Fraternity, it thus promised not to ignore its women and never to allow any discrimination on grounds of caste, creed, religion and sex. Various provisions, which provide equal status to women and safeguard their rights, comprise the Indian Constitution. Along with the specific chapters on fundamental rights and directive principles of state policy, the Constitution, according to Articles 325 and 326, declares that no person shall be ineligible for inclusion in, or for a claim to be included, in a special electoral roll on grounds of religion, race, caste or sex, and the elections to the house of people and to the legislative assemblies of states are to be on the basis of adult suffrage. The second step taken by the Government of India in the pursuance of the Constitution was to amend and repeal certain statutes, which violated the right of equality and discriminated against the female sex.

Women will have to fight for their proper image and make it clear that they no longer are to be thought of as a rib taken from Adam's side or as a kind of appendage to her husband, but as an adult human being in her own right with political rights and obligations. In the West, a step was taken in this direction by organising a movement known as 'Women's Liberation Movement' but it was confined only to a particular group of women and could not spread throughout the world. Another step was taken by the United Nations General Assembly by declaring the year of 1975 as an International Women's Year, focusing on three themes; i.e., promotion of equality between men and women, the integration of women into development, recognition of women's increasing contribution to strengthening world peace.

To sum up, it could be pointed out without any doubt that every society has been making use of women labour. They have always been engaged in some kind of job. Even when Adam delved and Eve Spun, woman was not a 'drove' in the household, but ail active 'bee' and had distinct functions to perform. In primitive societies, many instances of vigorous work in hunting and cultivation done by women are exemplified. Woman's role became more real and defined with the evaluation of an economy based on agriculture, because their functions, even if different from those of man were not of less importance. -After Independence, the status of Indian women was uplifted to a great extent, as equality in every sphere was sanctioned to them by the Constitution of 1950.

Today, there is no field barren, where women have not entered and excelled. But in spite of that, the concept of Indian women's approved traditional role of passivity and subservience has not yet been totally displaced and, in spite of the gradual liberalization in many spheres of activity, acceptance of total equality within the social sphere is not yet in sight, and in the professional field especially, they have to wage a greater battle against the male fortresses to get themselves accepted and derived. Ever since the freedom movement of the country the role that woman can play in every dimension of developmental activity has been recognised. The various Five Year Plan strategies have also emphasised on women's participation in the social and economic activities both within the family, in the community as also civil society. This is to enable them to inculcate a sense of confidence and bring about awareness about their own potential for development, rights and privileges. Although in recent years, some efforts have been made to rectify the low reflection of women's income and productive capabilities commensurate with their economic contribution in statistical returns, they have been inadequately covered by extension and skilled development programmes. Convergence of services at grass root level and integration of different programmes are bound to maximise the impact.

About the Study

The present set of elected women representatives in the Municipal Corporation, Shimla took over in the year 2020. On the working of the Municipal Corporation, Shimla there were divergent opinions ranging from praise to dissatisfaction. Those who praised their work mentioned that these members were doing their best under the present circumstances. They were sparing no efforts to provide better services to the people within the limited resources they had at their disposal. Those who criticized them said that these members were doing nothing and were only after their perks. They were helping only the rich and not the poor. The women councillors of the Municipal Corporation, Shimla were unanimous in pointing out the following difficulties in achieving the objectives of development.

- They did not have sufficient resources to execute various projects, which required immediate execution.
- They also did not have sufficient powers to carry out the functions assigned to them.

Number of respondents, who were interviewed through a questionnaire, were all elected and nominated women councillors w.e.f., 1986 till date. Since there were two women councillor during the 1992 to 1997 tenure of the Municipal Corporation, Shimla. One of the councillors Smt. Kamal Walia, who was also Deputy Mayor, passed away during the tenure of the Municipal Corporation. The other women councillor Smt. Jenny Prem was elected as Deputy Mayor in place of Mrs. Kamal Walia. Therefore total number of elected and nominated women councillor is 17 w.e.f., 1992 till date. All the elected and nominated women councillors interviewed from all the political parties.

Findings of the Study

Problem or obstacles being faced: Majority of the women did not face any problem being a women councillor. Women councillors feel otherwise in case of some untoward incident at night as they have to ask for others company to reach at the spot.

Delay Tactics: They do face administrative delay of the executive wing of the Municipal Corporation, Shimla. Majority of councillors were of the view that the problem raised by them are sometimes delay or abolished due to the some hidden pressures of the community in general and society in particular.

Unwanted Delay: Some women councilors find that centralised administrative structure is not working properly, but many have no problem with the centralised administrative structure. After taking any decision in the corporation these decision are sent to the government for their approval, which delays the projects / schemes.

Raising of Funds: A little number of respondents believe that Municipal Corporation raised the funds through the Government, but majority is of the opinion that Municipal Corporation raised the funds through the various sources i.e., Government grant, MPLAD (Member of Parliament Local Area Development), MLALAD (Member of Legislative Assembly Local Area Development) and through other agencies i.e., Deputy Commissioner, HUDCO and even foreign aids. The major part of funding of the Corporation is Governments grants-in-aids. The salaries of the Corporation are being disbursed from the grant received in lieu of octroi abolition.

Handpicked by Husband: All of the respondents are against the view that their husband handpicked them for the sake of political future. They told that their husbands are always there when they need help, but their husbands never handpicked them for their political future. In some cases the women representative has been forced to contest the election to safeguard the political future of the family.

Male Dominance: All the respondents told that they never felt marginalised by the male members or councillors. It is well known fact that the society is male dominated, but 74th Amendment has changed this myth with the passing of time. As only one woman councillor has told that she was marginalised because of political rivalry for mayor ship.

Participation in Dissuasions: Majority of the respondents is against the view and a few one is of the opinion that political party and pressure groups dissuaded them. Sometimes the issues raised by women councillors were against the ideology of particular political party or raised by opposing party that is why the political party dissuade them to consider these issues again.

Political, Administrative and Social Pressures: A little number of the respondents does find political, administrative and social pressures in the day-to-day decision making of the Municipal Corporation. The majority of decisions taken are discussed in the pre-house meetings only than these issues are taken to the general house meeting of the corporation which shows little political administrative and social pressure.

Male Attitude / Gender Bias: All the respondents did not find any gender bias. The men folk work with women members in a cordial manner. The respondents never faced negative attitude of the male colleagues.

Final Authority: Majority of the respondents is of the opinion that final authority to take decision lies with the Municipal Corporation, but just a lone respondent each believe that final authority to take decision is with the Mayor and give its answer in favour of the commissioner. Practically the final authority to consider any matter is with corporation, but in terms of implementation it is with the commissioner.

Consultation: Respondents are equally divided. One half opines that councillors are very much consulted by municipal officials; but other half believes that municipal official consult councillors considerably about implementation of any project.

Political Interference: About half of the respondents do find that administrators are very often more accommodating to the political interference/pressures. Another one-fourth find that sometimes administrator are more accommodating to the political interference/pressures; whereas equal number of the respondents are of the opinion that administrator are rarely accommodating to the political interference / pressures. It clearly indicates that there is likelihood of political interference. The political interference has affected the functioning of the Corporation.

Dominating Factors: Two-third of the respondents does face dominating factors during their tenure, but rest does not find any dominating factors in their tenure. The dominating factors in day-to-day functioning of the corporation are observed by the researcher is issue raised, discussed in pre-house meeting and even in sub-committees. After discussion the issue raised in these committee if find favour, sent to the corporation for ratification. Sometimes some issue raised by Government through MLAs plays dominating factor over any other decision considered by the corporation.

Involvement in Decision making: Almost all of the respondents got fully involved in the decision pertaining for the betterment of town/ her ward. Just a lone respondent feels ignored. In such cases the MLA and

Mayor plays vital role in preparing master plans etc, in consultation with councillors, NGOs and political party in power, which are to be finalised by the State Government. However majority was evident in the fact all the respondents felt that the allocation of licence, quotas and permits is the responsibility of executive branch of the Corporation.

Representation to sub Committees: All of the respondents are of the opinion that women councillors get enough representation in the various sub-committees and committees of the Municipal Corporation. Women councillor gets representation according to the Municipal Corporation Act.

Future Plan: Every women respondent has different opinion about her future plan. They want the problems like water, electricity, sanitation, drainage, traffic, street lightening etc., to be solved earnestly. In order to regulate traffic, these women counicllors emphasised on construction of flyovers/bridges etc. They are of the opinion that for proper sanitation private-public participation policy should be implemented vigorously. For beautification of Shimla as Queen of Hills their opinion are different. Their main stress is for construction of eco-gardens, preparation of master plan and regulating the unauthorized construction, removing the encroachment on government land, providing drinking water on regular basis, construction of lifts from Rivoli bus stand to the Ridge and pending proposal of Ropeway from U. S. Club to Jakhoo Hanuman Temple at the earliest. They have given more emphasize on time bound implementation of schemes and liberal grants in aids or financial assistance should be provided to the Municipal Corporation, Shimla so that the financial crunch be marginalised, urban development and beautification of this city be taken up.

Observations

It is pertinent to note that capacity building initiatives for elected representatives have yet to be undertaken in the state in spite of the fact that it is almost three years since they have been elected. The only initiative so far has been a workshop held for the councillors of Municipal Corporation, Shimla. A long-term strategy has to be worked out by the Directorate of Urban Development to address capacity building needs of elected representatives and bring about community participation and decision-making in local issues without which adequate progress may never be made in the sphere of urban governance.

The whole hearted participation of elected representatives is absolutely essential if urban governance is to take off in the manner envisaged in the 74th Constitution Amendment Act and if devolution is to become a functioning reality and not remain restricted to paper. Given the situation that many representatives are being elected for the first time and do not have much knowledge about their powers and responsibilities as out small survey in Shimla also indicates the issue of capacity building has to be tackled seriously. Specific areas of capacity building that need to be focused upon are their roles as elected representatives in various local bodies, municipal finance, information about various schemes and grants of the government in urban areas, micro planning, aspects of involving the community and community participation in ward level planning and privatisation. The impetus for community participation has to come from the councillors at various urban local bodies and this has been a missing ingredient in urban governance in the state. This is an area where urban governance can take some important lessons from the systematic training imparted to Panchayati Raj functionaries in the state, which has begun to pay dividends in the form of increased people's participation in various pockets and many women playing very effective leadership roles.

Thus a long-term strategy has to be worked out by the Directorate of Urban Development to address capacity building needs of elected representatives and bring about community participation and decision-making in local issues without which adequate progress may never be made in the sphere of urban governance. Every women councillor contributed for the development of the area being represented by her in the Municipal Corporation, Shimla. Ever since the freedom movement of the country the role that women can play in every dimension of developmental activity has been recognised. The various plan strategies have also emphasised on women's participation in the social and economic activities both within the family, in the community as also civil society. This is to enable them to inculcate a sense of confidence and bring about awareness about their own potential for development, rights and privileges. All the respondents highlighted some vital issues, which required immediate attention of the lawmakers, which are discussed below:

In view of the 74th Amendment the state government has legislated all the functions listed in the 12th Schedule as legitimate municipal functions. The Himachal Pradesh Municipal Corporation Act, 1994 provides the obligatory and discretionary functions to be performed by the Urban Local Bodies. There is overlapping of functions between urban local bodies and functional departments of State Government. The first item under 12th Schedule is "Urban Planning including Town Planning". However in Himachal Pradesh, these powers are vested with the Town and Country Planning Department. Similarly, for housing a separate authority, the Housing Board exists. Though these functions are mentioned in 12th Schedule of the Constitution and have been incorporated in the H.P. Municipal Corporation Act, 1994, they have not been entrusted to the Corporation, Councils and Nagar Panchayats. Some development programmes are out of pale of these bodies for example, augmentation of water supply. The sectoral programmes also create confusion at the local level, as responsibilities are not clearly defined. The administration of the programmes is also fragmented and overlapping. The Urban local bodies in Himachal Pradesh are under sever fiscal due to increasing expenditure responsibilities and lack of commensurate revenue. They are dependent upon grants from the government even for their day-to-day functioning. Where additional responsibilities and functions are given to these bodies it is without earmarking requisite additional resources. In the absence of a financial tie-up, functional decentralisation will simply lead to a worsening of the municipal problems.

In order to perform their functions effectively and as envisaged in the 74th Constitutional Amendment Act, the revenue of urban local bodies has to be increased substantially. While grants from the state government are one source of funds, in order to impart sustainability it is imperative that urban local bodies also tap all existing sources of revenue at their level. One of the ways to achieve this would be relax the currently existing upper limit cap on various fees and taxes such as that on electricity, which will ensure adequate recovery by local bodies. The other important aspect, which will considerably augment the revenue of local bodies, is to levy the various taxes leviable by local bodies, which is currently not being done by most local bodies.

The issue of alternative mechanisms to produce and deliver local public services has not been addressed by the conformity legislation. The provisions have not been made in the H.P. Municipal Corporation Act, 1994, H.P. Municipal Act, 1994 for institutional engagements, such as public private partnership, privatisation, etc. It is important to note that the discharge of municipal functions through official municipal machinery in only one of the options available to the urban local bodies. If efficient public service provision is the mandate of local self-Government then these local bodies should be enabled to choose the most appropriate production and delivery mechanism.

With the implementation of Himachal Pradesh Municipal Corporation Act, 1994 and Himachal Pradesh Municipal Act, 1994 elected urban local bodies will have the duration or continuity necessary for good performance. The provisions for reservations of seats will sensitise them to problems to important client groups. Thus, it is possible to achieve the political objectives of decentralisation. The next obvious step will be to develop autonomous, accountable and responsive urban local bodies which can achieve the mandate of local self-government, the most important being efficient provision of local public goods and services.

The 73rd and 74th Constitution Amendments - Panchayati Raj and Nagarpalika Acts have set in motion a revolution of great significance. Though decentralisation of power is enshrined in the Constitution, it took more than four decades for us to give statutory status to Panchayati Raj and Nagarpalika Institutions. It is significant to note that decentralisation at the grass-root level is no longer left to the whims and fancies of the state governments. What makes it more significant is that these two Amendments have ensured reservation of not less than one third of total seats for women members in all the three tiers of Panchayats Municipalities and Corporations and also in the offices of Presidents of Panchayats, Chairpersons of Municipalities and Mayors of Corpo-rations.

According to experts, ever since these Constitution Amendment Bills were introduced, two vital questions were raised: Why reservation through Amendments and; is one satisfied with 33 percent of seats for women at the level of local bodies? Though the Constitution has guaranteed that there should not be any discrimination between men and women on the basis of sex and provisions are included to ensure gender justice and equality, political empowerment of women remained elusive and representation of women in state legislatures and Parliament remained less than 10 percent. In the absence of proportional representation - remember women form half of the population - even after more than four decades of Independence it became imperative that reservation should be accepted as starting point to bring women into the main stream of political activity. It must be remembered that this is not a gift or a concession. This is our right and many women organisations have relentlessly to achieve this and the fight is still going on. All those believe in and committed to democracy and gender equity and justice should join hands and make concreted and coordinated effort to see that 'women get their due share not only in local bodies but in all law making bodies and decision making centres. If meaningful social changes are to forge and the equality of life is to be improved both men and women should get equal opportunities and act in unison, complementing each other.

All concerned should be aware of the fact that the Constitution Amendment Bill for the Women's Reservation which came up in the 11th, 12th and 13th Lok Sabha could not be enacted because some of the political parties tried to dilute the Bill for selfish political motives. To be very frank some of the men are afraid that they would lose their pocket boroughs. Whenever the question of political empowerment of women comes up, the argument leveled against it is that women have no political experience and most of them have no formal education. Arguments apply to them too. Another argument voiced by some of the political parties is that sufficient number of women candidates will not be available. But the elections to the Local Bodies, which took place after the implementation of Panchayatiraj and Nagarpalika Act, have proved that all political parties of national and local status were able to put up women candidates in all reserved seats.

It is the bias that prevails about the decision-making skill of women. In the existing social set up many of the issues in the society are women related where the burden of the problems directly falls on the shoulders of women e.g. drinking water, firewood and smokeless oven and toilet facilities. Their practical knowledge and experiences of various situations in relation to issues are underestimated. Given the opportunity and training women are sure to prove their skills and turn out to be good administrators. Democratic and secular India endeavours to provide the necessary conditions for greater participation of women in all spheres of life. Equality of opportunity is guaranteed, and discrimination on grounds of sex, language, region, class or creed is prohibited. Yet, in reality, women's participation in decision-making at all levels - national to local - is low. The challenges in seeking to redress this inequality in a diverse and complex country like India are enormous. They are related to overcoming attitudinal, institutional, cultural and social restrictions that have grown over centuries. There is now, however, an acceptance that women's participation in decision-making is large enough numbers at every level is needed. Women's unique experiences and perspectives would enhance and alter definitions of problems and solutions and would also empower them.

Participation of women is an integral part of democratic process and strengthening the quality of civic life. As they are half the population, women must be in decision making in all social economic and political organisations. Obstacles, which do not let women participate fully, need to be identified and removed. Often structures and social norms are barriers, and stem from social conditions, which inhibit women from aspiring to decision-making positions. Governmental and non-governmental interventions should facilitate and promote women's participation in decision-making. While women have often been in the forefront in mass movements, their presence has not been felt strongly in structured decision-making and institutions. Nor are they in positions of power. Even when they have not been a Prime Minister or Chief Minister, they have not been able to change the lives of the mass of women. Working in a predominantly patriarchal structure with no gender sensitivity has made it difficult to bring about real and sustained changes for women. Patriarchal control in all aspect of life severely limits the potential and scope of women's actual and de facto participation in public life. Multiple burdens make it difficult for women to avail completely of such politically significant change. The climate of present-day politics, dominated by elements of criminalization, corruption, muscle power and violence inhibits women's full participation in the political process, lack of awareness of the possibilities of political participation, means inadequate contribution to public affairs. Lack of orientation, training and preparation to fulfill the roles and responsibilities, as well as abrupt change in their lives further underscore the nature of challenges to be confronted.

Recognising these obstacles the Government, non-government organisations, women's groups and activists has been strategising to provide appropriate inputs to women. Women have been mobilised to participate in elections as candidates and voters, and to be vigilant citizens where elections have been held. Communities have received gender sensitisation to facilitate acceptance of the new roles assigned to women. Leadership and organisational training of women has been conducted to enable them to be dynamic change agents. Networks have been interacting; to influence mass based political structures to provide more space to women. Isn't it time that women are no longer marginalized and their potential is tapped in the developmental process and there is need to explore the extent to which they can be empowered and involved in formulation of plans and policies that have a direct or indirect bearing on their lives. To achieve these goals, active participation of women in the political processes is a must, which may be in any form of organised activity that seeks to influence the attitudes and behaviors of those who have powers of decision-making. Contrary to the political participation of women in the rural area, the voting trends in the urban areas show that the turnout of women is more because they are less influenced by the traditional factors like caste, religion, feudal and family status which are essentially patriarchal forces in favour of men. Despite the attitudinal transformation visible in women in the urban areas, there has been no serious effort to mobilize them as political pressure groups. So far, women have been largely employed in the informal / un-organised sector where there are no trade unions and they are subjected to exploitation due to absence of collective bargaining power. Legislations relating to women development need to be strengthened and vigorously implemented. Programmes need to be re-oriented to serve the aim of achieving parity between men and women and also between different sections of women themselves and where women are unable to absorb the benefits meant for them, they need to be empowered.

Stressing the vital role of education and training in moulding effective and dynamic women leaders, the political women leadership at the grass root level is the need of hour. Women should be given fair knowledge about the functioning of the political system. The trainer has a dual role of an educationist and catalyst in the process of empowering women. A new leadership of women provides constructive thinking in administration and ensures financial management. Urban administration areas of development have been identified in which the elected members have a free hand in planning and disbursement of funds. Obviously, all these are the activities in which the women have a crucial role to play despite several handicaps they are confronted with. The objective of enhanced representation in the executive bodies of local self-grass root institutions is to remove isolation of women from development and political process of the polity. It may be recalled that in earlier year of community development programme, Mahila Mandals were setup in villages with the help of women social education organisation. Similarly, the community-based organisations of women are being formed in urban areas also. Today there is a crying need for a platform where the women may interact among themselves for their own socialization and upliftment.

It is argued that for any meaningful participation of women in administration, gender equality is a pre-requisite. The women need to be trained in the art of administration, polity, finance and the cybernetic of development. Here the role of voluntary agencies must come into prominence. Local Self Government and co-operative are like twin sisters and they can be nourished equally well by our women folk. Planning from below should be stimulated and put in shape by simultaneous development of a powerful cooperative structure. In the matter of making Municipalities financially viable, women should take much interest and see that funds are not frittered away. They can serve as watchdogs in spending money and keeping accounts. The women vested with power have to function with great objectivity keeping in mind the overall interest of economic and social development of the area, where they live.

Decentralisation of structures and decision-making certainly has the potential and relevance in increasing response to grassroots initiatives of poor women. Municipalities are not minor political bodies. They constitute the first base to ensure that the voice of the women is heard. Women's views, which are increasingly articulated through grass root organisations and movement on issues such as environmental pollution, forestry, water management, land reforms, planning, slum improvement etc. have been virtually headed by men in local units of self governments and the bureaucracy.

It is observed that due to rapid industrial transformation, empowerment of women in Municipalities cannot be sufficient device for development of women. After all, empowerment of women is accomplished if they acquired necessary skills to initiate the changes, and not by calculating how much benefit they can earn for themselves from ongoing transformation process. In a country, like India, this is formidable challenge to be faced because majority of the people reside in rural areas and more than half of them are illiterate. The emergence of women power structure into Municipal institution is a milestone in achieving socio-economic development with a positive direction but to make it work needs sincere efforts from different quarters. The framers of the legislation have to ensure that undue difficulties are not created for women that may discourage them from participating in the political process of decision-making judiciously. It is due to absence of effective intent, commitment and sensibility, the programme meant for women, and financial allocations made for them remain unutilized or wrongly utilised. This can be stopped if there is adequate number of women participation in various implementing agencies, see to it that policies and programmes are implemented according to the prescribed manner with in the specified time frame. After entering into local grass root administration women become more confident that they can save the country from corruption, criminalisation of politics and other kinds of maladies. Women at large are more and more convinced that men have failed in governance especially in areas of education, health, environment, food production and development programmes. Empowerment of political power to women is extremely important for making progress. Once women get opportunity to participate in decision-making bodies, there would be spectacular change in social status of backward communities. Much of the effectiveness of this grass root local self-government would depend on the function assigned to them by the states. The role of women members would be important in identifying various resources and assessing various needs of the community so as to optimally use the scarce resources for the benefit of the people.

In this regard, the short-term training programmes, refresher courses, workshops, seminars etc., are sure to help them to understand and appreciate their responsibilities and obligation under the changed setup. Much would depend on the attitudinal and behavioural overtones of the varied functionaries involved in the functioning of these institutions because it is not the system but empowerment of women that really matters. This, in fact is the thrust of decentralised administration. Women in India are placed in a uniquely paradoxical position. For millions who have deeply internalised their subordinate position, there are those like Indira Gandhi, who have transcended these limitations to become its most powerful premiers. At the one hand they suffer discrimination because of their being female, and on the other they are worshipped as goddesses such as Durga and Kali that symbolises power. Saraswati is the goddess of learning, yet our country is home to millions of illiterate women. The crucial element in any decentralisation would be to identify the functions; responsibilities and powers a state government decides to devolve on the local bodies and what financial resources are placed at their disposal. Consequently, the restructuring of bureaucracy would be an essential part of any process of decentralisation. There would inevitably be some resistance from the bureaucracy to the attempt at restructuring. But the government cannot evade its responsibility much longer while expecting heroics from other sector. A greater degree of accountability is imperative that cannot be ignored.

Conclusion

In conclusion, it may be said that the Indian women today are not what they were ten years back. With the fast changing socio-economic scenario being witnessed today, coupled with the political empowerment, by the turn of the century, they are not going to be what they are today.

References

- Kanwar, Pamela,"Imperial Simla, The Political Culture of British Raj", (Delhi: Oxford University Press, 1990).
- Kapur, Promilla, "The Changing Status of the Working Women in India", (Delhi: Vikas Publishing House, 1974).
- Kaur, Harpreet, "Administration of Municipal Corporations in India", (New Delhi: H. K. Publications, 1992).
- Shastri, S. R., "Women in the Vedic Age", (Bombay: Bhartiya Vidhya Bhavan, 1960).
- Shridevi, S., "A Century of Indian Womenhood", (Mysore: Rao and Raghvan, 1965).
- Sharda, Sarita, "Finances of Shimla Municipal Corporation - An Analytical Study", (Shimla: Department of Public Administration, H.P. University, 1983.
- Banta, Pawan Kumar, A Study of Administration of Municipal Corporation, Shimla with Special Reference to 74th Amendment. (Unpublished dissertation), (Shimla: Himachal Pradesh University, Department of Public Administration, 2000).
- Banta, Pawan Kumar, A Study of Municipal Corporation, Shimla with Special Reference to 74th Amendment to Indian Institute of Public Administration, New Delhi, 1999.
- Banta, Pawan Kumar, Status of Urban Governance in Himachal Pradesh, PRIA, an NGO, New Delhi, 2004.
- Banta, Pawan Kumar, "Municipal Corporation, Shimla", (Lucknow: Journal Institute of Public Administration, Vol.6, No. 1 to 4, April 90 - March 91).
- Gautam, Padam Nabh, "Administrative History of Shimla Municipal Corporation", (Mimeo, July 1981).
- Gautam, Padam Nabh, "Municipal Corporation of Shimla - A Monograph", (Patiala: Punjabi University, 1983).
- Gautam, Padam Nabh, "Participation and Development - A Study of Municipal Corporation, Shimla", (Mimeo, 1995).
- Banta, Pawan Kumar, Women Empowerment: An Introduction, Department of Environment and Urban Studies, University of Lukhnow, 2002.
- Banta, Pawan Kumar, Municipal Corporation, Shimla, Journal of Institute of Public Administration, Lucknow, Vol. 6 No. 1 to 4, March 1991.
- Banta, Pawan Kumar, Urban Crisis, Civic Affair, Kanpur, Vol. 40, No. 1 August – 1992.
- Banta, Pawan Kumar, Urban Conflict, Civic Affair Kanpur, Vol. 40, No. 7, February – 1993.
- Banta, Pawan Kumar, Municipal Administration in Himachal Pradesh - Part 1. Civic Affairs, Kanpur, Vol.40, No. 11, June 1993.
- Banta, Pawan Kumar, Municipal Administration in Himachal Pradesh - Part 2. Civic Affairs, Kanpur, Vol.40, No. 12, July, 1993.

- Banta, Pawan Kumar, Historical Background of Shimla Municipal Corporation, Civic Affairs, Kanpur, Vol.40, No. 15, October - 1993.
- Banta, Pawan Kumar, Women in Panchayati Raj Institution: Beginning of New Era, Prashasnika, Vol. 25, No. 2 July December – 1998.
- Banta, Pawan Kumar, Municipal Finance: A Case Study of Municipal Corporation, Shimla, Journal of Institute of Public Administration, Lucknow, Vol. 1, January-December-2000, No. 1&2.
- Banta, Pawan Kumar, One Hundred and Fifty Years of Civic Administration in Shimla; Tiny Bits of England in U.B. Singh edited "Revitalized Urban Administration in India "Kalpaz Publication, New Delhi – 2002.
- Banta, Pawan Kumar, Civic Administration of Queen of Hill station: A Study of Imperial Rule, Nagarlok, Indian Institute of Public Administration, New Delhi, Vol. 34, April – June, 2002.
- Banta, Pawan Kumar, Participation and Development: A Study of Municipal Corporation, Shimla in U.B. Singh's (edited) book, Leaders in Making, Kalpaz Publications, New Delhi-2007.
- Banta, Pawan Kumar, Women Empowerment: An Introduction in Empowerment of Women in Urban Administration: Experiences and Expectations, edited by U.B. Singh, Serial Publications, New Delhi-2006.
- Banta, Pawan Kumar, Democratic Institutions, Political Representation and Women's Empowerment: The Quota Debate in India. in A K Singh, edited Gender Budgeting and Women Empowerment in India, Serials Publications, New Delhi, 2010.
- Banta, Pawan Kumar, Participation, Institute - Building and Social Change Development, Urban Panorama, Regional Centre for Urban and Environmental Studies, University of Lucknow, Lucknow.

19

Social Security: Issues & Challenges During Covid-19

— *Ravindra Singh*

Introduction

The Corona virus (Covid-19) has imposed a heavy cost on entire world and India too. In India especially poor, disabled and worker engaged in unorganized sector got affected due to this pandemic in many ways i.e. fall in incomes; loss of job; livelihood; many have seen their families uprooted; some have even lost their lives during amid lockdown by the Government of India. The Government of India has taken many important steps to reduce suffering of various stakeholders in this regard. However, more can and should be done based on demand and other situation. To overcome people who suffered due to this directly and indirectly various social groups, organizations, civil society organizations, NGO's, providing their services of social security in many ways i.e. to provide protection, prevention and rehabilitation of those suffered. It's very necessary that the dignity of person receiving social security be ensured. In characterising a person by his/her vulnerability or weaknesses, we tend to deprive that person of dignity and treat him/her as an object of charity, which arouses our feeling of pity.

This paper is an attempt to rethink social security in the context of Covid-19 pandemic and initiatives taken by the Government. Keeping in mind the changing conception as well as requirements of social security, especially for informal sector workers, this article reviews the social security status of Informal sector workers in India.

Social Security: Defining the Concept

The concept of social security is not static and has evolved over a period of time (Garcia and Gruat: 2003). One of the earliest definitions of the term social security was given in the Beveridge Committee Report (1942), where social security is defined as "freedom from want", where its provision was restricted to children's allowances comprehensive health and rehabilitation services and maintenance of employment; which implied avoidance of mass unemployment. (Borbora, 2013)

The concept of social security has been further widened so as to include the provisions for housing, safe drinking water, sanitation, health, educational and cultural facilities also as a minimum wage which can guarantee workers a decent life. (Mattoo: 2000)

The ILO has defined two broad groups according to the type of social security by which they are covered. They are: Social Assistance and Social Insurance. Social Assistance covers persons with various disabilities--old ages, sickness; and Social Insurance covers workers of various categories.

The ILO first proposed a comprehensive definition of Social Security as "The protection which society provides for its members, through a series of public measures, against the economic and social distress that otherwise would be caused by the stoppage or substantial reduction in earnings resulting from sickness, maternity, employment injury, unemployment, invalidity, old age and death; the provision of medical care; and the provisions of subsidies for families with children (Jhabvala, 1998)[28].

The above definition assumes that most persons are generally in a state of employment and that the employment ensures them enough earning to meet their basic needs. This view is not admissible for developing countries where workers' work is insecure and that yields too little to shield the cost of social security.

Hence, we may say the concept of Social Security in its broader sense should be understood as a mean to provide support to the individual by the society to enable him/her to attain a reasonable standard of living and to protect the same from falling due to the occurrence of any contingency.

Getubig proposed definition of Social Security with expansion in its element as "Any kind of collective measures or activities designed to ensure that members of society meet their basic needs (such as adequate nutrition, shelter, health care and clean water supply), as well as being protected from contingencies (such as illness, disability, death, unemployment and old age) to enable them to maintain a standard of living consistent with social norms (Getubig, 1992)[29].

According to Indira Hirway the concept of Social Security implies a broad pro-poor approach that has three major components namely, promotional component that aims at improving endowments, exchange entitlements, real incomes and social consumption; preventive component that seeks to avert deprivation in more specific ways; and protective component that is generating relief against deprivation. (Jhabvala, 1998)

Thus the programmes and activities connected with provision of employment, income and assets are termed as 'economic security', and those connected with other basic needs such as health care, child care, old age pensions, food etc be termed as 'social security'. So, economic security is the primary means by which persons are able to obtain their social security needs; while social security is a means to increase and maintain the productivity of the worker, so as to increase the economic security. (Borbora: 2013)

Social security can include social insurance programmes, social assistance programmes, universal programmes, mutual benefit schemes, national provident funds and other arrangements including market-oriented approaches, which in accordance with national law or practice.

Articles 41, 42 and 47 of the Directive Principles enshrined in Part IV of the Indian Constitution provide the basis for right to health and social security (Duggal, 2006). These provisions read as under:

Article-41— *Right to work, to education and to public assistance in certain cases:The state shall, within the limits of its economic capacity and development, make effective provision for securing the right to work, to education and to public assistance in cases of unemployment, old age, sickness and disablement, and in other cases of undeserved want.*

Article-42— *Provision for just and humane conditions of work and maternity relief: The state shall make provision for securing just and humane condition of work and for maternity relief.*

Article-47— *Duty of the state to raise the level of nutrition and the standard of living and to improve public health: The state shall regard the raising of the level of nutrition and the standard of living of its people and the improvement of public health as among its primary duties and, in particular, the state shall endeavour to bring about prohibition of the consumption except for medicinal purpose of intoxicating drinks and of drugs which are injurious to health.*

In India the history of social security provides clear evidence that social security mechanisms designed for the organized sector workforce have worked well and provided reasonable security to them but all other schemes designed for occupational groups under the numerous welfare funds have failed miserably.

In India, the term social security is used in its broadest sense, which may consist of all types of measures-- preventive, promotional and protective, as the case may be. The term encompasses social insurance, social assistance, social protection, social safety net, micro-insurance or insurance for the poor and other measures involved.(Sulzer : 2004)

In view of the growing informal sector in developing countries and the consequent increase in the number of people dependent on provisioning of social security, which is no longer seen as a burden to the exchequer, but as a boost to increase productivity. It is estimated that nearly two-fifth of India's gross domestic product originates from this sector. The prosperity of these enterprises and the well-being of its works along with production facilities provided to them at the workplace and their right remuneration have a significant impact on the productivity of the workers.

Social Security Measures

In India, joint family was considered as the best form of social security which makes the family members responsible to each other and is often considered as the best relief for the special needs and care required by children, the aged and those in poor health. With increasing migration, urbanisation and demographic changes, the system of joint families gives way to nuclear families and the importance to formal systems of social security gains (Social Security Division, GoI). Various laws were introduced to attend social security and welfare needs of organized workers. These are Workman's Compensation Act 1923, the Industrial Disputes Act 1947, the Employee's State Insurance Act 1948, the Minimum Wages Act 1948, the Employees Provident Fund and Miscellaneous Provision Act 1952, the Assam Tea Plantations Provident Fund Act 1955, the Maternity Benefit Act 1961, the Building and Other Construction Workers Act 1996 etc. The first National Commission on Rural Labour appointed in 1987 recommended old age pensions, life insurance, maternity benefits, disability benefits and minimum healthcare and sickness benefits to all rural workers (NCRL: 1991). The increased contractualisation, outsourcing, informalisation of industries had led to increase in size of unorganized sector. To address the social security concerns of unorganized sector Government took initiative in 10th Five Year Plan (2002-07) and promulgated the Unorganised Workers Social Security Act, 2008.To ensure social security of the poor onward for protecting the poor and destitute persons in the event of insecurity due to old age, death of prime breadwinner and maternity, the National Social Assistance Schemes are fully centrally funded social assistance programmes which include schemes such as Indira Gandhi National Old-Age Pension Scheme, Indira Gandhi Disability Pension Scheme, National Family Benefit Scheme and Annapurna.

There is a plethora of government-assisted social security schemes which have been provided to the citizens of India. However, the efficacy and coverage is always been subject to discussion for making it more efficient. The current situation of pandemic brought the hardest hit on economic activities across the globe and more evidently, forced more damage to the developing nations. The social security measures always meant to provide economic safety net to the population in uncertain catastrophes. In this pandemic situation, it is advertently needed for reviewing social security benefits to the target population that may help to evaluate and modify the social security schemes by the government with recommendations.

Measures taken by Government of India to minimize suffering during COVID-19 Pandemic[30]

1. **Food Security:** *Pradhan Mantri Garib Kalyan Anna Yojana* (Food scheme): Everyone under this scheme will get five kgs of wheat or rice for free in addition to the current five kgs allocation for the next three months. In addition, one kg of preferred pulse (based on regional preference) will be given for free to each household under this scheme for the next three months. This distribution will be done through Public Distribution Scheme (PDS) and can be availed in two installments. About two-thirds of population will be covered under this.
2. **Direct benefit transfer**
   - (i) PM-KISAN scheme (minimum income support scheme): Farmers currently receive INR 6,000/- every year in three equal installments. The government will now be giving the first installment upfront for fiscal year starting April 2020.
   - (ii) MNREGA workers: Wage has been increased to INR 202 from INR 182 per day. Such increase proposes to benefit 50 million families. The wage increase will amount into an additional income of INR 2,000 per worker.
   - (iii) Senior Citizens, Widows, Disabled will get one-time ex-gratia amount of INR 1,000 in two installments over the next three months.
   - (iv) *Jan Dhan* account: Woman *Jan Dhan* account holders to be given ex-gratia amount of INR 500 per month for the next three months, to run the affairs of their household.
   - (v) *Ujwala* scheme: Women in families below poverty line covered under will get free LPG cylinders for three months under this scheme.
   - (vi) Self-help Groups (SHGs): The government is doubling collateral-free loans to Rs200, 000.
   - (vii) Use of welfare fund for building and construction workers: The state governments have been directed to use The District Mineral Fund, worth about INR 310 billion, for helping those who are facing economic disruption because of the lockdown.

3. **Healthcare related:** The Finance Minister has announced medical insurance cover of Rs 5 million per healthcare worker. About 2 million health services and ancillary workers are expected to get benefit from such insurance scheme.

Measures taken by GoI to provide social security to those in organized sector

- The Employees Provident Fund Organization (EPFO) has announced that employees who contribute to EPF can withdraw up to 75 percent of the account balance or 3 months' basic salary and dearness allowance, whichever is lower.
- Establishments that employ up to 100 employees and if 90 percent of whom earn up to INR 15,000 per month, the government will pay the employee provident fund contribution both of the employer and the employee (12 percent each) for March 2020 to May 2020. This support is extended for another 3 months i.e. June to August 2020.
- Employer and employee contribution reduced to 10 percent each from 12 percent each currently for next 3 months (i.e. May, June and July 2020). This will be applicable to all employers (other than Government Company and other companies covered in preceding point).
- EPFO have extended the due date for payment of contribution for wage month of March 2020 from 15 April 2020 to 15 May 2020 (30 days grace period).
- Non-refundable advances may be granted to a member of a provident fund, subject to certain conditions.
- EPFO has issued the circular which states that no proceedings should be initiated on establishments covered under the EPF Act for levy of penal damages on account of any delay in the payment of any contributions or administrative charges due for any period during the lockdown.
- In view of the government's decision declaring COVID-19 as a pandemic, the Pension Fund Regulatory and Development Authority (PFRDA) have allowed partial withdrawals from the NPS to fulfill financial needs towards treatment of the COVID-19 illness of a member, his/her spouse, children (including adopted child), or dependent parents. The following documents must be provided to claim a partial withdrawal:
    - o medical certificate; and
    - o formal request for partial withdrawal

Measures taken to Strengthen Economy

(i) Relief to MSMEs

- INR3 Lakh crore (USD 39 bn) collateral free loan with 100% credit guarantee
- INR20k crore (USD 2.6 bn) subordinate debt for stressed MSMEs
- INR50k crore (USD 6.5 bn) equity infusion for MSMEs with growth potential and viability through Fund of Funds
- New definition of MSMEs – investment limit revised upwards; additional criteria of turnover introduced
- No global tenders for government contracts up to INR200 crore (USD 26 mn)
- E-market linkage to be promoted as replacement of trade fairs and exhibitions
- MSME dues to be cleared within 45 days

(ii) Relief for NBFCs

- INR30k crore (USD 3.9 bn) liquidity infusion for NBFCs/ HFCs/MFIs
- INR45k crore (USD 5.9 bn) partial credit guarantee scheme for NBFCs

(iii) Regulatory measures

- All lending institutions are being permitted to allow a moratorium of three months on repayment of installments for term loans outstanding as on March 1, 2020
- Lending institutions permitted to allow deferment of 3 months on payment of interest w.r.t all such working capital facilities o/s as of March 1, 2020
- Moratorium period to be excluded while computing 90 days NPA norm for asset downgrade
- Time period allowed under RBI framework for resolution extended by 90 days (210 + 90 days)
- Further deferring implementation of last tranche of 0.625 percent of capital conservation buffer to Sept. 30, 2020

(iv) Imports of medical equipment

- Exemption from customs duty and health cess, (w.e.f .9 April 2020 to 30 September 2020) on import of following:
    - o artificial respiration or other therapeutic respiration apparatus (ventilators), face masks and surgical masks, personal protection equipment (PPE), COVID-19 testing kits

- o inputs for manufacturing of aforesaid four items (subject to certain conditions)[31]

Plights of unorganized worker during Pandemic

The Government of India has responded to the crisis by announcing several social protection schemes, including direct benefit transfers for certain sections of the population and free LPG refills, grains and pulses for the poor as mentioned above. There has been migration of workers from cities due to employment drying up. Some of them travelled for long distances on foot or on bicycles. According to an assessment by the Centre for Monitoring Indian Economy, more than 120 million people lost their jobs in April due to the lockdown, 75 percent of whom were working in the un-organised sector. According to the National Commission for Enterprises in the Unorganized Sector, only about 8 percent of workers in the informal sector are covered under any social security scheme. Out of the total workforce of 47.41 crore, 82.7 percent is in the un-organised sector.

Amrita Sharma, who leads the Centre for Migration and Labour Solutions at *Aajeevika* Bureau, an organisation which works with migrant labourers, said, "Most of the social welfare schemes are linked to domicile certificates (a document of permanent residence). Migrant labourers do not have such residential documents...they often don't have employer IDs either, as they work in the un-organised sector. Many of them work in small factories, and are employed on a contract basis. Further, some states have been weakening existing labour laws. Workers don't even get dignified wages."Amrita Sharma added the rights of migrant workers are often ignored, she said, "Migrant labourers often do not vote in the states where they go in search of work. Perhaps this could be a reason why state governments do not pay attention to them. Migrant labourers do have some political agency, but unlike the middle class, livelihood is probably a more important issue for them."During the COVID-19 pandemic, many states, have suspended several labour laws to allow employers to reduce their workforce at will, and require workers to work for more than eight hours per day.

Nikhil De, allied with the *MazdoorKisan Shakti Sangathan,* said, "Despite having food grains in the buffer stock, the government have not been able to provide food grains to many needy people. Even cash assistance is very insufficient. The government has only given Rs 500 to women who have *Jan Dhan* accounts. Many families don't have any *Jan Dhan* account, and many accounts have been closed."[32]

Recommendations to Government

- Public Distribution System should be made available to all i.e. unconditional distribution of food grains.

- Some cash must be available to meet out essential need through Government and Non-Government Organisations.
- To build positive network among NGO's, SHG's, Labour Union and Government.
- Protect the rights of labour, any change in this drastically affects workers in unorganized sector.
- To establish linkages between policy and its implementation.
- More focus of economic development model based on *sui generis* means economy based on agriculture and rural industry.
- Create job at every level i.e. agri-based, manufacturing, service sector and small cottage industry based on local resources.
- To review the efficacy of the policy guidelines to ensure the coverage of social security that reach to maximum beneficiaries.

Role of Social Science Experts

- Work on to ensure well being of an individual by providing psychosocial support to strengthen mental health.
- Work on to promote social change, cohesion and empowerment of individual, group and community level.
- Engaging people and structures for the challenges in dissemination of social security benefits and accessing it by the beneficiaries.
- Advocacy on behalf of the most neglect means give voice to unheard.
- Engage in educational preparedness for public health.
- Addressing the social stigma of survivors.
- Access the need and plight of service provider while imparting their duties especially grass root level workers i.e. ANM, ASHA, *Aanganwadi* worker, Village development officer, manual scavenger.
- Help in Disaster preparedness, Disaster management and Disaster Mitigation.
- Mapping the impact of pandemic on the basis of gender, age, community etc.

References

- Borbora, A. M. (2013, October 19). Social Security System and the Informal Sector in India:A Review. Economic and Political Weekly, 48, 69-72.
- Duggal, R. (2006). Need to Universalise Social Security. Economic and Political Weekly Vol.41,No.32(Aug,12-18,2006), 3495-3497.
- Getubig, I. a. (1992). Social Security and the Poor: An Introduction Rethinking Social Security. Asian and Pacific Development Centre.

- Jhabvala, R. (1998). Social Security for Unorganized Sector. Economic and Political Weekly, L7-L11.

  1. Jhabvala, R. (1998). Social Security for Unorganized Sector. Economic and Political Weekly, L7-L11.
  2. (Getubig, 1992).
  3. https://home.kpmg/xx/en/home/insights/2020/04/india-government-and-institution-measures-in-response-to-covid.html
  4. https://home.kpmg/xx/en/home/insights/2020/04/india-government-and-institution-measures-in-response-to-covid.html
  5. Abstracted from article by Asheef Iqubbal entitled COVID-19 lockdown leaves Delhi migrant workers with neither jobs nor social security; experts blame political apathy, lack of legal protection", published in June, 2020.

20

Covid-19 Crisis— Governments' Responses and Administrative Challenges

— V. Anupama & V. Gnaneshwar

Introduction

Modern life is characterized by industrialization and urbanization. Industrialization which began during the 19th century continues through 20th century with more vigour. Scientific and technological advancements are guiding the industrial progress bringing structural and functional changes. Urbanization is the by-product of industrialization involving shift of people from rural to urban areas adopting non-agricultural occupations. At the society level, if industrialization facilitates consumerism demanding more and more products, urbanization involves lifestyle changes demanding new facilities and services. Industrialization and urbanization are closely linked twins shaping and promoting development in the world today.

At the other spectrum, unabated industrialization and urbanization disturbed the eco balances leading to global issues like ozone depletion, melting of glacier ice, rise of sea levels, deforestation, etc. The scientists and responsible elite groups worried over the disturbing eco changes continue warning countries time and again on the coming human calamities like flooding of cities due to increasing sea levels, changing weather patterns and increasing pollution-all impacting human well-being adversely. Of these, environmental pollution aspect has been widely discussed across the countries. Rising environmental pollution is critical for human health especially in urban areas. The emerging problem relating to human health is increasing virus attacks. Scientists have found close linkages between the deforestation and emergence of new viruses like Nipah, covid-1 and covid-2.

Covid-19 or covid-2 virus has turned into pandemic infecting large populations across the countries. Governments are struggling to control the covid-19 virus and deal with the related issues and problems. Covid or SARS group viruses are new to humans and scientists are busy understanding its growth, spread and health implications. In this context, this paper while tracing the linkage of deforestation and emergence of wildlife based viruses in human settlements attempts to discuss the covid-19 virus related issues and problems, and the efforts of the governments and administrative authorities in dealing with the problems in India in the light of some international experiences.

Tracing Deforestation-Wildlife Habitat Disruption-Virus Outbreak Linkage

The significant impact of industrialization and urbanization is deforestation. Ignoring the constant warnings of the world bodies like UN, countries are steadily destroying the forests to expand industrial and urban activities. This expectedly led to fast deforestation. Anthropogenic or human activities which contribute to deforestation include, small and large agricultural activities, cutting of trees, mining, and urban expansion. Disturbing the forest wildlife by steady deforestation by human activities led to migration of viruses from forests to human habitations, initially infecting the domestic animals and from animals to humans by zoonotic process. Rabbis is the most known zoonotic disease. As things turned-up, disturbing the wildlife habitats in fact became a threat to the human health. The governments unfortunately prefer to continue the disturbing activities in the name of development ignoring ecological issues and problems.

Several viruses grow and live in forests surviving on wildlife habitations. Deforestation process disturbs the wildlife habitats. Studies bring-out that various viruses which live on wild animals are slowly entering into human settlements affecting health of people adversely. For instance, in 1998, a novel paramyxovirus named Nipah virus, broke-out in Malaysia. Scientists have found link between the deforestation and outbreak of Nipah virus. The disease was transmitted from pigs to humans. It is observed that pteropid fruitbats were identified as a natural reservoir host[33]. This virus naturally lives in forests hosting on bats. It has been seen that the forest habitat of these bats in Southeast Asia has been substantially reduced by deforestation for pulpwood and industrial plantation. The study[34] therefore proposed that encroachment of Nipah virus-infected fruitbats throughout late 1997 and early 1998 led to initial transmission of the virus to pigs. The transmission of Nipah virus among pigs by amplification spread to human populations and other domesticated animals like dogs and cats which came into close contact with the infected pigs. Later, in September 1998, an outbreak of fatal febrile encephalitis occurred in inhabitants of Ampang village, Kinta district in the northern peninsular Malaysia.[35] Investigations found that the outbreak was preceded by the occurrence of respiratory illness and encephalitis in pigs in the same district and later in 1999 similar diseases in pigs and humans were recognized in the central and southern part of peninsular Malaysia due to movement of pigs outward. Slowly it travelled to Singapore. Eleven respiratory and encephalitis illness including a death were reported among abattoir workers in Singapore who handled pigs from the outbreak regions in Malaysia. The outbreak in Singapore ended when the importation of pigs from Malaysia was prohibited and the outbreak in Malaysia ceased with the culling of over a million pigs. A total of 265 cases of encephalitis including 105 deaths associated with the outbreak were recorded by May 1999 in Malaysia.[36] The virus outbreak was interlinked to several chain activities starting from disturbing the bat habitat to pigs and pig industry, food, migration, etc.

Scientists observe that many viruses exist harmlessly with their host animals in forests, because the animals have co-evolved with them. But humans can become unwitting hosts for pathogens when they venture into or change forest habitat.[37] Further, it is stated that malaria which kills over a million annually due to infection by Plasmodium parasites transmitted by mosquitoes, has long been suspected of going hand in hand with deforestation. In a study based on satellite and health data by MacDonald and Stanford University's Erin Mordecai[38] reported a significant impact of deforestation across the Amazon basin on malaria transmission. It is further estimated that between 2003 and 2015, on average10 percent yearly increase in forest loss led to a 3 percent rise in malaria cases. It is also brought-out that some viruses like Ebola or Nipah, can be transmitted directly between people allowing them to travel around the world as far as there are humans. Zika virus, which was discovered in Ugandan forests in the 20th century, could only cruise the world and infect millions because it found a host in *Aedes aegpti*, a mosquito that thrives in urban areas.[39]

The SARS-Severe Acute Respiratory Syndrome group is the latest viruses originated in China. Studies revealed that they SARS viruses thrive on bats as the bats developed immunity to the effect of these viruses. These viruses are transmitted to human first through wet markets which are popular in China. The first SARS virus surfaced in 2002-03 in humans and it was named as CoV-1. This virus is an enveloped virus containing a positive-sense single-stranded RNA Genome with a nucleocapsid of helical symmetry of – 120.[40] The virus infected large populations in China and Taiwan during its outbreak. The CoV virus, named as CoV-2, re-emerged in 2019 in Wuhan city, China. It is observed by scientific community that the CoV-2 or Covid-19 is very virulent compared to the Cov-1. Due high virulent nature it spreads very fast in humans. While spreading across the countries, the virus underwent several mutations to survive in different geographies and populations. As it spread to different countries fast through interpersonal contacts, it is declared a pandemic by the WHO.

The viral attack in humans is studied by the scientific communities across the world. The findings are helping us to understand the impacts of industries, urbanization, mining, and deforestation on emerging ecological imbalances. It is puzzling that industrialization and urbanization which brought-out modern development in the world also contributed to ecological disturbances affecting human life adversely either directly or indirectly. One of the crucial impacts is virus outbreaks causing human loss and suffering. The pandemic covid-19 virus has become the biggest health disaster witnessed by the countries across the world.

Impacts of Covid-19 Virus

Unlike other viruses, thecovid-19virusis more virulent spreading through world very fast. It is perplexing that modern transportation network which facilitated globalization and human travel across the countries and regions also became the passage for virus migration along with humans. Every country is facing problems in dealing with unfolding impacts of the covid-19. Surprisingly, even the developed countries are struggling to deal with the problems. The situation in India with poor healthcare facilities is more severe. Covid virus belonging to SARS group originated in Wuhan city, China like many other SARS viruses. There are mysteries to be uncovered about the actual origin of the virus. If China defends that it originated in the wet meat markets which are popular in the country, the countries like USA are suspecting that it might have leaked from research labs in Wuhan city. At the global level, countries are blaming China for its failure to control the spread into the other countries. Free international travel from Wuhan in the initial days of November and December, contributed for its transport to other countries from where it originated. While the political blame game continues, the countries should deal with the virus impacts on societies. The public health, economic and social impacts of covid-19 virus is discussed in the following.

Impact of Covid-19 on public health systems

Though world experienced virus outbreaks earlier in the form of Cov-1, Ebola, etc., covid-19 virus turned out to be more dangerous due to highly virulent nature, fast spreadand ability of the virus to survive in different environments adopting fast. In fact, the covid virus has taken entire world into its grip threatening lives of people and making governments struggle to control and deal with the problems. The worst affected are the public health systems which are fragile in the developing countries.

Public health status differs in rural and urban areas in India. At the outset, rural areas have deficient health infrastructure. Sanitation is simple problem due to lesser number of people in villages. In cities and megacities sanitation is a complex process and it is costly due to wide networks to be developed and maintained. As against this, simple and cost-effective solutions could be adopted in villages. Further, densities are very high in cities compared to villages. The covid-virus spread creates problems in villages and towns and cities, but administrative agencies face different problems in cities and villages.

In Indian cities and megacities, population densities are high. People live in congested areas with very less lung space. Several colonies lack basic infrastructure and civic facilities including health and sanitation. Slums have become common in core and developing areas in cities. At the other end, older parts of cities are overburdened with more population and deteriorating infrastructure urgently requiring redevelopment. The mindboggling human densities and congested living are ideal conditions for rapid spread of covid-19 virus in urban communities. Further cities are reeling under high pollution levels making people sick. Pollution also promotes air borne transmission of viruses including covid-19.

Managing cities is herculean task for the civic authorities even in the normal times in India. It is unfortunate that despite spending huge money for slum development, slum life has not changed much in India. Increasing urban growth put tremendous pressure on local authorities to maintain basic services. Sanitation and public health are the most affected areasdue to rapid growth of cities and towns. Overflowing drains and lack of basic facilities, staff, and medicines in primary health care are normal scenes in urban areas. In this grim urban situation where even, normal life has become problematic, covid virus spread is a big challenge. The congested living leaves very less scope for home isolation for infected persons and maintaining physical distance becomes difficult.

In villages, health infrastructure is very poor in India. Despite spending huge funds, public health remained weak in villages lacking necessary hospitals and medical care. People are compelled to travel long distances to reach hospitals located in towns/cities even for small health problems. In district level hospitals also, the facilities are poor. Ultimately, people flock to major cities where specialized health services are available. In this situation, spread of covid-19 virus is a great challenge.

As per the Indian Constitution, states are mainly responsibilities for public health. Traditionally, sanitation and preventive public health care are the responsibilities of local bodies. With Constitution 74th and 73rd Amendments, public health has also become the function of the local bodies-municipalities and *panchayats* through the 12th and 11thSchedules, respectively. If local bodies provide basic sanitation and primary health care systems in urban and rural areas, the state governments develop specialized and general health hospitals on a bigger scale, especially in the major cities. In line with privation, health facilities are also privatized in India leading to mushrooming of private hospitals in cities and towns. During seasonal disease periods, public and private hospitals find difficult to cope with the demand.

The local authorities should work hard not only performing normal civic functions but also attending to covid virus tasks. Frontline workers in the public health area should work hard putting their personal life at risk. Already many frontline public health workers in villages and cities were infected with covid-19. In this situation, these workers must be continuously motivated by the governments to keep their spirits.

The public health systems are designed to meet health needs of people in normal times and in times of seasonal diseases. But covid-19 is not normal health problem. It is pandemic threatening health of large populations, disaster creating health emergency and, a crisis for the health administration. Hence state and local governments must join and put combined efforts to deal with the covid virus health problems. The existing health system must be strengthened and streamlined to deal with the complex covid health issues. Committed funding is necessary to up-grade the hospitals, buy medical equipment, PPE kits, ventilators, etc. The testing facilities should be developed on wider scale, isolations centres should be provided to quarantine the infected persons and dedicated hospitals are also needed to treat covid patients, as covid virus spreads through human contacts.

Economic impact of covid virus

Rapid spread of covid-19 virus across the countries, not only affected public health systems, but also the economies of countries. The emergency health conditions led to imposition of lockdowns strictly curbing movement of people between states and within the cities and villages. This has forced industries, commercial establishments including retail sellers, public and private transport services, passenger travels, educational institutions, cinema halls, etc., to shut. In short, all the economic activity in the country came to standstill. In the process, if several people lost employment, commercial enterprises lost business and industries lost productive period booking heavy losses. Small businesses and MSMEs are the major sufferers due to their lower financial strength. Many small businesses could not even pay rents and maintain their families. The worst affected are people working in informal sector and migrant labour who form bulk of the labour force in India. These people being poor migrated to other states cities in search of employment. Loss of livelihood put them to unbearable family problems.

The central and state governments came forward to support unemployed and poor people to survive in difficult times. But even the governments' themselves became defunct and their own coffers got reduced due to halt of economic activities.

The economists warned that longer close-down of production and business activities will lead to severe recessions and hunger. But life is more precious and governments preferred life to livelihood in the initial period. As the livelihood issues and problems got intensified, the governments realized the futility of total lockdown for long periods. Slowly governments started easing lockdown controls opening the economy in stages. In the meantime, the repercussions of the lockdowns started showing in multiple ways. If unemployment led to psychological problems and family disturbances, reduced incomes compelled people to curtail their spending restricting to the necessities. Less spending led to less business even after the opening of businesses. Governments too reduced their spending due to decreased incomes. Industries moved slowly with covid constraints. Reducing GDPs and increasing government budgetary deficits are broader challenges facing the governments.

Social impact of covid virus

Social isolation and physical distance are essential safeguards during the covid times. Isolated working and living have become new lifestyles. Man is social animal and social isolation is a big threat to healthy society. As covid virus is infectious and spreads fast in communities through physical contact, isolation is suggested by the health authorities including the WHO. Losses of jobs are making people depressed. Psychologists are suggesting people to develop positivism to deal with isolation problems.

In India, the covid virus fear brought radical change in social relations. Communities are isolating covid infected people and families. It is distressing to hear the news that even family members are not coming forward to take the dead bodies from hospitals for last rights due to fear of virus. The virus fear is gripping people compelling to isolate. The social bonds are strong in Indian families. But the virus fear created panic behaviour among people affecting the normal social relationships. The governments are imposing restrictions on family and social gathering. This has affected the marriages and other ceremonies in Indian families where number of people gather and share. At present, nobody has ready answers to the critical problem of isolated living. It demands new relationship pattern-that is learning to maintain relationships even in distance. Going beyond the traditional beliefs, relationship in distance should be the new norm in covid times that is, physically distanced but socially connected. This requires mental change. It is really a big challenge in traditional societies like India.

On education front, the shutting of educational institutions has created problems to students. Online education is being promoted as alternate method. Though this may be workable in case of college students and high school students, it is not advisable to the kids. As there is no alternative, students are forced to adopt these methods. Educationists are divided on the efficacy of the method. Distance learning promoted for working people has now become inevitable for all students.

Distance living, distance working, and distance learning have become new social norms. Though this may be a temporary phenomenon, it may have long term impacts on people-their relationships, minds, and lifestyles. People should quickly adopt these lifestyles for better living.

Status of Covid Virus Spread in India

Survival of the covid-19 virus in humans depends mainly on the mutations in its genetic structure. Unfortunately, the virus has successfully mutated and survived in different regions. This has led to spread of covid virus into different regions and populations. The human transmission takes place mainly through two pathways-by interpersonal contact-based transmission and airborne transmission. The contact-based transmission could be either direct or indirect. Direct transmission takes place through deposit of virus on persons via coughing or sneezing or even by normal breathing. The indirect transmission takes via virus deposited on things. The airborne transmission takes place through aerosols deposited in air by infected persons. The aerosols released from infected persons stay suspended in air. These aerosols are very light and stay suspended in air for longer time in the closed spaces and polluted atmosphere. When people inhale, these aerosols enter the respiratory tracts directly.[41]

The urban link is significant in the covid-19 virus spread due to density factor. The prominence of covid cases in cities like New York, Chicago, Los Angeles, London, Delhi, Mumbai, Chennai, Hyderabad, etc. indicates this factor. If international travel across the cities contributed for migration of virus into other countries, higher densities of populations in cities have contributed for the spread of virus among communities. Wherever human densities are high, scope for rapid virus spread increases as humans are the prime carriers. The spatial nature of covid virus spread reveals that countries and regions/cities with large populations and densities have become super spreaders of covid. Cities have turned out to be epicentres of the virus due to slums and dense populations. In developing countries, urbanization in the last 3-4 decades led to growth of mega cities in countries like India, China and Brazil also indicate the intense and concentrated urban growth.

Urbanization in India has been fast in recent decades. Urban density is evident from the fact the rural areas which roughly occupy 90 percent of the area has about 70 percent of the population. States like Maharashtra and Tamil Nadu are more urbanized states in India. Expectedly, Maharashtra state contributes to 24 percent of the country covid cases and Tamil Nadu 14 percent. The rapid population growth in the country led to unprecedented migration to large cities like Delhi, Mumbai, Bangalore, Hyderabad, and Chennai turning them to mega cities. The mega cities lead in high population densities and growth of slums. The covid statistics are not maintained to differentiate between urban and rural areas. But the broad trends in the covid virus spread in mega cities including their vast urbanizing hinterlands, and the secondary cities in the districts undoubtedly prove the urban dominance.

Whether the covid pandemic is fatal to human life is debatable and there are different related issues and deciding factors. Apart from this discussion, the focus here is spread of covid-19 virus infections among communities. Even mild infections create health issues and leads to isolation. If isolation is neglected, virus will spread more rapidly infecting others. The spread is therefore a critical problem to the authorities dealing and the infected persons too. The status of covid-19 virus spread in India is discussed to trace the trends in the country, states, and cities.

The covid-19 virus arrived in India in January 2020 itself from its birthplace of Wuhan, China. The first case in India was confirmed on 30 January 2020 in Trissur district, Kerala through a student returned from Wuhan, China for vacation. The second and third cases were also reported in Kerala on 2nd February and 3rdFebruary from the same source. Source for all the first three cases was Wuhan, China from the students who returned for vacation to India. In February, the total cases in the country were these three only.

A significant incident that is a religious congregation event was organized in the first week of March by Tablighi Jamaat at Nizamuddin Markaz, in Delhi. In the same month, a cluster of covid virus was identified on 31st March by the government. In March itself more cases in Hyderabad, Delhi and Jaipur surfaced which were linked to the foreign travel. These initial events gave rise to a chain of covid cases in the country linked to foreign travel in different states. In Delhi, 141 cases linked to Nizamuddin Markaz were reported. If foreign linked cases dominated the entire March, the Nizamuddin Markaz linked cases dominated in April. Conducting meeting with thousands of members at Nizamuddin Markaz was a wrong decision which became a perfect platform for spread of virus among the members. As these people travelled to different parts of the country after the meeting it led to spread of the virus across the country. As per the Ministry of Health and Family Welfare, 4291 cases out of the country's total of 14,378 cases forming 29.8 percent were linked to the Nizamuddin Markaz cluster identified in 23 states. Majority of these cases were found in Tamil Nadu (84 per cent), Telangana (79 per cent), Delhi (63 per cent), Andhra Pradesh (61 per cent) and Uttar Pradesh (59 per cent).[42]

The above narration clearly show that lapses occurred in international travel screening and allowing a religious event with about 3,400 people including foreigners at Markaz in Delhi caused initial spread of the covid-19 virus across the states. Interestingly, even after ban imposed on any religious or other congregation of people over 50 in Delhi on 16th to 31st March, some people remained in the Markaz and police had to evacuate them forcefully. Despite these lapses, the virus spread was under control due to total lockdown. But, with the easing of lockdown controls since June, people started moving freely without proper care like maintaining social distance and wearing masks outside homes, the virus spread intensified. Now, it has spread to such an extent that some call it, community spread in several regions in the country. Further, about 80 percent of the confirmed cases are asymptomatic. The community spread and asymptomatic cases make people frightened to venture outside.

(a) National scenario

The virus confirmed cases which were just three in February, increased to 1,397 by March 31 before lockdown. During lockdown also there was gradual increase to 34, 863 cases in April 30 and 1,90,609 in May 31. During unlocking period, the cases spiked to 5,85,792 in June 30,to 16,97,054 in July and to 36, 87,939 in August (Chart:1).[43] The rapid hike in the number of cases over two times in June, three times July, and again two times in August is clear from the data.

Chart 1: Covid19-Total Cases

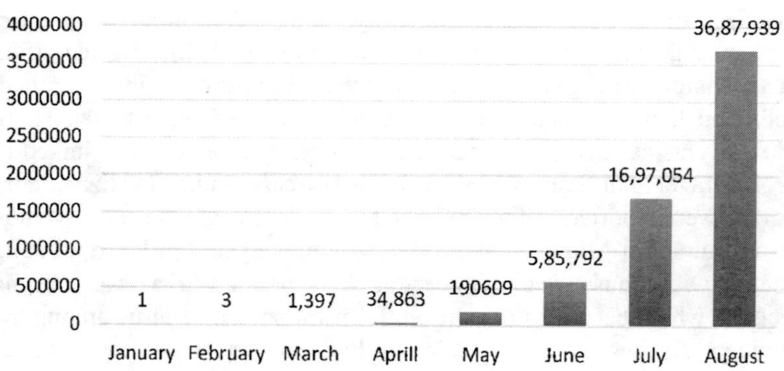

Source: (Worldometers.info)

Along with the total cases, the active cases also increased. The cases which were 1, 239 in March increased to 24,641 in April and to 93,349 in May. During unlocking period, the number increased fast to 2,20,546 in June, to 5,64,856 in July and to 7,85,127 in August (Chart-2). The increasing active cases put more pressure on the health administration and the hospitals.

Chart 2: Covid-19 Active Cases

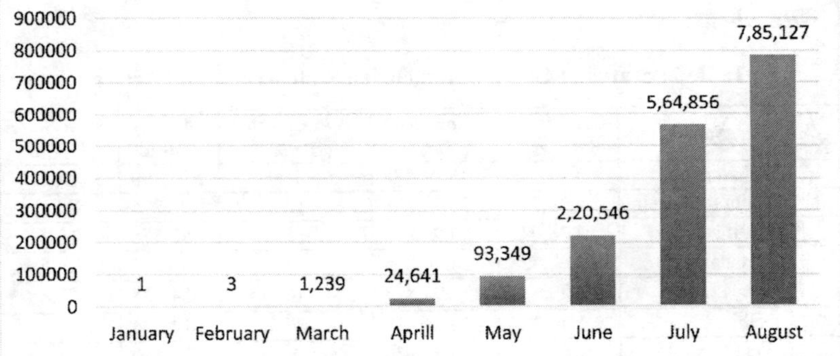

Source: Worldometers.info

The positive trends observed in India relate to high recovery and low fatality rates. The fatality rate which was April got reduced gradually to 1.8 percent by August (Table-1). Low recovery also means recoveries are better in covid infections. The recovery rate which was just 8.8 percent in March increased to 76 percent by August. These two aspects are positive trends in India.

Table 1: Covid19: Death Recovery Rates in India

Month	*No of Cases*	*Deaths*	*Death Rate*	*Recovered*	*Recovery Rate*
February	3	0	0.0	3	100.0
March	1,397	35	2.5	123	8.8
April	34,863	1,154	3.3	9,068	26.0
May	190609	5,408	2.8	91,852	48.2
June	5,85,792	17,410	3.0	3,47,836	59.4
July	16,97,054	36,551	2.2	10,95,647	64.6
August	36,87,939	65,435	1.8	28,37,377	76.9

Source: Worldometers.info

(b) State level trends

The covid virus has spread to entire India covering all states and Union Territories. However, the spread is not uniform across the country. Six states namely, Maharashtra, Tamil Nadu, Andhra Pradesh, Karnataka,

Uttar Pradesh and Delhi are worst affected as per the August data contributing 65 percent to country total. The states with over one lakh cases contributed 82 percent to country total (Table-2). Maharashtra tops the country list with 21 percent followed by Andhra Pradesh and Tamil Nadu each contributing 12 percent. West Bengal and Orissa lead in the active cases contributing 25 percent and 27 percent respectively. Orissa state is experiencing fast growth in recent months, hence high number of active cases. In terms of numbers Maharashtra and Andhra Pradesh lead (Table-2).

Table 2: Status of Covid in top eleven States-Total and Active

Sl. No	*State*	*Confirmed Cases*	*Country Total*	*% in Country Total*	*Active Cases*	*% in State Total*
1.	Maharashtra	7,92,541	36,94,878	21	1,94,399	24.5
2.	Andhra Pradesh	4,34,771	36,94,878	12	1,00,276	23.1
3.	Tamil Nadu	4,28,041	36,94,878	12	52,578	12.3
4.	Karnataka	3,42,423	36,94,878	9	87,254	25.5
5.	Uttar Pradesh	2,30,414	36,94,878	6	54,788	23.8
6.	Delhi	1,74,748	36,94,878	5	14,624	8.4
7.	West Bengal	1,62,778	36,94,878	4	25,280	15.5
8.	Bihar	1,36,337	36,94,878	4	16,071	11.8
9.	Telangana	1,27,697	36,94,878	3	31,699	24.8
10.	Assam	1,09,041	36,94,878	3	23,276	21.3
11.	Orissa	1,06,561	36,94,878	3	28,719	27.0
	Country Level	36,94,878			7,89,369	21.4

Source: Covid Statistics, Microsoft, Bing.[44] The data as on 01-09-2020.The actual data may vary slightly based on reporting timing in states.

In India, the high recovery rates and low death rates are the comforting numbers. National average is as high as 76.9% which is better than global average of 70.2 percent (Table-3).If Telangana reported highest recovery rate of 93.6 per cent, the states of Delhi, Tamil Nadu and West Bengal registered above 80 percent recovery rate. Further, all states discussed here reported about 70 percent recovery rates. The country fatality rate is just 1.8 percent which is far better than global average of 3.3 percent. If Assam report mere 0.3 percent fatality rate, Andhra Pradesh, Bihar, Telangana, and Orissa reported less than 1percent. Maharashtra however reported highest fatality rate of 3.1 percent Bihar on the other hand reported lowest fatality rate of 0.6 percent. Further, Maharashtra, Delhi, West Bengal, and Gujarat reported above national average figures. The low fatality and higher recovery rates give confidence to the authorities dealing with the covid virus infections in the country. Better treatment methods and medicines are being developed based on the last six months experiences. This might have contributed for improving fatality and recovery rates in India.

Table 3: Status of Covid in States-Recovery & Fatality Rates

Sl. No	*State*	*Confirmed Cases*	*Recovered Cases*	*Recovery Rate*	*Deaths*	*Fatality Rate*
1.	Maharashtra	7,92,541	5,73,559	72.4	24,583	3.1
2.	Andhra Pradesh	4,34,771	3,30,526	76.0	3,969	0.9
3.	Tamil Nadu	4,28,041	368141.0	86.0	7322.0	1.7
4.	Karnataka	3,42,423	2,49,467	72.9	5,702	1.7
5.	Uttar Pradesh	2,30,414	1,72,140	74.7	3,486	1.5
6.	Delhi	1,74,748	1,55,678	89.1	4,444	2.5
7.	West Bengal	1,62,778	1,34,270	82.5	3,228	2.0
8.	Bihar	1,36,337	95,162	69.8	836	0.6
9.	Telangana	1,27,697	1,19,572	93.6	694	0.5
10.	Assam	1,09,041	85,459	78.4	306	0.3
11.	Orissa	1,06,561	77,286	72.5	556	0.5
	Country Level	36,94,878	28,40,040	76.9	65,469	1.8

Source: The data as on 01-09-2020. The actual data may vary slightly based on reporting timing in states.

(c) City level picture

The WHO and ICMR reported in May, 2020 that 70 percent of cases and deaths are occurring in the 13 major cities viz., (i) Mumbai, (ii) Delhi, (iii) Kolkata, (iv) Bangalore, (v) Hyderabad, (vi) Chennai, (vii) Thane, (viii) Pune, (ix) Ahmedabad, (x) Indore, (xi) Jaipur, (xii) Jodhpur, (xiii) Chengalpattu (xiv) Tirunelveli. This clearly brings out the relation between population densities and the covid spread. A news report[45] brought-out on June 13 that 5 cities viz., Mumbai, Pune, Delhi, Ahmedabad, Chennai, and Jaipur contributed 50% of the corona virus cases in India.The ICMR India assessment that the risk of covid virus spread is 1.89 times more in slum areas is a caution to the cities. All this indicates that the cities with higher densities and congested living are more prone to rapid spread of corona virus.

Covid virus status in 11 million plus cities selected on random basis where significant virus infections are observed is discussed here. As the covid statistics are maintained by districts, city level figures may not be in line with the municipal limits. These figures pertain to the respective urban districts. The analysis done in eleven million plus cities has to be viewed within this limitation. Delhi state is totally urbanized hence it has 100 percent. Apart from Delhi, Telangana and Bangalore contributed 41 percent and 38 percent while Chennai and Ahmedabad contributed over 30 percent of the cases to their respective states. The city level covid spread in general indicates the urban dominance. Compared to the May and June figure, there has been lesser dominance of major cities due to fast spread of virus in the districts and rural areas (Table-4).

The burden of active cases is high in Pune and Bangalore with 52,712 and 37, 107 cases. The recovery and fatality rates are better in cities too. The Delhi recovery rate is about 90 per cent, while Mumbai Chennai, Thane, Ahmedabad, and Kolkata reported above national average of 76 percent. Kamrup Metro reported least recovery rate of 50 percent. The fatality rate is low in India but in 7 out of 11 cities observed here indicate that it is higher than the national average of 1.8 percent. The fatality rates reported are above 5percent in Ahmedabad and Mumbai (Table-4).

Above statistics relate to tested and confirmed cases only. The covid virus dynamics are changing fast in India and the situation may differ after a couple of months. The covid data analysis done here therefore should be considered as indicative of a continuing trend.The cities played major role in spreading the covid virus across the countries and it is same in India too. If the peripheral areas of major cities and other cities and towns are taken into consideration, the urban dominance will be more pronounced in spatial terms. Urban dominance largely remains in the spatial spread of covid virus even in the context of it spreading in districts and rural areas.

Table 4: Status of Covid Cases in Top Ten Million plus Cities

City	*Confirmed Cases*	*State Nos.*	*% in State*	*Active Cases*	*Recovered*	*Recovery Rate*	*Deaths*	*Fatality Rate*
1. Pune	1,75,105	7,92,541	22	52,712	1,18,324	67.6	4,069	2.3
2. Delhi	1,74,748	1,74,748	100	14,626	1,55,678	89.1	4,444	2.5
3. Mumbai	1,45,805	7,92,541	18	20,879	1,17,268	80.4	7,658	5.3
4. Chennai	1,35,597	4,28,041	32	13,227	1,19,626	88.2	2,744	2.0
5. Thane	1,32,640	7,92,541	17	21,376	1,07,455	81.0	3,809	2.9
6. Bangalore	1,29,125	3,42,423	38	37,117	90,043	69.7	1,965	1.5
7. Hyderabad	51,761	1,27,697	41	11,345	NA	0.0	NA	NA
8. Ahmedabad	31,519	96,435	33	3,433	26,371	83.7	1,715	5.4
9. Kolkata	40,157	1,62,778	25	4,709	34,158	85.1	1,290	3.2
10. Kamrup Metro	28,825	1,09,041	26	14,157	14,599	50.6	69	0.2
11. Lucknow	27,428	2,30,414	12	7,174	19,893	72.5	361	1.3

Source: Covid StatistSource: Covid statistics, Microsoft, Bing.[46] The data as on 01-09-2020.The actual data may vary slightly based on reporting timing in states.

Administrative Challenges in times of Covid Health Crisis

Epidemics and pandemics are abnormal crisis situations impacting multiple sectors including public health. Normally, national crises arise due to wars, economic recessions, and natural disasters. Health emergencies also arise due to outbreak of epidemics and pandemics. How governments respond and manage these crises is critical for human wellbeing, recovery and restoring normalcy in public life. Covid-19 pandemic has already led to global upheavals in various sectors. As the covid crisis turned into a longer than expected crisis, governments are struggling to deal with the covid pandemic each country following its own strategy depending on its national and local conditions. Covid crisis mainly affected three major areas-public health, livelihoods, and economies. How effectively the governments deal the emerging crises in these areas are significant in this context.

There are mainly three stages in any crisis namely, response stage, recovery stage and post crisis normalcy stage[47]. Governments should have advance plans, strategies, and institutional and management arrangements to deal with all these stages. As the covid crisis is continuing, the discussion here is mostly confined to response and recovery stages.

Administrative Response to Covid-19 Virus

Responding to covid crisis is a great administrative challenge to any country due to its long duration, novelty, and its pandemic nature. Some call the covid-19 a slow-motion disaster[48] extending into months which will test the administrative patience. Its pandemic nature makes it difficult to expect much international assistance as every country is struggling with the crisis. The novelty is that it is new disease of epidemic nature with changing effects and spread.

In response stage, the objective is containment of covid virus spread and mitigation of hardships of people. The concerned administration must be tuned to work toward this objective. The administrative approach should be crisis management. In health emergencies, main aim should be to prevent heavy human losses and livelihood suffering. Governments adopted certain emergency measures on war footing. The response strategies and tasks are discussed in detail to assess the situation in India.

(a) *Dealing with governance issues:* Each country has different governing system. Broadly, there are two governing systems - federal system and unitary system. The administrative system differs in federated structures compared to the unitary systems. Federation implies division of functions between centre and states and it differs from country to country. In unitary systems, the line of control is simpler compared to the federal system. Even within these broad systems, different countries may have some typical features. For instance, in US federation, the states have more autonomy and are independent in many aspects.

Lockdowns and closures of all official, business, and industrial activities are radical administrative measures taken-up to deal with health emergency conditions. The main purpose is control of the movement of people confining them to homes. The WHO has suggested this measure to all countries to control and flatten the covid virus spread curve. Most of the countries resorted to this extreme disruptive measure initially. This task demands cooperative functioning of central and state authorities.

In federations, managing national crisis is difficult task due to the functional division and intergovernmental jurisdictional issues. The governments, therefore, should adopt accommodative approach rather than usual confrontation modes to cooperate with one another. Frequent government level discussions and consultations are necessary to iron out the differences if any and deal with emerging problems effectively. Great efforts are needed at the political level to get necessary support. Political level understanding of the seriousness of the covid-19 problem is essential to enlist the required cooperation between the governments. Higher the understanding of the problems, higher is the cooperation.

(b) *Strengthening health administration:* Health administrative systems are designed to deal with health needs of the people in normal times. But pandemic and health emergency times are different. The foremost need is to strengthen and streamline the health care system urgently so that it can meet the demands of the covid health crisis. It involves developing hospital capacitiesto meet the medical needs like providing isolation spaces; medical equipment like bed strength, ventilators, ICU facilities, respirators; and essential personal protective kits including masks. Providing necessary specialized doctors, technical and nursing staffs are very significant to treat the covid patients. The nursing and technical persons so mobilized should be urgently trained to attend to covid tasks safely and effectively. The auxiliary services like ambulances and medicines should be streamlined properly. The deficiencies in this area will lead to more human loss and hardships to the patients.

As the medical needs like medicines, masks, PPE kits, ventilators, etc., are to be procured on emergency basis, concerned rules and regulations should be relaxed, as necessary. Dedicated funding is very important to avoid inadequacies and deficiencies. The active cooperation between the central and state governments is needed to ensure required health kits and equipment are procured and supplied to the hospitals concerned in time.

(c) *Containment of virus spread:* The most important and immediate measure needed in times of health crisis like epidemic or virus outbreak is containing the spread of infections among the people or flattening the curve. As the virus cannot be eradicated soon till the permanent solutions like vaccines are developed, the only alternative is containing the spread so that less and less people are affected. The main tasks needed for containment of the virus infections are testing and tracing. If testing identifies the infected persons, tracing the contacts of infected persons helps in identifying the potential victims. Different testing methods are being developed to test covid-19 virus infections. The molecular tests or polymerase chain reaction (PCR) tests which take sample from the throat of the infected persons with cotton swabs. The test becomes positive only when it identifies two specific genes in the genetic material. This test is a bit time consuming and tests the status of current infections only not past infections. The PCR test is the most reliable test in the world to identify the covid-19 virus infection in people. To detect past covid-19 infections, serological tests are conducted. These tests done with blood samples to detect the antibodies present in the people indicating the past virus infection. In view of delays in PCR testing time, rapid antigen tests are being promoted. Though this method may not be as accurate as the system, it will help in identifying the potential victims having mild systems or no symptoms at all. The WHO observed that the antigen tests could be used to rapidly identify the patients who are likely to have covid-19 and these tests reduce the need for expensive PCR tests. The antigen test identifies the foreign material in the like virus or bacteria with throat swab taken on specially treated strips. The test looks for a unique part of corona virus like specific protein on one of its namesake corona spikes. The material should be in detectable quantity to get positive result.

Isolation is the only solution to arrest the spread of virus among people. It is essential to identify the infected people and isolate them in the first instance. The covid virus will spread through human contacts and travel. Therefore, the first step needed was identifying the virus at the source itself that is, at the airports and seaports where international contact takes place. Countries started screening the foreign passengers at these points and identified the infected people. These infected people are quarantined, that is, isolated in some place. This isolation could either be home isolation or government provided isolation. On the people side, the main task is ensuring social distancing and wearing masks in public places. This will help the people in protecting from infected persons.

Monitoring the social isolation arrangements is important to serve its purpose. The lapses in isolation measures will leads to virus spread. Support of ground level community workers and police department are needed to ensure the isolation measures are strictly followed.The IT in present days has immense potential to support the covid activities. The mobiles and internet connectivity could be effectively used by developing specific apps for vital information dissemination and monitoring the movements of people under home isolation and quarantine. Modern governments are in fact fast adopting the digitalization process in general and this should be extended to the covid virus management activities on war footing basis. In fact, several countries are progressing well in this respect. The main advantage of digital applications is increasing the speed of response which is very important in times of crisis management. IT has greater role in monitoring and efficient execution of the tasks.

Media also plays an important role in times of crisis. Information is vital in times of crisis. Media is the best platform for dissemination of information across wider sections of the people. Through popular modes like TV and Newspapers, media not only can disseminate information but also can educate people on basics of dealing with covid virus and up-dating people about the things that are happening across the world. As people face psychological problems like depression, media can provide necessary moral support through arranging debates and discussions about the problems and means of overcoming them. More important, media can reach across the communities with their wide network and bring to the notice of the authorities concerned about problems and issues people are facing in dealing with covid health issues. Media can more effectively work on this aspect compared to government channels. Media not only bring-out peoples' problems to government attention but also will assist in disseminating information from government side to the people. Government must involve the media not only for information dissemination across communities but also for bringing-out ground level problems of people to their notice for taking corrective measures immediately. In crisis situations this is more essential.

(d) *Livelihood mitigation:* The total lockdowns are imposed to prevent the spread of the diseases by the countries. As the businesses, offices and all economic activities are closed during the lockdown extending into months, people lose their livelihoods and employment at least temporarily. This puts common man and poor under financial strain to maintain their families. In the circumstances, governments must provide temporary financial relief as social responsibility. Usually, the governments provide special assistance putting extra cash into peoples' hands. Measures like unemployment allowance either in the form of kind or cash, subsidies or financial assistance to self-employed and deferring loan repayments are adopted putting their own budgets under strain. Each country must devise its own strategy based on local conditions. For instance, USA provided direct deposits of emergency relief checks to the most affected tax papers and unemployment insurance to gig workforce for four months in addition to US$600 weekly payment. Canada provided an insurance assistance of CAD 500 per week up to 16 weeks. The UK government provided a lump-sum grant of up to 80% of average monthly profits to the self-employed. South Korean government provided emergency cash payments up to 1 million won for all families excluding the top 30 percent income earners. New Zealand provided one-time subsidy of NZD 7,000 to full-time employees.[49]

In developing countries like India, the governments face abnormal financial burdens and they must manage their resources judiciously not disrupting the covid related activities. Apart from the government measures, the NGOs also must be involved in providing the relief to the needy. Several NGOs normally provide charity to the poor people and in the crisis situations; they themselves may come forward to help. Their help will certainly supplement the government measures. Governments should monitor their activities too.

(e) *Coordination and monitoring of crisis management activities:* Covid crisis is a national calamity hence; it demands involvement of various public and private organizations working at the central and state government levels. At the country level, apart from the country head, health, home, port-air and sea authorities, and auxiliary institutions like research and scientific organizations are mainly involved. If the health department monitors the covid operations in the country, the country head should enlist the cooperation of various departments either directly or indirectly concerned, in the covid crisis management to provide necessary support. Similar arrangement is needed at the state level too in federations. In federations, higher responsibility lies at the state level as health subject belong to the state level. At the state level, health and home departments, hospitals, community workers, local bodies, police department, and the research and scientific institutions are important organizations involved in the process. Like health department at the centre, state level health department must play the key role in covid crisis management. The state head however provide the necessary coordinative help. In the private sector, private hospitals, airports, pharma industries, NGOs, etc., provide the necessary support to the government initiatives. Hence, coordination and monitoring of all these national and state level departments and agencies is must to the success of the covid crisis management.

Coordination is the most neglected aspect in public administration in modern times. Every country face coordination problem. Coordination is needed both at intra-departmental and inter-departmental levels. Interdepartmental coordination is the most critical area but normally neglected. In normal circumstances, the cost of ignoring coordination is delays and conflicts wasting scarce public resources. But covid crisis is an emergency and public administration cannot afford to ignore this aspect as usual. The government should give utmost importance to this area in dealing with the covid crisis. A team approach is far better that traditional bureaucratic approach.

Covid crisis management is a team work not confined to one or two organizations. It is herculean and challenging task indeed. It is dealing with abnormal and changing situations. Concerted efforts are needed to meet the demands. Dedicated teams are essential at country, state, and local levels. In modern times when each sector and department work differently, getting needed support in time is a challenging task. The teams must achieve this great task to succeed in the covid crisis management.

Recovery Initiatives

The covid pandemic is a slowly developing story. It is difficult for the governments to predict as to when the covid problem may end. It is true that the covid virus itself will make its own timeline as Anthony Fauci opined[50]. The responding measures like lockdowns which are strict and disruptive affect the entire national economies and businesses adversely. The dangers of long-term unemployment and recession are already looming across the countries with closure and disruptions in imports, exports, productions, and services. With these, the resources of governments themselves will deplete slowly making them handicapped in times of crisis. Governments and people cannot afford to closures for longer times. This situation demands urgent recovery measures. In view of the covid virus uncertainties, the governments must slowly move from responsive mode to recovery mode. Narendra Modi, Indian Prime Minister, while commencing the unlocking process observed that both lives and livelihoods are important, and government should slowly unlock the economy while giving top priority to the covid problems.

This unlocking process involves various recovery activities while focussing on covid activities. To be more specific, focussing is on life and livelihood. On the life side, the covid management structure established should be more strengthened to deal with the uncertain covid spread and possibly a second wave of the virus spread. The health care system capacity should be continuously built to deal with continuing virus infections effectively. Further, testing and tracing activities should be continued as per need. As the hospital care becomes overburdened with the increasing patients, alternate methods like home isolation and government provided isolation centres should be adopted to deal with mild cases. This will reduce burden on the hospitals. Adopting tele-medical services will help the covid victims in this regard. The health system must slowly move toward stabilization. Government should enlist the cooperation of the pharma industry in developing dependable drugs to treat the covid patients. Several initiatives are racing to develop effective vaccines as long-term solution to the covid virus. The focus in brief should be on rapid testing, incentivising medicine, and vaccine development, and providing medical equipment.

On the livelihood side, several economic measures should be taken to re-start the closed economic activities. Close downs naturally affects almost all sectors. Hence, each sector expects some assistance and relief from the government. For small and medium industries re-structuring loan repayment, relaxing rules for getting easy loans, etc., are adopted. Government should also focus creating more employment opportunities for the distressed people. Strategies for re-starting every sector must be planned at the national and state levels and executed with caution at every stage.

Indian Administrative Response to Covid Virus-Successes and Failures

Indian federation is unique in the sense; it tries to balance the autonomy of states and central control. Some thinkers feel that the federation is tilted towards Centre in the constitution itself in respect of functional and resource distributions. The typical three list structure with central list, state list and concurrent list, the balance is in favour of the Centre as both centre and states can legislate on subjects listed in the Concurrent List. Covid crisis is national health disaster and in Indian federalism, disaster management does not find place in any listed functions between the centre and states. The Union Government has the powers to legislate on the unlisted subjects under entry 91 of the Union List.[51] Further, the entry 29 of Concurrent List makes centre and states responsible for preventing spread of infectious diseases across the states and regions in the country. Added to this, the Union Government has also powers under emergency to give directions to the states in case of internal disturbances and external threat. Covid is considered internal threat arising out of health emergency in the country. Due to amendments to Article 352, emergency cannot be declared by the Centre. Under these circumstances, the Government of India utilized the old pre-independence period Act Epidemic Diseases Act, 1897 and the National Disaster Management Act, 2005 enacted under Concurrent List. The National Disaster Management Act empowers the centre to give directions to the states under security subject. The covid virus pandemic was thus dealt under different provisions by the Government of India. The management of disaster is normally the responsibility of the states. Thus, the legal provisions indirectly helped the central, state, and local governments to cooperate in dealing with the issues of covid in India.

In recent years, the relationships between the centre and the states have not been cordial. The reasons could vary from political to resource sharing. The states are demanding more functional and financial freedom especially in respect of the centrally sponsored schemes and programmes. Each party may have its own reasons, but the relationship scenario is not cordial. In the present covid crisis, it is expected that the centre and states cooperate well in dealing with the problems. Initially, the cooperation was good but as the crisis prolonged, the relational problems are surfacing. Though the governments agree at the discussions level, the actual execution level understanding is missing, and some states are openly expressing the displeasure against the centre especially issues pertaining to resource allocations and supply of medical equipment and tools. In a resource scarce country like India these issues may be normal. Despite these issues, the central government need cooperation of states to effectively deal with the national health crisis. The responses of the central and state governments in dealing with the covid-19 crisis are discussed here to assess their effectiveness.

Covid response strategies

Indian national spirit and democratic values are well appreciated globally since Independence. It is true that crisis situations bring-out the inherent national spirit in India. If wars and external threats brought-out that spirit on earlier occasions, it is the covid health crisis that stimulated the national spirit this time. Both governments and people displayed integrated spirit in responding to the covid virus which is not seen in recent years.

The central and state political leadership gave top priority to tackle the covid virus and cooperated with the centre while forgetting their usual issues and problems. Narendra Modi Hon'ble Prime Minister while explaining the immensity of covid virus problem made emotional appeal to provide moral support to people of the nation to be strong in dealing with covid virus problems. He coined the word "*Atmanirbhar*" emphasizing innovation and self-reliance. The Chief Ministers at the state levels too made appeals to people to cooperate with the government activities concerning covid virus. Intergovernmental cooperation during the initial period of covid outbreak was good. It is heartening that private sector, NGOs and the media focussed on covid related problems and supported the government initiatives. The measures adopted in containing the virus spread, improving the healthcare and financial reliefs are discussed in detail.

Containment of the covid virus spread

Though covid-19 virus surfaced in India in February itself from Wuhan, China, it was not significant with mere three cases registered in Kerala. But seriousness of the covid virus problem was recognized in March with several cases linked to foreign travel sprung in different parts of the country compelling the Government of India to bestow top attention on the problem. While recognizing the impending crisis, the first essential measure of screening of international travellers was introduced in airports on 6th March. Compulsory quarantine for the international travellers for at least 14 days which is considered incubation period for show of symptoms was followed. The first covid-19 death case was registered on 12th March. A day later, non-essential traveller visas were suspended followed by ban on border crossing. By March 15, first hundred cases were registered in India. Alerted by the increasing covid-cases in the country, a 14-hour *Janata* Curfew was observed on 22nd March based on the call given by Narendra Modi, Hon'ble Prime Minister of India. The Prime Minister gave a spirited speech to the people of India explaining about the problem of covid-19 and cautioning them about the need for taking strict personal measures to be safe. Immediately on same day, passenger air travel was completely banned in the country.

On the virus containment aspect, the strategy of lockdown as recommended by the WHO was adopted in India. The harsh measure of Nationwide lockdown was imposed in the country on 25th March initially till 14th April and lockdown continued through May too. In fact, the lockdown continues in India but with very few controls especially on mass gatherings, theatres, social ceremonies, public transport in cities, educational institutions, etc. The national lockdown was not done in a planned way. It was an emergency decision by the Government of India. The sudden lock down had put tremendous pressure on the state authorities to respond immediately. The states however came to terms and cooperated with central decision. The lockdown was total shutting down including businesses, offices, educational institutions, industries, and passenger travel. This curtailed the movement of people between states and in cities, towns, and villages. The police departments were streamlined and put into the task of monitoring the lockdowns strictly. The lockdown imposed in March was extended till first week of June.

The second task followed was identifying and isolating the infected persons. Testing and contact tracing were done to identify the infected persons. The infected persons were either sent to hospitals for treatment or put under isolation. The home isolation was allowed with necessary medical care and in cases where people needed help, government isolation centres were provided to the needy patients. In the areas where covid virus infections are more, they are designated as containment zones or hot spots to provide special care confining people strictly to homes. These measures were adopted as a national strategy through-out the country.

Spirited and coordinated efforts

India has shown much spirit and made coordinated efforts to tackle the covid crisis. Frequent political and administrative level consultations between centre and the states and concerned agencies at the state and local levels were done to chalk-out the plans and monitor the situation. At the national level, special covid team were created by the central government with agencies and departments dealing with covid problems either directly or indirectly under the headship of the Ministry of Health and Family Planning. This team coordinated and monitored covid activities at the national level and provided necessary policy guidance and directives to be followed by the states. The state health departments took the major task of implementing the national level strategies and prepared and implemented the state level plan of action. Coordinating teams were also formed under the headship of the Departments of Health at state level. This team monitored the activities of local bodies, hospitals, police, and district administration. The doctors, police, public health staff of the local bodies and the other health workers took main burden of the covid virus tasks. These were considered warriors to fight covid virus. The lockdown and efforts of central and state authorities effectively controlled the virus spread across the country.

Strengthening health care system

The network of health care system in India is spread at the central, state, and local levels. The central government maintains national level hospitals, and research and scientific institutions like the Indian Council of Medical Research (ICMR) to provide medical advice to the governments. The Ministry of Health and Family Welfare looks after the health subjects in the country. Public health is primarily a state function in India. The states provide government hospitals and higher health facilities while primary health centres are maintained by the local bodices. In times of national health emergency of covid virus outbreak, different levels of these health services must be fine-tuned and get connected properly.

The entire health system faced unprecedented pressure of work during the virus outbreak. The covid virus clearly brought-out glaring deficiencies of the local bodies and the governments in meeting the pandemic demands. This demanded immediate strengthening of health facilities. The medical facilities like beds, testing equipment and paramedical support was mobilized to tackle the problem. Dedicated covid hospitals were created in some cities and facilities like separate wards, kits, technical support, etc., in the hospitals were strengthened to treat the covid patients in isolation with special care. The hospitals were equipped with covid virus testing facilities. This apart, specialized scientific and research institutions were utilized for testing purposes. The focus was also made on mobilizing necessary doctors and nurses and para medical staff. Each state made efforts to strengthen health facilities.

Financial relief measures to overcome covid hardships

Covid-19 virus not only led to health and other related problems but also had adverse impact on employment and livelihood. The labourers in the informal sector and migrant labour lost livelihood due to lockdown and many people had food problems. Some NGOs and political parties helped by supplying free food. Many people working in small businesses also lost incomes staring at some body for help. Even the low-income people suffered income needing some financial help to meet their financial commitments. While responding to livelihood problems of the people, the Government of India announced some relief measures. These include food and cash transfers to the poor, daily wage increases, tax relief measures and insurance relief.[52]

(i) *Food and cash relief measures for poor:* Under *Pradhan Mantri Garib Anna Yojana*, every white card holder was provided 5 kg of rice or wheat and 1 KG pulses for three months. Same benefit was also extended to all migrant workers too. Direct cash benefit was also provided to poor people. Under PM Kisan scheme, every farmer was provided with Rs 6,000/- every year to be released in three instalments. One-time ex-gratia of Rs 1,000/- was provided to poor senior citizens, widows and disables persons to be paid in two instalments in three months. This was expected to benefit about 30 million poor people. Further, 200 million *jandhan* savings women account holders were provided Rs 500/- per month ex-gratia per month for three months.

(ii) *Relief under MNREGA wage employment scheme:* Under existing MNREGA wage employment scheme, the wages paid were increased from Rs 182/- to Rs 202/- putting additional money of Rs 2,000/- into workers pocket.

(iii) *Relief for organized sector:* Extra withdrawal facility including service tax waiver was provided to all EPFO contributors up-to 75 percent cash balance in their accounts. In respect of small enterprises employing up-to 100 employees if 90 percent of them getting below Rs 15,000/- monthly salary, the government agreed to pay both employer and employee contributions for six months. Further, partial withdrawal facility for covid victim families from the National Pension Scheme was provided to meet their immediate needs.

(iv) *Insurance relief to health workers:* Every health worker belonging to self-help groups (SHGs) who risk their life attending to the covid tasks were provided a special insurance coverage of Rs. 5 million under *Pradhan Mantri Garib Kalyan* Package. This was expected to benefit 2 million health workers. The benefit was provided initially for 90 days from30thMarch and later extended to 90 more days in June.[53]

(v) *Tax and other related reliefs:* Several reliefs were provided under tax category. Important of these include *Vivad se Vishwas* Scheme, a special tax dispute benefit was provided in respect of all tax disputes to settle the cases by paying only disputed amount till, March 2020. Other concessional measures include extending the filing of tax return dates for income tax, GST, etc., and other tax compliances and waiver of some charges for delayed payment. The delayed income tax payment interest rate was reduced from 12 percent to 9 percent. Immediate release of tax refunds to the tune of Rs 18,000 crores pending.

(vi) Relief for poor households: Poor households using 5kg cooking gas cylinders were provided additional eight free refills to be used in three months. This measure was taken to prove relief from the disruptions due to lockdown. Further, this benefit was reduced to three free cylinders for households using 14 kg cylinders.

All these measures were taken after imposing the lockdown to alleviate some financial pressure among the people especially, the poor people. Apart from these measures extended by the central government, the state governments also provided certain relief measures at their level. For instance, the Government of Telangana provided free ration even before the central government announced it to the poor workers including the migrant workers. Special financial incentives were also provided to the frontline workers like sanitation staff, health workers and even doctors in their salaries.

From lockdown to unlocking-the troubled journey

The imposition of lockdown caused severe hardships to all workers, industries, and governments. The pain was more to the poor people and daily wage earners who include migrant labourers. In India, urban migration for livelihood has been a steady process and reached high levels in recent years in large cities. Migrant workers have become the backbone of government and private sector projects. Bulk of the Government migrant labourers live in slums and sometimes on the project sites with temporary shelter. The migrant labourers suffered severely due to shut down of all projects. The suffering was not only income point of view but also mental as they are living away from their families. Despite government support, some workers could not receive the benefits and there was growing pressure among the migrant workers to return to their native places to be with their families in difficult times. Media reported several cases across the country where the hundreds of migrant workers with small kids walked hundreds of kilo meters to reach their families. Some unfortunately died on the way. Their situation was really appalling.

All commercial establishments, companies and construction works were shut completely. As the businesses were closed, many shop keepers could not even pay rents. Even the governments, guardians of the people, were affected financially as their income sources depleted fast with the shutting of economic activities. Some governments like Telangana and Andhra Pradesh could not even pay salaries for their employees. Employees and their families had to satisfy with half salaries only. All government works came to standstill.

With harsh shut down measures, the Indian economy started drifting toward crisis. Though all the countries faced this economic problem, India being a developing country with huge population burden could not bear total shut down long. While realizing the grave situation and severity of multiple problems, the Government of India started unlocking process in the first week of June 2020changing the earlier stance of *life first* to *life and livelihood slogan*. One after the other, all businesses and public activities were opened in stages. The unlocking process continued through July (unlock-2), and August (unlock-3) and September (unlock-4). Presently, few areas like passenger international travel, swimming pools and cinema halls and large public gatherings are not allowed. At every stage Government of India is issuing strict covid-19 guidelines to be followed by all in non-containment areas. In the containment areas however, strict lockdown measures should be adopted. While keeping in view the national level guidelines, the states are given autonomy to implement the guidelines according to local needs.

With unlocking process, the main covid-19 responsibilities are shifted to the states. The consequences of unlocking should have been properly taken care of with a clear strategy and action plan in many states. It was expected that the covid-19 activities and institutional arrangements made are continued with same tempo and commitment. Effective institutional arrangements should have been done to strictly monitor the implementation of the guidelines including the monitoring of home isolations. Further, health care facilities needed strengthening in terms of testing arrangements, hospital facilities and equipment, and home isolation kits and guidance to people under home isolation. The health infrastructure needed urgent up-gradation in the districts in the light of fast spreading covid infections in rural areas.

But the way unlocking is being done in states one thing is clear that the governments are in hurry to open-up economic activities. The removal of lockdowns controls and opening of the businesses led to free movement of people on the streets, especially in cities and towns. People as usual ignored the safety measures like maintaining social distancing and wearing masks in public places. Some influential people behaved irresponsibly by organizing large birthday parties and other functions ignoring guidelines. Though congregation of people was not allowed, some people managed to break the rules. Though governments issued state level guidelines and covid-19 safeguards to be followed by each sector, effective monitoring is missing. The health infrastructure and facilities remained fragile despite some improvements done during the initial period in many states. The unlocking was attempted without strengthening health care system, especially in districts. The deficient functioning of health administration is causing severe pain to the covid victims.

At the other end, the initial spirit, discipline, and commitment which were displayed by governments dissipated fast. The governments shifted their attention fast from covid to other areas. With the shift in the attention of the governments, the health machinery slowly fallen into their casual approach. Each organization started functioning in its own way. The casual and sometimes callous approach on the part of the public authorities has replaced the earlier spirit of concern for covid victims and cooperation among concerned functionaries. It appears that governments left the burden totally on the citizens.

Covid virus victims with mild symptoms and no symptoms are put under home isolation. Their number is increasing in recent years. One way it is good in the sense it reduces burden on the hospitals. The covid patients must behave responsibly and follow isolation rules strictly confining to home. It is reported that some people are not following isolation rules and roaming freely outside. This is another problem not taken seriously by authorities concerned. In covid virus situations, slackness in authorities adds to the problems. This is being reported frequently in the media. This problem could be solved by proper education of people and effective monitoring of the movements of the covid patients. The digital technology will provide solution for effective monitoring. But in populous countries like India where all people do not use smart phones, monitoring covid patients is a challenge to the authorities.

All these factors namely, lesser government attention, unresponsive public authorities, irresponsible peoples' behaviour, and increased peoples' movement contributed for the spread of covid virus rapidly overburdening the fragile health system. It is unfortunate that though some improvements are made to major hospitals, the status of primary health centres is very poor. In Hyderabad, it is reported that there is only one primary health centre for 2 lakh populations as against the national norm of one primary health centre for every 25,000 population[54]. Added to this, there are gross inadequacies in respect of qualified technicians and doctors to provide necessary medical services during the covid times. As the primary health care is in doldrums, people either flocking to large hospitals or private hospitals. If some states are conducting more tests, some are lagging. The biggest problem appears to be asymptomatic covid victims. Many people do not even know that the virus attacked them as they do not see any health issue; such people without knowing transmit the disease in the community. The doctors and scientists say that 80 percent of people do not show any symptoms. The spread of disease by such people is a big problem especially to their families and the close contact people. The doctors say that the most unfortunate covid victims are people having other health issues like blood pressure, sugar, cancer, etc. The fatality rate is high among these victims.

Another area of concern is that functioning of the private hospitals. The governments have allowed private hospitals to test and treat corona patients. Unfortunately, the private or so-called corporate hospitals started exploiting the patients by charging very high rates ignoring the government prescribed rates and creating artificial shortages of medicines and facilities. Due to lack of strict monitoring over them, the private hospitals continue to exploit people in multiple ways. The media is continuously highlighting this issue. Recently, thousands of complaints were received by the Government of Telangana on this problem and government is slowing waking-up to the problem and taking some measures to control the private hospitals.

It is unfortunate that the governments which displayed great spirit and attention to covid problems initially, are now giving superficial attention. As a result, health administration too became defective turning insensitive to covid problems adopting casual tendencies. One glaring administrative deficiency concerns with the monitoring of covid problems and activities. Most of the above discussed defects are related to slackness in coordination and monitoring. The entire covid burden is now on the respective health departments at the state level. But effective monitoring of covid guidelines requires cooperation of different sectors and organizations. A strong dedicated monitoring team at the state and district levels involving the concerned authorities is the need of the hour. Unfortunately, it is a serious miss in many states. The cumulative effect of the administrative deficiencies is reflected in increasing confusion and sufferings of the covid victims.

Another typical aspect of governments in India relates to downplaying the fast virus spread issue while projecting positive aspects like recovery and death rates. For instance, the Ministry of Health and Family Welfare, Government of India reported on 12th June that the rate of corona virus spread is coming down steadily in India. It was informed to the media that the daily growth rate which was 38.2 percent in March 2020 has come down to 3.24 percent by 12th July 2020. Further, it stated that much of the covid virus spread that is, 86 percent of the active cases are confined to ten more affected states with Maharashtra and Tamil Nadu contributing to about 50 percent of the cases. Karnataka, Delhi, Andhra Pradesh, Telangana, West Bengal, Uttar Pradesh, Gujarat, and Assam contributed to 36 percent of active cases. It is also said that the recoveries are overtaking daily cases in many states and in entire India by 1.8 times. The governments' continuous emphasis on low fatality and high recovery rates in comparison to other countries indirectly prompted the concerned authorities and people in general, and youngsters, to take covid problem lightly. If the authorities became less serious and sensitive to covid problems, people started ignoring the covid precautions.

Against the rosy government statistical information, the fact remains that the virus is spreading fast not only in the cities but also in districts which were safer in the early days. This is another emerging problem in India. Increasing covid infections in the country after easing lockdown restrictions indicate this trend. The number of daily casesin country which were below 8,000 before lockdown easing in May, increased to18,000-19,000 range in June, 40,000-50,000range in July, and to70,000-80,000 range in August. Current daily cases are higher than any other country faced so far including USA which is the worst victim of covid-19. The national level picture presented in chart-1 indicates the increasing trend of covid infections over 2-3 times in July and August during the unlocking period. The state level figures also indicate similar trend. As per analysis done by Indian Express daily[55], the share of additional cases in July ranged between 35 percent in Delhi to 89 percent in Andhra Pradesh. The Karnataka and Bihar states come in the higher range of 80-87 percent. In August, it ranged between 22 in Delhi and 68 percent in Andhra Pradesh. The addition was highest in Maharashtra with 3.7 lakhs followed by Andhra Pradesh with 2.9 lakhs and Karnataka with 2.1 lakh (Table-5). The increasing trend of covid virus infections in the country is thus very clear. If the governments downplay this increase or not is a different question.

Table 5: Trend of Increase of Cases in Ten States in July& August

Sl. No.	*State*	*Cases in July*	*Addition in July*	*% Share in July Cases*	*Cases in August*	*Addition in August*	*% Share in August Cases*
1.	Maharashtra	4,22,118	2,47,357	58.60	7,92,541	3,70,423	47
2.	Tamil Nadu	2,45,859	1,55,692	63.33	4,28,041	1,82,182	43
3.	Delhi	1,35,598	48,238	35.57	1,74,748	39,150	22
4.	Andhra Pradesh	1,40,933	1,26,338	89.64	4,34,771	2,93,838	68
5.	Karnataka	1,24,115	1,08,873	87.72	3,42,423	2,18,308	64
6.	Uttar Pradesh	85,461	61,969	72.51	2,30,414	1,44,953	63
7.	West Bengal	70,188	51,629	73.56	1,62,778	92,590	57
8.	Telangana	62,703	46,364	73.94	1,27,697	64,994	51
9.	Gujarat	61,438	28,992	47.19	96,440	35,002	36
10.	Bihar	50,987	40,999	80.41	1,36,337	85,350	63

Source: Compiled from Indian Express, 2nd August 2020 August numbers.

Economic recovery measures

As all economic sectors were affected adversely due to lockdown, the Government of India took some financial strengthening measures. The Prime Minister of India announced economic revival measures on May 12, 2020 under the clarion call of *Atmanirbhar* Mission focussing on self-reliance. It was stated that covid crisis not only led to severely battered economy and hardships to the people, it also provided opportunity to India to become self-reliant in all the sectors. He further explained that the economic package announced by the government is meant for cottage industry, home industry, small-scale industry and MSMEs which provide livelihood for millions of people in India. A massive package of Rs 20/- lakh crore equivalent to roughly 10 percent of the GDP was announced. It is observed that the package is comparable to USA which announced 13 percent economic stimulus package. It was further stressed that this package is based on four pillars-economy, infrastructure, technology driven system, vibrant demography and demand. As a follow-up to this, the Prime Minister also launched Innovation Challenge on July 4, 2020.It focuses on office productivity, work from home, social networking, e-learning, entertainment, health and wellness, business including aggro-tech and fin-tech, news, and games.

Following the Prime Minister's announcement, the Finance Minister, Ms Nirmala Sitaraman[56] explained the economic stimulus package details on May 13. The package broadly includes the *Pradhan Mantri Garib Kalyan* package a slightly revised programme of the earlier *Pradhan Mantri Garib Anna Yojana* and other financial relief measures announced in March. A sum of Rs 1.7 lakh crore was allocated for this component. The other components include several liquidity improvement measures of the RBI and assistance to MSMES. The food and cash scheme announced in March continued for another three months.

The MSME assistance of Rs 3.7 lakh crore financial package includes Rs 3 lakh crore collateral free loan with 100% credit guarantee, Rs 20,000 crore subordinate debt for stressed MSMEs and Rs 50,000 crore equity infusion for MSMEs which have growth potential viability through fund of funds. These apart, several incentives and concessions were provided to non-banking financial companies, housing agencies, real estate, banks, mutual funds, etc. Except the food and cash assistance programme, all other measures will be implemented in stages over a period.

Some critics argue that mu much of the May 12 *Atmanirbhar* package of Prime Minister Narendra Modi totalling Rs 20 lakh crore is liquidity driven, with little burden on the exchequer. For instance, the total financial burden on the Central Government comes to Rs 2,17,095 only. The remaining part goes as part of the running schemes and toward some reform measures in agriculture and public sector enterprises. The RBI in its August, 2020 monetary policy review announced one-time loan restructuring scheme for the individuals and companies whose loan defaults are of less than 30 days as on 1st March 2020. This is meant only for the companies and individuals suffered due to covid. The economic recovery is a long process. All the above measures are intended to re-start the economy and will be implemented in stages.

Focus on digital applications in health service

Modern IT services provide much scope for digitalization of government services. In times of covid-19 crisis social distancing and remote working are essential to protect from covid infections. In this situation, digitalization of health services is being adopted fast by the countries. India also took steps on this front. Three major digital missions namely, Covid-19 Tracker, e-*Sanjeevani* are formulated APPs like and e-*Sanjeevani* and National Digital Health Mission are introduced. The APP is devised to help people as covid-19 tracker. This AAP provides vital information on covid-19 virus, helps in tracking the covid patient movements, and warns people on their contacts with covid infected persons. This APP needs smart phones and registering on the APP to get the services. Many people in India are already using this APP in India.

The second initiative in digitalization process is launching of the National Tele -consultation Service. The APP titled e-*Sanjeevani* OPD. After registration, the APP provides remote tele-consultation with the doctor services. This facility provides remote help from doctors in respect of regular health issues of the people. Services like doctor consultations and prescriptions are available on this APP. This service will be utmost useful to the senior citizens avoiding frequent visits to the doctors for regular health problems like blood pressure, diabetes, etc.

Another unique initiative launched by the Prime Minister of India on the 74th Independence-day is National Digital Health Mission (NDHM). The Mission was designed and implemented by the National Health Authority. Digital Technology is the basis for NDHM. The main tool for its implementation is health ID card. The health card will be issued to every citizen of India and it is voluntary, option left to citizens to opt for the scheme. The Health ID card contains health information of the person like medical data, prescriptions, diagnostic reports, and summaries of previous discharge from hospitals[57]. The main purpose of the health ID card is to facilitate efficient and transparency in health services provided to the people by various hospitals in the country. The government said that the data so stored in the health cards will be totally protected. Further the digital health mission is expected to reduce the gap between various stakeholders like doctors, hospitals and other healthcare providers, pharmacies, insurance companies, and citizens by connecting through digital health infrastructure.

The Mission mainly comprises six key digital components namely, Health ID, Digi-Doctor, Health Facility Registry, Personal Health Records, e-Pharmacy, and Telemedicine[58]. It is further mentioned, the Mission will enable access to timely, safe, and affordable healthcare by citizen centric approach. Though private sector assistance is also taken for certain activities, the main responsibility rests with the government. Initially, a pilot roll-out is planned in the Union Territories viz., Chandigarh, Ladakh, Dadra and Nagar Haveli, Daman and Diu, Puducherry, Andaman and Nicobar Islands and Lakshadweep. Later, this will be extended to entire India with the cooperation of the states.

The Indian administrative response to the covid-19 virus reveals the typical Indian administrative style. Initially, the response was more spirited and cooperative but slowly the enthusiasm diluted. Several administrative lapses are found in airport screening and quarantine till the air travel was totally banned. Some people took it easy and organized various religious and social activities ignoring the government stipulations. The Markaz Nizamuddin event is often quoted in the media and states for its impact on the virus spread in the country. On the other hand, some states are following their own ideas for controlling the covid virus. Though the states are free to follow their own strategies, there appears to be difference of opinion on aspects like testing and quarantine. If some states are focussing more on testing, others are satisfied by doing the minimum. Telangana was slow on testing till it received directives from the High Court and the Governor to increase the tests. Some states are complaining about insufficient central aid and supply of medical equipment. In federations these issues are common but in crisis times there should be clarity and right understanding of the problems. False claims, lack of transparency and confusing covid data are often highlighted in the media.

The plans and programmes relating to covid-19 are high-sounding, but the implementation has been patchy. Several deficiencies are observed on the ground in states. The common concerns are lack of transparency; low testing; ineffective tracing and monitoring of home isolation cases; insufficient medical facilities like beds, ICUs, PPE kits, testing kits; and dilution of commitment. Finally, the economic revival measures are receiving more attention of the governments while the healthcare services continue to be deficient affecting common man in India in covid virus times. The correcting of the healthcare service deficiencies is crucial as the covid-19 virus is spreading fast in the country demanding continuous attention of the governments.

Covid Control Initiatives

A. International Experiences

At the global level, some countries like Germany, New Zealand, South Korea, Singapore, etc., did great efforts and successfully controlled the covid spread. The effective strategies normally adopted by the governments are mobilizing local level health facilities, better coordination, and monitoring of covid activities, testing, better contract tracing and isolation methods. Counties like India, Australia and USA followed lockdowns as a measure to control the covid virus. But Taiwan controlled the covid virus effectively without adopting disruptive lockdown approach. The cases of Taiwan and New Zealand are discussed to highlight their strategies which are well appreciated globally.

(a) ***Taiwan-case of undisruptive initiative:*** Taiwan is a small island country like Hongkong and Singapore. It has just about one million populations. The most important point here is Taiwan is just 130 KMs away from China where the virus generated and have active travel connections with China. In the light of its proximity and work connections with mainland China, it was expected that the country is more prone to covid virus reminding the SARS 2003 horrors. In 2003 Taiwan had highest mortality rate in the world. The earlier experiences might have warned Taiwan to take strict measures and strategies in the early stage itself. Result of these early strict measures is seen in the low covid virus infections in the country. The country had just 455 confirmed cases including 7 deaths as on 19th July 2020.[59] The globally appreciated strategies adopted are explained here.

Early containment measures and border control

Because of earlier SARS nightmare, the country has woken-up early on the day China reported the corona virus case to WHO on 31st December. Most of the other countries including USA at that time downplayed the issue and were not expecting it to spread into their countries on a significant scale. Another positive aspect was that the covid response team was led by the experts. The Vice-President Chen Chien-jen himself is epidemiologist from Johns Hopkins University with much experience in tackling the earlier SARS virus. The Vice-Premier Chen Chi-maiis a doctor himself and it was reported in Channel News Asia (CAN) on December, 31 that he had early knowledge of atypical cases of pneumonia virus which prompted him to take early responses to the emerging crisis. By January, 20 Taiwan's Central Epidemic Command Centre was activated.

Initially, the travellers from China were screened in early January 2020 itself. After thorough checks at airports, affected travellers were quarantined for 14 days strictly. Further, national health insurance data was integrated with the immigration database while allowing this data to all the hospitals treating the virus.[60] When the first confirmed case of covid virus was reported, level 3 travel alerts to Wuhan was announced and travel from Wuhan and Mainland China was bannedon 26th January, 2020[61]. As the virus started spreading across countries like Hongkong, Singapore and Malaysia travel of non-residents of Taiwan was totally banned.[62]

Avoiding shortage of PPE kits and masks

Effective measures were taken to prevent shortage of PPE kits and masks in hospitals. The supply chains were monitored strictly, and the prices of the essentials were totally controlled. Purchase of masks by people was rationed to avoid shortages. The manufacturing of masks was increased from 2 million per day to 16 million per day. The ban on surgical mask exports was also imposed against WHO advice.

Dedicated clinic for covid patients

In the Chang Gung Memorial Hospital, separate covid clinic was established exclusively for the covid patients with total isolation from other units. Apart from these, testing facilities were expanded. For this purpose, 50 regional hospitals and medical centres and 167 community hospitals and clinics were designated to test the patients. Special wards for covid patients were also provided in these medical centres for treating patients[63].

Effective utilization of technology

Digital health technology was used very effectively. The Chang Gung Memorial Hospital was provided with business intelligence (BI) to monitor healthcare to the patients by identifying the covid risk patients and isolating them to control the spread. Further, with the help of smart phone technology, quarantined patients were effectively monitored.

At the outset, these measures appear to be common being followed by other countries. The real difference is the early measures and strict implementation of the strategies on the ground. Controlling the virus spread without resorting to total lockdown is another achievement of Taiwan. It shows how strict the controls were. Finally, the citizen cooperation has been commendable.

(b) ***New Zealand-the case of early action:*** New Zealand is an island country with a population of 4.9 million in 2019 and has very less density of 17.3 persons per square kilo meter. The success of covid virus control in that country is really inspiring and a lesson to others. The early and strict measures in the beginning of February2020 itself were the key points there. The strictness of the measures and commitment of the government is visible from the point that when just two cases were reported in New Zealand in June due to control breaches, the Health Minister resigned taking the responsibility. The main points of the strategy adopted in the country outlined below.

Early international travel ban

The country started banning foreigners coming from or via Chinathe very next day when a person died of covid virus in Philippines on 2nd February 2020. Any New Zealander coming from China was put to 14-day compulsory quarantine. At that time there were no corona cases in New Zealand. It is really a great early precautionary measure when the other countries were taking covid virus issue lightly.[64]The moment first case was registered in New Zealand from a person coming from Iran, travel ban was extended to other countries like South Korea, Iran, etc., where the virus spread was observed. And from 16th March, except virus safe countries, all travellers were to go compulsory self-isolation on arrival. After few days only the New Zealand Prime Minister Ms Ardern decided to impose international travel ban to foreigners and residents too. This early measure largely stopped virus migration from other countries.

Early national lockdown

The national level lockdown with four-stage alert system was introduced in the country when the country just had 102 cases with no deaths reported on March 25 as against UK the country had over 6,500 cases and 330 deaths when the lockdown was imposed in the country. Further, UK never closed borders except bringing self-isolation controls. It was argued that the country had to bear economic pain, but the country experienced virus free and healthy life compared to other countries.

Proper utilization of lockdown period

The lockdown was used for conducting extensive testing and contact tracing for the virus. The victims were detected early and isolated for treatment. Though opposition leaders criticized the total lockdown for long periods, government continues the strategy. Interestingly, it is reported that 80% of the people supported the government measures. The Prime Minister announced officially on June 8 that the country has successfully eliminated the covid virus from the country at least for the time being.

Though the country experienced few cases later due to some lapses after lifting the lockdown, the situation is far better compared to the other countries which are still struggling. The international travel is still closed. Though critics lament on long period of travel ban and its economic impact, the country achieved success in controlling covid virus spread in the country, a great relief to its citizens.

B. Indian Experiences

(a) ***Dharavi, Mumbai-the unique success story:*** Mumbai is not only the financial capital of India but also most populated metropolis in the world. Even with geographical limitations, the city expanded on possible directions. The city grew into a large urban agglomeration with a population of 12 million populations, occupying 8^{th}place among the most populous cities in the world. The metropolis of Mumbai is the second biggest metropolis in India and includes cities of Navi Mumbai, Thane, Bhiwandi, and Kalyan apart from the Greater Mumbai. The UN estimated that the metropolis has a population of 25 million in 2014.

One of the main contributory factors for the rapid spread of covid is considered the density of population in the cities. In Mumbai, the density of population is very high with approximately 73,000 people per square mile as against densities of Tokyo 11,000 people per square mile and New York's 6,000people per square mile. In Asia, Shanghai has around 3,600 people per square kilometer as against 28,000 per square kilo meter in Mumbai. More significantly, the slum of Dharavi has mindboggling density of 3,34,728 people per square kilometer or 869,565 people per square mile. This statistical information is given only to show the level of density in Dharavi, a great risk factor for covid virus.

The famous Dharavi, Mumbai's biggest slum is also considered largest in Asia. It has over 10 lakh populations. Density in Dharavi is about six times more than the other areas in Mumbai. The slum is very congested with mixed residential and commercial activities. About 80% of people use community latrines and the streets are very narrow. Almost each home has small business. With these factors, it was feared that the covid outbreak in the slum may assume unmanageable dimensions.

But amidst fast growth of corona virus in other regions of Mumbai and Maharashtra, the Dharavi with several adverse civic exigencies, managed to control the covid spread in the slum to a great extent. This is evident from the following growth figures. In Dharavi[65],the daily growth was 12 percent in March, which reduced to 4.3 percent by May, 1.02 percent by June, and to 0.3% afterwards. The sustaining growth reduction is really a stupendous success in covid control. No doubt, the initiative of Dharavi and the strategies adopted are appreciated widely in India and even the WHO praised the controlling measures.

In Dharavi, the strategy included several local measures taken more effectively. The following specific measures were taken to control the pandemic.

- The foremost measure was aggressive testing and screening covering about 85 percent of the people in the slum. This has helped in tracing the potential covid victims. After tracing, rapid survey was done covering 3.6 lakh people to identify old people. About8246 old people were identified and isolated for special care.
- Another measure was setting-up fever clinics to identify the potential covid patients.
- Developing necessary medical facilities and health staff was done locally. For this support of private sector was sought. About 90% of treatment was done mostly in the local facilities.
- The other facilities like transporting the patients to the hospitals were also provided in local areas.
- As most of the people lived in very small tenements, home isolation was not feasible. To overcome this problem, several community level isolation centres were developed to isolate the people.
- Community participation is very important in the local level initiatives. Interestingly, local communities readily provided the needed support. To interact with communities, covid community leaders were identified who bridged the gap between the local people and health workers.

The case of Dharavi is a model for other cities with high slum populations because in most cases the initiative stops with planning in India. Well-planned and executed strategies are needed in other cities also to control the spread of corona virus. As the risk of covid virus spread is more in slum and congested areas, it is very important to control the virus by pragmatic and strict measures.

(b) ***Kerala-the case of lost opportunity:*** In Kerala, large number of people migrated to foreign countries for employment. As people started coming back India due to corona virus in other countries, the imported corona virus danger was imminent. The state foresaw such danger and made effective strategies to face the emerging problem. Kerala is the first state to experience the corona virus problem in India on January 30.[66] The state took effective measures like isolating the patients, contract tracing, quarantining the people coming from abroad which was the main source then, and streamlining the medical and hospital facilities and technical staff in the state to meet the health needs of the people. The earlier two Nipah out breaks guided the authorities to take early action on the Covid virus. The decentralized local government system in Kerala helped the authorities to control the virus. These measures were carried out more vigorously. The mobilization of resources from different departments was done to support the ground activities. Active people's participation, community kitchen to feed the poor, rationing of essentials and psycho-social counselling to alleviate victims stress were other supportive measures which worked well. With these measures Kerala could control the spread of virus to a large extent. In April, the covid cases were only 1,823 which increased to 8,380 in May. On May 4, there were just 16 active cases in the state.

The Kerala story gets reversed in the subsequent months. With the easing of lockdown controls, the Government of India started the repatriation missions to bring back Indian workers struck in other countries. Kerala has large number of people working abroad. As influx of people was expected, the Kerala government wanted to test the returnees at the airports itself to control the virus import. As this could not materialize, multilayer screening was adopted to identify and isolate the infected persons. The influx of migrant workers which started on 7th May already reached the 6 lakhs figure. The state and local authorities struggled to provide isolation centres to the migrant workers. In the meantime, there developed shortage of testing kits. The tests were restricted to only the highly risky sections of the people. Several types of tests like RT-PCR, antigen, antibody, TrueNat, CBNAAT, etc., were introduced to cover all the people having influenza like symptoms. The lockdown easing brought complacency among the authorities and the people throwing caution to winds. The influx of people from neighbouring regions accentuated the problem. The mitigation measures are being increased in recent days. With the resurgence of covid virus infections from unknown sources surfaced in Thiruvananthapuram. The Poonthura event triggered a chain of virus spread in about eight large community clusters in the capital city of

Thiruvananthapuram during July-August. The virus has steadily increased in the state. Initially, the government even declined to accept community spread, but continuing spread compelled the government to admit community spread in Kerala. Other covid clusters developed in Kasaragod district and Malappuram taluk. This fast increase is evident from the figures of 55,078 in July and in August. It appears that the unlocking effect was also experienced in Kerala. Kerala could control the corona spread effectively in the beginning till May but since then there has been sharp increase like other states. The only positive aspect is restricting the death cases in the state.

(c) ***Delhi-late but well-controlled initiative:*** Delhi experience is reverse of Kerala experience. Delhi is the capital of the country and hence needed increased efforts to control the covid. But initially the state administration showed laxity which led to spread of the covid. The incident of Markaz where thousands of foreigners assembled for religious purposes triggered the virus spread not only in Delhi but across the other states. The Delhi authorities could not cope with increasing spread of the disease due to coordination problems. The daily rate of growth was around 6% in June.

With the support of the Central Government, the state took some effective measures to control rapidly spreading disease. The medical infrastructure facilities were up-graded lot with developing a large medical facility in the Sardar Patel hall. This facility has 10,000 beds with latest medical equipment and facilities to meet demand of all the patients. The important measure was increasing the number of tests from 4-5 thousand daily to 20 to 25 thousand. This helped the authorities to trace the corona patients early and treat them in time. Another innovative measure was setting up of Plasma Bank to meet the needs of patients. Plasma treatment has shown some positive results in India in treating the critically ill patients. This facility has helped the plasma therapy on covid patients. This practice is being followed in other states too in India.

With all these stringent and coordinated measures, the virus spread is controlled. For instance, the daily growth rate has come down from 6 percent to 1.7 percent by July.[67] The recovery rate is also increased to over 90%. Resultantly, the recovery numbers are more than the daily detected cases. The efforts must be continued further to control the covid virus spread as any slackness may trigger virus surge again.

The above experiences reflect the responses of governments to cope with covid virus problems and to control its spread. Smaller countries like Taiwan, Singapore, Hongkong and New Zealand have responded more effectively achieving sustained results. Even bigger countries like Germany, Canada and Australia have done reasonably well in limiting the covid virus spread. USA and Russia in the developed world and countries like India, Iran and Brazil in the developing regions are still struggling with the covid crisis. Each country followed its own strategy based on local economic, political, and social conditions and limitations. The initiatives and experiences so far reveal the changing dynamics. If some countries like New Zealand and Taiwan succeeded in controlling the virus spread, other countries displayed mixed results. In India, controlling efforts varied from state to state. If Dharavi is a unique case of covid virus control in an extremely adverse condition, the experiences of Kerala and Delhi are typical. Kerala experienced earlier success which reversed during the later period. At the other end, Delhi which suffered fast virus spread in earlier months, took effective control measures, and succeeded in July. The current world picture shows that only few countries have been successful in controlling virus spread while others are experiencing different stages of ups and downs. The main lesson that emerges from this dynamic experiences is that as long as the effective administrative measures were put in place strictly, virus spread was controlled and the moment people and authorities became complacent, the virus surged again. The constant alertness and sustenance of strict measures are therefore essential till effective vaccine is developed.

Covid-19 Crisis-Administrative Dilemmas and Going Forward

The ticklish dialogue of development vs environment continues in the world forums. The global agendas are devised and revised periodically to balance development needs and the environmental demands. As not much progress is witnessed on the global front, countries should focus on the emerging problems like pollution, natural disasters, and health issues of the people. The era of viruses has begun on the global scene. The previous viruses like Ebola, Nipah and CoV-1 have shown us the extent of damage the viruses bring on humanity. As only few countries experienced the virus inflicted disasters, other countries just ignored the problem. To teach the world a hard lesson, the covid-19 virus turned into a pandemic infecting large populations across the countries assuming the dimension of global disaster. As every country tasted the virus impact, it is time to approach the covid-19 problem seriously by the governments. Underplaying and half-hearted attempts hoping that the covid virus will soon vanish from their territories may be just wishful thinking. The covid-19 virus may not be life threatening for many but its long-term impact on human health is still incomplete picture.

The mere scale of the spread and social and economic pain it is bringing are mindboggling. In this context, the governments have no other option but, strengthen their public health systems on a long-term perspective and guide the recovery process.

The covid-19 virus pandemic apart from unprecedented hardships to people also brought new global understanding and opportunities for future development. The limitations of much hyped globalization are exposed in recent years with increasing localism and restrictive international trade. The covid-19 crisis has further complicated these issues compelling the governments to look for indigenous solutions. Hence, the governments should prepare reconstruction plans while taking advantage of the emerging opportunities. The reconstruction plans broadly include economic revival plans and health sector capacity building. These plans could be long term and short term. Long term plans are future ready initiatives while the short-term plans are meant for meeting immediate needs.

The reconstruction strategies are discussed in the Indian context. As a preamble to the Indian reconstruction approach, the Indian Prime Minister has recently coined the terms "Global to Local" and "*Atmanirbhar*". If the former emphasizes local initiatives, the later meant to inspire people to become strong internally while focusing on innovation. The initiatives like *Ayushman Bharat* and National Digital Health Mission made recently are of long-term measures on health front. On economic front, the Prime Minister invited Indian entrepreneurs in various sectors to work toward self-reliant India. The re-discovered spirit of self-reliance after Independence is a welcome change, may be considered by-product covid-19 crisis. It is long term economic solution to make Indian economy strong enough to withstand the unforeseen upheavals that may come in future.

Apart from long term policy measures and plans, short term measures are needed to restart the Indian economy and to strengthen the health infrastructure to meet the demands of continuing covid crisis. Already, the government announced several measures to help the suffering sectors. These are already discussed in the above paragraphs. Special assistance and concessions announced to the housing, banking, and MSME sectors are some important steps in this direction. As the virus spread is expected in waves with occasional highs and lows, isolated temporary lockdowns and strict containing measures become necessary to deal with the situation in the areas where the virus spread becomes unmanageable to the authorities. This is already happening in India. Hence, the industries and offices should be ready with alternate plans to continue their businesses and reach targets with temporary interruptions either due to lockdowns or due to workers getting infected. This is a stupendous task for the businesses and industries. It also indicates longer than expected recovery.

On the health front, the health services namely, hospitals, pharma, and advanced healthcare facilities are dominated by the private players both in developed and developing countries. The government sector health services are very deficient in India. As the private sector is providing bulk healthcare, the government has confined its' role to insurance and providing free services for the poor people. In Telangana, the government bears the cost of health services taken by poor and government employees in private hospitals under the scheme "*Arogyasree*". The private hospitals are paid huge reimbursements every year. It has turned out into a good income source for private hospitals. But the pandemic covid-19 brought new understanding on the public healthcare dimension. It taught us that the governments should play more dominant role in public health in terms of resource allocation, infrastructure development, and quality services.

Covid-19 virus is a developing story. New knowledge and information are flowing across the globe pertaining to the sources, symptoms and impacts of the covid virus on human health. As the virus is behaving differently in different countries, each country has a story to tell. In India asymptomatic cases and recovery rate are on increasing trend giving the impression that covid virus is turning soft and less dangerous as initially believed. It is also argued that growth of asymptomatic cases may help in developing herd immunity among the people. Herd immunity is a controversial issue; some arguing herd immunity in humans takes longer times for a virus like covid-19. The surfacing re-infections of covid virus create doubts on antibodies and herd immunity. These questions about the covid-19 continue to haunt in future too till total knowledge is gained on the covid virus by the scientific community.

The level of asymptomatic covid infections is being assessed in India to understand the level of virus spread among the communities. The presence of covid virus antibodies in people is examined to verify this aspect. The presence of covid virus antibodies indicates that the person concerned already got covid infection and the body developed antibodies to fight the virus. It is clarified by the scientists that presence of covid virus in persons does not mean that they have become immune from further covid infection as the antibodies remain in the body for a short period only. Hence, antibody tests should be used only as surveillance method to assess the level of infections. Several serological surveys are done to assess the level of asymptomatic cases in India.

The ICMR has done a study in May 2020 to assess the anti-body levels in communities in 83 select districts covering 21 states affected by the covid virus. The antibodies were found only among 0.73 percent of the sample. Recent studies done indicate substantial increase in the percentage of people with antibodies. A sero survey was done in Delhi by the National Centre for

Disease Control (NCDC). It conducted the IgG antibody and infection survey using COVID KAVACH ELISA which is approved by Indian Council for Medical Research (ICMR) during June 27 and July 10. The survey was done across 11 districts in Delhi covering 21,387people. It was found that5,022 of the sample forming 23.48 percent developed antibodies against COVID-19.[68]Some private testing labs also did antibody tests on public. Thyrocare, a private testing lab has found antibodies in 1,340 of the 3,956 samples tested, indicating a positivity rate of 33.8% in Delhi. As the Delhi government decided to conduct serological tests to trace the movement of virus spread in communities the second serological survey was conducted in the last week of July and first week of August 2020. Second survey was conducted in all the districts of Delhi over a sample of 15,000 select people. The results which were announced on 20th August indicate that the extent of antibodies present in people increased from the level of 23 percent in June/July to 29 percent July/August.[69]The highest percentage of 32% anti bodies were in South Delhi. An increase of 6%in a month of people having antibodies is considered good. In Mumbai, two private labs namely, Thyrocare and Suburban Diagnostics Lab conducted the antibody tests. Thyrocare which tested 5,485 samples in the city found that 1,501 or 27.3 percent of the samples had antibodies. The Suburban Diagnostics lab also found that 830 or 20.2 percent of the 4,105 people it tested developed antibodies against COVID-19.Another Serological Surveillance for Sars-cov2 study was done in three wards covering 7,000 people in slum and non-slum areas in Mumbai.[70]The results show that 57 percent of people living in slum areas developed antibodies as against 16 percent in non-slum areas. The serological survey was also done in Pune by Indian Institute of Science Education and Research (IISER)[71]. The survey was done in five wards where the covid infections are high with sample of 1644. The findings indicate that 51 percent of the people have covid-19 antibodies. Similar survey done in Krishna district Andhra Pradesh found that 19.41 percent of people in Krishna district were infected by the covid. In Vijayawada urban area however, the percentage was high that is 40.51percent.[72]

Testing wastewater in a city is another indirect way of finding the extent of covid virus spread. Scientists claim that the covid virus will be released by infected persons into the wastewater or in sewerage systems in cities. Covid virus can stay alive in wastewater up-to 35 days. Testing untreated wastewater for covid-19 virus indicate the level of virus spread among the people. Based on this, a study was conducted by Centre for Cellular and Molecular Biology (CCMB) and Indian Institute of Chemical Technology (IICT) in Hyderabad[73]. Select untreated sources of wastewater were used to assess the extent of virus spread in Hyderabad. By this study, the scientists estimated that about 6.6 lakhs people in Hyderabad are already infected by covid virus and bulk of them are asymptomatic. On positive side, the scientists assure that the virus present in the wastewater do not infect people.

Another dimension of the asymptomatic cases is that more and more youngsters who work and move outside homes in the age groups of 21-50 years are getting infected and most of them remain asymptomatic. This is proved to be true as per an analysis by health department, Government of Telangana. It was observed that 65.27 percent covid victims were in the age group of 21-50 years[74]. One danger is that asymptomatically infected people may spread virus in others more specifically in their families.

The above discussed surveys and studies are indirect means of assessing the covid-19 virus spread and could be used only for surveillance purposes. Testing is a more reliable method of finding covid-19 infections in people. The government figures on covid-virus infections are based on the tests conducted. In respect of testing, USA stands first in the world as the country conducted83 million tests while India conducted 44 million tests as on 2rdSeptember 2020. Some argue that numbers of cases are increasing in these countries because of increased testing. Testing helps authorities to identify the infected persons and provide necessary treatment either in hospitals or home isolation depending on severity of the problem. At the other end, the percentage of cases turning positive also indicates the level of virus spread in more specific terms as it is the direct and reliable way of identifying covid virus infection. In India, the percentages are between 15 and 20. In states like Delhi, Tamil Nadu, and Andhra Pradesh where tests are increased the percentage of positive cases also increased. In USA too in some states like Florida where virus is spreading fast, the percentage of positive cases which were about 3.5 during May increased to 18.7 by July. Increasing covid-19 infections is a problem. Large number of people may be asymptomatic not requiring hospitalization. But along with the spread of the infections, number of people requiring hospitalization also increases which put more burden on the health infrastructure and services. The shortage of beds and ventilators become frequent occurrences wherever the virus victim number increase. Every country faces this problem, it is more critical in India with deficient health infrastructure.

In the context of prolonging covid-19 virus problem, living with covid virus, common slogan these days, is suggested. Living with covid-19 demands changing work styles. New patterns of work should be adopted focusing on social distancing, work from home and digitalization. The IT sector in India adopted more easily to this new work style. The government service sector however is struggling with restricted working days, staggered working days and work from home wherever possible. But industrial and construction sectors are facing problems as they need workers physically on the sites. On the social front, people are compelled to follow restrictive social and family gatherings, more tele/digital contacting, confining to simple personal needs. Whether people like it or not, these new lifestyles make the covid-19 virus periods tolerable.

At the other end, virus goes on spreading from urban to rural areas due to movement of people between rural and urban areas. Covid virus is travelling along with people to secondary cities and rural areas. This is already witnessed in India. The rural areas where health facilities are very poor, the spread of virus creates more severe problems to the people and authorities responsible to deal with the problem. Despite government claims of adequate facilities, instances of lack of hospital beds and medical facilities in urban as well as rural areas is witnessed which is highlighted by the media in India. In countries like India poor responses from authorities are common. Added to this, private hospitals keep busy in searching for opportunities to make money, even by adopting deviant and inhuman methods. Private hospital exploitation has reached peak in times of covid crisis, really an unfortunate trend in India. Cumulatively these problems put people to severe hardships and personal crises. Hence, people should become more responsible instead of just fighting with the overburdened and unresponsive authorities, strictly follow the minimum health directives given by the authorities and should take adequate personal care like wearing masks, avoiding crowd, and maintaining social distance which became new life style of the day. This is the only alternative left to people. If people ignore this, they not only suffer but also bring suffering to other people.

Governments cannot afford to ignore the covid virus issues in the critical covid virus scenario in India. Strengthening of the public healthcare should be on priority for governments with increased financial commitments. Half-hearted efforts, false claims and blame-game, the most common ills of Indian administration should be shunned. As the uncertain situation continues till a reliable vaccine becomes reality, the governments should continue the efforts and maintain the system set-up to tackling the covid virus problem with same initial spirit, commitment, and tempo. The following administrative measures are essential to tackle the covid problems in an effective and sustainable manner.

(1) It is observed that the governments are focusing more on economic revival plans and other developmental issues. This is no doubt, essential and a long-drawn process. At the same time, the governments should provide adequate resources and bestow attention to covid activities. In the light of weak public health infrastructure, financial allocations should be stepped-up substantially by central and state governments.

(2) The covid activities should be entrusted to dedicated full-time teams drawn from all the concerned executive authorities including

experts and NGOs. Involving the experienced NGOs and community-based organizations is essential to supplement the government efforts. The teams should be properly equipped with necessary staff and technical skills and formed at national, state, and local levels. The teams should be motivated with better facilities and benefits.

(3) In India, though the governments improved health infrastructure to some extent, there is still lot to be done in the face of increasing cases and rural spread. The governments focused more on cities in early stages of covid-19 crisis. The deficient health infrastructure is a big problem in rural areas.With the steady spread of covid virus in rural areas too, immediate upgrading the health infrastructure becomes essential. News reports are flowing daily in India about the poor facilities and services in the government hospitals in urban as well as rural areas. Even the doctors are complaining against shortage of essential staff, equipment, and facilities. The situation demands urgent attention of the governments to ensure timely supply of medical necessities in tune with the demand.

(4) Effective monitoring and coordination is great miss in Indian administration. The governments establish elaborate coordination mechanism, but it turns ornamental soon. This is witnessed in several government programmes and schemes. Many a time, problems arise due to neglect and lack of proper coordination among the agencies concerned. Authorities in India prefer to blame others whenever a problem arises than functioning responsibly. Integrated and shared work patterns among the concerned authorities are essential to deal with crisis situations. The central and state authorities should continuously monitor covid activities to ensure that they are on desired lines. Immediate corrective measures should be taken by the governments. The successful stories as discussed depict high level co-working and cooperation. Increased spending cannot benefit until it is supported by strict and effective monitoring at different levels. For countries like India, this is indeed a great challenge.

(5) Another area concerning monitoring relate to working of private hospitals which are permitted to conduct tests and treat the covid infected patients. Private hospitals operate on corporate methods and profit motive. This is their normal functioning. Unfortunately, certain inhuman practices are observed in some hospitals taking advantage of usual slackness in monitoring. As a result, covid patients are left to face much hardship and exploitation. Denying admissions to the needy patients under different pretexts and inflating the bills with unnecessary tests and procedures ignoring

the government fixed rates are the common complaints pouring across the country. This is a dangerous problem and should be corrected urgently. In times of health emergencies like covid virus, governments should adopt stringent approach. Strict monitoring is utmost important to ensure that the private hospitals follow minimum standards and rates fixed by government. At the other end, private hospitals working on corporate lines also have corporate social responsibility. Private hospitals though suffered during lockdowns along with other sectors should not be more exploitative, becoming a problem rather than support to the governments. Governments should monitor the functioning of private hospitals in more stringent manner to help suffering covid patients.

(6) Another crucial aspect concerns with transparency and fairness in covid-19 related data maintained by the concerned departments. The routine way of maintenance of covid data in a formal way cannot serve the purpose. It is pertinent to mention here recent directive of the High Court ordering the Telangana Government to prepare the covid data in more useful way including the necessary details of all covid patients not only at the state level but also in the districts and local bodies. The Court further ordered that the covid data in cities and towns must be maintained ward-wise. The covid data should be shared online 24 hours with all the stakeholders-government departments, hospitals, local bodies, airports, police, etc., in the country. The covid data should be fair and comprehensive in terms of its utility to the stakeholders.

(7) In India, the e-governance has become a catchword. It is good that government offices and services are being digitalized for efficiency. But the utilization of these IT models depends on the people manning the system. If it is effectively used by concerned people, it could yield the desired results. IT is only an administrative aid; by just installation it cannot yield the desired result unless authorities utilize it effectively and rightly. India has long way to go in this respect. In the emergency situations like Covid crisis, information sharing is vital for timely and right decisions not only to the authorities but also to the people. The IT enabled covid models have enormous scope here. It is imperative that India adopt this approach vigorously and benefit. The recent initiatives of the Government of India like *Arogya Setu*, e-*Sanjeevani* OPD and launching of the National Digital Health Mission are notable and they should be widely and appropriately adopted.

(8) In federal countries like India, the national level governments can devise national level guidelines, monitor state-wise progress,

provide technical and financial support to the states and take such other measures like ensuring enough PPE kits, surgical masks and ventilators are supplied to the needy states. The success ultimately depends on how effectively the state and local authorities are delivering the health services on the ground. Every state should prepare its own action plan and implement it strictly. Unfortunately, governments prepare good plans, but their implementation suffers. This style of functioning is seen even in covid crisis management in India. In health emergency times, the governments should adopt crisis management approach rather than following as usual approach. Proper resource mobilization-financial and human, providing necessary medical kits, strict monitoring of all covid activities including private hospital functioning and frequent consultation across the concerned authorities on day to day basis are essential to deal with covid crisis effectively.

Conclusion

To conclude, the countries which are doing well in crisis management are controlling the virus better compared to other countries. This is evident from the experiences of Taiwan and New Zealand globally and from certain local initiatives discussed in India. The struggling countries and regions could either follow these well appreciated models or devise their own innovative models to control the covid virus spread and mitigate the problems of the people till a permanent medical solution emerges. The present covid-19 issue is a long-drawn crisis. Some countries like South Korea managed the virus spread very effectively. In India, the state of Kerala has also controlled the covid virus effectively becoming a model to other states. But some unplugged loose ends developed later in some areas spoiled the good efforts leading to spiking of covid virus spread. Finally, administrative wisdom tells us that well planned and executed strategies, shared goals among the stakeholders and cooperative working are success mantra in covid virus control.

References

1. Anthropogenic deforestation, El Niiio and the emergence of Nipah virus in Malaysia.
2. *Ibid.*
3. Kaw Bing CHUA, Beng Hui CHUA and *Chew Wen WANG, Malaysian Journal of Pathol, 2002; 24 (1), 15-21.
4. *Ibid.*
5. Deforestation is leading to more infectious diseases in humans, Katarina Zimmer, https:// www.national geographicnationalgeographic.com/science/2019/11/ deforestation-leading-to-more-infectious-diseases-in-humans/

6. Published in Proceedings of the National Academy of Sciences, MacDonald and Stanford University's Erin Mordecai.
7. Ibid.
8. Renyi Zhang, Yixin Li, Annie L. Zhang, Yuan Wang, and Mario. J. Molina, Identifying airborne transmission as the dominant route for the spread of COVID-19 (A Research Article), Proceedings of the National Academy of Sciences, United States of America, June 30, 2020.
9. Renyi Zhang, Yixin Li, Annie L. Zhang, Yuan Wang, and Mario. J. Molina, op. cit.
10. The Hindu online news, thehindu.com, 18th April 2020
11. Worldometers.info
12. https://www.bing.com/search?q=Coronavirus+statistics
13. Covid Statistics, Microsoft, Bing. The data as on 01-09-2020.The actual data may vary slightly based on reporting timing in states
14. Hindustan Times, Delhi, June 13
15. https://www.bing.com/search?q=Coronavirus+statistics
16. Deloitte Insights, Governments' Response to Covid-19-from pandemic crisis to a better future, April, (https://www2.deloitte.com/content/dam/insights/us/articles/6724_government-response-to-covid 9/6724_Government-response-to-covid-19-exec-summ.pdf2010)
17. Ibid.
18. Deloitte Insights, Op.cit.
19. Anthony Fauci Director of National Institute of Allergy and Infectious Diseases, USA
20. V N Alok, Covid-19 and Multi-order Federalism in India, Nagarlok, vol LII, Part 1, January-March 2020, p. 1
21. https://www.hindustantimes.com/india-news/20-days-20-steps, April 13, 2020
22. F. No. Z 2120/ 16/2020-PH, Government of India, Department of Health and Family Welfare, Ministry of Health and Family Welfare, 26 June, 2020
23. Eenadu daily paper, 25 July 2020
24. Timesofindia.indiatimes.com, India, articles
25. https://indianexpress.com/article/explained/atmanirbhar-package-full-break-up-of-rs-20-lakh-crore-nirmala-sitharaman-lockdown-6414044/, VydyanadanIyer, The Indian Express, May 20, 2020
26. Ibid
27. Timesofindia.indiatimes.com, India, articles
28. Covid019 Pandemic in Taiwan, en.wikipedia.org
29. Healthcare IT News, Asia Pacific, by Roy Chiang, May 08, 2020. Healthcareitnews.com
30. Covid019 Pandemic in Taiwan, en.wikipedia.org
31. Rahul Kiran Reddy, Deccan Chronicle e-paper, May 13, 2020
32. The Hindu Chen Shih-chung, May 2nd, 2020, The Hindu.com
33. Anna Jones, BBC News, bbc.com, 10 July, 2020

34. Dr M Kiran, Eenadu daily, 18 July 2020
35. S. Anandan, the hindu.com, 26th July 2020
36. Indian Express, July,16, 2020
37. Financial Express online news, 22ndJuly, 2020
38. The Indian Express, https://indianexpress.com/article/cities/delhi/delhi-sero-survey-coronavirus-covid-cases-death-toll-6563510/
39. https://www.thehindu.com/news/national/coronavirus-57-of-mumbai-slum-population-has-developed-antibodies-study/article32216939.ece. The study is part of a wider study taken-up under a project jointly commissioned by NITI Aayog, the BMC and the Tata Institute of Fundamental Research (TIFR). It was done in collaboration with organisations like Kasturba Molecular Diagnostic Laboratory, Translational Health Science and Technology Institute (THSTI), A T E Chandra Foundation and IDFC Institute
40. Eenadu Daily, August 19, 2020
41. Eenadu Daily, August 20, 2020
42. Ibid
43. Eenadu Daily, August 26, 2020

Index

D

H

I

J

O

P

U

V

W

Y

Z